Essential
Windows® CE
Application
Programming

Robert Burdick

Wiley Computer Publishing

John Wiley & Sons, Inc.

NEW YORK • CHICHESTER • WEINHEIM • BRISBANE • SINGAPORE • TORONTO

Publisher: Robert Ipsen

Editor: Marjorie Spencer

Assistant Editor: Margaret Hendrey

Managing Editor: Brian Snapp

Electronic Products, Associate Editor: Mike Sosa

Text Design & Composition: NK Graphics

Designations used by companies to distinguish their products are often claimed as trademarks. In all instances where John Wiley & Sons, Inc., is aware of a claim, the product names appear in initial capital or ALL CAPITAL LETTERS. Readers, however, should contact the appropriate companies for more complete information regarding trademarks and registration.

This book is printed on acid-free paper. ∞

Published by John Wiley & Sons, Inc.

Published simultaneously in Canada.

This publication is designed to provide accurate and authoritative information in regard to the subject matter covered. It is sold with the understanding that the publisher is not engaged in professional services. If professional advice or other expert assistance is required, the services of a competent professional person should be sought.

Library of Congress Cataloging-in-Publication Data:

Burdick, Robert, 1965–
   Essential Windows CE application programming / Robert Burdick.
     p. cm.
   ISBN 0-471-32747-6 (pbk. : alk. paper)
   1. Microsoft Windows (computer file)   2. Operating systems
(Computers) I. Title.
QA76.76.063B856   1999
005.4′469—dc21   98-50484
                                         CIP

Printed in the United States of America.

10 9 8 7 6 5 4 3 2 1

To my wife Katy, for urging me ever onward.

I started working on this book back in April of 1998, when I wrote the original proposal. Since that time a number of people have contributed in various ways to its successful completion.

Great thanks go to Marjorie Spencer and Margaret Hendrey, and Brian Snapp at John Wiley and Sons. Their thoughtful and professional assistance in every aspect of preparing the manuscript of this book are deeply appreciated. Pam Masara of John Wiley and Sons also deserves many heartfelt thanks for encouraging me to contact Marjorie about the idea for this book. Thanks also go to Rob Vermeulen and Peter van der Linden, both accomplished writers in their own right, for their advice and encouragement.

On the technical front, special thanks go to Martin Heller for his thorough critique of the manuscript. Thanks also to John Ruley for his review of my original proposal and his suggestions for how to improve the focus of the book. I must also thank everyone at UpperCase Software for their patience and understanding during my writing of this book. I would particularly like to thank Frank Halasz and Kim McCall for the opportunity to work for them part time while spending the majority of my time writing, and Tom Zurkan for helping me sort out various ActiveSync issues. I would also like to thank Tor Amundson of Navitel Communications for his help with various hardware issues. Former Navitel compatriot Dianna Tai also deserves thanks for her input on data synchronization.

Thanks also go to several people at Philips Mobile Computing Group. David Hargis and James Beninghaus provided me with some great opportunities to write Palm-size PC applications for the Philips NINO. Also, Michael Croot, Benjamin Beasley, and Sathish Damodaran have been instrumental in helping me meet my deadlines.

I must of course add special thanks to Mom and Dad for all of their love and moral support over the years. I also want to thank my mother-in-law,

Olga Disney, for making the best polenta. I cannot forget John and Katrina Staten for giving me the key to their house in Carmel that week in April, where the outline for this book was conceived.

Thanks also go to my two cats, Boots and Luigi, for their company on many late nights while working on this book. Jumping up on the keyboard aside, thanks for the support. (Any last minute typos are entirely their fault!)

Finally, and most importantly, I owe a debt of gratitude to my wife Katy for all of her support and encouragement. There is no way I could have done this without you. Thanks for enduring with me all of the stress, occasional depression, and of course the jubilation that went along with getting this done.

The Windows CE operating system has been available to application programmers for over two years. Independent software vendors have been writing applications for platforms such as the Handheld PC ever since Windows CE was born. At the same time, original equipment manufacturers have been designing and implementing all kinds of new devices based on the operating system. But despite the growth of the operating system and the number of software developers writing applications for it, there are still only a handful of books on the subject of Windows CE programming.

My interest in writing this book comes from over two years of Windows CE programming experience, during which I have been involved in a number of Windows CE development efforts. I am writing this book out of a desire to share with readers the insights I have gained from these experiences.

As the market for mobile and handheld computing devices continues to grow, Windows CE will continue to change. The features present in Windows CE today may not be there tomorrow. Windows CE features will be shaped by the demands of the users of the devices powered by the operating system.

But certain core technologies will always be a part of Windows CE. This book is a guide to the essential features of Windows CE programming.

How This Book Is Organized

This book is organized into four parts which focus on the following Windows CE application programming topics:

- Windows CE programming fundamentals
- Windows CE persistent storage

- User interface programming techniques
- Desktop connectivity, memory, and power management

Part I

Part I of the book covers Windows CE programming fundamentals and contains five chapters. Chapter 1 describes the architecture of the Windows CE operating system. The various Windows CE subsystems are described. In addition, Chapter 1 takes a look at how to use some of the development tools available for writing Windows CE applications. The chapter takes you through a sample session in which you learn how to build a Windows CE application for emulation as well as for a real hardware platform.

Chapter 2 covers the main ingredients of a Windows CE application. Through the example of a generic template application, the chapter introduces the concepts of the Windows CE entry point, registering window classes, writing window procedures, and creating windows. It also points out some of the fundamental differences between Windows CE windows and windows created for desktop Win32 platforms.

Next, Chapter 3 discusses the fundamentals of programming Windows CE controls and dialog boxes. The chapter introduces the basic concepts you need to use Windows CE child and common controls. It also covers how to program modal and modeless dialogs and how to write and use dialog procedures. Chapter 3 finishes with a discussion of programming the Windows CE common dialogs.

Chapter 4 covers Windows CE menus. The majority of the chapter is devoted to a discussion of Windows CE command bars. The command bar control is an essential part of using menus in Windows CE applications.

Part I concludes with a more detailed discussion of programming the Windows CE common controls. In particular, Chapter 5 covers the month calendar control, the date time picker control, rebar controls, and command bands.

Part II

Part II of this book is dedicated to Windows CE persistent storage. The three chapters in this part are your resource for learning how to program the various features of the Windows CE object store.

Chapter 6 covers using the Windows CE file system and how to program the file system API. You will learn about using files and directories, as well as how to access storage cards attached to Windows CE devices. The concepts of this chapter are made clear with the Windows CE File System Explorer sample application.

Chapter 7 discusses Windows CE database technology. You will learn how to create custom databases for your applications and how to read and write database records. You will also learn how to search for database records, and how to sort databases. In addition, Chapter 7 introduces the Windows CE contacts database.

The last chapter of Part II covers the Windows CE registry. Chapter 8 shows you how to use the registry for persistent storage of small amounts of information when a complete database or directory structure is not necessary.

Part III

Part III concentrates on various Windows CE user interface programming techniques. An entire book could easily be devoted to this subject. The five chapters in this section cover some of the more important and common user interface programming subjects.

Chapter 9 begins the discussion by introducing the concept of owner draw controls. With specific examples of programming owner draw buttons, the chapter provides an overview of how Windows CE owner draw controls can be used to customize the appearance of your applications. This chapter also covers the use of offscreen bitmaps. Chapter 10 expands on the owner draw concept with its treatment of the Windows CE custom draw service

Chapter 11 shows you how to take complete control of the appearance and behavior of your controls by describing how to create Windows CE custom controls. This chapter also provides a valuable review of how to program and use dynamic link libraries.

Chapter 12 is about using the Windows CE HTML viewer control. It shows you how to use this control to add HTML viewing capabilities to your Windows CE applications.

Finally, Chapter 13 introduces various nontraditional Windows CE input techniques. In the context of programming applications for the Palm-size PC, this chapter shows you how to program the rich ink control and how to add voice recording capability to applications using the voice recorder control. Chapter 13 also describes how to take advantage of the Palm-size PC navigation buttons.

Part IV

The last part of this book discusses programming some of the desktop connectivity features provided by the Windows CE operating system. This section is invaluable if you are interested in writing Windows CE applications that can share data with desktop PCs.

Chapter 14 covers the ActiveSync technology for data synchronization. You will learn how to program ActiveSync service providers for both a desktop PC and a Windows CE device.

Chapter 15 shows you how to use the remote application programming interface, or RAPI, in order to allow your desktop applications to access Windows CE devices. This chapter also covers file filter programming.

The last chapter of the book introduces Windows CE memory management concepts. Chapter 16 also discusses Windows CE power considerations.

Who Should Read This Book

This book is intended primarily for readers with some Windows programming experience. It assumes that you are familiar with the basic components of a desktop Windows application. It assumes that you have written applications for Windows NT, Windows 95, or Windows 98. It also assumes that you already have some experience with Windows graphics programming topics, such as the Graphics Device Interface (GDI) functions.

However, you do not need to be a Windows expert to use this book for your Windows CE programming needs. In fact, the emphasis in this book is on programming Windows CE at the application programming interface (API) level. This book is perfectly suited, therefore, for a programmer with experience using the Microsoft Foundation Classes (MFC), but whose understanding of how the underlying API works is a bit rusty.

This is why, for example, I cover topics such as window procedures, message loops, and dialog box programming early in the book. Many

Windows programmers successfully write applications with MFC, but do not really understand how that class library works. And since Windows CE is for many reasons not particularly well suited to MFC, this book will provide many intermediate level Windows programmers with a thorough understanding of the internal workings of Windows CE.

Experienced Windows programmers will also find this book valuable because it discusses features specific to Windows CE application programming. Many of the advanced topics in this book, such as data synchronization or programming the remote API, may be unfamiliar to the most experienced Windows NT or Windows 98 programmer.

This book is intended, then, for intermediate level and advanced Windows programmers interested in writing Windows CE applications. Advanced readers may find that they want to skip the chapters that cover subjects they are familiar with from programming desktop Windows applications. For example, chapters covering Windows CE dialog box programming, custom controls, or the Windows CE file system can safely be skipped by advanced readers. However it is worth pointing out that although many Windows CE concepts are similar to their Windows NT or Windows 98 counterparts, there are often subtle differences specific to Windows CE programming. More experienced programmers will therefore find all of the chapters of this book useful.

With few exceptions, all of the examples in this book and all of the code samples on the companion CD-ROM are written in C. C++ is only used for some of the code required for the ActiveSync service providers in Chapter 14, and for the file filter examples of Chapter 15.

Tools You Will Need

To use this book, it is assumed that you have a desktop PC running Windows NT version 4.0 or later with Microsoft Developer Studio Visual C++ version 5.0 or later. It also assumes that you have installed the Windows CE Toolkit for Visual C++ version 2.0 or later.

The companion CD provides a number of sample applications illustrating the programming concepts discussed in this book. Read the appendix, "What's on the CD-ROM?" to find out more about it. If you are interested in running any of these on a Windows CE device such as a Handheld PC or Palm-size PC, it is assumed that you have installed Windows CE Services on your desktop PC. This book also assumes that you are familiar with concepts such as connecting the device to the PC and copying files to the device.

NOTE

DEVELOPMENT MUST BE DONE ON WINDOWS NT

Your Windows CE applications must be developed on Windows NT. The emulation environment only works under Windows NT, and the Windows CE Toolkits and SDKs are only supported for Windows NT.

Before We Begin

This book covers a lot of material. However, no single book can possible discuss all aspects of a subject as vast as Windows CE programming. It is my hope that this book will become your primary reference for understanding the most essential features of Windows CE programming.

As such, this book concentrates on those subjects that are most fundamental to Windows CE. As with any software product, Windows CE will see features come and go. But the fundamental building blocks on which Windows CE applications are based are sure to be around for a long time to come. It is the goal of this book to introduce you to these core Windows CE programming concepts.

Windows CE Application Programming Fundamentals

A thorough understanding of Windows CE programming requires a firm grasp of the fundamentals. We therefore begin our exploration of Windows CE application programming with a discussion of the core Windows CE topics.

We start with a brief look at the overall architecture of the Windows CE operating system. We continue with the anatomy of a typical Windows CE application. Next, programming application building blocks such as Windows CE controls and dialog boxes are covered.

Part I continues with a look at how menus are included in Windows CE applications. We will see that this is very different from how menus are added to Windows 98 or Windows NT applications. The Windows CE command bar control is presented in this discussion. Part I closes with a description of programming Windows CE common controls.

After completing the chapters in Part I, you will have a solid understanding of the basic principles required to write more complex Windows CE application programming.

CHAPTER 1

Getting Started with Windows CE

I n this chapter we take a brief look at the architecture of the Windows CE operating system. We also discuss some of the software development tools available to help you write Windows CE applications.

What Is Windows CE?

Windows CE is a compact, modular 32-bit operating system designed for use on devices with small memory requirements. Windows CE is very similar in design to its larger desktop cousin, Windows NT. Windows CE is a multitasking, multithreaded operating system like Windows NT. It includes most of the user interface features of Windows NT so that software developers can take advantage of most users' familiarity with Windows applications.

Storage on Windows CE devices is a combination of random access memory (RAM) and read-only memory (ROM). Devices can also include expansion flash memory storage cards for additional storage space. PCMCIA cards can be added to many devices, and Windows CE provides full support for such cards.

Since storage is all memory based, the contents of the Windows CE file system is stored in RAM. The operating system and all applications which ship with Windows CE devices are in ROM. The ROM software components are run in place, instead of being paged into RAM, so that they run faster.

Windows CE application programmers get a huge productivity boost because Windows CE is based on the Win32 API. This means that programmers who are familiar with programming for traditional Windows platforms like Windows NT can begin programming Windows CE applications with very little additional training. Certainly there are features that are unique to Windows CE. But understanding traditional Windows programming is a big advantage when moving to the Windows CE operating system.

Architectural Considerations

Windows CE consists of seven subsystems. Each of these subsystems is further broken down into smaller components. The GWE subsystem, for example, consists of smaller components including the window manager and the dialog manager. The seven Windows CE subsystems are:

- The kernel
- The Graphics, Windowing, and Event Subsystem (GWES)
- The object store (including the file system)
- The OEM Adaptation Layer (OAL)
- The device driver layer
- The communication APIs
- Custom shells and the Internet Explorer

The Kernel

The Windows CE kernel is similar to the kernel in Windows NT. It uses the same thread and process model as Windows NT. It supports the same file formats as Windows NT. Additionally, Windows CE uses a virtual memory model similar to Windows NT. You can write Windows CE applications that share memory across multiple processes using memory mapped files.

The Windows CE kernel also implements the object manager. As is the case with Windows NT, windows, GDI objects such as brushes and bitmaps, files, and all other such objects are manipulated by applications through object handles. The handles, as well as the underlying objects they correspond to, are managed by the object manager.

The Graphics, Windowing, and Event Subsystem

Windows CE has combined the user and GDI components into one subsystem. This subsystem, the Graphics, Windowing, and Event Subsystem, is sometimes abbreviated as GWES, or even GWE.

Windows CE behavior such as creating a window, painting a window, or loading a string resource is handled somewhere within the code of this subsystem. All of the Windows CE child controls, such as buttons, list boxes, and the like, are implemented in GWES.

GWES also contains the event manager. This is where the Windows CE messaging capabilities are implemented.

The Object Store

Random access memory in a Windows CE device is divided into two sections. The first is program memory. The other part contains the Windows CE object store. The object store contains the Windows CE file system and the registry. The object store also contains Windows CE databases such as the Contacts database and custom databases created by applications.

The OEM Adaptation Layer

The OEM adaptation layer, or OAL, consists of all of the pieces of software that an original equipment manufacturer (OEM) must implement to port Windows CE to new hardware.

If you are interested in creating a new class of Windows CE products, such as a point-of-sale terminal for ordering parts at the local auto repair shop, you need to get Windows CE to run on your custom hardware. The OAL is where you customize the interrupt service routines and hardware interfaces that allow hardware to communicate with Windows CE.

Programming the OEM adaptation layer is one of the many aspects of Windows CE embedded systems programming. As this subject deserves an entire book of its own, it is not covered in this book, which is devoted to application programming.

The Device Driver Layer

This layer of the Windows CE operating system contains all of the drivers for peripherals that are included with a particular device. These might include flash memory card drivers, video drivers, and keyboard drivers. Detailed coverage of this subject, like the OAL, belongs in an embedded systems programming book.

The Communication APIs

Windows CE includes many of the communication APIs that you might be familiar with from Windows NT. For example, sockets, serial communication, TAPI, and the WinINet APIs are all supported under Windows CE.

One of the most important features of many Windows CE devices is their ability to share data with a desktop PC. Windows CE therefore supports ActiveSync technology. ActiveSync allows application programmers to write service providers for synchronizing application-specific data between Windows CE devices and desktop computers. Additionally, there is file filter support for transferring files between platforms.

Custom Shells and the Internet Explorer

OEMs can use the Windows CE shell component to write their own custom shells for their devices. For example, if you do not want the standard Handheld PC shell, you can write your own.

Windows CE also supports a version of the Internet Explorer.

Windows CE Modularity

One of the nicest features of Windows CE from the OEM point of view is the modularity of the operating system. Each of the various subsystem components can be added or removed as needed. If you are designing a product that does not need any of the Windows CE child controls, for example, you can remove them from the ROM operating system image that runs on your hardware. This allows OEMs to shrink the memory footprint of the operating system by removing any components that are not needed for a particular product.

The SYSGEN tool that ships with the Windows CE Platform Builder makes this possible. When OEMs license Windows CE, they get all of the operating system component libraries. They must, however, build their own operating system image.

Part of this process involves writing a file, called CESYSGEN.BAT, that specifies which component libraries to include in the image. The SYSGEN tool then links those pre-compiled libraries into the operating system image.

Windows CE Programming Tools

Microsoft designed Windows CE with existing Windows programmers in mind. We have already discussed how Windows CE is based on the Win32 API. Programmers can also use many of the same programming tools that they are already familiar with.

This is because Microsoft Developer Studio can be used for writing and debugging Windows CE applications. Emulators for the various Windows CE platforms allow developers to write and debug applications on a desktop PC. The Windows CE Toolkit includes utilities for allowing the Microsoft Developer Studio debuggers to remotely debug applications running on Windows CE hardware. Developers can therefore begin writing and debugging Windows CE applications without learning a new set of development tools.

A Sample Session

To demonstrate the Windows CE programming tools, let's see how to build a sample Windows CE application. We will build the TEMPLATE.EXE application for the Handheld PC emulation environment. Then we will see how to build the same application for real HandheldPC hardware and download it to a device. The project files for this application can be found on the companion CD under \Samples\ template.

Building for Emulation

The first step in building a Windows CE application for any target is to open the workspace file for that application. Choose the Open Work-

Figure 1.1 The Open Workspace menu option.

space option from the Microsoft Developer Studio File menu (Figure 1.1). From the Open Workspace dialog, find and open the file TEMPLATE.DSW (Figure 1.2).

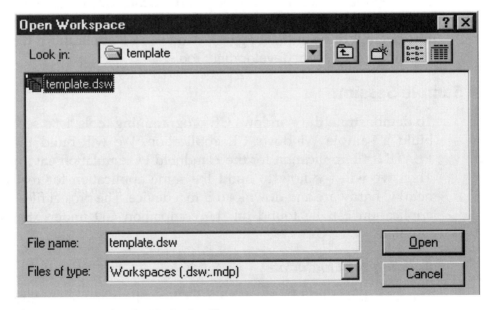

Figure 1.2 Opening the Workspace file.

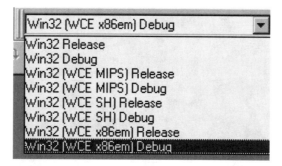

Figure 1.3   Selecting a target build configuration.

You must now specify which *configuration* to build the application for. This is done by making a selection from the combo box shown in Figure 1.3. You can specify whether to build TEMPLATE.EXE for the debug emulation environment. Or you can build the release or debug versions of the application for any of the processors for which you have installed compilers. As we want to build for debug emulation, select the "Win32 (WCE x86em) Debug" option.

If you have installed more than one Windows CE Platform SDK, a second combo box will be included in the Developer Studio toolbar which lets you select the product to build for. For this example, make sure you pick a Handheld PC version.

NOTE
▬▬▬ WHAT IF I DON'T SEE THE CONFIGURATION COMBO BOX?

If the configuration combo box does not appear somewhere in the Developer Studio toolbar, you may need to add it manually. Select the Customize... option from the Tools menu. Then click on the Commands tab. From the Category combo box, select Build. The Buttons group will include the configuration combo box. Simply drag it to your toolbar and drop it where you want it.

Now that you have specified the configuration to build, build the application by choosing the Rebuild All option from the Build menu. The application will compile and link. During the link phase, the Handheld PC emulation environment will start up (Figure 1.4). This simulates a real Handheld PC shell.

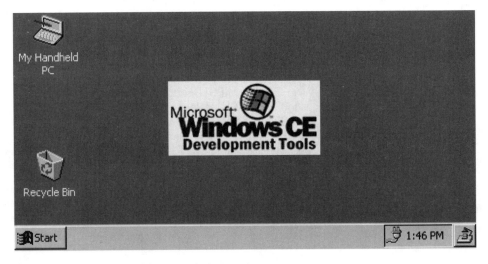

Figure 1.4   The Handheld PC emulation environment.

Now you can run and debug the application just as you would any other Windows application. When you run the TEMPLATE.EXE application in the emulator, you should see something like Figure 1.5.

Building for a Real Device

Building an application for a real Windows CE device configuration is similar to building for the emulator. The differences come in when it's

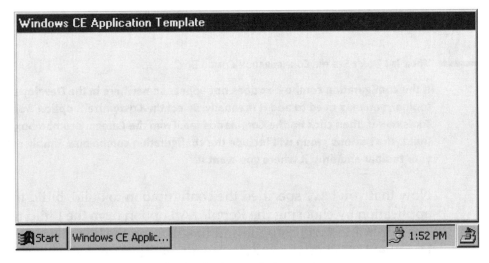

Figure 1.5   Running an application in the emulation environment.

time to transfer the executable image from the desktop PC to the hardware.

Let's say you want to build the release version of TEMPLATE.EXE for a Handheld PC running on an SH3 processor. You simply select "Win32 (WCE SH) Release" from the configuration combo box and rebuild the application (see Figure 1.3).

Now you have to get the application to the Handheld PC. Assuming that you have already connected your Handheld PC to the desktop computer, open the Mobile Devices folder on the desktop PC. You will see a window that looks something like the one in Figure 1.6. The name of the Handheld PC icon will be whatever name you gave your device when you configured it.

Double-click on the icon corresponding to your Windows CE device, and a window similar to that in Figure 1.7 will appear. This window shows the contents of your Handheld PC desktop.

To copy the TEMPLATE.EXE image to your Handheld PC, open Windows NT Explorer and drag the executable you just built to the desired location on the Handheld PC. To place it on the desktop, drop the file in the desktop window shown in Figure 1.7. To copy the file to the Windows directory, double-click the My Handheld PC icon in the Mobile Devices window displaying your Handheld PC desktop. Sev-

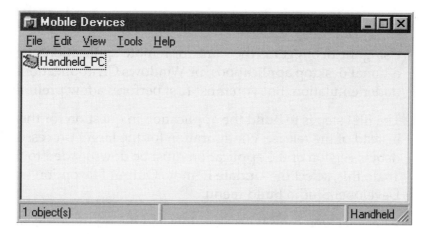

Figure 1.6 The Mobile Devices folder.

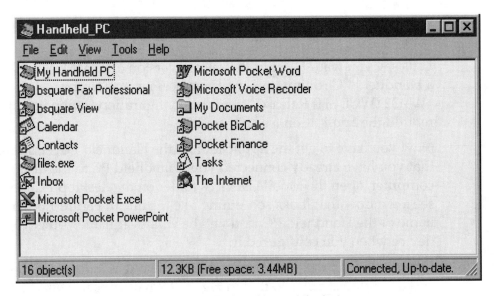

Figure 1.7   A Handheld PC desktop displayed by mobile devices.

eral folders, including the Windows folder, will appear. Drag and drop
TEMPLATE.EXE to the Windows folder.

Debugging on the Windows CE Device

Now that you have successfully built a Windows CE application and
downloaded it to your Handheld PC, let's take a quick look at how to
remotely debug the application using the Visual C++ debugger.

Using the debugger is the same for remote applications as it is for traditional desktop applications, or Windows CE applications running
under emulation. But you must first perform a few preliminary steps.

The first step is to build the application in question for the debug,
instead of the release, configuration for the target processor. Next, this
debug version of the application must be downloaded to the device.
To do this, select the Update Remote Output File option from the
Developer Studio Build menu.

After that, you can set break points and debug the application just as
you would a Windows NT or Windows 98 application.

NOTE
▬▬▬▬ AUTOMATIC DOWNLOADING

It is possible to have Microsoft Developer Studio automatically download release and debug application images. If you select the Always Download option from the Build menu, compiled executables are downloaded to the appropriate target automatically. This also includes "downloading" applications to the emulation object store.

Other Tools

There are many other development tools that can be used for Windows CE programming. For example, the Windows CE Toolkits include Spy, a process viewer, and a heap walker, to name a few. These tools are not covered in this book. Readers are referred to the on-line documentation for details on using the other Windows CE development tools.

Before We Move On . . .

Companies that hire my Windows CE consulting services quickly learn one very important thing about me: Like it or not, I tell it like it is. Being in the business of helping companies succeed in their development efforts requires nothing less.

The hard part of this is that it often means telling people what they least want to hear. Pointing out serious problems with development plans or software designs can mean a lot of reengineering and taking large steps backward on a project. On the positive side, however, willingness to rethink products realistically is a key ingredient to getting a successful product to market.

So, before we turn our attention to the primary purpose of this book, writing Windows CE applications, I want to take a few pages to describe in general terms some of the biggest mistakes that are made which prevent successful Windows CE–based products from getting to market.

The State of the Art

As this book goes to press, Windows CE finds itself in a somewhat precarious situation. The number of shipping Windows CE–based product categories is small. The currently available ones include PC companion devices such as Handheld and Palm-size PCs. The Auto PC platform hopes to make it into all of our cars. Windows CE Jupiter class products fall somewhere between the Handheld PC and a laptop computer in features and complexity. And none of these are selling in droves.

About two years ago I had the opportunity to discuss Windows CE at the Windows Hardware Engineering Conference (WinHEC) in Taipei with Frank Fite, director of the Windows CE Product Unit at Microsoft. Frank discussed the interest customers were expressing in Windows CE for products as diverse as slot machines, golf carts, and refrigerators. Today, Microsoft still discusses the queries it is receiving from companies interested in some day putting Windows CE in slot machines, golf carts, and refrigerators.

I do not make these statements to be glib. I make them to point out that to date, no one has come up with a product based on Windows CE that has generated a huge compulsion to buy in consumers.

What Happened to the Customer?

Each new version of the Windows operating system has been released to try and capture a new segment of the computer market. Windows 98 is intended to be the consumer desktop operating system of choice. Windows NT targets the business and software development communities.

Windows CE was intended to take Microsoft into the brave new world of consumer electronics. Furthermore, many of the products based on Windows CE were meant to target consumers with very little experience with (or interest in using) computers.

This presents an enormous challenge for Microsoft. The majority of the products the company sells are software packages. And despite the fact that consumers use products like Microsoft Office for personal business, the majority of users of Microsoft software are paid between eight and twelve hours a day to use computers in their daily jobs.

Moving the Windows model to products aimed at the less computer-literate segment of the population has thus proved a very daunting task. And in my opinion, based on experience with numerous Windows CE software and hardware vendors, the reason for this

difficulty is simple: Windows CE products today are far too complicated to use.

Build Benefits, Not Features

Many years ago, while working for Integrated System Corporation
(ironically, a real-time operating system vendor and embedded systems
integrator), the team I worked with was treated to an off-site meeting at
our manager's beach house. As part of the work portion of the trip, he
invited a speaker to discuss various topics with us, including how to
sell a product.

This speaker made a simple, yet for many companies, elusive point
which has been forever indelibly imprinted in my brain. He said that
no customer will care how high-tech a product is, how state-of-the-art
the software behind it is, or how sexy the user interface is, if that customer does not get some benefit from using the product. In short, we
won't care about the space-age metal used in a new line of ballpoint
pen if it leaks ink all over our clothes.

Most Windows CE products suffer from such feature distraction. And
nowhere is the problem more pronounced than in the area of Windows CE application user interface design. A trend is evolving where
companies place more power and decision-making authority in the
hands of user interface design teams than in the hands of the very
engineering teams that must make products a reality. Time and again,
features are insisted upon which, given the current limitations of Windows CE, draw out development schedules and cause deadlines to
slip. And worse, such features are sometimes added to product
requirements without a single potential customer expressing a desire
for the feature.

The result is late products that are user interface–intensive and far too
difficult to use by the inexperienced customers to whom they are supposed to appeal.

Ironically, the most successful PC companion product to date, the
PalmPilot, is not based on Windows CE. It has a very boring text-
based user interface. But users love it. The reason is that the PalmPilot
only tries to do a few things for the user. And the tasks it does do are
very easy to perform. My wife used my PalmPilot for the first time to

look up the phone number of our doctor. In ten seconds, she found the phone number she needed. That's a product benefit.

While writing and testing the applications in this book on Handheld and Palm-size PCs, I occasionally handed the devices over to my wife so she could see what was distracting me from spending more time with her. Just figuring out how to launch these applications required the assistance of the author of an entire book about Windows CE.

So Why Use Windows CE?

The foregoing discussion might prompt readers to wonder why I am writing a Windows CE book at all. The reason is that Windows CE is a great platform for building small, easy-to-use devices that do a few things well for their users.

I hope to encourage you to constantly think about the customer for whom you are developing your Windows CE–based products. Desktop software users have (for better or worse) become used to occasionally rebooting a PC when their software crashes. But the user of a consumer electronics product heads straight back to the store for a refund if something goes wrong.

The best advice I can give to companies considering entering the Windows CE market is to keep product designs simple. The success of Windows CE as a consumer product operating system depends on the introduction of products that consumers feel compelled to buy. Have your potential customers define the minimum set of features they would need in order to buy your product. Then incorporate those features into the product with simple user interfaces.

Next, add new features only when enough customers will pay for them. Browsing the Internet on a four-inch screen sounds like a good idea to whom? If the idea originated in the marketing or engineering department, beware. If large numbers of focus group members said it would be nice, start drawing up a new requirements document. In other words, let the customer drive the design.

Now Let's Get To Work

I'll get off my soapbox now and turn my attention to the real objective of this book. In the chapters that follow, we will explore how to program the various features of the Windows CE operating system. It is my belief that after mastering the concepts presented in this book, you will have a good grasp of the essential elements of writing Windows CE applications.

2

A Windows CE
Application Template

It is a bit difficult to know how much to say about the fundamentals of Windows CE programming. It is true that the Windows CE application programming interface (API) is a subset of the traditional Win32 API. It is also true that a majority of application programmers who are interested in developing software for Windows CE–based devices come to this new platform with some level of Windows programming experience.

A detailed introduction to Windows CE programming concepts such as window classes and window procedures would therefore be wasted on programmers with a lot of Win32 experience. On the other hand, not covering these topics at all might alienate those developers whose primary Windows experience is with class libraries such as the Microsoft Foundation Classes (MFC). All of the code samples in this book use the Windows CE API directly in order to promote a solid understanding of Windows CE programming from the most fundamental level. Some coverage of basic concepts is therefore necessary.

In order to strike a compromise, this chapter presents a basic Windows CE template application. This application can be used as the boilerplate for any other application that you may wish to write. It does nothing but display a main application window and implement the most rudimentary window procedure. I promise that nowhere in this application will you find words even remotely reminiscent of "Hello World"!

In fact, the template application presented in this chapter is the foundation of all the other sample applications presented in this book. Each of the applications was written by taking the template source code and adding functionality specific to the topics and techniques under discussion.

This chapter serves a dual purpose. In addition to describing the basic framework of all the applications to follow in this book, it also introduces the basic ingredients of a complete Windows CE application.

Experienced Win32 API programmers and MFC programmers alike will get something out of the presentation of this template application. For example, the Win32 programmer will benefit from seeing the differences in window styles and window messages between Windows CE and desktop Windows platforms. At the same time, MFC programmers will get a refresher on the underlying mechanics of the Windows programming model.

AFTER COMPLETING THIS CHAPTER YOU WILL KNOW HOW TO . . .

Register a window class

Write a window procedure

Create instances of a window class

Write a message loop

What Is a Window, Anyway?

To users of Windows CE–based devices and applications, a window is one of those things on the screen that contains buttons, scroll bars, and all of the other components that are used as the interface to the functionality of the device. To Windows programmers, however, windows have multiple levels of meaning.

One of these levels is that which the user ends up seeing: the user interface aspect of windows. The "look and feel" of an application is defined primarily by the appearance of the application's windows. As application developers and user interface designers, we must constantly think about windows in these graphical terms.

Then there are the behavioral aspects of windows. Users interact with windows by pressing buttons, selecting menu items, and so forth, and the windows in our applications respond by performing actions.

But as programmers, we also think of windows at the more mechanical level. This level, which the users of our software probably never contemplate, is concerned with the way in which Windows CE represents windows.

The Window Class

To Windows CE, all windows are described in terms of a *window class*. The window class describes all of the attributes of the window, from the background color and the window title text to the way in which the window responds to user input. Every Windows CE window, from the most exalted main application window to the lowliest button or edit box, has a window class lurking somewhere behind it. More than one window can be based on the same window class.

A window based on a particular window class is called an *instance* of that window class. Windows CE applications reference individual windows (i.e., window class instances) via their *window handle*. Window handles are defined by the type HWND.

Instances of a window class are created with the Windows CE functions *CreateWindow* or *CreateWindowEx*. We will see *CreateWindow* in action a bit later in the template application.

Windows CE application programmers work with window classes in the form of the WNDCLASS structure, defined as follows:

```
typedef struct _WNDCLASS {
  UINT style;
  WNDPROC lpfnWndProc;
  int cbClsExtra;
  int cbWndExtra;
  HANDLE hInstance;
  HICON hIcon;
  HCURSOR hCursor;
  HBRUSH hbrBackground;
  LPCTSTR lpszMenuName;
```

```
    LPCTSTR lpszClassName;
  } WNDCLASS;
```

The members of the WNDCLASS structure define the attributes of any instance of this class.

lpszClassName points to a null-terminated Unicode string which contains the name of the window class. Applications create instances of a particular window class using this name.

style contains all of the class styles. The styles supported under Windows CE are described in Table 2.1. The *style* parameter is one or more of the values shown in that table, bitwise-ORed together.

lpfnWndProc is a pointer to the *window procedure* for this window class. The subject of window procedures is discussed later.

cbClsExtra specifies the number of extra bytes that Windows CE is to allocate for the WNDCLASS structure. These bytes can be used to define additional class attributes over and above those provided for in the WNDCLASS structure. If used, this value must be a multiple of four. This means that any value stored as an extra class word must be a 32-bit integer.

Extra class words are accessed and set using the Windows CE functions *GetClassLong* and *SetClassLong*. A value assigned to a particular extra class word is the same for all instances of the class.

For example, let's say that every window based on a particular window class needs to have the same caption. This window caption is an

Table 2.1 Windows CE Window Class Styles

STYLE	MEANING
CS_DBLCLKS	Window receives double-click messages (corresponding to double-tapping on the device touch screen).
CS_GLOBALCLASS	Instances of the window class can be created by applications that are not in the same module (.EXE or .DLL) as the window class.
CS_HREDRAW	Redraws the entire window if a movement or size adjustment changes the width of the client area.
CS_NOCLOSE	Close command on the system menu is disabled.
CS_PARENTDC	Sets the clipping region to that of the parent window. This lets instances of this class draw on their parent.
CS_VERDRAW	Redraws the entire window if a movement or size adjustment changes the height of the client area.

attribute that is constant across all instances of the window class. A pointer to the window caption string could therefore be stored as an extra window class word.

Similarly, *cbWndExtra* can be used to specify extra bytes to be allocated for each instance of a window class. In this way, applications can assign unique attributes to each window using the *GetWindowLong* and *SetWindowLong* functions. Each instance of a window class can thus have different values for a particular extra window word. *cbWndExtra*, like *cbClsExtra*, must be a multiple of four.

hInstance identifies the HINSTANCE of the Windows CE module that contains the window procedure of the class.

hIcon and *hCursor* are the icon and mouse cursor to use with instances of the class, respectively. These members can be NULL.

hbrBackground is used to represent the background color of windows based on the particular window class.

The *lpszMenuName* member of WNDCLASS is not supported under Windows CE and therefore must be NULL. This does not exactly mean that Windows CE windows cannot have menus. But menus are added to windows quite differently under Windows CE than under other Windows platforms. Menus in Windows CE are included in *command bar controls*. Command bars are the subject of Chapter 4.

NOTE
ALL WINDOW CLASSES ARE GLOBAL

Under Windows CE, all window classes are global by default. The CS_GLOBALCLASS style is included for compatibility with other Windows platforms.

Registering a Window Class

Simply defining a window class with a WNDCLASS structure does not mean that the class can be used to make instances of that class. Before a Windows CE application can create a window of a particular window class, the window class must be registered.

Window class registration is the mechanism by which the class is made available to the Windows CE operating system. *CreateWindow* requires the window class description in order to successfully create a window instance.

The function used to register a window class is *RegisterClass*:

```
RegisterClass(const WNDCLASS *lpWndClass);
```

RegisterClass takes one argument, a pointer to the WNDCLASS structure representing the window class to be registered. If the function succeeds, it returns an atom representing the registered class. Otherwise it returns zero. An atom is an integer that uniquely identifies a string. In this case, the string identified is the name of the window class, specified in the *lpszClassName* member of the *lpWndClass* parameter.

NOTE

■■■■■ *REGISTERCLASSEX* Is NOT SUPPORTED

The function *RegisterClassEx* is not supported under Windows CE.

The Window Procedure

Windows CE uses the same message-based architecture that the desktop Windows platforms such as Windows NT use. This means that the Windows CE operating system interacts with the windows in the various applications it is running by sending Windows CE messages.

The window procedure for a given window class is the function that implements the response of each instance of that class to every Windows CE message that it receives. Every window class has a window procedure. It can be implemented by the application programmer, in the case of application-defined window classes. In other cases the window procedure is part of Windows CE. For example, all of the child control window classes such as buttons and list boxes have window procedures that are implemented in the Graphics, Windowing, and Events Subsystem of Windows CE.

Window procedures have the following function signature:

```
LRESULT CALLBACK WndProc(hwnd, uMsg, wParam, lParam);
```

The first parameter is the HWND of the window to which a specific Windows CE message is sent. *uMsg* is a UINT containing the message identifier of the message. *wParam* and *lParam* are 32-bit parameters whose values depend on the message being sent.

A window procedure is a *callback function* (as indicated by the CALL-BACK specifier in the function prototype). This means that the function is called by Windows CE, instead of being called directly by an application.

For example, if an application wants to get the font being used by a particular window, it does so by sending the WM_GETFONT message to the window in question. Windows CE then calls the window procedure of the window class from which the window is derived:

```
HFONT hFont;
hFont = (HFONT)SendMessage(hwndSomeWindow, WM_GETFONT,
          0,0L);
```

Window procedures return an LRESULT, which is simply a LONG integer. This return value allows a window procedure to return message-specific information for any message posted or sent to it. If the message is sent via *PostMessage* or *SendMessage*, this result is passed back to the sender through the return value of these functions. The *SendMessage* and *PostMessage* functions are discussed in detail later in this chapter.

Window procedure return values can indicate success or failure of a message, or return requested information. In the WM_GETFONT example above, the value returned from the window procedure of *hwndSomeWindow* is the current window font.

As an application programmer, you will be implementing window procedures of your own. These will often be for application main windows, but you will also implement them for custom controls and other Windows CE window classes that you design. It would seem that it would be quite a challenge to implement responses for all of the hundreds of Windows CE messages that might be sent to your windows.

Luckily, Windows CE takes care of a lot of the default message handling for you. The function *DefWindowProc* is used to call Windows CE and have the operating system provide default behavior for any specified message:

```
DefWindowProc(hWnd, uMsg, wParam, lParam);
```

DefWindowProc has the same arguments as any window procedure. You pass it the corresponding parameters from your window procedure, and Windows CE performs the default processing for the given message. This greatly simplifies the implementation of window behavior. It allows you to concentrate on the messages that have a unique or specific meaning to your particular window classes, and not think about the rest.

For example, in the template application, the only message that we handle ourselves is WM_LBUTTONDOWN. We want the template application to shut down whenever the user taps in the client area of the main window. The window procedure for the main application window class therefore look like this:

```
LRESULT CALLBACK WndProc(
   HWND hwnd,
   UINT message,
   WPARAM wParam,
   LPARAM lParam)
{
  switch(message)
  {
   case WM_LBUTTONDOWN:
    DestroyWindow(hwnd);
    PostQuitMessage(0);
    return (0);
   default:
    return (DefWindowProc(hwnd, message, wParam,lParam));
  }
}
```

All of the several hundred Windows CE messages that can possibly be sent or posted to this window are handled by these few lines of code. All but one are handled by *DefWindowProc*.

NOTE
EACH MESSAGE RETURNS A VALUE

For every message handled by a window procedure, some appropriate value must be returned. The Windows CE on-line documentation specifies the values to return for each message under various circumstances.

Windows implement their specific behavior by responding to the various Windows CE messages. There are literally hundreds of messages in Windows CE, representing user input, window painting, and updating, and all of the other interactions that go on in Windows CE applications. In some sense, the essence of Windows CE programming is mastering these messages and their meanings, and implementing the responses to them to enable your applications to behave in the ways that make them unique and interesting. This book is full of sample applications that will help you get started.

Creating Windows

So much for the window theory. How does an application actually create windows?

Windows CE provides two functions, *CreateWindow* and *CreateWindowEx*, for this purpose. These functions are used extensively in Windows CE applications to create everything from main application windows to child and common controls.

CreateWindow has the following form:

```
CreateWindow(lpClassName, lpWindowName, dwStyle, x, y,
    nWidth, nHeight, hWndParent, hMenu, hInstance, lpParam);
```

CreateWindow creates an instance of a particular window class. *lpClassName* specifies the window class to use. This parameter is the Unicode string name of the class that was used to register the window class (i.e., the *lpszClassName* member of the WNDCLASS structure).

lpWindowName points to a null-terminated Unicode string that contains the window text. For example, in a window with a caption, this string is used as the caption text. For a button, the string is the button text.

dwStyle is a set of one or more window styles. (See Table 2.3 later for a complete list of window styles supported under Windows CE.)

x, *y*, *nWidth,* and n*Height* specify the position and dimensions of the window: *x* and *y* are the x and y coordinates of the upper left corner of the window in screen coordinates. *nWidth* and *nHeight* are the width and height in screen coordinates.

hWndParent is the parent window of the window being created.

hMenu should be NULL for top-level windows. For child windows, such as Windows CE controls, this parameter specifies the child window identifier. This is the value used, for example, to identify the control sending a WM_COMMAND message.

hInstance is the HINSTANCE of the module in which the window is created.

Finally, *lpParam* is the value sent as the *lpCreateParams* member of the CREATESTRUCT sent with the WM_CREATE message that is triggered by the *CreateWindow* call. This parameter can be NULL. We take a closer look at the WM_CREATE message in the next section.

I should point out here that all text in Windows CE is Unicode, not ANSI. Therefore, any string function parameter will be Unicode for Windows CE. All text rendered in any application is Unicode. In short, if it's text, it's Unicode.

NOTE

CREATEWINDOW AND CREATEWINDOWEX ARE NOT REALLY FUNCTIONS

CreateWindow and **CreateWindowEx** are macros that call the **CreateWindowExW** function, the Unicode-based window creation function. Applications should never call **CreateWindowExW** directly, since porting this code to other versions of Windows may be problematic. For example, as Windows NT applications can be built with Unicode support disabled, CreateWindowExW may not be defined. The **CreateWindow** and **CreateWindowEx** macros, however, are guaranteed to resolve to the correct supported API.

CreateWindowEx is the same as *CreateWindow* except that it allows you to specify various *extended window styles* in the first parameter. The rest of the parameters are the same. The extended window styles supported under Windows CE are listed in Table 2.4 (shown later).

The WM_CREATE Message

The *CreateWindow* and *CreateWindowEx* functions both send a WM_CREATE message to the window procedure of the window being created. This message is sent after the window has been created but before it becomes visible. Furthermore, the WM_CREATE message is sent before the *CreateWindow* and *CreateWindowEx* functions return.

As Table 2.2 shows, the WM_CREATE message passes a pointer to a CREATESTRUCT structure containing information about the window being created. Here is the definition of the CREATESTRUCT structure:

```
typedef struct tagCREATESTRUCT
{
  LPVOID lpCreateParams;
  HINSTANCE hInstance;
  HMENU hMenu;
  HWND hwndParent;
```

Table 2.2   The WM_CREATE Message Parameters

PARAMETER	MEANING
wParam	Not used
(LPCREATESTRUCT)lParam	Pointer to the CREATESTRUCT structure containing information about the window being created

```
        int cy;
        int cx;
        int y;
        int x;
        LONG style;
        LPCTSTR lpszName;
        LPCTSTR lpszClass;
        DWORD dwExStyle;
    } CREATESTRUCT, *LPCREATESTRUCT;
```

The *lpCreateParams* member of CREATESTRUCT contains the *lpParam* passed to the *CreateWindow* or *CreateWindowEx* call that generated the WM_CREATE message. If you use the *lpParam* parameter of *CreateWindow* or *CreateWindowEx* to pass some application-specific value for use during window creation, your application extracts it from this member.

hInstance identifies the module (application or dynamic link library) that owns the window that was just created.

hMenu identifies the window menu. As we'll see later in Chapter 4, windows do not support menu bars under Windows CE. The *hMenu* member will therefore be NULL unless the window created is a child window. In that case this member will contain the child window identifier.

hwndParent contains the HWND of the parent of the newly created window.

cx, *cy*, *y*, and *x* are the width, height, y position, and x position of the window, respectively. For top-level windows such as overlapped or pop-up windows, these values are given in screen coordinates. For child windows, these coordinates are relative to the upper left corner of the window's parent.

The *style* and *dwExStyle* members are DWORD values containing the style and extended style bits defined for the newly created window. In other words, these members are exactly the same as the *dwStyle* and *dwExStyle* values passed to *CreateWindow* or *CreateWindowEx*.

Adding or Removing Styles after a Window Has Been Created

It is common to want to add or remove window styles or extended styles from windows after they have been created. You can do this using the *GetWindowLong* and *SetWindowLong* functions.

For example, let's say you want to disable scrolling in a window programmatically. An application would do this:

```
//hwndNoScroll is the window of interest
DWORD dwStyle;
//Get the current set of window style bits
dwStyle = GetWindowLong(hwndNoScroll, GWL_STYLE);
//Disable WS_VSCROLL, WS_HSCROLL
SetWindowLong(hwndNoScroll, GWL_STYLE,
    (dwStyle & ~(WS_VSCROLL | WS_HSCROLL))
```

Finally, *lpszName* and *lpszClass* contain the window caption and window class name, respectively, of the newly created window.

The value that an application returns in response to the WM_CREATE message controls the value returned by the *CreateWindow* and *CreateWindowEx* functions that triggered the WM_CREATE message. If an application returns 0 (zero) in response to this message, *CreateWindow* and *CreateWindowEx* continue with their normal execution. When the functions finish, they return the HWND of the window that was created.

On the other hand, if the application returns –1 in response to WM_CREATE, the new window is destroyed and *CreateWindow* and *CreateWindowEx* return NULL.

Applications respond to the WM_CREATE message to implement custom window creation behavior or to take more control of the window creation process.

As a very contrived example, let's say that we are writing an application that includes a registered window class with a window procedure named *WideWndProc*. Our application wants to refuse to create any instance of this class that is not at least 300 pixels wide.

To implement this feature, the WM_CREATE message handler of *WideWndProc* would look like this:

```
LRESULT CALLBACK WideWndProc(
  HWND hwnd,
```

```
      UINT message,
      WPARAM wParam,
      LPARAM lParam)
{
  switch(message)
  {
   case WM_CREATE:
    LPCREATESTRUCT lpcs;
    lpcs = (LPCREATESTRUCT)lParam;
    if (lpcs->cx < 300)
    {
     return (-1);
    }
    return (0);
   ...
}
```

For future reference, Table 2.3 lists all of the window style values that can be specified in calls to CreateWindow. Similarly, the extended style values that can be used in CreateWindowEx calls are shown in Table 2.4.

NOTE

■■■■■ MDI WINDOWS ARE GONE

Windows CE currently does not support Multiple Document Interface (MDI) windows.

NOTE

■■■■■ MAXIMIZED/MINIMIZED WINDOWS

Windows CE does not support the Windows NT/Windows 98 concepts of maximizing or minimizing windows. This is why you see none of the window styles for including a maximize or minimize box in the style tables in this chapter.

The Windows CE Application Entry Point

As you might remember, back in the days of C programming in non-Windows environments, programs started with a line that looked something like this:

```
void main(int argc, char** argv)
```

This function, *main*, was called the *program entry point*. To make a long story short, this was the function that the operating system called to start the program execution.

Table 2.3 Windows CE Window Styles

STYLE	MEANING
WS_BORDER	Window has a thin border.
WS_CAPTION	Window has a title bar. This style also includes the WS_BORDER style.
WS_CHILD	Window is a child window. Cannot be used with WS_POPUP style.
WS_CLIPCHILDREN	Excludes the area occupied by child windows when drawing occurs within window.
WS_CLIPSIBLINGS	Clips child windows relative to each other.
WS_DISABLED	Window is initially disabled when created.
WS_DLGFRAME	Window has a dialog box style border. Windows with this style cannot have title bars (i.e., cannot have WS_CAPTION style).
WS_GROUP	Identifies the window as the first in a group of controls.
WS_HSCROLL	Window has a horizontal scroll bar.
WS_OVERLAPPED	Window has a title bar and a border.
WS_POPUP	Creates a pop-up window.
WS_SYSMENU	Window has a system menu in its title bar. Such windows must also have the WS_CAPTION style.
WS_TABSTOP	Specifies a control that can receive the keyboard focus when the user presses the Tab key. Pressing the Tab key changes the keyboard focus to the next control with the WS_TABSTOP style.
WS_VISIBLE	Window is initially visible when created.
WS_VSCROLL	Window has a vertical scroll bar.

NOTE

THE WINAPI SPECIFIER

The WINAPI specifier is an alias for the _stdcall calling convention.

The various Win32-based operating systems also need an entry point. For the Win32 operating systems, including Windows CE, the entry point is called *WinMain*. The prototype of *WinMain* is:

```
int WINAPI WinMain(hInstance, hPrevInstance,
    lpCmdLine,nCmdShow);
```

Under Windows CE, multiple copies, or instances, of an application may be launched at a time. The *hInstance* and *hPrevInstance* parameters

Table 2.4 Windows CE Extended Window Styles

EXTENDED STYLE	MEANING
WS_EX_NOACTIVATE	A top-level window created with this style cannot be activated. If a child window has this style, tapping it will not cause its top-level parent to be activated. A window that has this style will receive stylus events, but neither it nor its child windows can get the focus.
WS_EX_NOANIMATION	A window created with this style does not show animated exploding and imploding rectangles when created, closed, or deleted, and does not have a button on the taskbar.
WS_EX_CLIENTEDGE	Specifies that a window has a border with a sunken edge.
WS_EX_CONTEXTHELP	Includes a question mark in the title bar of the window. When the user clicks the question mark, the cursor changes to a question mark with a pointer. If the user then clicks a child window, the child receives a WM_HELP message. The child window should pass the message to the parent window procedure, which should call the WinHelp function using the HELP_WM_HELP command. The Help application displays a pop-up window that typically contains help for the child window.
WS_EX_CONTROLPARENT	Allows the user to navigate among the child windows of the window by using the Tab key.
WS_EX_DLGMODALFRAME	Creates a window that has a double border; the window can, optionally, be created with a title bar by specifying the WS_CAPTION style in the dwStyle parameter.
WS_EX_NODRAG	Creates a window that cannot be dragged
WS_EX_STATICEDGE	Creates a window with a three-dimensional border style, intended to be used for items that do not accept user input.
WS_EX_TOPMOST	Specifies that a window created with this style should be placed above all non-topmost windows and should stay above them, even when the window is deactivated. To add or remove this style, use the SetWindowPos function.
WS_EX_WINDOWEDGE	Specifies that a window has a border with a raised edge.

are both HINSTANCE values. *hInstance* is the handle of the current application instance. *hPrevInstance* is always NULL.[1]

[1]In older versions of Windows, if multiple instances of an application were running, *hPrevInstance* specified the instance of an application that was launched prior to the current one. Under Windows CE you can determine if another instance is running by calling the *CreateMutex* API function and then calling *GetLastError*. If *GetLastError* returns the error code ERROR_ALREADY_EXISTS, there is another instance of the application running.

Windows CE Non-Client Messages

Unlike other Win32-based platforms, Windows CE does not expose any of the non-client area window messages to the application programmer. Non-client area operations, such as painting the non-client area and non-client area stylus tap hit testing, are all performed exclusively by the operating system.

This means that your Windows CE applications cannot include handling for any non-client messages. For example, the following code in the window procedure of a main application window would result in a compilation error:

```
switch(message)
{
case WM_NCPAINT:
//Custom window border drawing code
   return (0);
...
}
```

Specifically, the compiler will issue an error 2065 (undeclared identifier) when it tries to compile the line that contains WM_NCPAINT. Not only are the non-client messages not forwarded to the window procedure, they are actually excluded from the WINUSER.H public header file.

lpCmdLine is a null-terminated Unicode string containing the command line with which the application was launched, if any.

nCmdShow specifies how the main application window is to be shown.

NOTE
WinMain Signature Is A Bit Different In Windows CE

Please note this subtle difference between the Windows CE *WinMain* signature and that for other Win32 platforms: The *lpCmdLine* parameter under Windows CE is a LPTSTR, whereas on Windows NT and Windows 98 it is an LPSTR.

The Message Loop

How do Windows CE messages end up getting to your window procedure if you never call your window procedure directly?

Messages can get to windows in a couple of different ways. One common way is for an application or Windows CE to send messages directly to a window using the *SendMessage* function:

```
SendMessage(hwnd, uMsg, wParam, lParam);
```

Does this look familiar? The parameters of *SendMessage* are the same as the parameters of any Windows CE window procedure. This is because *SendMessage* immediately turns around and calls the window procedure of the window class of which *hwnd* is an instance.

For example, if I wish to change the text in a button in one of my applications, I can do something like this:

```
SendMessage(hwndButton, WM_SETTEXT, 0,
    (LPARAM)(LPCTSTR)TEXT("New Text"));
```

SendMessage has the same function signature as a window procedure. In fact, *SendMessage* calls the window procedure for the specified window. It does not return until the message specified in the second parameter is processed by the window procedure of the window to which the message is sent.

SendMessage processes messages *synchronously*. That is, the message is processed by the window it is sent to immediately. The other way that Windows CE handles messages is *asynchronously*. Many messages, such as requests to update or repaint a window or notifications that the user has tapped the touch screen, are often sent by the operating system to an application faster than the application can process them.

For this reason, when an application starts running, Windows CE creates a *message queue* for that application.[2] The message queue is a place where messages can be put by the operating system or an application to be processed asynchronously, that is, when the application gets around to it.

To process asynchronous messages, an application implements a *message loop*. This is a simple piece of code that continuously looks for messages in the application's message queue. When the message loop finds a message, it gets processed. Otherwise the message loop just keeps on looping.

---

[2]Actually, Windows CE creates a message queue for every thread created by an application. But for the sake of this discussion, we'll think of each application as having only its main thread. The meaning of the application's message queue is therefore unambiguous.

A typical message loop looks like this:

```
while (GetMessage(&msg, NULL, 0, 0) == TRUE)
{
  TranslateMessage(&msg);
  DispatchMessage(&msg);
}
```

That's a pretty short while loop for processing a whole lot of messages. The *GetMessage* function gets a message from the message queue. This message is contained in a message structure of type MSG. This structure includes information such as which message was sent and which window it was intended for. Once a message is retrieved, *DispatchMessage* calls the window procedure corresponding to the window class of the window specified in the message structure.

GetMessage returns TRUE until it receives a WM_QUIT message from the message queue. The *GetMessage* function has the following syntax:

```
GetMessage(lpMsg, hWnd, wMsgFilterMin, wMsgFilterMax);
```

The lpMsg parameter to *GetMessage* is a pointer to a message structure that receives the information about the message retrieved from the message queue. *hwnd* specifies the window for which messages are to be retrieved. In other words, only messages sent to the specified window are removed from the message queue. If this parameter is NULL, messages for any window created by the calling thread are retrieved. *wMsgFilterMin* and *wMsgFilterMax* specify a range of window message identifiers to look for. Setting these both to zero tells *GetMessage* to look for all messages.

We skipped over the *TranslateMessage* step. This function converts virtual key messages into regular key messages before they are dispatched by *DispatchMessage*. We glossed over this because the main point of the discussion is how messages get pulled from the message queue and sent off to the proper window procedure. Once translated, virtual key messages get handled just like any other messages. The use of the *TranslateMessage* function is discussed when we introduce the concept of accelerator tables in Chapter 4.

Adding an asynchronous message to the message queue is called *posting* the message. As was mentioned above, Windows CE posts many messages to an application. However, applications can also post messages to an application or thread using the *PostMessage* function.

The MSG Structure

The MSG structure used by functions like *GetMessage* contains all of the information about a message that was posted to an application's message queue. The structure is defined as:

```
typedef struct tagMSG { // msg
HWND hwnd;
UINT message;
WPARAM wParam;
LPARAM lParam;
DWORD time;
POINT pt;
} MSG;
```

The first four members of this structure are the same parameters that ultimately get sent to the window procedure. *time* specifies the time at which the message was posted. *pt* takes on a meaning under Windows CE that is somewhat different from its meaning under other Win32 platforms. Since Windows CE devices don't use a mouse, there is no concept of a current point. Therefore, rather than indicating the current cursor position, *pt* indicates the last point touched by the user on the touch screen before the message was posted.

PostMessage has the same argument list as *SendMessage*. The message posted is added to the message queue of the thread that created the window specified by the *hwnd* parameter.

The Template Application

Now that we have a basic understanding of how windows are represented in Windows CE and how they respond to messages, we can present the template application, shown in Figure 2.1.

This application creates a main application window and nothing more. Pressing the left mouse button when the cursor is anywhere inside the window while running the application in emulation (or tapping on it with the stylus if it's running on a real device) terminates the application. Terminating the application is accomplished with a call to the Windows CE API *PostQuitMessage*.

You can use this application as the foundation for other real Windows CE applications that you write. It contains all of the boilerplate needed

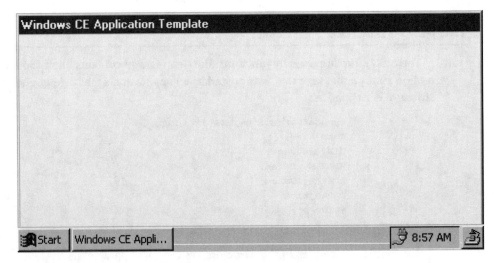

Figure 2.1 The Windows CE Template application.

for any Windows CE application: a *WinMain* function, a message loop, and a main window procedure. Of course you will probably replace the WM_LBUTTONDOWN handler with code of your own.

The project files for this application can be found in the \Samples\ template directory of the companion CD. The application that results from building the project is called TEMPLATE.EXE. The complete source code for the template application is shown in Figure 2.2.

template.h

```
#ifndef __TEMPLATE_H_
#define __TEMPLATE_H_
TCHAR szAppName[] = TEXT("TEMPLATE");
TCHAR szTitle[] = TEXT("Windows CE Application Template");
/* Define the global application HINSTANCE */
HINSTANCE ghInst;
/* Define the HWNDs used by this application
  hwndMain  ->  Main application window
 */
HWND hwndMain;
/* Define the main application window procedure */
LRESULT CALLBACK WndProc(HWND hwnd,
          UINT message,
```

```
                    WPARAM wParam,
                    LPARAM lParam);
    #endif
```

main.cpp

```cpp
#include <windows.h>
#include "template.h"
int WINAPI WinMain(HINSTANCE hInstance,
          HINSTANCE hPrevInstance,
          LPTSTR lpCmdLine,
          int nCmdShow)
{
   MSG msg;
   WNDCLASS wndClass;
   /* Save application instance in ghInst for
    possible use by other functions, such as
    the main window's window procedure.
   */
   ghInst = hInstance;
   /* Register the main window class */
   wndClass.style       = 0;
   wndClass.lpfnWndProc  = WndProc;
   wndClass.cbClsExtra   = 0;
   wndClass.cbWndExtra   = 0;
   wndClass.hInstance    = hInstance;
   wndClass.hIcon        = NULL;
   wndClass.hCursor      = NULL;
   wndClass.hbrBackground = (HBRUSH)(COLOR_WINDOW+1);
   wndClass.lpszMenuName = NULL;
   wndClass.lpszClassName = szAppName;
   RegisterClass(&wndClass);
   /* Create the application's main window */
   hwndMain = CreateWindow(szAppName,
             szTitle,
             WS_VISIBLE|WS_OVERLAPPED,
             0,0,
             GetSystemMetrics(SM_CXSCREEN),
             GetSystemMetrics(SM_CYSCREEN),
             NULL,
             NULL,
             hInstance,
             NULL);
   while (GetMessage(&msg, NULL, 0, 0) == TRUE)
   {
     TranslateMessage(&msg);
     DispatchMessage(&msg);
   }
   /* Return the wParam associated with the WM_QUIT message
    that got us out of the while loop above. This wParam
```

```
     contains the exit code passed to PostQuitMessage.
  */
  return (msg.wParam);
}
LRESULT CALLBACK WndProc(HWND hwnd,
          UINT message,
          WPARAM wParam,
          LPARAM lParam)
{
  switch(message)
  {
  case WM_LBUTTONDOWN:
    DestroyWindow(hwnd);
    PostQuitMessage(0);
    return (0);
  default:
    return (DefWindowProc(hwnd, message,
            wParam,lParam));
  }
}
```

Figure 2.2   TEMPLATE.EXE source code.

Concluding Remarks

In this chapter we have covered the basic window and message handling concepts you need to understand in order to write Windows CE applications. To make your applications more useful, you will want to use Windows CE controls and dialog boxes to allow users to interact with your applications. The next chapter describes how to program Windows CE controls and various kinds of dialog boxes.

3

Controls and Dialog Boxes

I n this chapter, we look at how to program some of the most fundamental ingredients of Windows CE applications. Specifically, this
chapter introduces Windows CE child and common control programming. After that, it describes how to include dialog boxes in your
applications. It finishes with an introduction to the Windows CE
common dialog library.

AFTER COMPLETING THIS CHAPTER YOU WILL KNOW HOW TO . . .

Program child controls

Program common controls

Use modal and modeless dialogs

Use the Windows CE common dialogs

Programming Child Controls

A crucial part of almost every Windows CE user interface is the set of
child controls with which users interact. Windows CE child controls

include push buttons, list boxes, and edit controls, as well as all of the other control types listed in Table 3.1.

Child controls are created by calling *CreateWindow* or *CreateWindowEx*, just as top-level application windows are created. The window class name to use for a given control type is given in Table 3.1.

Child controls communicate with their parent window by sending WM_COMMAND messages. These messages include the *control identifier* associated with the control, and a *notification code* that indicates what sort of action the user performed with the control. All of this information is sent to the parent window in the WM_COMMAND message parameters, as shown in Table 3.2.

The command identifier is an integer specified in the *hMenu* parameter of the *CreateWindow* call. For example, to create a push-button control with command identifier IDC_BUTTON and the string "Exit" inside, you could write:

```
#define IDC_BUTTON 1028
HWND hwndButton;
hwndButton = CreateWindow(
   TEXT("BUTTON"),             //Control class name
   TEXT("Exit"),              //Button text
   WS_CHILD|WS_VISIBLE|WS_PUSHBUTTON, //Button styles
   0,0,75,35,                 //x, y, width, height
   hwndParent,                //Parent window
   (HMENU)IDC_BUTTON,          //Command identifier
   hInstance,                 //Application HINSTANCE
   NULL);
```

Note that both the control window class name and the button text specified are Unicode strings.

Table 3.1 Windows CE Child Control Classes

CONTROL	WINDOW CLASS NAME
Button control	BUTTON
Edit control	EDIT
Combo box control	COMBOBOX
List box control	LISTBOX
Scroll bar control	SCROLLBAR
Static control	STATIC

Table 3.2 The WM_COMMAND Message

PARAMETER	MEANING
HIWORD(wParam)	Notification code. If the message is from a menu item, this value is 0.
LOWORD(wParam)	Specifies the command identifier of the control (or menu item) sending the WM_COMMAND message.
(HWND)lParam	The HWND of the control sending the message. If the WM_COMMAND message is not sent by a control, this value is NULL. For example, this is the case if the message is sent by a menu item.

Responding to WM_COMMAND Messages

As noted earlier, controls send WM_COMMAND messages to their parent windows to tell them that some action has taken place. For example, when a button is pushed, the button sends a WM_COMMAND message with a notification code BN_CLICKED.

The window procedure of the parent window of the button IDC_BUTTON we created in the previous section might include the following code. This code implements the window's response to the button being pressed:

```
LRESULT CALLBACK WndProc(
   HWND hwnd,
   UINT message,
   WPARAM wParam,
   LPARAM lParam)
{
   switch(message)
   {
   //Other window messages
   //...
   case WM_COMMAND:
    UINT nID;
    nID = LOWORD(wParam);
    switch(nID)
    {
    case IDC_BUTTON:
     DestroyWindow(hwnd);
     PostQuitMessage(0);
     break;
    default:
     break;
    }   //End of switch(nID) statement
```

```
     return (0);
   default:
    return (DefWindowProc(hwnd, message, wParam, lParam));
   }   //End of switch(message) statement
 }
```

The identifier of the control sending the WM_COMMAND message is assigned to *nID*. The switch statement that follows then tests for the identity of the control, and performs whatever action that control specifies. In this case, the Exit button terminates the application.

From the example above, you can see that applications should return zero if they handle the WM_COMMAND message.

Notice that we ignored the notification code. Although not perfectly legitimate, this is usually the only button control notification of interest to applications. It is therefore common practice to ignore the notification code in the case of button WM_COMMAND messages.

At other times the notification code is important. For example, assume that you want to know when an edit control receives input focus. Assuming the edit control command identifier is specified by IDC_EDIT, your application could test for this in the parent window procedure as follows:

```
LRESULT CALLBACK WndProc(
  HWND hwnd,
  UINT message,
  WPARAM wParam,
  LPARAM lParam)
{
  switch(message)
  {
  //Other window messages
  //...
  case WM_COMMAND:
   UINT nID, nNotify;
   nID = LOWORD(wParam);
   switch(nID)
   {
   case IDC_EDIT:
    nNotify = HIWORD(wParam);
    if (nNotify == EN_SETFOCUS)
    {
      //Do something
    }
    break;
   default:
    break;
```

```
    }    //End of switch(nID) statement
    return (0);
  default:
    return (DefWindowProc(hwnd, message, wParam, lParam));
  }    //End of switch(message) statement
}
```

For a complete list of the notification codes sent by the various Windows CE child controls, refer to the Microsoft Developer Studio Windows CE on-line documentation.

The complete sample application from which the examples in this section come can be found on the companion CD in the directory \Samples\controls.

Programming Common Controls

Back in the days before there were 32-bit versions of Windows, the Windows user interface was limited to the child controls. Custom controls could be implemented by ambitious programmers. But the core control set was the child controls.

When Windows 95 and Windows NT came out, however, a brand new set of controls was included with the operating systems. The common control library contains the controls that were added to Windows for Windows 95 and NT. Today, this library is still around, and there is a version of it for Windows CE. The library includes controls like list view controls and tree view controls. Table 3.3 lists the Windows CE

Table 3.3 The Windows CE Common Control Classes

CONTROL	WINDOW CLASS NAME
Date Time Picker	DATETIMEPICK_CLASS
Header control	WC_HEADER
Month calendar control	MONTHCAL_CLASS
Progress bar	PROGRESS_CLASS
Rebar control	REBARCLASSNAME
Tab control	WC_TABCONTROL
Trackbar control	TRACKBAR_CLASS
Tree view control	WC_TREEVIEW

common control classes. Note that Table 3.3 does not include those controls that have their own unique API. Such controls are not created using *CreateWindow,* and hence the window class names of these controls are not included.

Programming these controls is very similar to using the child controls. However, you must link with the common control library and initialize this library from your application. Also, the common controls do not communicate with their parent windows via WM_COMMAND messages. These controls send notifications by means of the WM_NOTIFY message.

NOTE
WINDOWS CE COMMON CONTROLS PROGRAMMING DETAILS

This section is only intended as an introduction to the mechanism by which common controls communicate with applications. Refer to Chapter 5 for a more detailed description of programming the Windows CE common controls.

Using the Common Controls Library

To use any of the Windows CE common controls, an application must link with the library COMMCTRL.LIB. It must then initialize the library by calling the function *InitCommonControls.*

Calling *InitCommonControls* further requires the application to include the header file COMMCTRL.H. *InitCommonControls* is typically called in an application's *WinMain* function.

Responding to Common Control Notifications

Common control notifications are a bit more complex than notifications sent by child controls. Notifications are sent in the form of the WM_NOTIFY message. This message includes a pointer to an NMHDR structure, which contains information about the notification being sent.

```
typedef struct tagNMHDR {
    HWND hwndFrom;
    UINT idFrom;
    UINT code;
} NMHDR;
```

hwndFrom is the window handle of the common control sending the notification. *idFrom* is the identifier of the control.

code indicates the notification code identifying the particular notification being sent. This value is used like the notification code sent by a child control.

Let's look at a typical example of how an application responds to common control notifications. Assume that a main window wants to know when the selected tab of a tab control in that window is changed. The main window procedure would respond to the WM_NOTIFY message as follows:

```
LRESULT CALLBACK WndProc(
   HWND hwnd,
   UINT message,
   WPARAM wParam,
   LPARAM lParam)
{
   switch(message)
   {
   //Other window messages
   //...
   case WM_NOTIFY:
    LPNMHDR lpnmhdr;
    lpnmhdr = (LPNMHDR)lParam;

    switch(lpnmhdr->idFrom)
    {
    case IDC_TAB:
     switch(lpnmhdr->code)
     {
     case TCN_SELCHANGE:
     //Perform some action
      break;
     default:
      break;
     }   //End of switch(lpnmhdr->code) statement
     break;
    default:
     break;
    }   //End of switch(lpnmhdr->idFrom) statement
    return (0);
   default:
    return (DefWindowProc(hwnd, message, wParam, lParam));
   }   //End of switch(message) statement
}
```

The window procedure determines which control is sending the notification by looking at the command identifier in *lpnmhdr->idFrom*. It then checks the notification code and responds accordingly to the tab control notification it is interested in.

The complete sample application from which this code sample comes is found on the companion CD in the directory \Samples\tab.

Dialog Boxes

Many operations in Windows CE applications require user input to perform properly. Opening or saving files generally requires that the user specify a file name. To search a file for a specific string, a user enters text that the application uses to perform the search. A *dialog box* is a window through which users enter information required by an application to perform some task.

Dialog boxes can be either *modal* or *modeless*. A modal dialog box is displayed temporarily to accept user input (Figure 3.1). An important characteristic of a modal dialog box is that its owner window is disabled while the dialog box is present. Thus a modal dialog gives the effect of suspending an application until the user dismisses it.

A modeless dialog box, on the other hand, does not prevent users from interacting with the owner window (Figure 3.2). Modeless dialog boxes are often used in cases where the application may require frequent user input. Reopening the dialog box in such cases would be needlessly inconvenient. The dialogs that many applications use to provide text searching capability are often implemented as modeless dialog boxes.

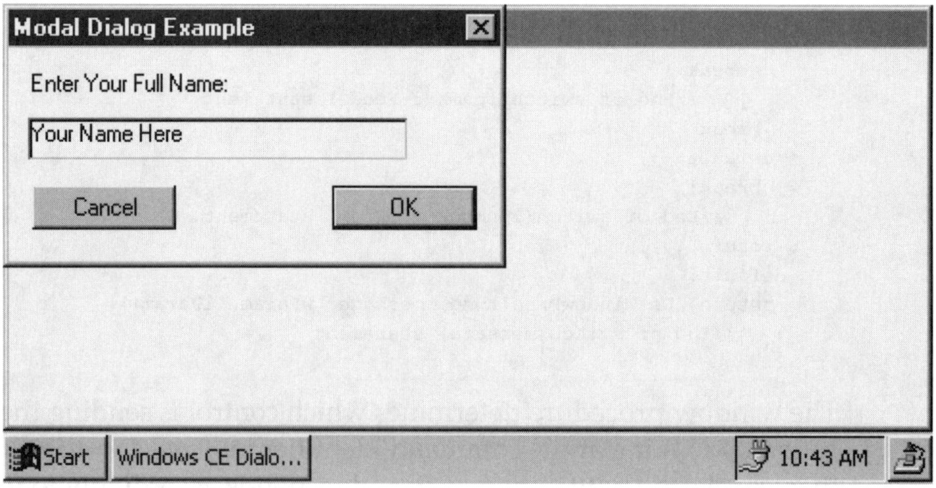

Figure 3.1 A modal dialog box example.

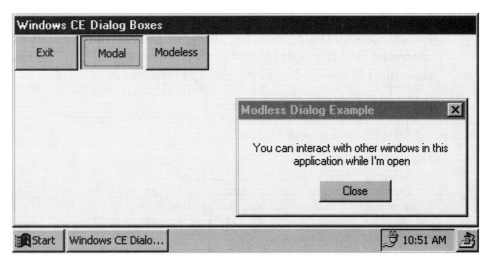

Figure 3.2 A modeless dialog box example.

Despite their differences, adding modal or modeless dialog boxes to your Windows CE applications involves the same basic steps. In the case of modeless dialogs, there are some additional programming requirements, but the basic idea is the same. Adding dialog boxes to an application involves these basic steps:

- Designing the dialog box and adding its dialog resource definition to the application's .rc file
- Programming the dialog procedure that handles Windows CE messages sent to the dialog box
- Invoking the dialog box at the appropriate times from the application

This chapter includes a sample application on the companion CD that demonstrates many of the concepts covered in this chapter. The application is called DIALOGS.EXE and can be found in the directory \Samples\dialogs. This application includes the implementations of the dialog boxes shown in Figures 3.1 and 3.2.

Dialog Box Resources

The appearance of the dialog boxes in Figures 3.1 and 3.2 was defined in a dialog box resource. The dialog box resource definition determines where the various controls appear. It also specifies the dialog box caption text, the dialog box size, and the font used when rendering text in the dialog box.

Dialog box resource definitions appear in the resource file (.RC file) of an application. Dialog box resources can be created manually or by means of the Microsoft Developer Studio Dialog Editor. The resource definition of the modal dialog box in Figure 3.1 is:

```
IDD_MODAL DIALOG 0, 0, 170, 66
STYLE DS_MODALFRAME | WS_POPUP | WS_CAPTION | WS_SYSMENU
CAPTION "Modal Dialog Example"
FONT 8, "MS Sans Serif"
BEGIN
  DEFPUSHBUTTON  "OK",IDOK,112,43,50,14
  PUSHBUTTON    "Cancel",IDCANCEL,8,43,50,14
  LTEXT       "Enter Your Full Name:",IDC_STATIC,7,7,70,8
  EDITTEXT    IDC_NAME,7,22,132,14,ES_AUTOHSCROLL
END
```

The first line of this definition contains the resource identifier of the dialog (IDD_MODAL) and the dimensions of the dialog box in *dialog units*. Dialog units are defined in terms of the system font used by the particular Windows CE device. These units are interpreted by the system such that the dimensions of a dialog box are the same regardless of the resolution of the display.

Dialog box and dialog box child control identifiers are typically defined in the application's RESOURCE.H file. Some standard command identifier definitions, such as IDOK and IDCANCEL, are defined in the Windows CE header file WINUSER.H.

The next line defines the styles assigned to the dialog. Line 3 specifies the dialog box caption text, and line 4 specifies the font to be used by the dialog box.

The most interesting part of the dialog box resource definition lies between the BEGIN and END statements. The lines that appear between these statements specify the Windows CE controls that will appear in the dialog box.

The most general way to define a dialog box control is with the CONTROL statement:

```
CONTROL text,control identifier,class name,
  style,x,y,width,height
```

As an example, a push-button control with control identifier IDC_EXIT might be defined as follows:

```
CONTROL "Exit", IDC_EXIT, "BUTTON",
  WS_CHILD|WS_VISIBLE|BS_PUSHBUTTON,
  0,0,65,35
```

Windows CE also defines a number of aliases for many of the child controls commonly used in dialog boxes. For example, in the case of the resource definition of the dialog in Figure 3.1, DEFPUSHBUTTON specifies a push button control that is the default button. The PUSHBUTTON control specifies a button control with style BS_PUSHBUTTON. The on-line documentation defines the full set of resource definition keywords.

The Dialog Box Procedure

To Windows CE, a dialog box is like any other window. Whenever an application creates a dialog box, deep in the implementation of Windows CE a call to *CreateWindowExW* is made. Similarly, dialog boxes respond to Windows CE messages. This implies that dialog boxes have a function for responding to messages similar to the window procedure discussed in the previous chapter.

A *dialog procedure* is an application-defined function that is assigned to a dialog box for responding to Windows CE messages. Programming a dialog procedure is very similar to coding the window procedure of a standard window. There are, however, a few subtle and very important differences.

When you use dialog boxes in your applications, you generally do not define a window class for the dialogs as you do for other windows. The dialog box window class for most types of dialog boxes available in Windows CE is defined by the operating system. This means that the true window procedure used by a dialog box is defined and provided by Windows CE.

The dialog procedure that you define as an application programmer and assign to a dialog box is simply a hook into the real dialog box window procedure. The dialog box window procedure defined in Windows CE receives all dialog box messages. The operating system then passes the messages to the application-defined dialog procedure, giving the application the first opportunity to handle them. If the application does not handle a particular message, it is handled by Windows CE.

A dialog procedure has the following prototype:

```
BOOL CALLBACK DlgProc(HWND hwndDlg, UINT message,
    WPARAM wParam, LPARAM lParam);
```

This is almost exactly the same as the standard window procedure definition. The only difference is the return type. Dialog procedures return a BOOL instead of an LRESULT. This return value tells Windows CE whether or not to pass handling of a particular message on to the default dialog box message handler. Returning FALSE means that your dialog procedure did not handle a message. TRUE means it did.

This brings us to another important difference between dialog procedures and regular window procedures. A regular window procedure typically calls *DefWindowProc* to make Windows CE perform default processing for any unhandled Windows CE messages. A dialog procedure should return FALSE for any unhandled messages. The Windows CE API does include the function *DefDlgProc* for performing default message processing. This function should only be used in conjunction with private dialog classes.

Private Dialog Classes

The window classes associated with the majority of the dialog boxes you will use in your applications are defined by Windows CE. Invoking a modal dialog by calling *DialogBox* or displaying a message dialog with a call to *MessageBox* creates an instance of an operating system–defined window class.

This is generally adequate for most applications. Programmers create customized dialog boxes by specifying the contents and appearance of a dialog via a resource template. Custom behavior is provided by the dialog procedure implementation.

It is possible to completely define the dialog box window class within an application, however. *Private dialog class* is the term used to describe any such dialog class. A private dialog class is similar to a regular window class. The application defines the dialog procedure and specifies how all messages are handled. The Windows CE–defined dialog procedure plays no part in processing private dialog class messages.

Using private dialog classes in your applications is the only time you should ever call *DefDlgProc*. This function is the dialog box equivalent of *DefWindowProc*. It performs default processing for unhandled dialog messages. Calling this function from any other dialog procedure will cause your application to misbehave in very unexpected ways.

Table 3.4 The WM_INITDIALOG Message

PARAMETER	MEANING
(HWND)wParam	Window handle of the control to which Windows CE will assign default focus. Focus is assigned only if the dialog procedure returns TRUE in response to this message.
lParam	Initialization parameter passed by DialogBoxParam or Dialog-BoxIndirectParam.

The WM_INITDIALOG Message

A dialog box procedure typically implements custom responses to fewer messages than a standard window procedure. Most message processing for a typical dialog box is performed by Windows CE.

Since most dialog boxes are used for collecting user input, they generally respond to WM_COMMAND messages sent by their child controls. They also typically handle a message that is only sent to dialog boxes called WM_INITDIALOG. This message is used to initialize the contents of a dialog box, and is sent by Windows CE after the dialog box window is created but right before the dialog box is displayed. WM_INITDIALOG can be thought of as the dialog box equivalent of WM_CREATE. Table 3.4 lists the WM_INITDIALOG parameters and their meanings.

Returning FALSE after processing WM_INITDIALOG tells Windows CE not to set the default focus. *lParam* can contain an application-specific parameter used to initialize the dialog box. We will discuss this in greater detail later when we talk about how to invoke a dialog box.

An Example

Let's take a look at an example modal dialog procedure. This example comes from the sample application DIALOGS.EXE. The dialog box that corresponds to this code is shown in Figure 3.1. IDC_NAME is the command identifier of the edit control.

```
#define MAX_STRING_LENGTH 129
TCHAR pszUserText[MAX_STRING_LENGTH];
BOOL CALLBACK ModalDlgProc(HWND hwndDlg,
          UINT message,
          WPARAM wParam,
          LPARAM lParam)
{
```

```
    UINT nID;
    HWND hwndEdit;
    switch(message)
    {
    case WM_INITDIALOG:
     hwndEdit = GetDlgItem(hwndDlg, IDC_NAME);
     SetWindowText(hwndEdit, TEXT("Your Name Here"));
     return (FALSE);
    case WM_COMMAND:
     nID = LOWORD(wParam);
     switch(nID)
     {
     case IDOK:
      hwndEdit = GetDlgItem(hwndDlg, IDC_NAME);
      GetWindowText(
        hwndEdit,
        pszUserText,
        MAX_STRING_LENGTH);
     case IDCANCEL:
       EndDialog(hwndDlg, nID);
       break;
     default:
       break;
     }    //End of switch(nID) block
     return (TRUE);
    default:
     return (FALSE);
    }      //End of switch(message) block
  }
```

This dialog procedure is pretty simple. The WM_INITDIALOG handler sets the edit control text to a default string. It uses the *GetDlgItem* function:

```
GetDlgItem(hDlg, nIDDlgItem);
```

This function returns the window handle of the control with control identifier *nIDDlgItem* contained by the dialog box specified by the window handle *hDlg*.

The WM_COMMAND handler responds to the OK button by reading the edit control text into the string *pszUserText* by calling *GetWindowText*. Both the OK and Cancel buttons end up closing the dialog box by calling *EndDialog*. More on this function in the next section.

The WM_COMMAND handler returns TRUE to tell Windows CE that this particular message has been handled. You will often see dialog box procedures return FALSE at the end of their WM_COMMAND handlers, instead of TRUE. Many programmers prefer this, since returning FALSE is consistent with returning zero from a standard window procedure. And since the default WM_COMMAND processing is to do nothing, returning FALSE instead of TRUE produces no ill effects.

Invoking and Destroying Modal Dialogs

We have yet to discuss how an application displays a modal dialog box. Windows CE provides four functions for invoking modal dialog boxes. We will discuss the two most common of these functions.[1]

The first of these functions is aptly named *DialogBox*:

```
DialogBox(hInstance, lpTemplate, hWndParent, lpDialogFunc);
```

This function displays the modal dialog specified by the resource template *lpTemplate*. *hInstance* is an HINSTANCE identifying the module that contains the dialog resource definition. *hWndParent* is the dialog box parent window. *lpDialogFunc* is a pointer to the dialog procedure to use with the modal dialog.

The second function is *DialogBoxParam*. This functions works just like *DialogBox*, except that it includes an extra parameter:

```
DialogBoxParam(hInstance, lpTemplate, hWndParent,
   lpDialogFunc, lpInitParam);
```

The additional parameter *lpInitParam* is passed to the dialog procedure *lpDialogFunc* as the *lParam* of the WM_INITDIALOG message. This parameter can be used to pass application-specific initialization information to the modal dialog box.

A modal dialog is destroyed by calling *EndDialog*:

```
EndDialog(hDlg, nResult);
```

hDlg is the window handle of the dialog box. *nResult* specifies the value to be returned to the application by the function that invoked the dialog, such as *DialogBox* or *DialogBoxParam*. In other words, whatever value is passed to *nResult* is the value returned by *DialogBox* or *DialogBoxParam*.

[1]The other two functions are *DialogBoxIndirect* and *DialogBoxIndirectParam*. These functions are used to display modal dialog boxes defined by dialog templates contained in program memory instead of in a resource file. This technique is uncommon enough to leave out of our discussion with no disservice to the reader.

This return value is typically used to tell the application which dialog box button was pressed. For example, here is how DIALOGS.EXE calls *DialogBox* to invoke the modal dialog whose resource identifier is IDD_MODAL. The return value is used to determine what action to perform after the dialog box is closed.

```
if (IDOK==DialogBox(ghInst, MAKEINTRESOURCE(IDD_MODAL),
  hwnd, (DLGPROC)ModalDlgProc))
{
  //Do something
}
```

Modeless Dialog Boxes

Modal dialogs are designed to collect user input and to not go away until the user dismisses them in some way. This behavior is no accident. When an application calls *DialogBox* (or any of the other functions that invoke a modal dialog box), Windows CE creates a new message loop specifically for the dialog box. This loop does not exit until the *EndDialog* is called for the dialog box. Hence the *DialogBox* call does not return until the dialog box is closed.

The fundamental difference between modeless dialogs and modal dialogs is that modeless dialog messages are put on the message queue of the thread that creates them. Therefore, modeless dialog box messages get dispatched by the message loop of the same thread that creates the dialog. In most cases, this means that the message loop in your application's *WinMain* function processes modeless dialog box messages.

The IsDialogMessage *Function*

Windows CE does not create a separate message loop for modeless dialogs or take care of the details of dispatching messages intended for modeless dialogs. So to use modeless dialogs, your application will clearly have to do more work that it does for modal dialogs.

This is where the *IsDialogMessage* function comes in. This function determines if a particular message is intended for the specified dialog. If so, *IsDialogMessage* processes the message.

```
IsDialogMessage(hDlg, lpMsg);
```

hDlg is the HWND of a modeless dialog, and *lpMsg* is a pointer to a MSG structure. If *IsDialogMessage* processes the message, it returns TRUE. Otherwise it returns FALSE.

This leads us to the time-tested technique for handling modeless dialog messages in message loops. Let's assume that a Windows CE application has created a modeless dialog with window handle *hwndModeless*. (We'll get to how to create modeless dialogs in the next section.) So that the application and the modeless dialog can share the same message loop, the message loop is rewritten as shown in Figure 3.3:

```
while (GetMessage(&msg, NULL, 0, 0) == TRUE)
{
  if (!hwndModeless ||
    !IsDialogMessage(hwndModeless, &msg))
  {
    TranslateMessage(&msg);
    DispatchMessage(&msg);
  }
}
```

Figure 3.3 Modifying the message loop to accommodate a modeless dialog box.

We have given *IsDialogMessage* the first chance to handle each and every message on the application's message queue. If the modeless dialog is not NULL and the message was indeed meant for the dialog, *IsDialogMessage* will process it and return TRUE.

IsDialogMessage evaluating to TRUE means that the code inside the if statement is skipped. If it returns FALSE, the message is processed in the normal way by *TranslateMessage* and *DispatchMessage*.

Creating and Destroying Modeless Dialog Boxes

The message loop modification discussed above is the most important thing to grasp about programming modeless dialog boxes. But we still have to see how to invoke and dismiss them.

There are four functions available for creating modeless dialogs, as there were for creating modal dialogs. We will discuss *CreateDialog* and *CreateDialogParam*. (*CreateDialogIndirect* and *CreateDialogIndirectParam* are analogous to *DialogBoxIndirect* and *DialogBoxIndirectParam*. These functions are not covered here. See the footnote in the section "Invoking and Destroying Modal Dialogs" for the reason.)

CreateDialog creates a modeless dialog and returns the HWND of the dialog if successful:

```
CreateDialog(hInstance, lpTemplate, hWndParent, lpDialogFunc);
```

The arguments have exactly the same meaning as they do in the function *DialogBox*.

Similarly, *CreateDialogParam* is used just like *DialogBoxParam*:

```
CreateDialogParam(hInstance, lpTemplate, hWndParent,
   lpDialogFunc, lpInitParam);
```

Again the difference is the return value. If successful, *CreateDialogParam* returns the HWND of the dialog it creates. Both *CreateDialog* and *CreateDialogParam* return NULL if they fail.

Dismissing modeless dialogs is done by calling *DestroyWindow*. An application should never use *EndDialog* to destroy a modeless dialog.

We can now see how to get the window handle of the modeless dialog required for the message loop. When using a modeless dialog, an application typically maintains a global HWND variable that is set to NULL as long as the modeless dialog does not exist. Once the dialog is created, the global variable is assigned the dialog's window handle.

The application DIALOGS.EXE provides an example. The application initializes *hwndModeless* to NULL. The if statement in the message loop of Figure 3.3 therefore never gets to call *IsDialogMessage*. All messages posted to the application's message queue therefore get handled the usual way.

But once the modeless dialog is created, hwndModeless is no longer NULL. The modeless dialog IDD_MODELESS is displayed when a user presses the Modeless button in the main application window. The portion of the main window procedure that responds to the corresponding WM_COMMAND message is:

```
HWND hwndModeless; /Modeless dialog window handle
//Inside the main window WM_COMMAND handler
case IDC_MODELESS_BUTTON:
  hwndModeless = CreateDialog(
  ghInst,
  MAKEINTRESOURCE(IDD_MODELESS),
  hwnd,
  (DLGPROC)ModelessDlgProc);
```

Messages intended for the dialog box are now processed by *IsDialogMessage*.

To dismiss the modeless dialog, the user taps the Close button. Here is how the modeless dialog procedure responds:

```
//Inside the dialog procedure WM_COMMAND handler
case IDCANCEL:
  DestroyWindow(hwndDlg);
  hwndModeless = NULL;
  break;
```

After destroying the actual dialog window, the global variable *hwnd-Modeless* is set back to NULL. Thus the application's message loop doesn't send messages to *IsDialogMessage* until a user again creates the modeless dialog box.

The Windows CE Common Dialogs

If you have been using applications written for the various versions of Windows for awhile, you have no doubt noticed that certain features, such as opening and saving files, are often the same from one application to another.

In fact, software users have come to expect that the user interfaces for performing such operations will look the same. The widespread acceptance of computers is in part due to the fact that most users can figure out how to use new software quickly because the user interfaces for such fundamental features are often the same.

The common dialogs provide a way for Windows CE applications to quickly include a standard user interface for various operations common to many applications. Specifically, the standard dialog boxes for opening and saving files and choosing colors can be easily included in Windows CE applications.

Each of these dialogs has come to be known by a unique name. For example, the dialog for opening files is called the File Open dialog. Table 3.5 lists the common names for the dialogs in the Windows CE common dialog library.

Figure 3.4 shows an example of the File Open dialog in use.

Table 3.5 The Windows CE Common Dialogs

DIALOG NAME	USE
File Open dialog	Dialog used for opening files.
Save As dialog	Dialog used to save a file under a new name.
Color dialog	Dialog providing a user interface for selecting a color.

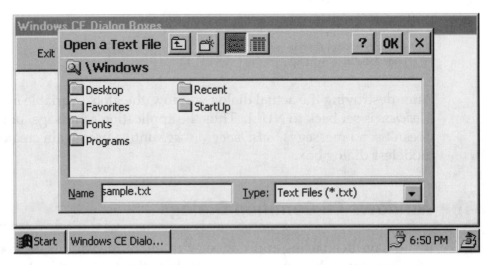

Figure 3.4   The File Open common dialog.

NOTE
COMMDLG.DLL

The Windows CE common dialog library is implemented in COMMDLG.DLL. To use the dialogs, an application must include the header file COMMDLG.H and link with COMMDLG.LIB. Under Windows CE emulation, the DLL is called COMMDLGM.DLL, and the import library to link with is COMMDLGM.LIB.

These dialogs are implemented in a library called the common dialog library, which is a part of the Graphics, Windowing, and Event Subsystem.

Each of the common dialogs is invoked by a single function call. Furthermore, each common dialog has an associated data structure that an application fills with parameters specifying various attributes about the dialog to be displayed.

For example, an application invokes the File Open dialog by filling an OPENFILENAME structure and then calling *GetOpenFileName*.

NOTE
COMPATIBILITY: *FindText* **and** *ChooseFont* **Are Not Supported**

The functions *FindText* and *ChooseFont* are not currently supported under Windows CE. This means that the corresponding Find Replace and Font Chooser common dialogs are not available.

NOTE
■■■■ COMMON DIALOGS ARE MODAL

All of the common dialogs supported under Windows CE are modal dialogs. The functions that invoke them therefore do not return until the user dismisses them by pressing the OK or Cancel (X) button.

Common Dialog Programming

The following sections give the details of how to program each of the common dialogs supported under Windows CE.

The File Open and Save As Dialogs

The File Open and Save As common dialogs under Windows CE look very similar. The difference between them is how your applications use the information that they provide.

The File Open common dialog is invoked by calling the function *GetOpenFileName*:

```
GetOpenFileName(lpofn);
```

The Save As dialog is invoked with *GetSaveFileName*:

```
GetSaveFileName(lpofn);
```

Each of these functions displays the respective dialog box. The functions do not return until the user dismisses the dialog by pressing the OK or Cancel (X) button.

The single argument to each of these functions is a pointer to an OPENFILENAME structure. This structure contains information used by *GetOpenFileName* or *GetSaveFileName* to control the appearance and behavior of the resulting dialog box.

The OPENFILENAME structure is defined as follows:

```
typedef struct tagOFN
{
    DWORD lStructSize;
    HWND hwndOwner;
    HINSTANCE hInstance;
    LPCSTR lpstrFilter;
    LPSTR lpstrCustomFilter;
```

```
        DWORD nMaxCustFilter;
        DWORD nFilterIndex;
        LPSTR lpstrFile;
        DWORD nMaxFile;
        LPSTR lpstrFileTitle;
        DWORD nMaxFileTitle;
        LPSTR lpstrInitialDir;
        LPCSTR lpstrTitle;
        DWORD Flags;
        WORD nFileOffset;
        WORD nFileExtension;
        LPCSTR lpstrDefExt;
        DWORD lCustData; //
        LPOFNHOOKPROC lpfnHook;
        LPCSTR lpTemplateName;
    } OPENFILENAME;
```

This structure looks pretty complicated, but in reality you generally do not use all of the members. In fact four of them, *lCustData*, *lpfnHook*, and *lpTemplateName*, and *hInstance*, are never used by Windows CE. These members appear in the Windows CE definition of the OPEN-FILENAME structure because the definition was taken from the Windows NT implementation.

While reading the description below, keep in mind that this structure is used for both the File Open and File Save dialogs.

lStructSize must contain the size in bytes of the OPENFILENAME structure.

hwndOwner specifies the owner of the dialog box. This can be NULL if the dialog box has no owner.

lpstrFilter is used to specify the *filter strings* to be used when displaying the dialog box. These strings determine the contents of the Type: combo box (see Figure 3.4). They also tell the dialog box to display only those files with the specified extensions. This member can be NULL. You specify *lpstrFilter* as pairs of NULL-terminated strings. The first string in each pair is the descriptive text, such as the text "Text Files (*.txt)" that appears in the Type: field in Figure 3.4. The second string is the filter pattern, such as "*.htm".

lpstrCustomFilter is used by *GetOpenFileName* or *GetSaveFileName* to return the filter chosen by the user. This can be NULL. If not NULL, you must specify the length of the buffer that you are passing in the *lpstrCustomFilter* member in the *nMaxCustFilter* member.

nFilterIndex specifies the 1-based index of the pair of *lpstrFilter* strings with which to initialize the Type: combo box.

lpstrFile is used to specify the file name to initially display in the Name field. It also returns the name of the file specified by the user if the user presses the OK button.

nMaxFile specifies the size of the buffer passed in *lpstrFile*.

Similarly, *lpstrFileTitle* defines a buffer that receives the name of the selected file without the full path name. *nMaxFileTitle* is passed to specify the size of the buffer pointed to by *lpstrFileTitle*. *lpstrFileTitle* can be NULL, in which case *nMaxFileTitle* is ignored.

The *lpstrInitialDir* member is a string that specifies the directory whose contents are displayed by the File Open or Save As dialog when it first appears. This member can be NULL.

lpstrTitle is the string used as the dialog box caption text. This member can be NULL.

nFileOffset specifies a zero-based offset from the beginning of the path to the file name in the string pointed to by *lpstrFile*. Similarly, *nFileExtension* is the zero-based offset to the file extension.

lpstrDefExt is a string containing the default file extension. This is the extension that is appended to the selected file name if, for example, a user types a file name into the Name field but does not supply an extension. This member can be NULL.

We left out the *Flags* member. This member is used to specify a set of bit flags that determine various attributes of the File Open dialog box. This member is also used as a return value. *GetOpenFileName* returns one or more flags to report information about the user's input.

There are many flags that can be specified in the Flags member of an OPENFILENAME structure. The most common flags and their meanings are given in Table 3.6.

An Example

All of the foregoing has no doubt caused your eyes to glaze over. Let's take a look at how the DIALOGS.EXE application creates a File Open dialog to make it all more clear.

Table 3.6   OPENFILENAME Flag Values

FLAG	MEANING
OFN_CREATEPROMPT	If the user specifies a file that does not exist, this flag causes the dialog box to prompt the user for permission to create the file. If the user chooses to create the file, the dialog box closes and the function returns the specified name. Otherwise, the dialog box remains open. This flag is only used with GetSaveFileName.
OFN_EXTENSIONDIFFERENT	Specifies that the user typed a file-name extension that differs from the extension specified by lpstrDefExt. The function does not use this flag if lpstrDefExt is NULL.
OFN_FILEMUSTEXIST	Specifies that the user can type only names of existing files in the File Name entry field. If this flag is specified and the user enters an invalid name, the dialog box procedure displays a warning in a message box. If this flag is specified, the OFN_PATHMUSTEXIST flag is also used.
OFN_HIDEREADONLY	Hides the File Open dialog's read-only check box.
OFN_NOCHANGEDIR	Restores the current directory to its original value if the user changed the directory while searching for files.
OFN_NODEREFERENCELINKS	Directs the dialog box to return the path and file name of the selected shortcut (.LNK) file. If this value is not given, the dialog box returns the path and file name of the file referenced by the shortcut.
OFN_NONETWORKBUTTON	Hides and disables the Network button.
OFN_OVERWRITEPROMPT	Causes the Save As dialog box to generate a message box if the selected file already exists. The user must confirm whether to overwrite the file.
OFN_PATHMUSTEXIST	Specifies that the user can type only valid paths and file names. If this flag is used and the user types an invalid path and file name in the File Name entry field, the dialog box function displays a warning in a message box.
OFN_SHOWHELP	Causes the dialog box to display the Help button.

The most important part of creating the File Open dialog is filling an OPENFILENAME structure with the right values. To render the dialog in Figure 3.4, DIALOGS.EXE executes the following code in the function *OnFileOpen*:

```
void OnFileOpen(HWND hwnd)
{
  OPENFILENAME ofn;
```

```
    TCHAR pszName[256];
    DWORD dwSize;
    dwSize = sizeof(ofn);
    lstrcpy(pszName, TEXT("sample.txt"));
    memset(&ofn, 0, dwSize);
    ofn.hwndOwner = hwnd;
    ofn.lStructSize = dwSize;
    ofn.lpstrFilter = TEXT("Text Files (*.txt)\0*.txt\0");
    ofn.nFilterIndex = 1;
    ofn.lpstrFile = pszName;
    ofn.nMaxFile = 256;
    ofn.lpstrTitle = TEXT("Open a Text File");
    ofn.lpstrInitialDir = TEXT("\\Windows");
    ofn.lpstrDefExt = TEXT("txt");
    GetOpenFileName(&ofn);
}
```

The *hwnd* parameter of *OnFileOpen* is the main application window. This value is the owner of the File Open dialog. Hence the *hwndOwner* member of *ofn* is set to this window.

The filter strings are assigned to *ofn.lpstrFilter*. The first null-terminated string is used as the contents of the dialog Type: field. The second specifies that the File Open dialog should only display files with the .txt extension.

nFilterIndex specifies the 1 -based index of the filter string pair to initially use with the dialog. Setting *nFilterIndex* to 1 tells the dialog box to use the first filter string pair, the string "Text Files (*.txt)\0*.txt\0."

Assigning a string to *ofn.lpstrFile* means that the File Open dialog will be initialized with that string in the Name field of the dialog box. In this case, the file name "sample.txt" will initialize this field.

Finally, the string "Open a Text File" will be the File Open dialog box title, and "txt" will be used as the default file name extension. If a user types a file name in the name field without an extension, .txt will be automatically appended.

This is all the hard work. To display the dialog box, the application simply calls *GetOpenFileName*. When *GetOpenFileName* returns, the *lpstrFile* member of *ofn* contains the fully qualified file name of the selected file.

OnFileOpen doesn't do anything once a user selects a file. It just shows you how to use the File Open dialog. A real application would proceed by, for example, reading the file and displaying the contents in the main application window.

Programming the Save As common dialog is very similar. An OPEN-FILENAME structure is filled as in this example. The application then simply calls *GetSaveFileName* to display the dialog.

The Color Dialog

Now we take a very brief look at using the Color dialog. Figure 3.5 shows an example of the Color dialog. Applications use this dialog as a user interface for making color selections. Pressing the Define button causes the dialog to expand into the form shown in Figure 3.6.

This dialog box is created with one function call, just like all the other common dialogs. In the case of the Color dialog, you call the *ChooseColor* function:

```
ChooseColor(lpcc);
```

The single argument in this case is a pointer to a CHOOSECOLOR structure. The various members of this structure are initialized to control the appearance of the Color dialog.

To create the Color dialog in Figure 3.5, an application only needs six lines of code:

```
CHOOSECOLOR cc;
COLORREF cr[16];
memset(&cc, 0, sizeof(cc));
cc.lStructSize = sizeof(cc);
```

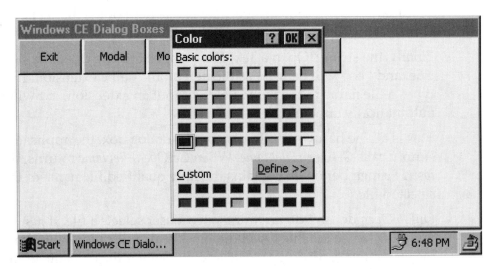

Figure 3.5   The Color common dialog.

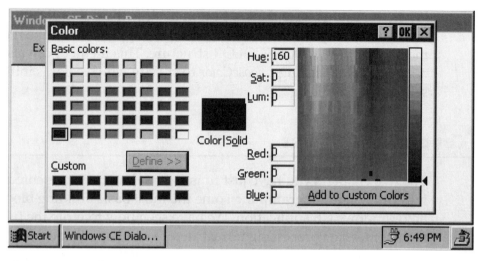

Figure 3.6 A fully expanded Color dialog.

```
cc.lpCustColors = cr;
ChooseColor(&cc);
```

The *lpCustColors* member of the CHOOSECOLOR structure can be used to specify the 16 colors displayed in the custom colors fields at the bottom of the dialog box in Figure 3.5. This allows the application to specify colors of its own for users to choose from other than the basic colors at the top.

Note that *lpCustColors* cannot be NULL. Since this member is used to return any custom colors specified by the user, it must be initialized with a valid COLORREF array.

These custom colors can also be changed by the user. If the Define button is pressed, the user sees the fully expanded Color dialog like the one in Figure 3.6. Colors can be entered in the Red, Green, and Blue edit boxes. Or the user can tap points on the large field above the Add To Custom Colors button to select colors. The hue, saturation, and luminance of the colors in this field can also be changed via the corresponding edit boxes.

The point of all of this is that if the user taps the Add To Custom Colors button, the color currently selected in the right half of the dialog is added to the *lpCustColors* array. This provides a mechanism for the application to store the user's custom color selections and put them in the custom color fields the next time the dialog is created.

When the user presses the OK button to close the Color dialog, the color selected by the user is returned to the application in the *rgbResult* member of the CHOOSECOLOR structure. This member can also be assigned before calling *ChooseColor* to specify which color is initially selected in the dialog.

Concluding Remarks

The two chapters you have just finished reading have presented an introduction to programming some the most basic building blocks of any Windows CE application. We have seen how to write the fundamental message processing infrastructure of an application. We know how to add child and common controls, as well as various types of dialog boxes.

In the rest of Part I, we add to this knowledge by investigating how menus are added to Windows CE applications. And we look at how to program some of the common controls that are of particular interest to Windows CE applications.

Menus and the Windows CE Command Bar

One of the biggest challenges that Windows application programmers have traditionally faced is designing a user interface that is intuitive and easy to use. Keeping the computer screen organized and free of the clutter of lots of buttons and other controls gets more difficult as Windows programs become more complex and feature-rich.

If this is a challenge on desktop Windows platforms, it is even more problematic when designing applications for Windows CE-based devices. With screen sizes that are typically a mere fraction of their desktop computer siblings, Windows CE devices are much more susceptible to problems of screen clutter and confusing user interfaces.

Fortunately, Windows CE provides extensive support for including menus and menu accelerators in your applications. Menus provide the application programmer and user interface designer with a convenient way to include a large number of user command options in a small amount of screen real estate. Accelerators allow applications to translate simple keyboard actions into menu item equivalents. Of course, Windows CE devices are not required to have a keyboard. Palm-size PCs have no use for menu accelerators. But the support for accelerators is provided by Windows CE for use by those devices that do include a keyboard.

Central to the discussion of Windows CE menus is the command bar control. In this chapter we will introduce this control, which is used for holding menus as well as other child controls. Command bars give Windows CE application programmers a way to include menus and other controls in an application without using large amounts of screen space.

I Repeat Myself When under Stress . . .

It cannot be stressed enough here that menus under Windows CE are fundamentally different from menus under Win32. Menus in Windows CE applications can still be defined in terms of menu resources just as they can on desktop Windows platforms. However, there is no concept of a menu bar, and Windows CE menus are not part of the non-client area of a window. Menus under Windows CE must be embedded within a control, most commonly a command bar. (Menus can also be inserted into command bands, a control discussed in the next chapter.) The controls that contain Windows CE menus are child controls, and therefore reside in their parent window's client area.

Another implication of the absence of menu bar support under Windows CE is that the *hMenu* parameter of *CreateWindow* and *CreateWindowEx* has no meaning for a top-level window. Therefore code like the following will fail:

```
HWND hwndMain;
HMENU hMenu;
/* Assume that IDR_MENU identifies a legitimate menu
   resource contained by the module hInstance.
 */
hMenu = LoadMenu(hInstance, MAKEINTRESOURCE(IDR_MENU));
hwndMain = CreateWindow(
  TEXT("MYWNDCLASS"),
  NULL,
  WS_VISIBLE|WS_OVERLAPPED,
  0,0,100,100,
  NULL,
  hMenu,
  hInstance,
  NULL);
```

CreateWindow in this case will most assuredly return NULL. Menus for top-level windows are not supported.

For the same reason, creating instances of a window class registered with a non-NULL *lpszMenuName* WNDCLASS member works, but the *lpszMenuName* attribute has no effect.

Of course you can still use non-NULL values for the *hMenu* parameter of *CreateWindow* and *CreateWindowEx* to specify the identifier of child windows. For example, as we saw in the previous chapter, whenever you create a Windows CE control, you use the *hMenu* parameter to specify that control's identifier.

AFTER COMPLETING THIS CHAPTER YOU WILL KNOW HOW TO . . .

Create a command bar control and insert it into a window

Add a menu to a command bar

Add controls like buttons and combo boxes to a command bar

Add adornments to a command bar

Add tool tips to a command bar

Add menu accelerators to a command bar menu

Add a window menu (system menu) to a window

The Command Bar Control

On desktop Windows platforms, menus are contained in a *menu bar*. Windows CE does not support the concept of a menu bar. Menus are instead contained by a Windows CE control called the *command bar* control.

One exception to this is pop-up menus. Pop-up menus in Windows CE are implemented just as they are on desktop Windows platforms. We will see an example using pop-up menus later in this chapter.

Command bars are one of the common controls. Their implementation lives in the COMMCTRL.DLL dynamic link library. To use them, an application must therefore initialize the common control library with a call to *InitCommonControls* or *InitCommonControlsEx*. Furthermore,

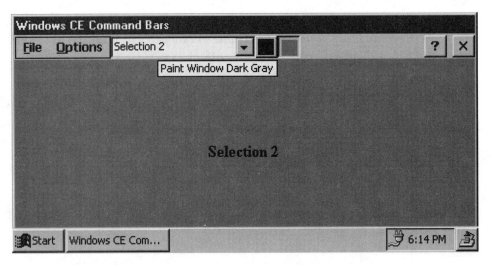

Figure 4.1   A command bar with menu, controls, and adornments.

applications must include the file COMMCTRL.H. This header file contains the definitions of the *InitCommonControls* and *InitCommon-ControlsEx* functions. It also defines all of the command bar API functions that we will use in this chapter.

Since command bars often contain menus, it is very easy to think of them as menu bars. But it is important to keep in mind that command bars, just like buttons or list boxes, are child controls. This means that a command bar is part of the client area of the window that owns it. Your application needs to account for the space used up by any command bars in the client area. The sidebar that follows points out a good way to do this.

Command bar controls are actually a type of toolbar control. As such, you can use any of the toolbar messages, styles, and the like with command bars. Toolbar messages can be sent directly using *SendMessage*. Toolbar styles can be added with *SetWindowLong*.

The details of creating and working with command bars will be introduced later. We first describe some menu basics. Because Windows CE menu concepts are similar to their desktop Windows counterparts, this discussion will be brief.

The sample application in this chapter, shown in Figure 4.1, wins "The World's Most Useless Windows CE Application" award. It implements a command bar with a menu, combo box, and two buttons that change

What Happened to the Button?

Command bars are part of the client area of the windows that contain them. This point can be driven home by the following code example:

```
/* IDCB_MAIN is the command ID of the command bar
   IDC_BUTTON is the command ID of a button
   hwndMain is the main application window
   hInstance is the application instance
*/
HWND hwndCB;          //Command bar HWND
HWND hwndButton;      //Button HWND
// . . .other WinMain application code . . .
hwndCB = CommandBar_Create(hInstance, hwndMain, IDCB_MAIN);
hwndButton = CreateWindow(TEXT("BUTTON"),
             TEXT("Button"),
             WS_VISIBLE|WS_CHILD|
             BS_PUSHBUTTON,
             0,0,65,35,
             hwndMain,
             HMENU)IDC_BUTTON,
             hInstance,
             NULL);
```

The button will be obscured by the command bar because the command bar takes up client area just like any other control.

Windows CE applications must account for the space used up by command bars. This is done using the *CommandBar_Height* function. This function returns the height of the specified command bar. This value can be used to offset any y dimension in the client area.

More generically, you can define the following macro:

```
#define MAKEY(y, hwndCB) (y+CommandBar_Height(hwndCB))
```

The button could then be created like this:

```
hwndButton = CreateWindow(TEXT("BUTTON"),
             TEXT("Button"),
             WS_VISIBLE|WS_CHILD|
             BS_PUSHBUTTON,
             0,MAKEY(0, hwndCB),65,35,
             ...);
```

The button control will be positioned just below the command bar control.

the color of the main window client area. The buttons also include *tool tips*, which are little pop-up windows containing strings that describe the button functionality. At least this application is useful in introducing command bar concepts. The application is in the directory \Samples\cmdbar on the companion CD, and generates an application named CMDBAR.EXE.

Windows CE Menu Basics

Windows CE applications can include four types of menus:

- drop-down menus
- cascading menus
- scrolling menus
- pop-up menus

Drop-down menus are the standard pull-down menus as shown in Figure 4.1. Cascading menus are menus that contain items that open menus of their own. An example is shown in Figure 4.2.

Windows CE introduces scrolling menus. A scrolling menu is simply a menu that can scroll vertically. If an application creates a menu that contains more items than fit in the vertical screen space, Windows CE makes the menu scrollable. Users can then scroll the menu to expose menu items that do not fit in the screen area.

Pop-up menus are similar to their desktop Windows counterparts. They can be used to implement menus that do not live on the command bar, but that temporarily appear as the result of some user action. An example of a pop-up menu is given later in this chapter.

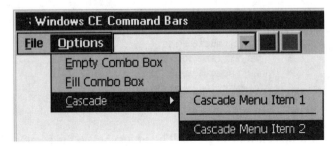

Figure 4.2 A cascading menu.

Menus can be defined in your applications by means of menu definitions in resource files. They can also be defined programmatically using the menu API. The examples in this chapter will all use the resource file approach. The complete set of Windows CE–supported menu functions is shown at the end of the chapter.

Windows CE also supports owner draw menus. We will not cover owner draw menus in this book, except to discuss the basic concepts of owner draw control programming in Chapter 9.

A Menu Resource Refresher

Just in case your memory is a bit rusty, here's a quick refresher course on how menu resources are described in resource files.

The general syntax of a menu resource is shown below. Items in uppercase are required keywords. Items in italics are supplied by the application programmer. Items in square brackets are optional values.

```
MenuName MENU [DISCARDABLE]
BEGIN
  POPUP SubMenu1Name [, options]
   BEGIN
    MENUITEM MenuItemName, id [, options]
    ... //More MENUITEMs
   END
  POPUP SubMenu2Name [, options]
   BEGIN
    MENUITEM MenuItemName, id [, options]
    ...
   END
END
```

MenuName is the name of the menu. Generally this is a resource identifier, but it can be a string menu name.

The optional DISCARDABLE keyword tells Windows CE that the menu resource can be discarded from memory automatically when no longer needed.

The POPUP keyword indicates that a new submenu is being defined. These POPUP definitions define the individual submenus. *SubMenu1Name, SubMenu2Name*, etc. are the names of the submenus. In the example in Figure 4.1, these would be "&File" and "&Options".

Cascading menus can be defined by nesting submenus within other submenus.

The MENUITEM keyword inserts a new item in the submenu. The *MenuItemName* values represent the individual pull-down menu choices.

id is the *command identifier* for the particular menu item. The use of this identifier is described in the next section, where we describe how applications respond to menu item selections.

The menu resource identifier and menu item command identifiers are typically defined in the application's RESOURCE.H file.

Various options can be specified for submenus and for menu items. More than one of these options can be specified by bitwise-ORing them together. For submenus, these option include:

GRAYED. The text is grayed; the menu is inactive, and does not generate WM_COMMAND messages.

INACTIVE. The text is displayed normally, but the menu is still inactive. No WM_COMMAND messages are generated.

MENUBREAK. This option is supported, but has no effect in the context of menus in command bars.

HELP. This option is supported, but has no effect in the context of menus in command bars.

Menu item options include the following:

CHECKED. Places a check mark to the left of the menu item text.

GRAYED. Same meaning as for submenus; see the list above.

INACTIVE. Same meaning as for submenus; see the list above.

MENUBREAK. The menu item and all items that follow appear in a new column in the menu.

MENUBARBREAK. Same as MENUBREAK, except that a vertical line separates the menu columns.

As an example, here is the menu resource definition for the cascading menu shown in Figure 4.2:

```
IDR_MENU MENU DISCARDABLE
BEGIN
  POPUP "&File"
  BEGIN
    MENUITEM "&Exit",   IDC_EXIT
  END
  POPUP "&Options"
```

```
      BEGIN
       MENUITEM "&Empty Combo Box",   IDC_EMPTY
       MENUITEM "&Fill Combo Box",    IDC_FILL
        POPUP "&Cascade"
         BEGIN
          MENUITEM "Cascade Menu Item 1", IDC_SUBITEM1
          MENUITEM SEPARATOR
          MENUITEM "Cascade Menu Item 2", IDC_SUBITEM2
         END
      END
   END
```

Responding to Menu Items

The usefulness of menus comes from the ability to map the various menu items in a menu to actions. This is done by assigning a command identifier to each of the menu items that an application is meant to respond to. The previous section described how a command identifier is assigned to a menu item.

This command identifier performs the same role as control identifiers for Windows CE controls. Specifically, whenever a menu item is selected, Windows CE sends a WM_COMMAND message to the parent of the command bar control. The low word of the *wParam* parameter contains the menu item identifier. The WM_COMMAND message notification code is zero, indicating that the message is sent as a result of a menu item selection.

Creating a Command Bar

Creating a command bar control is a little different from creating other Windows CE controls. Instead of using *CreateWindow* or *CreateWindowEx* as when creating child and common controls, Windows CE provides a separate API for creating and working with command bar controls.

To create a command bar control, an application calls *CommandBar_Create*:

```
CommandBar_Create(hInst, hwndParent, idCmdbar);
```

This function is a wrapper for the *CreateWindow* call that ultimately creates the actual command bar window. *hInst* is the application instance of the application in which the control is being created.

hwndParent is the command bar's parent window. *idCmdBar* is the control identifier of the command bar.

If *CommandBar_Create* is successful, it returns the HWND of the newly created command bar control. Otherwise the function returns NULL. Thus creating a command bar is semantically similar to creating any other Windows CE window or control.

Creating the command bar control is only the beginning. The command bar in Figure 4.1 contains a menu and various child controls. After calling *CommandBar_Create*, your application is left with nothing more than the HWND of an empty command bar control.

Adding useful things like menus and buttons to a command bar control requires using the various *CommandBar_Insert* functions.

Inserting a Menu into a Command Bar

An application adds a menu to a command bar with the function *CommandBar_InsertMenubar*. After all the caveats about how Windows CE does not support menu bars, the command bar API still thinks it is inserting a menu bar. In any of its incarnations, consistency in function naming has never been a strong point with Windows.

CommandBar_InsertMenubar takes four parameters:

```
CommandBar_InsertMenubar(hwndCB, hInst, idMenu, iButton);
```

hwndCB is the HWND of the command bar into which the menu is inserted. *hInst* is the application instance. *idMenu* is the resource identifier of the menu to insert.

iButton identifies where in the command bar the menu is to be inserted. A command bar can contain buttons and command bars as well as a menu. *iButton* is the zero-based index of the control to the left of which the menu is inserted. Since controls are typically inserted into command bars after the menu, *iButton* for menus is typically zero, putting the menu at the very left of the command bar.

MAKING SENSE OF *IBUTTON*

iButton is best thought of as the position index of a control in a command bar. In the example shown in Figure 4.1, the menu has index 0, the combo box index 1, and so forth.

CommandBar_InsertMenubar internally loads the menu resource corresponding to *idMenu* from the module identified by *hInstance*. *CommandBar_InsertMenubar* returns TRUE if successful. Otherwise it returns FALSE.

An alternative way to insert a menu into a command bar is with *CommandBar_InsertMenubarEx*. This function is exactly the same as *CommandBar_InsertMenubar*, except that the third parameter is not a menu resource identifier. Instead, this parameter can be passed the menu resource name, or a menu handle.

Here's an example of how you might insert a menu into a command bar. In this example, IDR_MENU is the resource identifier of a menu resource, defined in the file RESOURCE.H:

```
#define IDCB_MAIN   0   //Command bar control command ID
int WINAPI WinMain(
  HINSTANCE hInstance,
  HINSTANCE hPrevInstance,
  LPTSTR lpCmdLine,
  int nCmdShow)
{
  HWND hwndCB;  //Command bar window
  HWND hwndMain; //Main application window
  /* Register main window class and create main window here
  ... */
  /* Create the command bar control */
  hwndCB = CommandBar_Create(hInstance, hwndMain, IDCB_MAIN);
  /* Insert the menu into the command bar */
  if (hwndCB)
  {
   CommandBar_InsertMenubar(hwndCB, hInstance,IDR_MENU,0);
  }
  /* The rest of the WinMain code here
  ... */
}
```

Adding Controls to a Command Bar

The example in Figure 4.1 shows a command bar with a menu as well as a combo box and a set of buttons. Also, at the right of the command bar you can see a small Close button and Help button. How did the Windows CE child controls get there?

This section presents the command bar API functions that are used to insert controls into the command bar. It also describes how to add

Table 4.1 Command Bar Functions for Adding Controls and Adornments

FUNCTION	MEANING
CommandBar_AddAdornments	Used to add OK, Close, and/or Help buttons to a command bar.
CommandBar_AddBitmap	Adds images to a command bar to use with command bar buttons.
CommandBar_AddButtons	Inserts one or more buttons (not adornments) to a command bar.
CommandBar_AddTooltips	Inserts tool tip strings into a command bar for use with command bar buttons.
CommandBar_InsertButton	Inserts a single button into a command bar.
CommandBar_InsertComboBox	Inserts a combo box into a command bar.

adornments, the Close, Help, and OK buttons that often appear in command bars. Adding tool tips to command bar buttons is also described.

As a quick reference, Table 4.1 lists these functions and their use.

Inserting Buttons

Buttons can be inserted into a command bar with two different functions. *CommandBar_AddButtons* inserts one or more buttons into the specified command bar. *CommandBar_InsertButton* is the same except that it inserts only one button at a time.

The buttons that you insert into a command bar control send WM_COMMAND messages just like standard Windows CE child control buttons. The only difference is that instead of sending the message to their parent, which would be the command bar control, the message is sent to the command bar control's parent. In this way, your window procedure can handle WM_COMMAND messages from command bar buttons just as it responds to such messages from other buttons.

In order to add any buttons to a command bar, an application must define an appropriate button structure for each button to be added. The button structure used for this purpose is TBBUTTON. This is the same structure used in toolbar controls to describe toolbar buttons.

```
typedef struct _TBBUTTON
{
```

```
        int iBitmap;
        int idCommand;
        BYTE fsState;
        BYTE fsStyle;
        DWORD dwData;
        int iString;
    } TBBUTTON, NEAR* PTBBUTTON, FAR* LPTBBUTTON;
```

iBitmap is the zero-based index of the bitmap to use with the button. *idCommand* is the button control identifier. This value is the value of the control identifier that Windows CE sends with WM_COMMAND messages whenever this particular button is pressed.

fsState defines the *button state*. This can be one or more of the values defined in Table 4.2. Some of these states refer to toolbar button styles, which are described in Table 4.3.

The *fsStyle* member of TBBUTTON specifies the various styles of a command bar button. This member can be one or more of the values in Table 4.3.

dwData is used to store application-defined data with the button. This member can be zero.

Finally, *iString* is the zero-based index of the string to use as the button's text. As command bar buttons do not use text, this member is ignored.

Let's see how to use the TBBUTTON structure to insert buttons into a command bar. The sample application for this chapter has a command bar with two buttons (see Figure 4.1). They are placed to the right of the command bar menu. One has a black square bitmap, the other a

Table 4.2 Command Bar/Toolbar Button States

STATE	MEANING
TBSTATE_CHECKED	The button is checked. Button must have the TBSTYLE_CHECK style to support this state.
TBSTATE_ENABLED	The button accepts user input, i.e., is not disabled.
TBSTATE_HIDDEN	The button is not visible.
TBSTATE_INDETERMINATE	The button is grayed out.
TBSTATE_PRESSED	The button is pressed.
TBSTATE_WRAP	A line break follows the button. The button must also have the TBSTATE_ENABLED state.

Table 4.3 Command Bar/Toolbar Button Styles

STYLE	MEANING
TBSTYLE_BUTTON	Specifies a standard push-button–style button.
TBSTYLE_CHECK	Specifies a button that looks like a push button, but that behaves like a check button. That is, it toggles between the pressed and unpressed states each time it is tapped by the user.
TBSTYLE_GROUP	Specifies a group of TBSTYLE_BUTTON buttons.
TBSTYLE_CHECKGROUP	Specifies a group of TBSTYLE_CHECK buttons. If a button in the group is pressed, it stays pressed until another button in the group is tapped. Unlike standard controls, all buttons in toolbar button group or check group must have the TBSTYLE_GROUP or TBSTYLE_CHECKGROUP style.

dark gray square bitmap. Pressing either of these buttons changes the background color of the main window's client area to the color shown in the button. The WM_COMMAND handler code for the buttons is not shown.

```
/* Define the command bar button command IDs */
#define IDC_CMDBAR_BUTTON1    1028
#define IDC_CMDBAR_BUTTON2    1029
/* Define the button bitmap image indices */
#define IDI_BUTTON1    0
#define IDI_BUTTON2    1
HWND hwndCB;    //The command bar HWND
/* Define the button structures associated with the
  command bar buttons
 */
TBBUTTON tb[2] = { {IDI_BUTTON1,IDC_CMDBAR_BUTTON1,
  TBSTATE_ENABLED,TBSTYLE_BUTTON,0,0},
    {IDI_BUTTON2,IDC_CMDBAR_BUTTON2,
      TBSTATE_ENABLED,TBSTYLE_BUTTON,0,0}};
//Create the command bar control
hwndCB = CommandBar_Create(...);
if (hwndCB)
{
  //Other command bar code
  //...
  CommandBar_AddBitmap(hwndCB, hInstance, IDB_BUTTONS,
    2, 0, 0);
  CommandBar_AddButtons(hwndCB, 2, &tb);
  //...
}
```

The pertinent pieces of the previous sample are the definition of the TBBUTTON array *tb*, and the *CommandBar_AddBitmap* and *CommandBar_AddButtons* calls.

The array *tb* contains two TBBUTTON structures, one describing each of the buttons to be inserted into the command bar. The buttons are both enabled, push-button–style command bar buttons. The control identifiers are ID_CMDBAR_BUTTON1 and ID_CMDBAR_BUTTON2, respectively.

The only part that still might need some clarification is the *iBitmap* value of the elements of the array.

Each command bar control maintains its own internal image list. This image list is what the control uses to figure out what bitmap to display on a particular command bar button. The *iBitmap* member of the TBBUTTON structure used to describe a particular button is the index into the image list.

An application sets the bitmap of images in this image list by calling *CommandBar_AddBitmap*:

```
CommandBar_AddBitmap(hwndCB, hInst, idBitmap, iNumImages,
        iReserved, iReserved);
```

hwndCB and *hInst* have the usual meanings. *idBitmap* is the resource identifier of the bitmap to add. *iNumImages* contains the number of 16-by-16-pixel button bitmap images contained in the bitmap referred to by *idBitmap*.

The last two parameters of the function are reserved and should be zero.

The bitmap referred to by the resource identifier IDB_BUTTONS is shown in Figure 4.3.

After the bitmap has been added to the command bar, the *Command-Bar_AddButtons* call adds the buttons to the command bar:

```
CommandBar_AddButtons(hwndCB, uNumButtons, lpButtons);
```

The second parameter specifies the number of buttons to be added. *lpButtons* is a pointer to the array of TBBUTTON structures that define the command bar buttons.

Note that no matter how many buttons are added to a command bar control, only one bitmap resource is specified in the call to *Command-*

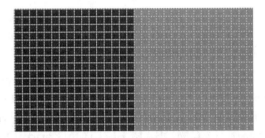

Figure 4.3 The CMDBAR application button bitmap.

Bar_AddBitmap. Each command bar button bitmap is expected to be 16 by 16 pixels, and *iNumImages* specifies the number of such images. The *iBitmap* value in a given TBBUTTON description can then reliably identify which 16-by-16 bitmap to associate with the particular button.

When a button is added with *CommandBar_AddButtons* or *Command-Bar_InsertButton*, the command bar looks at the *iBitmap* member of the button's TBBUTTON definition. If this value is 2, for example, the command bar uses the second 16-by-16 section of bits from the bitmap resource added to the control by the *CommandBar_AddBitmap* call as the button image.

Inserting Combo Boxes

Combo boxes can be inserted into command bar controls using the function *CommandBar_InsertComboBox*:

```
CommandBar_InsertComboBox(hwndCB, hInst, iWidth, dwStyle,
   idComboBox, iButton);
```

hwndCB and *hInst* are the same as with the other command bar functions we've seen. *iWidth* specifies the width, in pixels, of the combo box control to be inserted. *dwStyle* defines the style of the combo box. This value can be one or more of the styles used for other combo box controls. *idComboBox* is the control identifier of the combo box, and *iButton* specifies where to put the control.

If *CommandBar_InsertComboBox* is successful, it returns the HWND of the combo box that is created. If the function fails, the return value is NULL.

Applications interact with combo boxes in command bars just as they do with other combo box controls. All messages and notifications that are generated by a command bar combo box are sent to the command bar control's parent window. The application's main window procedure therefore handles these events in its WM_COMMAND handler.

Inserting Adornments

Adornments are the Help, OK, and Close buttons that are often found in command bars. The Help button is used as a standard way to invoke help features in an application. The Close button closes the window that contains the command bar. The OK button sends a WM_COMMAND message to the parent of the command bar. The control identifier sent with this message (i.e., the LOWORD of *wParam*) in this case is IDOK.

A command bar can include one or more adornment buttons. Any command bar that has adornments must have a Close button. You have no choice in this, and Windows CE will add it for you automatically. The Help and OK buttons can be specified optionally.

The function for doing all of this is *CommandBar_AddAdornments*:

```
CommandBar_AddAdornments(hwndCB, dwFlags, dwReserved);
```

hwndCB identifies the command bar, and *dwReserved* is reserved and must be set to zero.

That leaves the *dwFlags* parameter. This parameter is used to specify which optional adornment buttons to add to the command bar. This parameter can be CMDBAR_HELP, CMDBAR_OK, or both. CMDBAR_HELP adds the Help button, and CMDBAR_OK adds the OK button.

As an example, here's how an application would add the Help and OK buttons to a command bar with an HWND identified by *hwndMyCB*:

```
CommandBar_AddAdornments(hwndMyCB,(CMDBAR_HELP|CMDBAR_OK), 0);
```

If the function is successful, it returns TRUE. Otherwise it returns FALSE.

COMMANDBAR_ADDADORNMENTS MUST BE LAST!

Any call to *CommandBar_AddAdornments* must come after all other functions that insert menus or controls into a particular command bar.

Table 4.4 summarizes the Windows CE messages generated when the various adornment buttons are pressed. These messages are sent to the command bar control's parent window.

Adding Tool Tips to Command Bar Buttons

Windows CE supports tool tips in command bar buttons (see Figure 4.4). A tool tip is a little pop-up window that is displayed when a user presses a command bar button and holds it down for more than half of a second. The tool tip contains an application-specified Unicode string that is used as a description of the command bar button. Tool tips are a good way to provide users of your Windows CE applications with a description of what action is performed by command bar buttons without taking up a lot of valuable screen space.

Tool tips are inserted with the function *CommandBar_AddToolTips*:

```
CommandBar_AddToolTips(hwndCB, uNumToolTips, lpToolTips);
```

uNumToolTips specifies the number of tool tip strings in *lpToolTips*. *lpToolTips* is an array of null-terminated Unicode strings. One of these strings is displayed for each command bar button.

This sounds pretty simple, but there is a catch. Windows CE does not allow tool tips for menus or combo boxes in command bars. However, it does assume that *lpToolTips* contains a string pointer for each item in the command bar. This is strange indeed. In order to add tool tips to two command bar buttons that come after a menu and combo box, *uNumToolTips* would have to be 4, and *lpToolTips* would have to contain two NULL pointers for the menu and combo box.

Table 4.4   Adornment Button Messages

BUTTON	MESSAGE GENERATED
Help	WM_HELP
OK	WM_COMMAND, with IDOK as the command identifier
Close	WM_CLOSE

Figure 4.4   A command bar with Help, OK, and Close button adornments.

To be more specific, here's how the sample application for this chapter (shown in Figure 4.1) defines the tool tips it uses:

```
TCHAR* pszTips[] = {NULL,
  NULL,
  TEXT("Paint Window Black"),
  TEXT("Paint Window Dark Gray")};
```

The first two string pointers are NULL. These correspond to the menu and combo box. The next two strings are the command bar button tool tip strings. If not defined this way, *CommandBar_AddToolTips* will produce unexpected results.

With this definition for *pszTips*, the application adds the tool tips with this function call:

```
CommandBar_AddToolTips(hwndCB, 4, pszTips);
```

The basic rule of thumb for adding tool tips is that you must specify as many strings as components in your command bar (menus, combo boxes, and command bar buttons). Additionally, these strings must be specified in *lpToolTips* in the same order as the command bar components.

The *CommandBar_AddToolTips* function returns TRUE if successful. Otherwise, it returns FALSE.

Other Command Bar Functions

There are some other command bar functions we have not yet covered. These remaining functions provide functionality for such things as showing or hiding command bars, determining if a command bar is visible, and so on.

The remaining functions are pretty self-explanatory. They are listed in Table 4.5.

Table 4.5 Miscellaneous Command Bar Control Functions

FUNCTION	MEANING
CommandBar_Destroy	Destroys the specified command bar without destroying the parent window.
CommandBar_DrawMenuBar	Used to redraw or reposition the menu in the specified command bar.
CommandBar_GetMenu	Retrieves the menu handle (HMENU) of the specified command bar menu.
CommandBar_Height	Gets the height of the specified command bar.
CommandBar_IsVisible	Determines if the specified command bar is visible or not.
CommandBar_Show	Shows or hides the specified command bar.

Using Accelerators in Windows CE Applications

Desktop computers have relied heavily on keyboard accelerators for years. A *keyboard accelerator* is a keystroke combination that duplicates the behavior of a menu item or control.

Keyboard accelerators are a useful feature of many popular Windows applications. After becoming familiar with the keyboard equivalents of common menu selections, users can greatly increase the speed at which they use applications.

Windows CE provides the same keyboard accelerator support as desktop versions of Windows. Since Windows CE devices are not required to have a keyboard, accelerators don't make sense for all devices. But many devices do have keyboards, so briefly covering the subject of keyboard accelerators is worthwhile. And you never know when the Palm-size PC application that you write today will need to be ported to run on Handheld PCs.

Accelerator tables are pretty small, so the memory they consume is minimal. And compiling out the application code that enables them with preprocessor symbols is easy. As we will see, once the accelerators are defined, enabling them can be done with exactly five lines of code.

Accelerator Resources

Like menus, keyboard accelerators are a type of Windows CE resource. They are defined in a resource file as an *accelerator table*. An accelerator table has the following general syntax:

```
TableName ACCELERATORS [DISCARDABLE]
   BEGIN
    [Acclerator definitions]
   END
```

TableName is either the resource identifier or a string name identifying the resource. The accelerator table for this CMDBAR.EXE is defined as follows:

```
IDR_ACCELERATOR ACCELERATORS DISCARDABLE
BEGIN
   "E",      IDC_EMPTY,   VIRTKEY, CONTROL, NOINVERT
   "F",      IDC_FILL,    VIRTKEY, CONTROL, NOINVERT
   "Q",      IDC_EXIT,    VIRTKEY, CONTROL, NOINVERT
END
```

Each of the accelerator definitions identifies the keyboard key that must be pressed to invoke the accelerator.

The second item in each definition is the control or menu item identifier to which the accelerator corresponds. This is the command identifier that Windows CE sends with the WM_COMMAND message to the window that owns the accelerators.

The VIRTUAL keyword indicates that Windows CE is to use the virtual key code, not the ASCII key code, for the key specified in the accelerator definition.

CONTROL indicates that the Control key must also be pressed to invoke the accelerator. So the first definition means that the key combination Ctrl+E must be pressed. Other keywords of this type are SHIFT and ALT, indicating that the Shift or Alt key must be pressed. For example, to define an accelerator for the key combination Alt+Shift+X, the accelerator table would include this line:

```
"X",   SomeID, VIRTKEY, SHIFT, ALT, NOINVERT
```

The NOINVERT keyword says that the menu containing the menu item corresponding to the accelerator's control identifier is not inverted (i.e., not highlighted) when the accelerator key combination is pressed. Leaving out this keyword forces Windows CE to try to invert the menu.

The identifiers such as IDR_ACCELERATOR and IDC_EMPTY are typically defined in the application's RESOURCE.H file.

Loading and Translating Accelerators

To use keyboard accelerators, an application must load the accelerator table resource. Windows CE represents keyboard accelerators using an *accelerator handle* of type HACCEL.

Accelerators are loaded using the *LoadAccelerators* function:

```
LoadAccelerators(hInstance, lpTableName);
```

hInstance specifies the application instance or dynamic link library instance that contains the accelerator table resource. *lpTableName* is the name of the accelerator table resource. If the accelerator table was given a string name when it was defined in the resource file, this is the string that you pass to *lpTableName*.

If, on the other hand, the table is identified by a resource identifier, you can use the Windows CE macro MAKEINTRESOURCE to convert the identifier into the suitable string value. For example, CMDBAR.EXE loads its accelerators as follows:

```
#define IDR_ACCELERATOR  102
HACCEL hAccel;
hAccel = LoadAccelerators(hInstance,
   MAKEINTRESOURCE(IDR_ACCELERATOR));
```

If *LoadAccelerators* is able to load the accelerator table, it returns a handle to the table. Otherwise the function returns NULL.

Once an accelerator table is loaded, an application needs to know how to respond to accelerator keystrokes. This is done by the function *TranslateAccelerator*:

```
TranslateAccelerator(hWnd, hAccelTable, lpMsg);
```

The parameters passed to *TranslateAccelerator* are an HWND, an accelerator table (HACCEL), and a pointer to a message structure. The function first determines if the message specified by *lpMsg* is a WM_KEYDOWN or WM_SYSKEYDOWN message. If it is, it looks in the accelerator table specified by *hAccelTable* to see if the virtual key code sent with the message corresponds to any of the accelerator keys. If so, the message is converted into a WM_COMMAND message and sent to the window procedure of the window specified by the *hWnd* parameter, and then returns TRUE. Otherwise *TranslateAccelerator* returns FALSE.

So how does an application use this function to continually monitor the keyboard for accelerator keystrokes?

Handling accelerators is generally done by modifying an application's message loop. Consider what happens when the standard message loop code is changed by first checking for accelerators:

```
while (GetMessage(&msg, NULL, 0, 0) == TRUE)
{
  if (!TranslateAccelerator(hwndMain, hAccel, &msg))
  {
   TranslateMessage(&msg);
   DispatchMessage(&msg);
  }
}
```

As described above, *TranslateAccelerator* turns any WM_KEYDOWN or WM_SYSKEYDOWN message that corresponds to an accelerator into the equivalent WM_COMMAND message and sends it off to the appropriate window procedure. For every message that gets into the application's message queue, this new message loop code first gives *TranslateAccelerator* a chance to process the message. If the message does not correspond to an accelerator keystroke (i.e., if *TranslateAccelerator* returns FALSE,) the message is processed in the usual way by *TranslateMessage* and *DispatchMessage*.

NOTE

<hr>

COMPATIBILITY: **WM_SYSCOMMAND MESSAGES**

Unlike on desktop versions of Windows, under Windows CE *TranslateAccelerator* does not generate WM_SYSCOMMAND messages, only WM_COMMAND messages.

Using the Window Menu

The window menu (or system menu, as it used to be called) is the little menu that appears in some windows when you tap the window icon in the upper left corner of the title bar. A window with a window menu is shown in Figure 4.5.

You include a window menu in a window by specifying the WS_SYS-MENU style when the window is created:

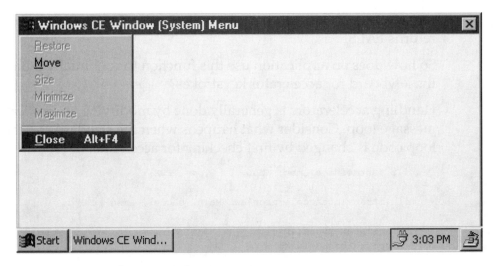

Figure 4.5 A Windows CE window (system) menu.

```
HWND hwndSysMenu; //Handle of window with a window menu
hwndSysMenu = CreateWindow(
  TEXT("MyWndClass"),
  TEXT("My Window"),
  WS_VISIBLE|WS_OVERLAPPED|WS_SYSMENU,
  ...);
```

The window menu notifies its parent window that an item has been selected from the window menu by sending WM_SYSCOMMAND messages to the window. This is analogous to the command bar menu behavior of sending WM_COMMAND messages when items are selected. Table 4.6 details the WM_SYSCOMMAND message parameters.

Table 4.6 WM_SYSCOMMAND Message Parameters

PARAMETER	MEANING
wParam	Specifies the system command. Value can be SC_CLOSE or SC_KEYMENU.
LOWORD(lParam)	Specifies the x component of the point where the stylus tapped the screen if the menu item was selected with the stylus.
HIWORD(lParam)	Specifies the y component of the point where the stylus tapped the screen if the menu item was selected with the stylus.

The SC_CLOSE system command indicates that the Close item was selected from the window menu. SC_KEYMENU means that the menu has been activated by a keystroke.

Notice in Figure 4.5 that including a system menu in a window also includes a Close button in the upper right corner of the title bar.

A window procedure should return zero for any WM_SYSCOM-MAND message that is handled. All other WM_SYSCOMMAND messages should be passed on to *DefWindowProc*.

NOTE

SYSTEM COMMANDS

Under Windows NT and Windows 98, there are many more possible system command values that can be sent with WM_SYSCOMMAND messages. Under Windows CE, only the SC_CLOSE and SC_KEYMENU values are supported.

The Complete Windows CE Menu API

So far we have been describing menus that are created in Windows CE resource files. The typical use of menus has been to create the desired menu in a menu resource and then insert it into a command bar with *CommandBar_InsertMenubar*. The application then responds to menu item selections with the appropriate WM_COMMAND message handler.

Windows CE also provides a rich set of functions for working with menus more directly. This API is very similar to the traditional Win32 menu API. Since there are already numerous resources that describe these functions in detail, this section will simply summarize the Windows CE menu API and point out where particular functions differ from their Win32 siblings. We also demonstrate some of the functions by showing how to add a context-specific pop-up menu to the CMD-BAR.EXE sample application.

Adding Pop-up Menus

Menus in Windows CE applications do not have to reside on a command bar menu. Applications often implement *pop-up menus* that are temporarily displayed when the user performs some specified action, like tapping the screen while pressing the Alt key on the keyboard. Some devices such as Palm-size PCs have hardware navigation buttons that can be used in various combinations to invoke pop-up menus. For the example in this section, it is assumed that a keyboard is present.

Pop-up menus are extremely useful in Windows CE applications to present users with lists of options that depend on the context in which the menu is invoked. For example, in a word processing application a pop-up menu might contain one set of choices when a document is open in the application, a completely different set of menu items when the application has no documents open.

Pop-up menus behave pretty much like regular command bar menus. Once displayed, the user can select menu items as in any other menu. Pop-up menus notify their parent that an item has been selected via the WM_COMMAND message. When displayed, a pop-up menu generally stays open until the user makes a menu item selection or taps outside the menu.

In this section we add context-specific pop-up menus to CMDBAR.EXE. One of these menus is shown in Figure 4.6. The menus are invoked by tapping the client area of the main application window while pressing the Alt key. If the client area is black, the menu offers the choice of painting the client area gray, or reverting to white. If the

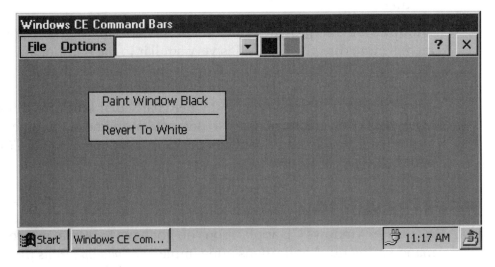

Figure 4.6 A Windows CE Pop-up menu.

client area is gray, the menu allows the user to paint it black or revert to white. If the client area is white, the pop-up menu offers the choice of painting black or gray, and the revert-to-white option is disabled.

We define the basic pop-up menus in this menu resource:

```
IDR_POPUPS MENU DISCARDABLE
  BEGIN
    POPUP "Popup1"
    BEGIN
      MENUITEM "Paint Window Gray", IDC_SET_COLOR_GRAY
      MENUITEM SEPARATOR
      MENUITEM "Revert To White",  IDC_CLEAR
    END
    POPUP "Popup2"
    BEGIN
      MENUITEM "Paint Window Black", IDC_SET_COLOR_BLACK
      MENUITEM SEPARATOR
      MENUITEM "Revert To White",  IDC_CLEAR
    END
  END
```

Each of the individual pop-ups in this menu definition will be used as the pop-up menu that is displayed for a particular application context, i.e., current client area color. Each pop-up statement in the resource definition above defines a *submenu*.

NOTE

▬▬▬ **MENUS CAN BE CREATED PROGRAMMATICALLY**

The examples in this chapter all use menu resources to define the menus that they use. The Windows CE menu API also provides functions that allow applications to create menus programmatically. See Table 4.9 for a complete list of menu functions.

Programmatically, the process of creating and displaying a pop-up menu and then detecting a user's menu item selection can be summarized with these three steps:

- Loading the menu resource that contains the pop-up menu to be displayed
- Obtaining a menu handle to the appropriate submenu
- Tracking the user's menu item selection

The menu resource is loaded using the *LoadMenu* function:

```
LoadMenu(hInstance, lpMenuName);
```

LoadMenu returns a menu handle (HMENU) to the specified menu. If it fails, *LoadMenu* returns NULL.

hInstance is the HINSTANCE of the application or DLL that contains the specified menu resource. *lpMenuName* is the name of the menu resource to be loaded. As with all of the resource loading functions, this parameter can be obtained by passing the menu resource identifier to the macro MAKEINTRESOURCE. Refer to the section "Loading and Translating Accelerators" for details.

The next step in the process, obtaining a submenu handle, is done by calling *GetSubMenu*:

```
GetSubMenu(hMenu, nPos);
```

Like *LoadMenu*, *GetSubMenu* returns a menu handle to the specified submenu if it succeeds. Failure results in a NULL return value.

hMenu specifies the menu containing the submenu of interest. This value generally comes from a previous *LoadMenu* call. *nPos* is the zero-based index of the submenu to be extracted from *hMenu*.

For example, to get a menu handle to the Popup2 submenu defined in the resource definition above, an application would do this:

```
#define IDR_MYMENU 1028   //Resource ID of the menu,
                //typically defined in
                //resource.h
HMENU hMenu, hSubMenu; /Define the menu handles
hMenu = LoadMenu(hAppInstance, MAKEINTRESOURCE(IDR_MYMENU));
if (hMenu)
{
   hSubMenu = GetSubMenu(hMenu, 1);
}
```

After the application has a handle to the submenu it wants to use as a pop-up, all that is left to do is display that submenu and track user selections. Menu tracking is the menu behavior that includes displaying and hiding the menu and highlighting menu items that are pressed. Menu tracking is implemented by the operating system. All that an application needs to do to display a pop-up menu and track selections is to call *TrackPopupMenu*:

```
TrackPopupMenu(hMenu, uFlags, x, y, nReserved, hWnd, prcRect);
```

hMenu is the menu handle of the submenu to track. *x* and *y* determine where the menu is displayed, specifying the x and y coordinates of the top left corner of the menu. These coordinates are assumed to be given in screen coordinates, not in client coordinates. *nReserved* must be set to zero.

hWnd specified the HWND of the menu's parent window. *prcRect* points to a RECT that specifies the area of the screen which the user can tap without closing the pop-up menu. If this parameter is NULL, the pop-up menu is always closed if the user taps anywhere outside the open menu.

uFlags is a UINT that specifies various flags controlling the position and behavior of the pop-up menu. *uFlags* can be one or more of the values in Table 4.7. The *uFlags* parameter of *TrackPopupMenu* can include only one of the values TPM_CENTERALIGN, TPM_LEFT-ALIGN, and TPM_RIGHTALIGN. These values are used to specify the horizontal alignment of the pop-up menu. Likewise, only one of the values TPM_BOTTOMALIGN, TPM_TOPALIGN, and TPM_VCENTERALIGN may be specified for vertical alignment.

TrackPopupMenu does not return until a menu item is selected or the menu is closed by tapping a point on the screen not contained by the RECT in *prcRect*. If the TPM_RETURNCMD flag is set, the return value is the command identifier of the selected menu item. If this style is not set, the return value of *TrackPopupMenu* is treated like a BOOL:

Table 4.7 TrackPopupMenu Flags

FLAG	MEANING
TPM_CENTERALIGN	Centers the menu horizontally with respect to the x parameter.
TPM_LEFTALIGN	Positions the menu so that the left side is aligned with the x parameter of TrackPopupMenu.
TPM_RIGHTALIGN	Positions the menu so that the right side is aligned with the x parameter of TrackPopupMenu.
TPM_BOTTOMALIGN	Positions the menu so that the bottom edge is aligned with the y parameter of TrackPopupMenu.
TPM_TOPALIGN	Positions the menu so that the top edge is aligned with the y parameter of TrackPopupMenu.
TPM_VCENTERALIGN	Centers the menu vertically with respect to the y parameter of TrackPopupMenu.
TPM_RETURNCMD	If this style is set, TrackPopupMenu returns the identifier of the selected menu item.

That is, it returns TRUE if the function completes successfully, and FALSE otherwise.

NOTE
TrackPopupMenu Flags

Windows CE does not support the TPM_NONOTIFY flag. Also, as Windows CE devices do not support a mouse, the TPM_LEFTBUTTON and TPM_RIGHTBUTTON flags are not supported.

The pop-up menus in CMDBAR.EXE are displayed by holding the Alt key and tapping the screen. All of the pop-up menu code is therefore implemented in the WM_LBUTTONDOWN message handler in the main window procedure. In the code below, *bWhite* and *bBlack* are BOOL global variables that indicate if the window is painted white or black, respectively.

```
case WM_LBUTTONDOWN:
  POINT pt;
  SHORT nState;
  int nSubMenuIndex;
  HMENU hPopupMenu, hSubMenu;
  pt.x = LOWORD(lParam);
  pt.y = HIWORD(lParam);
  ClientToScreen(hwnd, &pt);
  nState = GetKeyState(VK_MENU);
  if (nState&0x80)
  {
   hPopupMenu = LoadMenu(ghInst,
    MAKEINTRESOURCE(IDR_POPUPS));
   if (hPopupMenu)
   {
    nSubMenuIndex = (bBlack ? 0 : 1);
    hSubMenu = GetSubMenu(hPopupMenu, nSubMenuIndex);
    /* Insert the menu item for painting the window
      gray. Also disable the revert to white
      menu item if the client area is already
      painted white.
     */
    if (bWhite)
    {
     InsertMenu(hSubMenu, 1, MF_BYPOSITION,
      IDC_SET_COLOR_GRAY, TEXT("Paint Window Gray"));
     EnableMenuItem(hSubMenu, IDC_CLEAR,
      MF_BYCOMMAND|MF_GRAYED);
    }
    TrackPopupMenu(hSubMenu, TPM_TOPALIGN|TPM_LEFTALIGN,
     pt.x, pt.y, 0, hwnd, NULL);
```

```
    }        //End of if (hMenuPopup) block
    }        //End of if (nState & 0x8000) block
return (0);
```

The WM_LBUTTONDOWN message is sent with the client coordinates of the point where the screen was tapped in the window that receives the message. These coordinates are immediately converted to screen coordinates with a call to *ClientToScreen*. This is because the *TrackPopupMenu* call that comes later expects its *x* and *y* parameters in screen coordinates.

The next interesting part of this piece of code tells us if the Alt key is being pressed. The call to *GetKeyState* does this for us. This function takes a virtual key code as its only parameter. If the corresponding key is pressed, *GetKeyState* returns a SHORT whose high-order bit is 1.

If the Alt key is pressed, the code proceeds to load the pop-up menu resource and get a handle to the proper submenu, and the menu is displayed and tracked with *TrackPopupMenu*.

Two other interesting menu functions are demonstrated in the piece of code above. In the case that the window was already painted white, a menu item for painting the window gray is added to the pop-up menu with a call to *InsertMenu*. Otherwise the only choices will be for painting it black and reverting to white. Also, if the window is white, the application disables the "Revert To White" option by calling *Enable-MenuItem*. The next two sections discuss how these features are implemented.

Inserting New Menu Items

New menu items can be inserted into existing menus at run-time with the function *InsertMenu*:

```
InsertMenu(hMenu, uPosition, uFlags, uIDNewItem,lpNewItem);
```

The *hMenu* parameter specifies the HMENU of the menu into which the new menu item is inserted. *uPosition* specifies the menu item which the new menu item is to be inserted before. This value is interpreted depending on the *uFlags* parameter.

uFlags must be either MF_BYCOMMAND or MF_BYPOSITION, combined with at least one of the values in Table 4.8. MF_BYCOMMAND means that *uPosition* gives the identifier of the menu item to be

Table 4.8 InsertMenu Flags

FLAG	MEANING
MF_CHECKED	Draws a check mark to the left of the menu item text.
MF_ENABLED	Enabled the menu item. Item can be selected and the item text is not grayed.
MF_GRAYED	Disables the menu item and grays the item text.
MF_MENUBREAK	Places the item in a new column.
MF_MENUBARBREAK	Same as MF_MENUBREAK , except columns are separated by a vertical line.
MF_OWNERDRAW	Specifies the menu item as owner draw.
MF_POPUP	Indicates that the menu item is a submenu.
MF_SEPARATOR	The item inserted is a horizontal menu item separator.
MF_STRING	Indicates that the lpNewItem parameter is a string.
MF_UNCHECKED	Opposite of MF_CHECKED, i.e., a check mark is not drawn next to the item text. This flag is set by default.

inserted. MF_BYPOSITION says that *uPosition* is the zero-based index of the new item. MF_BYCOMMAND is the default.

uIDNewItem indicates the command identifier of the new menu item. If *uFlags* includes the MF_POPUP flag, *uIDNewItem* is the menu handle of the menu or submenu to be inserted.

lpNewItem specifies the contents of the new menu item. Generally *lpNewItem* points to a null-terminated Unicode string used as the menu item text. This parameter can also contain information for drawing owner draw menu items. But as we are not covering owner draw menus in this book, we don't discuss this.

NOTE

INSERTMENUITEM

The function *InsertMenuItem* is not supported under Windows CE.

Enabling and Disabling Menu Items

We have described the pop-up menus that were added to the CMD-BAR application as context-specific. That means that the particular pop-up menu that is displayed depends on the state of the application at the time the menu is displayed.

Individual menu items can also be displayed differently depending on the state of an application. For example, a word processor typically grays out the Cut and Copy menu items in the Edit menu if no text is selected in a document. But when text is selected, those menu items become enabled.

The CMDBAR.EXE application pop-up menus have a Revert To White menu item that is only enabled when the main window background is not already painted white. Menu items are enabled or disabled with the *EnableMenuItem* function:

```
EnableMenuItem(hMenu, uIDEnableItem, uEnable);
```

hMenu is the menu handle of the menu or submenu that contains the item to disable or enable.

uEnable is similar to the *uFlags* parameter of the *InsertMenu* function. It is a combination of one of the flags MF_COMMAND or MF_BYPOSITION, and one of the flags MF_GRAYED or MF_ENABLED. These flags have the same meanings as in the *InsertMenu* function.

uIDEnableItem indicates which menu item to enable or disable. As with the *uFlags* parameter of *InsertMenu*, *uIDEnableItem* specifies the command identifier of the menu item if *uEnable* includes the MF_COMMAND flag. If *uEnable* instead contains MF_BYPOSITION, *uIDEnableItem* is the zero-based index of the menu item to enable or disable.

NOTE

MF_DISABLED NOT SUPPORTED

Under Windows CE, the menu flag MF_DISABLED is not supported. To disable menu items using functions like *InsertMenu* and *EnableMenuItem*, applications must use the MF_GRAYED flag.

The Complete Windows CE Menu API

The Windows CE menu API includes many more functions than those few detailed above. However, their usage is generally similar to those functions which we have discussed in detail.

Table 4.9 The Windows CE Menu Functions

FUNCTION	MEANING
AppendMenu	Inserts a new menu item at the end of the specified menu.
CheckMenuItem	Used to add or remove a check mark from a menu item.
CheckMenuRadioItem	Draws a bullet next to the specified menu item and removes any previously drawn bullets from all other items in the menu item group.
CreateMenu	Creates an empty menu.
CreatePopupMenu	Creates an empty pop-up menu.
DeleteMenu	Deletes an item from the specified menu.
DestroyMenu	Destroys the specified menu and frees any memory used by the menu resource. The menu analogue of DestroyWindow.
DrawMenuBar	Redraws the menu in the specified window. The window is a command bar window.
EnableMenuItem	Enables or disables the specified menu item.
GetMenuItemInfo	Gets information about the specified menu item in the form of a MENUITEMINFO structure.
GetSubMenu	Gets a handle to the specified submenu.
GetSystemMenu	Gets a handle to the window menu (system menu) in the specified window.
InsertMenu	Inserts a new menu item into the specified menu.
LoadMenu	Loads the specified menu resource.
RemoveMenu	Deletes a menu item from the specified menu.
SetMenuItemInfo	Changes menu item information.
TrackPopupMenu	Displays a pop-up menu and tracks user selections.
TrackPopupMenuEx	Similar to TrackPopupMenu, but passes the exclusion RECT in a TPMPARAMS structure instead of as an individual LPRECT.

Table 4.9 can be used as a quick reference for the menu operations provided by the operating system. Now that you have a good understanding of Windows CE menu basics, understanding how to use these functions when needed should be straightforward with the help of the Windows CE on-line documentation.

The Complete CMDBAR Sample Application

All of the concepts presented in this chapter are pulled together in the sample application, CMDBAR.EXE. Complete source code for this application is included on the companion CD under the directory \Samples\cmdbar. The command bar button bitmap file and all of the project files needed to build the application are included there as well.

Concluding Remarks

In this chapter, we discussed how to add menus and accelerators to Windows CE applications. We introduced the Windows CE command bar control, and showed how menus, controls, and tool tips can be added to command bars. This chapter also presented the Windows CE menu API.

At this point, you should be able to write some fairly complex applications that include menus, modal and modeless dialogs, and the standard Windows CE child controls. In the next chapter, we will explore programming the Windows CE common control library in greater detail. You will then be able to add even more rich features, such as calendar functionality, to your applications very easily.

CHAPTER 5

Windows CE Common Controls

This chapter discusses programming Window CE common controls. It concentrates on the *month calendar* control, the *date time picker* control, *rebar* controls, and *command bands* (Table 5.1). But the basic common control programming concepts covered here, such as how to respond to common control notifications, can be applied to programming all Windows CE common controls.

Like the other common controls, each of the controls listed in Table 5.1 resides in COMMCTRL.DLL. To use one or more of them in an application, the COMMCTRL.DLL must be loaded. The application then creates the controls using *CreateWindow* or *CreateWindowEx* calls with the appropriate control class name in the *lpClassName* parameter. Care must be taken to load COMMCTRL.DLL properly. See the section called "Why Are My HWNDs Always NULL?" in this chapter for details.

For any Windows CE common control, there are a number of messages that an application can send to the control to take advantage of various features and control functionality. In addition, there are many notifications that a common control can send to its parent window via the WM_NOTIFY message.

Table 5.1 Windows CE Common Controls Covered in This Chapter

CONTROL	USE
Month Calendar	A complete month view calendar control. User interface allows for easy selection of one or more dates.
Date Time Picker	Displays dates and times, and provides a convenient user interface for changing the date and time information displayed.
Rebars	Resizable child control container.
Command Bands	A special rebar containing close, help, and OK buttons.

The programming model of all common controls is basically the same. Applications create controls with various control styles to enable various control features. Then parent windows send the controls messages to program their behavior. Controls also send notifications to their parent window to alert the parent that some action has been performed or some other occurrence of interest has taken place. It is therefore more economical to present a sample application for each control that highlights some of the more interesting features of the particular control.

After understanding the sample application, you can delve into other messages, notifications, or styles that might be of interest to you for your specific application programming needs. Using the samples as a model, you should find that taking advantage of the other Windows CE common controls not covered in this chapter will not present any serious challenges.

At the end of each section covering a control, a brief description of all messages and notifications for the particular control is given.

AFTER COMPLETING THIS CHAPTER YOU WILL KNOW HOW TO . . .

Program month calendar controls

Program date time picker controls

Program rebar controls

Program command band controls

Why Are My HWNDs Always NULL?

There is a serious discrepancy between the on-line documentation and the reality of creating any of the Windows CE common controls covered in this chapter.

The documentation states that applications can create these controls by loading COMMCTRL.DLL with *InitCommonControls*, and then calling *CreateWindow* or *CreateWindowEx* with the appropriate control window class name. Alternatively, the documentation states, an application can load just the control classes it needs with *InitCommonControlsEx*, and then proceed with *CreateWindow* or *CreateWindowEx*.

It turns out that you *must* use the latter method with either *CreateWindow* or *CreateWindowEx*.

For example, I tried the following:

```
#include <commctrl.h>
HWND hwndMonth;
InitCommonControls();
//Code to create main application window, etc, removed
hwndMonth = CreateWindowEx(0, MONTHCAL_CLASS,...);
```

To my surprise, *hwndMonth* was NULL after the *CreateWindowEx* call executed. To try and figure out what was going on, I put a call to *GetLastError* right after creating the control and got back error code 1407, which stands for ERROR_CANNOT_FIND_WND_CLASS.

This can only mean that *InitCommonControls* in fact does not register the window class for the month calendar control. This error also occurred for other common control classes covered in this chapter.

When doing the following, however, everything worked as expected:

```
#include <commctrl.h>
HWND hwndMonth;
                INITCOMMONCONTROLSEX icex;
icex.dwSize = sizeof(icex);
icex.dwICC = ICC_DATE_CLASSES;
InitCommonControlsEx(&icex);
hwndMonth = CreateWindowEx(0, MONTHCAL_CLASS,...);
```

The Month Calendar Control

The month calendar control provides a quick way to include full-featured calendar functionality in your applications. It can display dates over any specified range of dates, and automatically accounts for the

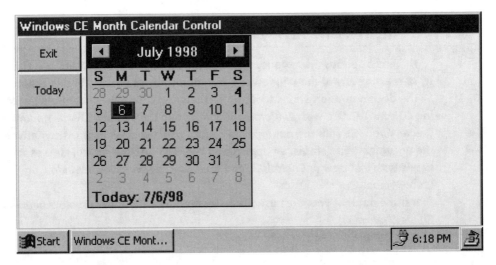

Figure 5.1 The month calendar control.

day of week variations for dates in different years, as well as for leap years. An example of the month calendar control is shown in Figure 5.1.

The control allows users to move backward or forward through the months of the year by clicking the left or right arrow button in the control title. If the device on which the application is running has a keyboard, users can also move through the months using the Page Up (to advance) and Page Down (to go back) keys.

As an alternative, if the user taps the name of the month in the control title, a pop-up menu appears listing all of the months in the year. Selecting a month from this menu tells the control to display the selected month.

The current year can also be changed. Tapping on the year in the title of the control forces an up-down control to appear that can be used to change the year. On devices with a keyboard, CTRL+Page Up and CTRL+Page Down also move the year forward or back.

A number of features of the month calendar control are programmable, such as whether the control indicates the current date, and various control color options.

Writing personal information management applications such as an appointment book or meeting scheduler is made much easier given the functionality of the month calendar control.

The control class for the month calendar control, which you need to pass to *CreateWindow* or *CreateWindowEx* when creating an instance of this control, is MONTHCAL_CLASS.

Month Calendar Control Styles

There are five control styles that can be used with the month calendar control:

MCS_DAYSTATE. Indicates that the control is capable of drawing specific dates in bold text.

MCS_MULTISELECT. Indicates that the control can select a range of dates. The default is that month calendar controls can only select one date at a time.

MCS_NOTODAY. Control does not display "Today is . . ." text at the bottom.

MCS_NOTODAYCIRCLE. Control does not box the current date.

MCS_WEEKNUMBERS. Control displays the number of each week (1–52) to the left of each week.

Day States

Month calendar controls can be made to display dates of interest in bold text. For example, you may want an appointment calendar application to display holidays in bold to make them easier to identify.

Highlighting dates in bold in a month calendar control is done using the *day state* mechanism. A day state is a data type called MONTH-DAYSTATE which is simply a DWORD. Each of the 32 bits of a MONTHDAYSTATE is used to represent the state of the corresponding day in a particular month. If, for example, bit 5 is set to 1, day 5 in the corresponding month is displayed in bold on the month calendar control. Zero values in MONTHDAYSTATEs mean the corresponding dates are not bold.

Applications typically tell month calendar controls which dates to display in bold in response to the MCN_GETDAYSTATE notification. We will look at the specifics of responding to this and other month calendar control notifications a little later.

An Example

In this example, we create a month calendar control that highlights a limited set of holidays. For the sake of simplicity, the holidays it highlights are among those that always fall on the same date every year. This prevents me from having to implement an algorithm that can do things such as determine what date the third Sunday in June is in any given year (sorry, Dad).

Our application uses a month calendar control that only allows users to select a single date at a time. It displays the currently selected date in the main application window title bar. Also, the application has a button labeled Today which sets the current selection to today's date.

To pick the holidays, I sat down with my wife's "Cat Lover" calendar and chose seven holidays at random (I wouldn't have picked January 22, "Answer Your Cat's Question Day," any other way). Here's what I came up with:

- January 1: New Year's Day
- January 22: see above
- February 14: Valentine's Day
- March 17: St. Patrick's Day
- July 4: Independence Day
- October 31: Halloween
- December 25: Christmas

Our month calendar control will display each of these holidays in bold. Therefore, our application needs to use day states. Let's look first at how to do this.

Recall that for any given month, a month calendar control uses a MONTHDAYSTATE 32-bit integer to represent the dates to display in bold. The least significant bit represents the first of the month, the next bit represents the second, and so on. Since the control keeps track of the number of days in a given month for a particular year, the last day of the month may be bit 28, 29, 30, or 31. Defining a day state for Christmas, for example, could be done like this:

```
MONTHDAYSTATE mdsXMas;
mdsXMas = (MONTHDAYSTATE)(0x01 << 24);
```

Since bit zero of a MONTHDAYSTATE represents the first of the month, bit 24 corresponds to the 25th. Shifting the number 0x01 24 bits to the left sets that bit.

The application defines an array of MONTHDAYSTATE values to represent all of the holidays I picked. Notice that the first entry of this array, representing the month of January, has two holidays:

```
#define ONE     0x01
MONTHDAYSTATE mdsHoliday[12] = {(ONE | (ONE<<21)), //January
  (ONE<<13),   //February
  (ONE<<16),   //March
  0,           //April
  0,           //May
  0,           //June
  (ONE<<3),    //July
  0,           //August
  0,           //September
  (ONE<<30),   //October
  0,           //November
  (ONE<<24)    //December};
```

The next interesting thing that the application does is to create the month calendar control and set some of its visual properties. *hwnd-Main* and *hInstance* are the main application window and the application HINSTANCE, respectively.

```
#define IDC_MONTH   1026
HWND hwndMonth;
hwndMonth = CreateWindowEx(
  MONTHCAL_CLASS, NULL,
  WS_VISIBLE|WS_BORDER|WS_CHILD|MCS_DAYSTATE,
  0,0,0,0,
  hwndMain,
  (HMENU)IDC_MONTH,hInstance, NULL);
OnInitMonthCalendar(hwndMonth, 70, 0);
```

The MCS_DAYSTATE creates a month calendar control that can use day states, which we need in order to highlight our holidays.

The only funny thing here is that all of the window position parameters passed to *CreateWindowEx* are zero. The reason for this is that a month calendar control can be made to display more than one month at a time. The control therefore leaves it to the application to set the size of the control to accommodate the number of months to display.

This is made easier by the MCM_GETMINREQRECT message. This message is sent to a month calendar control to determine the minimum height and width required to display one calendar month. When an application sends this message to a month calendar control, the control returns a RECT through the *lParam* parameter of *SendMessage*. The *right* and *bottom* members of this RECT contain the minimum width and height required, respectively.

Let's look at the *OnInitMonthCalendar* function to see how to use the MCM_GETMINREQRECT message:

```
void OnInitMonthCalendar(HWND hwndCal, int nLeft, int nTop)
{
  RECT r;
  SendMessage(hwndCal, MCM_GETMINREQRECT,
    0,(LPARAM)(LPRECT)&r);
  /* Resize the month calendar control window
    to accommodate one full calendar month.
   */
  SetWindowPos(hwndCal, NULL,
    nLeft,nTop,
    r.right, /cx, new width
    r.bottom, /cy, new height
    SWP_NOZORDER);
}
```

If an application wanted to display more than one month at a time, it could pass integer multiples of *r.right* and *r.left* as the *cx* and *cy* parameters of *SetWindowPos*.

The next interesting part of the application is in the main window's window procedure, where we handle the control notifications we are interested in (Figure 5.2). In our example, we respond to the MCN_SELCHANGE and MCN_GETDAYSTATE notifications. The pertinent part of the window procedure is shown in Figure 5.2.

The MCN_SELCHANGE notification is sent by the month calendar control to its parent window whenever the date selection in the month calendar control is changed by some user interaction with the control. Furthermore, as the name implies, this notification is only sent when the selected date or dates change. For example, tapping a date in the control and then tapping the same date again results in an MCN_SELCHANGE notification only for the first tap.

There is a related notification called MCN_SELECT. This notification is sent by the month calendar control only when the user explicitly taps a date or selects a date range. It is not sent any other time, for example

```
case WM_NOTIFY:
  LPNMHDR lpnmhdr;
  nID = (UINT)wParam;
  switch(nID)
  {
  case IDC_MONTH:
   lpnmhdr = (LPNMHDR)lParam;
   switch(lpnmhdr->code)
   {
   case MCN_SELCHANGE:
    LPNMSELCHANGE lpsel;
    lpsel = (LPNMSELCHANGE)lParam;
    OnSelect(lpnmhdr->hwndFrom, hwndMain, lpsel);
    break;
   case MCN_GETDAYSTATE:
    LPNMDAYSTATE lpds;
    lpds = (LPNMDAYSTATE)lParam;
    OnGetDayState(lpds);
    break;
   default:
    break;
   }        //End of switch(lpnmhdr->code) block
   return (0);
  default:
   return (0);
  }          //End of switch(nID) block
```

Figure 5.2 Handling month calendar control notifications.

when the date changes by selecting a month from the pop-up menu or tapping the month scroll buttons. In the example described above where a user taps the same date multiple times, an MCN_SELECT notification would be sent for each of the taps.

Since the MCN_SELCHANGE notification is sent upon any user interaction that changes the date selection in the control, we only need to respond to MCN_SELCHANGE.

When either the MCN_SELCHANGE or MCN_SELECT notification is sent, the *lParam* of the parent window's window procedure is an NMSELCHANGE structure. This structure is defined as:

```
typedef struct tagNMSELCHANGE
{
  NMHDR nmhdr;
  SYSTEMTIME stSelStart;
  SYSTEMTIME stSelEnd;
} NMSELCHANGE, FAR* LPNMSELCHANGE;
```

The two notification-specific members of this structure, *stSelStart* and *stSelEnd*, are SYSTEMTIME structures containing date information about the first and last dates in the new date selection range. If the control does not have the MCS_MULTISELECT style, *stSelStart* and *stSelEnd* will be the same.

In our sample application, we change title bar text to display the currently selected date in response to these notifications. The application code for handling this notification is the *OnSelect* function:

```
#define IsMultiSelect(hwnd) \
   (GetWindowLong(hwnd, GWL_STYLE) & MCS_MULTISELECT)

void OnSelect(HWND hwndCal,HWND hwndParent,
   LPNMSELCHANGE lpsel)
{
   TCHAR pszText[64];
   //Set caption text only if control is single select
   if (!IsMultiSelect(hwndCal))
   {
    wsprintf(pszText, TEXT("Selected Date: %d\\%d\\%d"),
     lpsel->stSelStart.wMonth,
     lpsel->stSelStart.wDay,
     lpsel->stSelStart.wYear);
    SetWindowText(hwndParent, pszText);
   }
}
```

The *IsMultiSelect* macro just tests if the month calendar control specified has the MCS_MULTISELECT style. *OnSelect* says if the control only allows single selection, set the current selected date in the application's main window caption. The selected date in this case is either of the SYSTEMTIME members of the NMSLECHANGE structure sent by the control with the MCN_SELCHANGE notification.

The second notification we respond to is MCN_GETDAYSTATE. This notification is sent by the month calendar control to request the day state information, which it uses to determine which dates to display in bold text.

Along with the MCN_GETDAYSTATE notification, the control sends an NMDAYSTATE structure in the *lParam* of the parent window's window procedure. This structure is defined as:

```
typedef struct tagNMDAYSTATE
{
```

```
   NMHDR nmhdr;
   SYSTEMTIME stStart;
   int cDayState;
   LPMONTHDAYSTATE prgDayState;
} NMDAYSTATE, FAR* LPNMDAYSTATE;
```

The month calendar control requires that applications supply day state information for more than just the current month. For example, if the current month (as determined by the date that the control is currently using as today's date) is June, the control will want day state information for May, June, and July. The *cDayState* member of this structure tells the application exactly how many months' worth of day state information is needed. The *stStart* member indicates the first month for which the control wants day state information. This month is found in the *wMonth* member of the *stStart* SYSTEMTIME structure. *prgDayState* is an array of MONTHDAYSTATE values that the application fills in with the application specific day state information.

Looking at our sample application's *OnGetDatState* function will make this much clearer. As the code in Figure 5.2 previously showed, this function is called in response to the MCN_GETDAYSTATE notification:

```
void OnGetDayState(LPNMDAYSTATE lpds)
{
  int i, nStart;

  nStart = lpds->stStart.wMonth-1;
  for (i=0; i<lpds->cDayState; i++)
  {
  //Account for month roll over, i.e., nStart > 11.
   if (nStart>11)
   {
    nStart = 0;
   }
   lpds->prgDayState[i] = mdsHoliday[nStart++];
  }
}
```

nStart is the index into our *mdsHoliday* array. It is initialized to the starting month indicated by the NMDAYSTATE structure, minus 1. The minus 1 accounts for the fact that in *mdsHoliday*, January corresponds to index 0, but SYSTEMTIME month values are 1-based. Then for each of the months for which the month calendar control is requesting day state information, we assign the holiday day state information for that month to the corresponding MONTHDAYSTATE value in the *prgDayState* member of the NMDAYSTATE structure.

When the window procedure returns after processing this MCN_GET-DAYSTATE notification, the month calendar control uses the day state information in the NMDAYSTATE structure to display the appropriate dates in bold.

Finally, the sample application allows the user to return to today's date by tapping the Today button. This is done in the *OnGotoToday* function:

```
void OnGotoToday(HWND hwndCal)
{
  SYSTEMTIME stToday;
  SendMessage(hwndCal, MCM_GETTODAY, 0, (LPARAM)&stToday);
  SendMessage(hwndCal, MCM_SETCURSEL, 0, (LPARAM)&stToday);
}
```

This function simply determines the date that the control currently uses as today's date with the MCM_GETTODAY message, and then sets the current month calendar control selection by sending MCM_SETCURSEL. MCM_GETTODAY returns a SYSTEMTIME structure representing today's date. MCM_SETCURSEL takes a SYS-TEMTIME telling the control what day to set the current selection to.

The Today Button Doesn't Work, Right?

Click on the Today button in the sample application. The month calendar control switches to today's date, but the application caption text doesn't change. This "bug" was left in the sample application to highlight a subtle undesirable feature of the month calendar control.

It turns out that programmatic changes to the current selection in a month calendar control do not trigger MCN_SELECT or MCN_SELCHANGE notifications. Therefore, the MCM_SETCURSEL message sent in the *OnGotoToday* function does not cause the MCN_SELECT or MCN_SELCHANGE notifications to be sent. Hence, the main application caption text does not change when the Today button is pressed.

This is a serious oversight in the design of the month calendar control. The application developer must manually trigger the notification handlers for each of these notifications.

One method for fixing this bug is presented in the next section.

Before We Move On, Let's Fix the Bug

In the previous section, we pointed out a small bug with the Today button in the month calendar control sample application. This section describes one way to fix this bug.

The caption text in the main window of the application is changed by the *OnSelect* function. Pressing the Today button results in a call to the *OnGotoToday* function. Fixing the bug is as simple as making *OnGotoToday* appropriately call *OnSelect*.

OnSelect requires handles to the month calendar control and the parent window. These are global variables available to any function in the application. Additionally, *OnSelect* needs a pointer to an NMSELCHANGE structure. Actually, it only needs the *wMonth*, *wDay*, and *wYear* components of the *stSelStart* member of such a structure. *OnGotoToday* already obtains this information by sending an MCM_GETTODAY message. The bug can thus be fixed by replacing the original *OnGotoToday* function with the following:

```
void OnGotoToday(HWND hwndCal)
{
  SYSTEMTIME stToday;
  NMSELCHANGE nmsel;
  memset(&nmsel, 0, sizeof(nmsel));
  SendMessage(hwndCal, MCM_GETTODAY, 0, (LPARAM)&stToday);
  SendMessage(hwndCal, MCM_SETCURSEL, 0, (LPARAM)&stToday);
  nmsel.stSelStart = stToday;
  OnSelect(hwndMonth, hwndMain, &nmsel);
}
```

There are very few changes to the *OnGotoToday* function here. We declare an NMSELCHANGE structure, *nmsel*, and initialize its contents to zero. After sending the MCM_SETCURSEL message to the month calendar control, we assign the *stSelStart* member of *nmsel* to the DATETIME structure retrieved by the MCM_GETTODAY message.

hwndMonth and *hwndMain* are the global variables containing the window handles of the month calendar control and the main application window, respectively. The *OnSelect* call therefore has all the information it needs to update the main window caption correctly.

Month Calendar Control Messages and Notifications

The complete list of the control messages and notifications associated with the month calendar control are described in Tables 5.2 and 5.3.

Table 5.2 Month Calendar Control Messages

MESSAGE	MEANING
MCM_GETCOLOR	Retrieves the color of the specified part of the control.
MCM_GETCURSEL	Gets the SYSTEMTIME structure corresponding to the currently selected date.
MCM_GETFIRSTDAYOFWEEK	Returns the first day of the week displayed for each week in the control.
MCM_GETMAXSELCOUNT	Returns the maximum number of days that can be selected at one time in the control.
MCM_GETMAXTODAYWIDTH	Returns the maximum width of the Today string displayed at the bottom of month calendar controls.
MCM_GETMINREQRECT	Returns the minimum width and height required to display one full calendar month.
MCM_GETMONTHDELTA	Returns the number of months that the control advances or retreats when the user taps the right or left month scroll button.
MCM_GETMONTHRANGE	Returns SYSTEMTIME structures representing the maximum and minimum dates that can be displayed by the control.
MCM_GETRANGE	Retrieves the maximum and minimum allowable dates set for the control.
MCM_GETSELRANGE	Gets the range of dates currently selected in a control with the MCS_MULTISELECT style.
MCM_GETTODAY	Retrieves the date currently set as today's date in the control
MCM_HITTEST	Determines which part of the control contains the specified point.
MCM_SETCOLOR	Sets the color of the specified part of the control.
MCM_SETCURSEL	Sets the current date selection in the control. Cannot be used with controls with the MCS_MULTISELECT style.
MCM_SETDAYSTATE	Sets the day state information for days that are currently visible in the control.
MCM_SETFIRSTDAYOFWEEK	Sets the day (Monday, Tuesday, etc.) to use as the first day of each week displayed in the control.
MCM_SETMAXSELCOUNT	Sets the maximum number of days that can be selected in a control.
MCM_SETMONTHDELTA	Sets the number of months the control advances or retreats when a user taps the right or left month scroll button.

(Continues)

Table 5.2 Month Calendar Control Messages (Continued)

MESSAGE	MEANING
MCM_SETRANGE	Sets the maximum and minimum dates for a control.
MCM_SETSELRANGE	Sets the range of currently selected dates for a control. Message only applies to controls with the MCS_MULTISELECT style.
MCM_SETTODAY	Sets the date that the control specifies as today's date.

The Complete Sample Application

The complete source code for the month calendar control sample application is shown below.

month.h

```
#ifndef __MONTH_H_
#define __MONTH_H_
#define MAX_STRING_LENGTH   129
#define IsMultiSelect(hwnd) \
  (GetWindowLong(hwnd, GWL_STYLE) & MCS_MULTISELECT)
/Child control IDs
#define IDC_EXIT        1024
#define IDC_TODAY  1025
#define IDC_MONTH  1026
#define ONE     0x01
TCHAR pszAppName[] = TEXT("MONTHSAMPLE");
TCHAR pszTitle[] = TEXT("Windows CE Month Calendar Control");
HINSTANCE ghInst;
int nWidth;
int nHeight;
/* Define the various windows used in this application:
  hwndMain -> The main application window.
```

Table 5.3 Month Calendar Control Notifications

NOTIFICATION	MEANING
MCN_GETDAYSTATE	Sent by a control to request day state information used to determine which dates to display in bold.
MCN_SELCHANGE	Sent by a control anytime the currently selected date or range of dates changes.
MCN_SELECT	Sent by a control whenever the user explicitly selects a new current date or range of dates, i.e., the user taps a specific date in the calendar.

```
  hwndExit -> Exit button
  hwndToday -> Goto Today button
  hwndMonth -> Month calendar control
 */
HWND hwndMain;
HWND hwndExit;
HWND hwndToday;
HWND hwndMonth;
//MONTHDAYSTATEs for holidays
MONTHDAYSTATE mdsHoliday[12] = {(ONE | (ONE<<21)), //January
  (ONE<<13),   //February
  (ONE<<16),   //March
  0,           //April
  0,           //May
  0,           //June
  (ONE<<3),    //July
  0,           //August
  0,           //September
  (ONE<<30),   //October
  0,           //November
  (ONE<<24)    //December};
void OnInitMonthCalendar(HWND hwndCal, int nLeft, int nTop);
void OnSelect(HWND hwndCal,
  HWND hwndParent,
  LPNMSELCHANGE lpsel);
void OnGetDayState(LPNMDAYSTATE lpds);
void OnGotoToday(HWND hwndCal);
LRESULT CALLBACK WndProc(HWND hwnd, UINT message,
  WPARAM wParam, LPARAM lParam);
#endif
```

main.cpp

```
#include <windows.h>
#include <commctrl.h>
#include "month.h"
int WINAPI WinMain(HINSTANCE hInstance,
  HINSTANCE hPrevInstance,
  LPTSTR lpCmdLine,
  int nCmdShow)
{
  MSG msg;
  RECT rc;
  INITCOMMONCONTROLSEX icex;
  WNDCLASS wc;
  ghInst = hInstance;
  wc.style = 0;
  wc.lpfnWndProc = WndProc;
  wc.cbClsExtra = 0;
  wc.cbWndExtra = 0;
```

```
wc.hInstance = hInstance;
wc.hIcon = NULL;
wc.hCursor = NULL;
wc.hbrBackground = (HBRUSH)GetStockObject(WHITE_BRUSH);
wc.lpszMenuName = NULL;
wc.lpszClassName = szAppName;
RegisterClass(&wc);
icex.dwSize = sizeof(icex);
icex.dwICC = ICC_DATE_CLASSES;
InitCommonControlsEx(&icex);
SystemParametersInfo(SPI_GETWORKAREA, NULL,
 &rc, NULL);
nWidth = rc.right;
nHeight = rc.bottom;
hwndMain = CreateWindow(szAppName, szTitle,
 WS_VISIBLE|WS_BORDER|WS_CAPTION,
 0,0,nWidth, nHeight,
 NULL, NULL, hInstance, NULL);
hwndExit = CreateWindow(TEXT("BUTTON"),TEXT("Exit"),
 WS_VISIBLE|WS_CHILD|BS_PUSHBUTTON,
 0,0,65,35, hwndMain,
 (HMENU)IDC_EXIT, hInstance, NULL);
hwndToday = CreateWindow(TEXT("BUTTON"),
 TEXT("Today"),
 WS_VISIBLE|WS_CHILD|BS_PUSHBUTTON,
 0,37,65,35,
 hwndMain, (HMENU)IDC_TODAY,
 hInstance,NULL);
hwndMonth = CreateWindowEx(MONTHCAL_CLASS,
 NULL,
 WS_VISIBLE|WS_BORDER|WS_CHILD|MCS_DAYSTATE,
 0,0,0,0,
 hwndMain,(HMENU)IDC_MONTH,
 hInstance, NULL);
OnInitMonthCalendar(hwndMonth, 70, 0);
while (GetMessage(&msg, NULL, 0, 0))
 {
 TranslateMessage (&msg);
 DispatchMessage(&msg);
 }
 return(msg.wParam);
}
LRESULT CALLBACK WndProc(HWND hwnd,
 UINT message,
 WPARAM wParam,
 LPARAM lParam)
{
 UINT nID;
 switch(message)
 {
```

```
    case WM_NOTIFY:
     LPNMHDR lpnmhdr;
     nID = (UINT)wParam;
     switch(nID)
     {
     case IDC_MONTH:
      lpnmhdr = (LPNMHDR)lParam;
      switch(lpnmhdr->code)
      {
      case MCN_SELCHANGE:
       LPNMSELCHANGE lpsel;
       lpsel = (LPNMSELCHANGE)lParam;
       OnSelect(lpnmhdr->hwndFrom, hwndMain, lpsel);
       break;
      case MCN_GETDAYSTATE:
       LPNMDAYSTATE lpds;
       lpds = (LPNMDAYSTATE)lParam;
       OnGetDayState(lpds);
       break;
      default:
       break;
      }      //End of switch(lpnmhdr->code) block
      return (0);
     default:
      return (0);
     }      //End of switch(nID) block
    case WM_COMMAND:
     nID = LOWORD(wParam);
     switch(nID)
     {
     case IDC_TODAY:
      OnGotoToday(hwndMonth);
      break;
     case IDC_EXIT:
      DestroyWindow(hwnd);
      PostQuitMessage(0);
      break;
     default:
      break;
     }      //End of switch(nID) statement
     return (0);
    default:
     return (DefWindowProc(hwnd,message,wParam,lParam));
    }      //End of switch(message) statement
}
void OnInitMonthCalendar(HWND hwndCal, int nLeft, int nTop)
{
  RECT r;
  SendMessage(hwndCal, MCM_SETCOLOR, MCSC_MONTHBK,
    (LPARAM)RGB(192,192,192));
  SendMessage(hwndCal, MCM_SETCOLOR, MCSC_TITLEBK,
```

```
     (LPARAM)RGB(0,0,0));
   SendMessage(hwndCal, MCM_SETCOLOR, MCSC_BACKGROUND,
     (LPARAM)RGB(128,128,128));
   SendMessage(hwndCal, MCM_GETMINREQRECT,
     0,(LPARAM)(LPRECT)&r);
   SetWindowPos(hwndCal, NULL, nLeft,nTop,
     r.right, r.bottom, SWP_NOZORDER);
}
void OnSelect(HWND hwndCal,
  HWND hwndParent,
  LPNMSELCHANGE lpsel)
{
  TCHAR pszText[64];
  //Set caption text only if control is single select
  if (!IsMultiSelect(hwndCal))
  {
   wsprintf(pszText, TEXT("Selected Date: %d\\%d\\%d"),
     lpsel->stSelStart.wMonth,
     lpsel->stSelStart.wDay,
     lpsel->stSelStart.wYear);
    SetWindowText(hwndParent, pszText);
  }
}
void OnGetDayState(LPNMDAYSTATE lpds)
{
  int i, nStart;
  nStart = lpds->stStart.wMonth-1;
  for (i=0; i<lpds->cDayState; i++)
  {
   //Account for month roll over, i.e., nStart > 11.
   if (nStart>11)
   {
    nStart = 0;
   }
   lpds->prgDayState[i] = mdsHoliday[nStart++];
  }
}
void OnGotoToday(HWND hwndCal)
{
  SYSTEMTIME stToday;
  SendMessage(hwndCal, MCM_GETTODAY, 0, (LPARAM)&stToday);
  SendMessage(hwndCal, MCM_SETCURSEL, 0, (LPARAM)&stToday);
}
```

The Date Time Picker Control

The date time picker control is closely related to the month calendar control. Since we spent so much time and effort describing the month calendar control, we will not spend as much time on the date time picker control.

The window class for this control is DATETIMEPICK_CLASS.

A date time picker control is an editable text field that can display date and time information in a variety of formats (Figure 5.3). Predefined formats include the long and short formats—for example, "Thursday, July 04, 1776" and "7/4/76" respectively (beware Year 2000-aware folks!).

The control also supports time format. This means that the control just displays time in hh:mm:ss format.

Application-specific display formats can be defined in a number of ways. Applications set the format using the DTM_SETFORMAT message. With this message the application specifies a format string that the control uses to format its display. This format string can include *callback fields*. In this case, the control sends notifications to which the parent window responds by telling the control what text to display in a particular callback field.

By default, date time picker controls include an arrow button similar to that found in combo boxes. When this button is pressed, a month calendar control appears from which users can then select the current

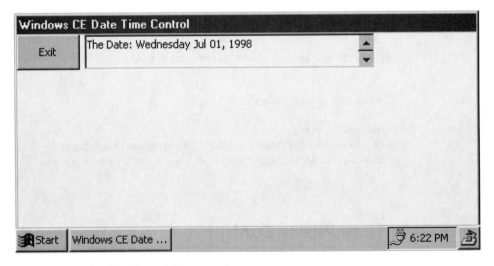

Figure 5.3 The date time picker control.

date. Alternatively, date time pickers can include an up-down control for picking the current date.

The date time picker control also allows the user to type into the edit field of the control.

DROP-DOWN MONTH CALENDAR CONTROL VERSION OF THE DATE TIME PICKER

The drop-down month calendar control version of the date time picker control is a good choice for Windows CE applications running on devices with limited touch screen sizes. Applications that require the ability to display dates and times can do so with a minimum of screen real estate using this control style by creating small date time picker controls.

When the control is closed, the date and time information takes up very little space. The more detailed month calendar control only appears temporarily when dropped down by the user.

Date Time Picker Control Styles

The six styles that can be specified for a date time picker control are shown below. Only one of DTS_LONGDATEFORMAT, DTS_SHORT-DATEFORMAT, and DTS_TIMEFORMAT can be used with a particular control.

DTS_APPCANPARSE. Indicates that the control can parse strings entered into the control by users. After the user edits the contents of the control, a DTN_USERSTRING notification is sent, to which the parent window can respond by interpreting the string in some way.

DTS_LONGDATEFORMAT. Specifies that the control is to display dates in the long date format.

DTS_SHOWNONE. Allows the control to display no date. Used with the DTM_SETSYSTEMTIME and DTM_GETSYSTEMTIME messages.

DTS_SHORTDATEFORMAT. Specifies that the control is to display dates in the short date format.

DTS_TIMEFORMAT. Specifies that the control displays the time, instead of dates. If this style is specified, the control does not include

A Note on Date Time Picker Controls That Include Month Calendar Controls

Date time picker controls do not keep a static month calendar control. So, for example, if you wrote the following code, you should not expect *hwndCal* to be a valid window:

```
HWND hwndCal, hwndDateTime;
//Init common controls, etc.
//Create the date time picker control...
hwndDateTime = CreateWindow(DATETIMEPICK_CLASS,
            NULL,
            WS_CHILD|WS_VISIBLE|
            DTS_SHORTDATEFORMAT,
            ...);
//...and extract the month calendar control associated with it
hwndCal = (HWND)SendMessage(hwndDateTime,
            DTM_GETMONTHCAL,
            0, 0L);
```

hwndCal will be NULL. The reason is that the month calendar control associated with the date time picker is only around between the times that the date time picker sends the DTN_DROPDOWN and DTN_CLOSEUP notifications.

Therefore, your applications must initialize the month calendar control in response to the DTN_DROPDOWN notification, the indication that the month calendar control is being displayed. And yes, this initialization must include proper positioning of the month calendar control window using the MCM_ GETMINREQRECT technique we saw in the application in the previous section.

a month calendar control, but only an up-down control for time selection.

DTS_UPDOWN. Specifies that the control include an up-down control for date selection instead of a month calendar control. This style is always included for date time picker controls with the DTS_ TIMEFORMAT style.

An Example

In this section we present a very simple example of how to use the date time picker control. All the example does is create a control that displays dates in the long date format and that responds to some basic text editing user input. Specifically, if the user types "Today" in the display area of the control, the control sets its current selection to today's date.

The date time picker control in this example uses an up-down control for moving through dates. Since the month calendar control was described in detail in the previous section, including an example of a date time picker using a month calendar control would be redundant.

The control is created with the following *CreateWindow* call. *hwndMain* and *hInstance* are the main application window and the application HINSTANCE, respectively.

```
#define IDC_DATETIME    1025
HWND hwndDateTime;
hwndDateTime = CreateWindow(DATETIMEPICK_CLASS,
  TEXT("DateTime"),
  WS_VISIBLE|WS_BORDER|WS_CHILD|DTS_LONGDATEFORMAT|
  DTS_APPCANPARSE|DTS_UPDOWN,
  70,0,300,35,
  hwndMain,
  (HMENU)IDC_DATETIME,
  hInstance,
  NULL);
```

The DTS_APPCANPARSE style is set to allow the control's parent to respond to user text input.

The most interesting feature of our application is that if the user types "Today" into the contents of the date time picker, the date time picker sets its date to today's date. The ability of the application to respond to user text input was enabled by the DTS_APPCANPARSE style. The control informs its parent that the user has entered text by sending the DTN_USERSTRING notification. The application's main window procedure is responsible for responding to this notification. Here is the portion of the window procedure that handles WM_NOTIFY messages:

```
case WM_NOTIFY:
  nID = (UINT)wParam;
  switch(nID)
  {
  case IDC_DATETIME:
   lpnmhdr = (LPNMHDR)lParam;
   switch(lpnmhdr->code)
   {
   case DTN_USERSTRING:
    LPNMDATETIMESTRING lpstr;
```

```
    lpstr = (LPNMDATETIMESTRING)lParam;
    if (!lstrcmp(lpstr->pszUserString,TEXT("Today")))
    {
     GetLocalTime(&lpstr->st);
     lpstr->dwFlags = GDT_VALID;
    }
    break;
   default:
    break;
   }    //End of switch(lpnmhdr->code) block
   return (0);
  default:
   return (0);
  }    //End of switch(nID) block
```

The DTN_USERSTRING notification is accompanied by an
NMDATETIMESTRING structure:

```
typedef struct tagNMDATETIMESTRING
{
  NMHDR nmhdr;
  LPCTSTR pszUserString;
  SYSTEMTIME st;
  DWORD dwFlags;
} NMDATETIMESTRING, FAR* LPNMDATETIMESTRING;
```

pszUserString is the string entered by the user. *st* is a SYSTEMTIME
structure that is filled in by the parent of the date time picker control.
The date specified will be the date displayed by the control after
the main window procedure returns from processing the
DTN_USERSTRING notification.

dwFlags can be set to GDT_VALID, indicating that the *st* member of
the NMDATETIMESTRING structure is valid and that the control
should display this date in the control's current date format. Alternatively, *dwFlags* can be GDT_NONE to tell the control to show no date,
which is valid only if the DTS_SHOWNONE style is used.

Our sample application responds to DTN_USERSTRING by comparing the user input string to "Today". If the user typed "Today", the
application calls *GetLocalTime* to determine today's date, and sets the *st*
member of the NMDATETIMESTRING to this value. Thus the date
time picker knows to display today's date.

Specifying Custom Date Time Formats

Date time picker controls are capable of displaying dates and times in
formats other than the predefined short, long, and time formats. Speci-

fying such formats, however, requires some extra work on the part of the application programmer.

The simplest way to specify a different format is to use the DTM_SET-FORMAT message. This message allows the application to specify a format string to be used by a particular date time picker control. Format strings can include any of a set of predefined format codes. For example, "MMM" tells the control to display the three-character abbreviation for the month, and "dddd" tells it to display the full weekday name. (A full list of these codes is contained in the on-line documentation for the DTM_SETFORMAT message.) To embed literal strings inside a format string, enclose the desired text in single quotes.

For example, if the date was Thursday, July 2, 1998, and we wanted our date time picker to display this date as "The Date: Thursday July 02, 1998," our application could set the format string as follows:

```
SendMessage(hwndDateTime, DTM_SETFORMAT, 0,
    (LPARAM)TEXT("'The Date: 'ddddMMMdd', 'yyy"));
```

Another way that applications can customize date time picker display formats is by means of callback fields. The application adds "X" characters to the format string specified with the DTM_SETFORMAT message. Then, whenever the control needs to display the date time information, it sends its parent DTN_FORMAT and DTN_FORMAT-QUERY notifications. The application responds to these notifications by specifying the text to use in place of the callback fields, and to indicate the physical size of the text to be displayed.

The application must allow users to enter text in the regions of the string displayed by the date time picker that corresponds to the callback fields. The application handles the DTN_WMKEYDOWN notification to respond to user input in callback fields.

Date Time Picker Control Messages and Notifications

Tables 5.4 and 5.5 give a complete list of date time picker control messages and notifications, along with their meanings.

The Complete Sample Application

I'll be the first to admit that this application won't be making any headlines, but it will help make you more familiar with how to use date time picker controls.

Table 5.4 Date Time Picker Control Messages

MESSAGE	MEANING
DTM_GETMCCOLOR	Retrieves the color of the specified part of the month calendar child control contained by the date time picker. Message is only supported for date time pickers that do not have the DTS_UPDOWN style bit set, i.e., that have month calendar controls. Compare to MCM_GETCOLOR.
DTM_GETMCFONT	Retrieves the font currently in use by the month calendar child control contained by the date time picker. Message is only supported for date time pickers that do not have the DTS_UPDOWN style bit set.
DTM_GETMONTHCAL	Retrieves the HWND of the month calendar child control contained by the date time picker. Only supported for date time pickers that do not have the DTS_UPDOWN style bit set.
DTM_GETRANGE	Message gets the range of date time values that the date time picker can display.
DTM_GETSYSTEMTIME	Retrieves the time currently displayed in the date time picker. Time is returned as a SYSTEMTIME.
DTM_SETFORMAT	Message sets the date time picker control's display format string.
DTM_SETMCCOLOR	Message sets the color of the specified part of the month calendar child control contained by the date time picker. Message is only supported for date time pickers that do not have the DTS_UPDOWN style bit set. Compare to MCM_SETCOLOR.
DTM_SETMCFONT	Message sets the font used by the month calendar child control contained by the date time picker. Message is only supported for date time pickers that do not have the DTS_UPDOWN style bit set.
DTM_SETRANGE	Message sets the range of date time values that the date time picker can display.
DTM_SETSYSTEMTIME	Message sets the date and time to be displayed by the date time picker.

datetime.h

```
#ifndef __DATETIME_H_
#define __DATETIME_H_
//Child control IDs
#define IDC_EXIT   1024
#define IDC_DATETIME 1025
```

Table 5.5 Date Time Picker Control Notifications

NOTIFICATION	MEANING
DTN_CLOSEUP	Sent by the control when the user closes the drop-down month calendar child control contained by the date time picker. Only applicable to date time pickers that do not have the DTS_UPDOWN style bit set.
DTN_DATETIMECHANGE	Sent by the control whenever the date time display changes.
DTN_DROPDOWN	Sent by the control when the user opens the drop-down month calendar child control contained by the date time picker. Only applicable to date time pickers that do not have the DTS_UPDOWN style bit set.
DTN_FORMAT	Sent by the control for each callback field in a format string. The application responds by providing the text to display in the callback fields.
DTN_FORMATQUERY	Sent by the control for each callback field in a format string. The application responds by specifying the maximum pixel width of the text that can be displayed in the corresponding callback field.
DTN_USERSTRING	Sent by the control after the user edits text in the date time picker's date time display.
DTN_WMKEYDOWN	Sent by the control whenever the user types in a callback field. Responding to this notification allows the control owner to implement custom behavior for keystrokes such as arrow keys.

```
TCHAR pszAppName[] = TEXT("DATETIMESAMPLE");
TCHAR pszTitle[] = TEXT("Windows CE Date Time Control");
HINSTANCE ghInst;
int nWidth; //Main window width
int nHeight; //Main window height
/* Define the various windows used in this application:
  hwndMain -> The main application window.
  hwndExit -> Exit button
  hwndDateTime -> Date time picker control
 */
HWND hwndMain;
HWND hwndExit;
HWND hwndDateTime;
LRESULT CALLBACK WndProc(HWND hwnd,
  UINT message,
  WPARAM wParam,
  LPARAM lParam);
#endif
```

main.cpp

```cpp
#include <windows.h>
#include <commctrl.h>
#include "datetime.h"
int WINAPI WinMain(HINSTANCE hInstance,
  HINSTANCE hPrevInstance,
  LPTSTR lpCmdLine,
  int nCmdShow)
{
  MSG msg;
  RECT rc;
  INITCOMMONCONTROLSEX icex;
  WNDCLASS wc;
  ghInst = hInstance;
  wc.style = 0;
  wc.lpfnWndProc = WndProc;
  wc.cbClsExtra = 0;
  wc.cbWndExtra = 0;
  wc.hInstance = hInstance;
  wc.hIcon = NULL;
  wc.hCursor = NULL;
  wc.hbrBackground = (HBRUSH)(COLOR_WINDOW+1);
  wc.lpszMenuName = NULL;
  wc.lpszClassName = pszAppName;
  RegisterClass(&wc);
  icex.dwSize = sizeof(icex);
  icex.dwICC = ICC_DATE_CLASSES;
  InitCommonControlsEx(&icex);
  SystemParametersInfo(SPI_GETWORKAREA,NULL,
    &rc, NULL);
  nWidth = rc.right;
  nHeight = rc.bottom;
  hwndMain = CreateWindow(pszAppName,
    pszTitle,
    WS_VISIBLE|WS_BORDER|WS_CAPTION,
    0,0,nWidth,nHeight,
    NULL, NULL, hInstance, NULL);
  hwndExit = CreateWindow(TEXT("BUTTON"),
    TEXT("Exit"),
    WS_VISIBLE|WS_CHILD|BS_PUSHBUTTON,
    0,0,65,35,
    hwndMain, (HMENU)IDC_EXIT,
    hInstance,NULL);
  hwndDateTime = CreateWindow(DATETIMEPICK_CLASS,
    TEXT("DateTime"),
    WS_VISIBLE|WS_BORDER|WS_CHILD|
    DTS_LONGDATEFORMAT|DTS_APPCANPARSE|DTS_UPDOWN,
    70,0,300,35,
    hwndMain, (HMENU)IDC_DATETIME,
```

```
        hInstance,NULL);
    SendMessage(hwndDateTime, DTM_SETFORMAT, 0,
     (LPARAM)TEXT("'The Date: 'ddddMMMdd', 'yyy"));
    while (GetMessage(&msg, NULL, 0, 0))
    {
     TranslateMessage (&msg);
     DispatchMessage(&msg);
    }
    return(msg.wParam);
}
LRESULT CALLBACK WndProc(HWND hwnd,
    UINT message,
    WPARAM wParam,
    LPARAM lParam)
{
    UINT nID;
    LPNMHDR lpnmhdr;
    switch(message)
    {
    case WM_NOTIFY:
     nID = (UINT)wParam;
     switch(nID)
     {
     case IDC_DATETIME:
      lpnmhdr = (LPNMHDR)lParam;
      switch(lpnmhdr->code)
      {
      case DTN_USERSTRING:
       LPNMDATETIMESTRING lpstr;
       lpstr = (LPNMDATETIMESTRING)lParam;
       if (!lstrcmp(lpstr->pszUserString, TEXT("Today")))
       {
        GetLocalTime(&lpstr->st);
        lpstr->dwFlags = GDT_NONE;
       }
       break;
      default:
       break;
      }    //End of switch(lpnmhdr->code) block
      return (0);
     default:
      return (0);
     }    //End of switch(nID) block
    case WM_COMMAND:
     nID = LOWORD(wParam);
     switch(nID)
     {
     case IDC_EXIT:
      DestroyWindow(hwnd);
      PostQuitMessage(0);
```

```
     break;
    default:
     break;
    }       //End of switch(nID) statement
   return (0);
  default:
   return (DefWindowProc(hwnd, message, wParam, lParam));
   }       //End of switch(message) statement
 }
```

Rebar Controls

Rebar controls are those nice little draggable strips with buttons or other controls that appear all over applications like Microsoft Developer Studio and Microsoft Word. Applications use rebar controls as an attractive and flexible way to group and arrange related sets of child controls. Figure 5.4 shows this section's sample application using a rebar control.

Rebar controls act as containers for other Windows CE child controls. A rebar control can contain one or more *bands*, each of which in turn can contain one child control. The control contained by a rebar band can be a toolbar, giving the impression of multiple controls in a single

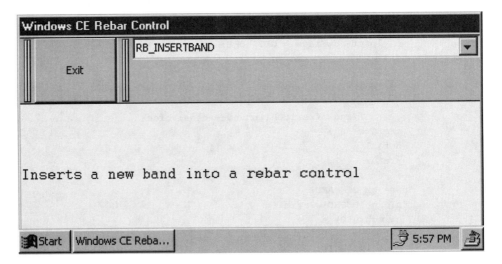

Figure 5.4   Rebar control with two bands.

band. Rebar controls can also include image lists. Bands in a rebar control can display a particular image list bitmap.

Each band in a rebar control can also include a *gripper bar*. A gripper bar appears as two vertical lines that can be used to drag the band.

Rebar Control Styles

There are seven styles that can be used to specify various rebar control characteristics:

CCS_VERT. Causes the control and the bands it contains to display vertically instead of horizontally.

RBS_AUTOSIZE. Rebar band layout automatically updates when child control size or position changes.

RBS_BANDBORDERS. Draws borders around rebar bands.

RBS_FIXEDORDER. Bands can be moved to different rows, but band order is fixed.

RBS_SMARTLABELS. If a band has an icon, the icon is only displayed when the band is minimized. If a band has a text label, the label is only displayed when the band is either in its restored or maximized state.

RBS_VARHEIGHT. Displays bands at the minimum required height if possible. If this style is not set, the height of all bands in the control is set to the height of the tallest band.

RBS_VERTICALGGRIPPER. Displays the gripper bar vertically instead of horizontally. Style is ignored if the rebar does not also have the CCS_VERT style.

Applications interact with the controls contained by rebar bands in the same way as with any other child control. The application can send the same child control messages to rebar band child controls. The child controls in rebar bands send WM_COMMAND messages to the parent of the rebar control. As this is normally the main application window, applications can respond to user interaction with the child controls as they would if the controls were not contained by a rebar control band.

As with most Windows CE controls, there are a number of messages and notifications used by rebar controls. These include functionality for inserting and deleting bands, getting the number of bands in a rebar control, resizing the rebar control, and the like. Text and background bitmaps can also be added to rebar control bands to further customize their appearance.

It's a safe bet that on the majority of occasions that you choose to use rebar controls, you will use them to group the child controls that drive the functionality of your Windows CE applications, relying on the default behavior of rebar controls to provide other functionality such as moving them with the gripper bar. It is therefore most useful to discuss the procedure for creating rebar controls and inserting bands with child controls into them. This will be the focus of this section.

The sample application for this section demonstrates a rebar control with two bands (see Figure 5.4). The first band contains the omnipotent "Exit" button. The second band contains a combo box. This combo box provides us some relief from the monotony of listing the messages and notifications supported by rebar controls at the end of chapter. Instead, the combo box lists all of the rebar control messages and notifications. Selecting an item in the combo box causes the application to display a description of the corresponding message or notification.

All of the new functionality presented in the sample application is related to creating rebar controls and inserting bands. Since this is described in detail in the pages that follow, listing the entire sample application at the end of the chapter is unnecessary.

Creating Rebar Controls

A rebar control is created using the REBARCLASSNAME control class.

The control is created with the following *CreateWindow* call. *hwndMain* and *hInstance* are the main application window and the application HINSTANCE, respectively.

```
#define IDC_REBAR  1024
HWND hwndRebar;
hwndRebar = CreateWindow(REBARCLASSNAME, NULL,
    WS_CHILD|WS_VISIBLE|WS_BORDER|
    RBS_VARHEIGHT|RBS_BANDBORDERS,
    0,0,0,0,
    hwndMain, (HMENU)IDC_REBAR,
    hInstance,NULL);
```

As was the case with the month calendar control, the *x*, *y*, *nWidth*, and *nHeight* parameters can be set to zero. The dimensions of the bands are what really matter, and these are inserted after the rebar control is created.

Rebar Control Bands

Bands are the real nucleus of a rebar control. The bands are what contain the child controls and define the appearance of the rebar control.

To fully understand bands, we must first look at how Windows CE represents bands. We can then explore how to add bands to rebar controls.

The REBARBANDINFO Structure

All information describing a band is specified in terms of a REBARBANDINFO structure. REBARBANDINFO information is supplied by applications when inserting bands into rebar controls. It can also be queried by an application to get information about existing rebar control bands. The structure is defined as:

```
typedef struct tagREBARBANDINFO
{
  UINT cbSize;
  UINT fMask;
  UINT fStyle;
  COLORREF clrFore;
  COLORREF clrBack;
  LPTSTR lpText;
  UINT cch;
  int iImage;
  HWND hwndChild;
  UINT cxMinChild;
  UINT cyMinChild;
  UINT cx;
  HBITMAP hbmBack;
  UINT wID;
  UINT cyChild;
  UINT cyMaxChild;
  UINT cyIntegral;
  UINT cxIdeal;
  LPARAM lParam;
} REBARBANDINFO, FAR* LPREBARBANDINFO;
```

cbSize just indicates the size of the REBARBANDINFO structure. Applications set this value using the *sizeof* function.

The rest of the members of this structure are used to describe various characteristics of a particular rebar band. Not all of the members are necessarily used. The *fMask* member defines which members are valid for a given instance of the structure. *fMask* can be one or more of the following values (the RBBIM prefix stands for "rebar band info mask"):

RBBIM_BACKGROUND. Indicates that the *hbmBack* member is valid.

RBBIM_CHILD. The *hwndChild* member is valid.

RBBIM_CHILDSIZE. The *cxMinChild* and *cyMinChild* members are valid.

RBBIM_COLORS. The *clrFore* and *clrBack* members are valid.

RBBIM_IDEALSIZE. The *cxIdeal* member is valid.

RBBIM_ID. The *wID* member is valid.

RBBIM_IMAGE. The *iImage* member is valid.

RBBIM_LPARAM. The *lParam* member is valid.

RBBIM_SIZE. The *cx* member is valid.

RBBIM_STYLE. The *fStyle* member is valid.

RBBIM_TEXT. The *lpText* member is valid.

The *fStyle* member is used to specify various styles for the band in question. Just as the parent rebar control has a set of styles associated with it, each band in a rebar control can have its own style attributes. The *fStyle* member can be one or more of the following (the RBBS prefix stands for "rebar band style"):

RBBS_BREAK. Indicates that the band is on a new line, i.e., in a new row.

RBBS_CHILDEDGE. The band has an edge at the top and bottom.

RBBS_FIXEDBMP. If the band has a background bitmap, the bitmap does not move when the band is resized.

RBBS_FIXEDSIZE. The band cannot be moved/sized, and no gripper bar is displayed.

RBBS_GRIPPERALWAYS. The band always displays a gripper bar, even if the RBBS_FIXEDSIZE style is set.

RBBS_HIDDEN. Makes the band invisible.

RBBS_NOVERT. The band will not be displayed if the parent rebar control uses the CCS_VERT style.

RBBS_VARIABLEHEIGHT. The band can be resized by the rebar control. The *cyIntegral* and *cyMaxChild* members of the corresponding REBARBANDINFO structure control the resizing.

The *clrFore* and *clrBack* members specify the band's foreground and background colors, respectively. These colors are ignored if the *hbmBack* member is valid.

lpText contains the text label used with the band. *cch* specifies the size of *lpText* in bytes.

iImage is the zero-based index of the image to display with the band. The rebar control must be using an image list in this case.

The *hwndChild* member specifies the HWND of the child control contained by the band. *cxMinChild* and *cyMinChild* specify the minimum width and height of the control. The band cannot be smaller than these values. Similarly, *cyMaxChild* specifies the maximum child control height, and hence the maximum band height. This value is ignored if the band does not have the RBBS_VARIABLEHEIGHT style. *cx* specifies the width of the band. *cyChild* specifies the initial height of the band. It is also ignored if RBBS_VARIABLEHEIGHT is not set.

The *hbmBack* member specifies a bitmap to use as the band background.

wID is used to identify the band in Custom Draw notifications.

The *cyIntegral* member defines the smallest number of pixels that the band grows or shrinks when resized. This member is ignored if the band does not have the RBBS_VARIABLEHEIGHT style.

cxIdeal specifies the ideal band width. If the band is maximized to its ideal width via the RB_MAXIMIZEBAND message, the rebar control tries to make the band this size.

Finally, *lParam* is a 32-bit value which the application can use to store any other application-defined information with the corresponding rebar control band.

Inserting Bands into Rebar Controls

Now that we understand how Windows CE represents bands, adding bands to a rebar control is straightforward.

Bands are inserted by sending the message RB_INSERTBAND to the rebar control. The *wParam* of this message is a UINT specifying the zero-based index of the band. The *lParam* is a pointer to a REBAR-

BANDINFO structure which contains all the characteristics of the band to be inserted.

For example, to create the band containing the Exit button shown in Figure 5.4, the application includes the following code. *hwndRebar* is the HWND of the rebar control created previously:

```
HWND hwndExit;
REBARBANDINFO rbbi;
hwndExit = CreateWindow(TEXT("BUTTON"),
  TEXT("Exit"),...);
memset(&rbbi, 0, sizeof(rbbi));
rbbi.cbSize = sizeof(rbbi);
rbbi.fMask = (RBBIM_CHILD|RBBIM_CHILDSIZE|
  RBBIM_STYLE|RBBIM_SIZE);
rbbi.fStyle = (RBBS_GRIPPERALWAYS);
rbbi.hwndChild = hwndExit;
rbbi.cxMinChild = 30; //Band, button min width
rbbi.cyMinChild = 65; //Band, button min height
rbbi.cx = 100;     //Band width
SendMessage(hwndRebar, RB_INSERTBAND,0, (LPARAM)&rbbi);
```

The *fMask* member of *rbbi* indicates that the band will have a child control (RBBIM_CHILD) and that the *cxMinChild* and *cyMinChild* members of *rbbi* are valid (RBBIM_CHILDSIZE.) *rbbi.fStyle* is also valid, as indicated by the RBBIM_STYLE mask bit. RBBIM_SIZE indicates that the *cx* member of *rbbi* is used to specify the width of the band.

The *fStyle* member of *rbbi* specifies that the band to be inserted will always display a gripper bar.

The band will contain the "Exit" button because *rbbi.hwndChild* is set to the HWND of that button. The code goes on to specify that this button (and therefore the band) cannot be smaller than 30 pixels high and 65 pixels wide, and that the band will be 100 pixels wide.

That's all there is to it. With this brief introduction, and a quick look at the sample application to familiarize yourself with rebar control messages and notifications, you are well on your way to enhancing your Windows CE applications with rebar controls.

Command Bands

A command band control is a fancy rebar control that can contain OK, Close, and Help buttons, called *adornments*, which rebar controls alone do not support (Figure 5.5). Like command bars, command bands can

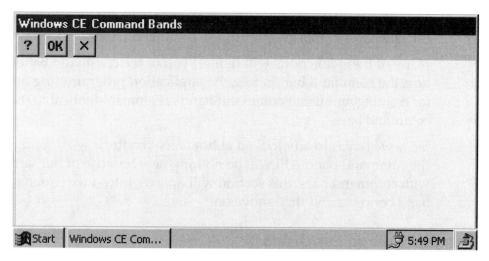

Figure 5.5   Command band with adornments.

contain child controls (Figure 5.6). In addition, each band in a command band control contains a command bar control by default. This means that a programmer can use command bands to construct windows containing multiple menus (Figure 5.6). In the Windows CE control hierarchy, we can think of command band controls as a superset of command bar controls.

All of the operations you might want to perform with command band controls have been wrapped into command band API functions.

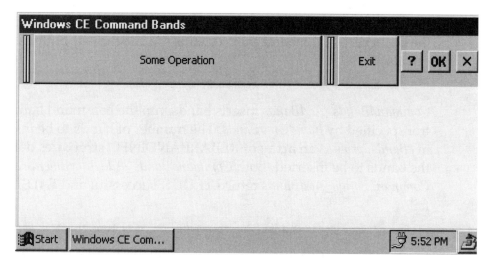

Figure 5.6   Command band with adornments and child control bands.

Instead of sending messages to the control explicitly, your application calls these functions in order to use command bands.

Many of these functions will remind you of the command band's sibling, the command bar. In fact, the application programming interface for creating and using command bands is almost identical to that for command bars.

Since we have already looked at how rebar controls work, and using the command band API will be nothing new because of our familiarity with command bars, this section will quickly introduce command band concepts and then move on.

Command Band Functions

The command band API is very similar to the command bar API in both form and usage. For example, usage of *CommandBands_ AddAdornments* is the same as *CommandBar_AddAdornments*.

In all of the functions that follow, the *hinst* parameter (if present) is the application HINSTANCE.

```
CommandBands_AddAdornments(hwndCmdBands,hinst,dwFlags,prbbi);
```

CommandBands_AddAdornments inserts the Close button into the command band control specified by the *hwndCmdBands* parameter. Additionally, a Help or OK button (or both) can be inserted by specifying the appropriate values in *dwFlags*: CMDBAR_HELP adds the Help button, and CMDBAR_OK adds the OK button. *prbbi* points to a REBARBANDINFO structure. This structure can be used to customize the properties of the band that contains the adornment buttons. *prbbi* can also be NULL.

```
CommandBands_AddBands(hwndCmdBands, hinst, cBands, prbbi);
```

CommandBands_AddBands inserts bands into the command band control specified by *hwndCmdBands*. The number of bands to be inserted is in *cBands*. *prbbi* is an array of REBARBANDINFO structures defining the bands to be inserted. Both *CommandBands_AddAdornments* and *CommandBands_AddBands* return TRUE if successful and FALSE if they fail.

```
CommandBands_Create(hinst, hwndParent, wID, dwStyles, himl);
```

CommandBands_Create creates a new command band control. *hwndParent* is the parent of the control. *wID* is the command band control identifier. *dwStyles* contains the command band control styles. Command bands use the same style specifiers as rebar controls. *himl* is the handle of an image list containing the images to be used with the bands. This parameter can be NULL.

If successful, *CommandBands_Create* returns the HWND of the newly created command band control. Otherwise it returns NULL.

```
CommandBands_GetCommandBar(hwndCmdBands, uBand);
```

CommandBands_GetCommandBar is the poorly named function that retrieves the HWND of the band specified by the zero-based index *uBand*. If unsuccessful, this function returns NULL.

```
CommandBands_Height(hwndCmdBands);
```

CommandBands_Height returns the height in pixels of the specified command band control.

```
CommandBands_IsVisible(hwndCmdBands);
```

CommandBands_IsVisible determines whether the specified control is visible. The function returns TRUE if the control is visible and FALSE if not.

```
CommandBands_GetRestoreInformation(hwndCmdBands, uBand, pcbr);
```

CommandBands_GetRestoreInformation gets a COMMANDBANDSRE-STOREINFO structure for the band specified by *uBand*. This structure, returned in the *pcbr* parameter, contains size, maximized/minimized state information, and the like for the band. This information is usually obtained by an application before it closes. This information can then be held in persistent storage so that the next time the application starts, command bands can be restored to their previous states. The function returns TRUE if successful and FALSE if it fails.

```
CommandBands_Show(hwndCmdBands, fShow);
```

CommandBands_Show is used to show or hide the specified command band control. *fShow* is TRUE to make the control visible, FALSE to hide it. The previous state of the control is returned.

Concluding Remarks

The discussion of command band controls concludes our introduction of Windows CE application building blocks. At this point, you have enough background to build the framework for a huge number of useful Windows CE programs.

Part II of this book shows you how to take advantage of the various persistent storage options available in Windows CE. We will look at the Windows CE file system and registry, as well as how to use Windows CE database technology. These components give you a wide variety of options for storing, retrieving, and organizing the information used by your Windows CE applications.

Windows CE Persistent Storage

Memory in Windows CE devices consists of some amount of read-only memory, or ROM, and some amount of random access memory, also known by its acronym RAM. ROM is where the Windows CE operating system and applications that ship with Windows CE devices are stored.

RAM on a Windows CE device is divided into two sections. The first section is used as *program memory*. This memory is used, for example, by heaps and stacks. For example, whenever your Windows CE applications call *LocalAlloc* to reserve memory on the application's default heap, the memory that is reserved is in program memory. The applications that you write and download to devices also reside in program memory.

The other section of Windows CE RAM is devoted to the *object store*. The object store is used for persistent storage. Persistent storage in Windows CE consists of files and directories, databases and database records, and the Windows CE registry. All of these types of storage objects are called persistent because powering off the Windows CE device on which they are stored does not cause the data they contain to be lost.

In the following chapters, we will discuss Windows CE persistent storage in detail. Each chapter is dedicated to one of the persistent storage classes, such as databases or the registry, and to programming techniques and the various APIs for using them in your applications. But before exploring each of these specific items in detail, we must first discuss the general features of the Windows CE object store.

Object Identifiers

Any object that resides in the Windows CE object store is assigned a unique *object identifier* by the operating system. This identifier is used, for example, to specify a database to be opened or a database record to delete. This object identifier is of type CEOID, one of the basic Windows CE data types.

Given the unique identifier of any object in the object store, an application can extract all of the other information about the object. For instance, given the object identifier of a particular file, the application can determine such information as the name of the file or the directory that contains the file. From a database identifier, an application can determine the number of records stored in the database or the total number of bytes of object store memory used by the database.

The *CeOidGetInfo* Function

Information about a particular object in the object store is retrieved using the function *CeOidGetInfo*. Because it can be used to get information about so many types of objects, this function is of paramount importance when working with the Windows CE object store.

It is important to keep in mind that this function does not retrieve the *contents* of an object store object. For example, it cannot be used to directly read the data contained in a particular Windows CE database record. A useful analogy is to think of the information obtained by *CeOidGetInfo* as similar to the kind of information you get from the Windows NT Explorer on a desktop PC. *CeOidGetInfo* can give you information about an object's relationship to other objects in the object store, as well as information such as file length, database size, or object names. Other Windows CE API functions must be used to access or modify the data represented by an object identifier.

The syntax of *CeOidGetInfo* is:

```
CeOidGetInfo(oid, poidInfo);
```

oid is the object identifier of the object of interest. *poidInfo* is a pointer to a CEOIDINFO structure through which the function returns all the information about the object identified by *oid*. The CEOIDINFO structure is defined as:

```
typedef struct _CEOIDINFO
{
  WORD wObjType;
  WORD wPad;
  union {
   CEFILEINFO infFile;
   CEDIRINFO infDirectory;
   CEDBASEINFO infDatabase;
   CERECORDINFO infRecord;
  };      //End of union
} CEOIDINFO;
```

wObjType identifies the type of object represented by the object identifier passed to *CeOidGetInfo*. *wObjType* can be one of the following values:

OBJTYPE_INVALID	Specified object identifier not found in the object store
OBJTYPE_FILE	Object specified by object identifier is a file
OBJTYPE_DIRECTORY	Object specified by object identifier is a directory
OBJTYPE_DATABASE	Object specified by object identifier is a database
OBJTYPE_RECORD	Object specified by object identifier is a database record

The *wPad* member is a WORD that is in the structure only to align the structure on a double-word boundary. It therefore contains no information about the object queried with *CeOidGetInfo*.

The last member of the CEOIDINFO structure is a union containing an object information structure with the attributes of the object being queried. Which member of this union is valid depends on the value of *wObjType*. For example, if the object queried is a database (as indicated by a *wObjType* value of OBJTYPE_DATABASE), the member you would use is *infDatabase*.

In all there are four such object information structures: CEFILEINFO, CEDIRINFO, CERECORDINFO, and CEDBASEINFO. In the next three chapters the use of these structures will be covered in greater detail. The definition of each is given in the following sections.

The CEFILEINFO Structure

CEFILEINFO structures are used to describe files in the object store:

```
typedef struct _CEFILEINFO
{
  DWORD dwAttributes;
  CEOID oidParent;
  WCHAR szFileName[MAX_PATH];
```

```
    FILETIME ftLastChanged;
    DWORD dwLength;
} CEFILEINFO;
```

dwAttributes contains the attributes of the file. *oidParent* is the object identifier of the file's parent directory. If NULL, the file is at the top level of the file system. *oidParent* can be passed to a subsequent call of *CeOidGetInfo* to get information about a file's parent directory. *szFile-Name* is a null-terminated Unicode string containing the full path and file name of the file. *ftLastChanged* indicates when the file was last modified, and *dwLength* gives the length of the file in bytes.

The CEDIRINFO Structure

Directories are described with CEDIRINFO:

```
typedef struct _CEDIRINFO
{
  DWORD dwAttributes;
  CEOID oidParent;
  WCHAR szDirName[MAX_PATH];
} CEDIRINFO;
```

dwAttributes contains the attributes of the directory. *oidParent* is the object identifier of this directory's parent. If NULL, the directory is in the root directory of the file system. *szDirName* contains the full path name of the directory.

The CERECORDINFO and CEDBASEINFO Structures

The CERECORDINFO structure contains information about a particular Windows CE database record:

```
typedef struct _CERECORDINFO
{
  CEOID oidParent;
} CERECORDINFO;
```

This structure contains only one member, *oidParent*. *oidParent* contains the object identifier of the Windows CE database to which this record belongs.

A CEDBASEINFO structure contains details of a Windows CE database object. This structure will be defined and discussed in detail in the Chapter 7.

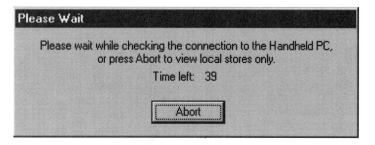

Figure II.1   Connecting to the Remove Object Viewer.

Viewing the Windows CE Object Store

The Windows CE Toolkit provides a tool for visually examining the object store on either a Windows CE device or the Windows CE emulator. To invoke it, select the Remote Object Viewer options from the Tools menu in Microsoft Developer Studio. The dialog box shown in Figure II.1 will appear.

If you have a Window CE device connected to your PC, the Remote Object Viewer will connect to it and display the object store on the device. Otherwise, to view the emulator's object store, press the abort button.

The Remote Object Viewer works much like the Windows NT Explorer. It contains a tree view user interface that allows you to browse the hierarchy of files on the drives attached to the Windows NT machine on which you are running the Remote Object Viewer.

For example, in Figure II.2 you can see a root item in the tree labeled C:Drive. Expanding this node would display all of the directories on my C: drive.

More interesting, however, is that the Remote Object Viewer allows you to browse both the Windows CE file system and all of the databases contained in the object store. This tool is very useful for quickly creating folders, moving and deleting files, or viewing database records.

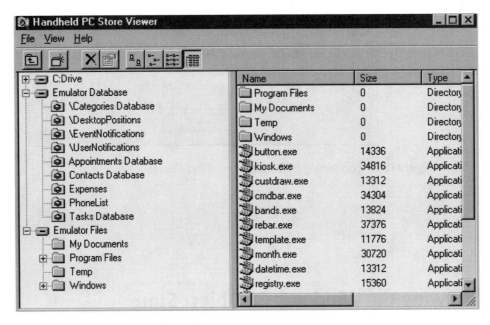

Figure II.2 The Remote Object Viewer.

In Figure II.2, the Emulator Database tree view item contains all of the databases currently stored by the Windows CE emulation object store. Similarly, the Emulator Files item contains the hierarchy of directories and files in the emulation file system. If the host Windows NT PC were connected to a Windows CE device such as a handheld PC or a palm-size PC, the Remote Object Viewer would instead show the databases and file system on that device.

Using the Remote Object Viewer is very much like using the Windows NT Explorer. You can view the contents of directories by expanding the corresponding folder icon. Menu options allow you to rename and delete files or folders. You can also create new folders. You can change the way the contents are displayed with the various View menu options.

The Remote Object Viewer also allows you to transfer files between your desktop computer and the Windows CE emulation environment. If your computer is connected to an actual Windows CE device, you

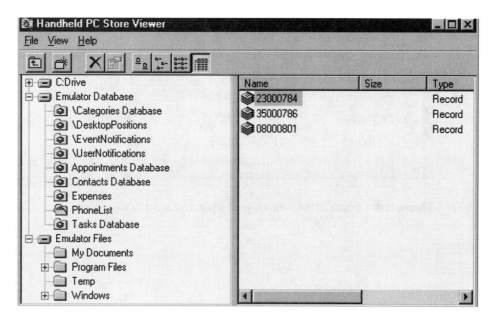

Figure II.3 Browsing the contents of the phone list database with the Remote Object Viewer.

can also transfer files between the computer and the device. As with the Windows NT Explorer, simply drag the icon representing the file to be transferred to the folder where you wish the file to reside.

For databases, the Remote Object Viewer allows you to look at all of the records in a particular database. For example, Figure II.3 shows the contents of the phone list database associated with an application we will see in Chapter 7. Each item in the right-hand pane of the Remote Object Viewer is a database record labeled with its unique CEOID object identifier.

If you select an individual database record in the right-hand pane and then select the Properties option from the File menu, the window in Figure II.4 is displayed. This window details the contents of the selected database record. It displays the record property data types and values. The subjects of Windows CE database records, record properties, and the like are covered in detail in Chapter 7.

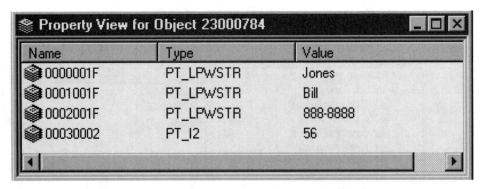

Figure II.4 A look at the properties of a phone list database record.

CHAPTER 6

Working with the Windows CE File System

T he concepts of files and directories under Windows CE are the same as on other Windows platforms. A *file* is defined as a named collection of information. Files can contain data, as do the document files created by a word processor or notepad application. Files can also be executable programs or dynamic link libraries. The essential point is that the file is the most basic unit of storage that allows Windows CE to distinguish one set of data or information from another. A *directory* is a named group of files or other directories.

Files and directories on a traditional Windows NT or Windows 98 desktop computer have always been closely linked to the presence of permanent storage in the form of floppy disks or hard disks. Computer users are used to using utilities such as Windows Explorer to browse the contents of a physical disk on their own PC or on a PC to which they have access via a computer network.

Devices running under Windows CE do not use floppy or hard disks as storage media. Under Windows CE, files and directories are one of the object types supported by the object store. Files and directories are therefore stored persistently in device RAM, along with databases and database records and the Windows CE registry.

Despite this difference, working with files under Windows CE is very much like working with files under Windows NT or Windows 98 on a desktop PC. Although some file system features are not supported, the file system application programming interface and its semantics are much the same. Hence your understanding of working with the file system API on Windows NT or Windows 98 will go a long way in helping you learn how to work with the Windows CE file system.

AFTER COMPLETING THIS CHAPTER YOU WILL KNOW HOW TO . . .

Create and delete files and directories

Open and close files and directories

Read and write files

Copy files and directories

Rename files and directories

Search for files and directories

Access persistent storage on flash cards

The File System Explorer Application

The file system programming concepts covered in this chapter will be illustrated with the example of a simple File System Explorer application. The application files are found in the \Samples\filesys directory of the companion CD. The application that is generated by the project is called FILESYS.EXE.

You can certainly already use the Remote Object Viewer to browse the file system on your Windows CE device or on the Windows CE emulator. But developing an explorer application from scratch is a good way to learn how to use the file system API.

The application interface is a tree view control that displays the contents of the Windows CE file system hierarchically as shown in Figure 6.1. The folder at the top of the tree view display represents the *root directory* of the file system. All other directories and files reside somewhere under the root directory.

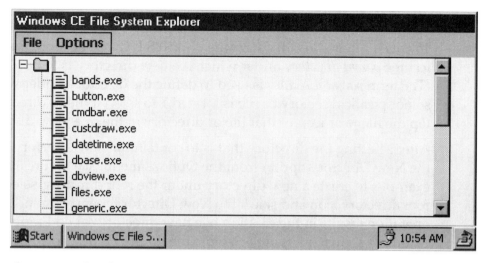

Figure 6.1   The File System Explorer application.

The FILESYS.EXE application allows users to create, delete, and rename files and directories. It also provides very primitive file editing. File properties such as file attributes and file size can also be determined using the application.

Most of these features are accessed through the Options menu shown in Figure 6.2.

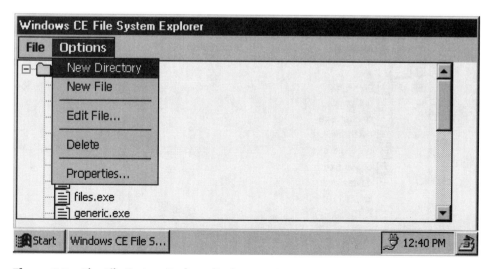

Figure 6.2   The File System Explorer Options menu.

Creating and Deleting Files and Directories

To create a new directory with the FILESYS.EXE application, first select the *parent directory* under which the new directory is to be located. (The term *parent directory* is used to define the directory under which some specific directory or file is located.) To select a file or directory, tap the name or icon of that file or directory in the tree view display.

After selecting the directory that is to contain the new directory, select the New Directory option from the Options menu (see Figure 6.2). For example, to create a new directory under the root directory, select the root directory icon and select the New Directory menu option. This operation results in the creation of a new directory called Empty Folder, as shown in Figure 6.3. Note the Empty Folder icon.

New files are created in much the same way. To create a file under a particular directory, select the directory and then choose the New File option under the Options menu. A file called Empty File will appear. Deleting files and directories is straightforward. Simply select the file or directory you wish to delete, and then select the Delete option from the Options menu.

Renaming Files and Directories

Another common file system operation is renaming files or directories. The names Empty Folder and Empty File are not very useful for real-

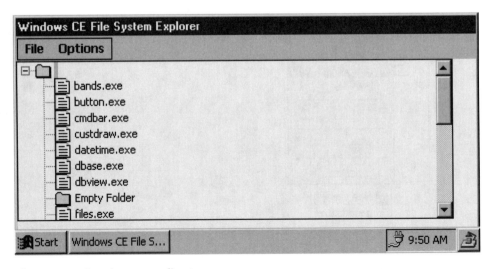

Figure 6.3 Creating a new directory.

world directories and files. To rename a file or directory in the File System Explorer application, double-tap on the file or directory to be renamed. A small text entry field appears containing the name of the selected file or directory. You can then type the new file or directory name in this field. Press the Enter key to make the name change take effect. If the application is running on a Windows CE device that does not have a keyboard, simply tap a different part of the screen and your change will take effect.

As an example, let's say that you want to change the name of the Empty Folder directory in Figure 6.3 to Acme Corp. Simply double-tap on the name Empty Folder, and type Acme Corp in the edit field. The File System Explorer display should then look as shown in Figure 6.4.

Files are renamed the same way. Double-tap the file you wish to rename and type the new name in the edit field that appears.

For example, let's create a file called Expenses under the Acme Corp directory. Tap the Acme Corp directory to select it, and then choose New File from the Options menu. A new file, called Empty File, appears under the Acme Corp directory as shown in Figure 6.5.

Rename this file by tapping it twice and then typing the name Expenses into the edit field that appears. The contents of the Acme Corp directory will then appear as shown in Figure 6.6.

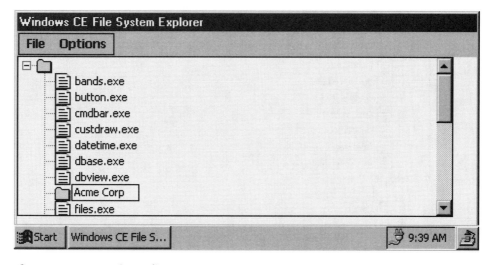

Figure 6.4 Renaming a directory.

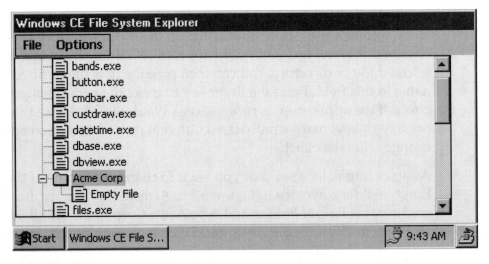

Figure 6.5 Creating a new file.

Editing Files

Another important set of file system functions we will cover in this chapter lets your applications write data to and read data from files. To demonstrate these features, the File System Explorer application provides very rudimentary file editing capabilities. You will not be tempted to delete your current word processing software from your Handheld PC when you see this feature. However, after finishing this

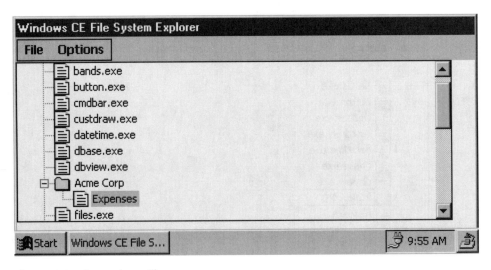

Figure 6.6 Renaming a file.

chapter you will know how to use the file system API to read and write files.

To edit a file in the FILESYS.EXE application, select the file you wish to edit by tapping it once. Then press the Enter key on your keyboard. (For devices that do not include a keyboard, you can use the Edit File menu option in the Options menu to invoke this feature.) The dialog box shown in Figure 6.7 appears.

Text entered in the edit field of this dialog is written to the file if the user presses the Save button. Pressing Cancel aborts file editing.

Examining File Properties

The final notable feature of the File System Explorer application is invoked by the Properties option of the Option menu. Choosing this menu option retrieves and displays various features of the currently selected file. The dialog box shown in Figure 6.8 appears, showing which file attributes are set for the selected file, as well as the size of the file in bytes.

File Handles

The Windows CE file system API functions access files and directories by means of a *file handle*. Like any other Windows CE handle type,

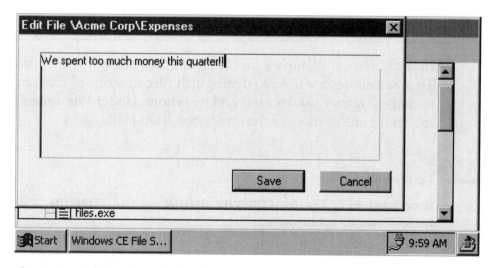

Figure 6.7 Editing a file with the file system explorer.

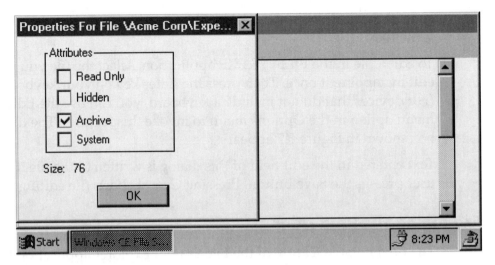

Figure 6.8 Displaying the properties of a file.

such as a window handle, a file handle is an identifier for referencing an object managed by the Windows CE kernel. In this case the object is a file or directory.

As we will see, the function used for opening and creating files returns a handle to the specified file. Functions for reading and writing files require a file handle in order to access the right file. In short, any operation that a Windows CE application may perform on a file or directory requires a valid file handle.

File Attributes

Every file in the Windows CE file system has one or more *attributes*. These attributes are used to distinguish files in terms of characteristics such as how they can be used and by whom. Under Windows CE, files may have one or more of the attributes listed in Table 6.1.

NOTE
FILE ATTRIBUTES

Under Windows CE, the FILE_ATTRIBUTE_OFFLINE and FILE_ATTRIBUTE_TEMPORARY file attributes are not supported.

An application typically sets the attributes of a file when the file is created. However, it may be necessary to change or determine the attrib-

Table 6.1 Windows CE File Attributes

ATTRIBUTE	MEANING
FILE_ATTRIBUTE_ARCHIVE	Used by applications to mark a file that has not been backed up.
FILE_ATTRIBUTE_COMPRESSED	File or directory is compressed. For files, this means that all of the data in the file is compressed. For directories, this means that by default all files or subdirectories created in this directory are created with the compressed attribute.
FILE_ATTRIBUTE_HIDDEN	The file is marked as hidden.
FILE_ATTRIBUTE_NORMAL	This attribute cannot be used with any other attribute. Hence, if set, it means that no other attribute is set.
FILE_ATTRIBUTE_READONLY	Applications can only read this file. They cannot write to or delete it.
FILE_ATTRIBUTE_DIRECTORY	Indicates that the particular file is a directory. Note: This attribute cannot be set. It can be returned by GetFileAttributes.
FILE_ATTRIBUTE_SYSTEM	Indicates the file is a system file, i.e., it is intended to be used only by the operating system.
FILE_ATTRIBUTE_INROM	Indicates the file is a read-only operating system file stored in ROM.
FILE_ATTRIBUTE_ROMMODULE	Indicates the file is an in-ROM DLL or EXE.

utes of a file after it has been created. Applications might even need to determine the attributes of files they did not create.

The Windows CE file system API provides two functions to read and modify the attributes of a file, *GetFileAttributes* and *SetFileAttributes*. The first of these functions has the following form:

```
GetFileAttributes(lpFileName);
```

This function takes the Unicode string name of the file of interest in the parameter *lpFileName*. If successful, it returns a DWORD containing the file attributes that are set for the file. The return value is the bitwise OR of one or more of the file attribute values specified in Table 6.1. In addition, Windows CE provides for two additional return values for this function, FILE_ATTRIBUTE_INROM and FILE_ATTRIBUTE_ROMMODULE. The first of these indicates that the file in question is a read-only operating system file stored in ROM. The second indicates that the file is a DLL or executable (.EXE) file stored in ROM and intended to execute in place. This means that files with the FILE_ATTRIBUTE_ROMMODULE attribute do not need to be copied into RAM in order to run. Files of this type are typically libraries and applications that ship with the Windows CE operating system.

The attributes of a file can be set using the *SetFileAttributes* function:

```
SetFileAttributes(lpFileName, dwFileAttributes);
```

This function returns TRUE if the attributes are successfully set, and FALSE if the function is unsuccessful.

As an example, let's assume that we want to mark as hidden all files that are read-only. The piece of code responsible for testing if a file is read-only and then setting the hidden file attribute would look something like this:

```
//File name is in lpFileName
DWORD dwAttributes;
dwAttributes = GetFileAttributes(lpFileName);
if (dwAttributes & FILE_ATTRIBUTE_READONLY)
{
  dwAttributes |= FILE_ATTRIBUTE_HIDDEN;
  SetFileAttributes(lpFileName, dwAttributes);
}
```

Note that as in Windows NT and Windows 98, *SetFileAttributes* cannot be used to set the FILE_ATTRIBUTE_COMPRESSED attribute of a file. If this attribute is not set when the file is created, you must use the *DeviceIoControl* function to set it.

Searching for Files

It may seem a little strange to discuss searching for files in the Windows CE file system this early in the chapter. Certainly, operations such as creating and deleting files must be more fundamental than file searching!

While this may be true in some sense, it is also the case that many file operations are iterative. For example, deleting a directory requires recursively deleting all files and subdirectories contained by the directory to be deleted. Such an iterative process entails file searching operations to look for files to delete.

As another example, consider how an application might determine if a particular directory is empty. There is no Windows CE API function *IsDirectoryEmpty*. Writing such an operation from scratch involves searching the directory in question to see if it contains any files.

In fact, file searching is so fundamental to many file system operations that understanding how these features are implemented requires that we first understand file searching under Windows CE.

Windows CE provides three functions for such operations: *FindFirstFile*, *FindNextFile,* and *FindClose.*

The first two of these functions return a data structure containing information about the files that they retrieve. Before discussing the find functions in detail, let's first look at this structure.

NOTE FINDFIRSTFILEEX

The function *FindFirstFileEx* is not supported under Windows CE.

The WIN32_FIND_DATA Structure

The WIN32_FIND_DATA structure is used by Windows CE to provide information about a file located by one of the find functions.

```
typedef struct _WIN32_FIND_DATA
{
  DWORD dwFileAttributes;
  FILETIME ftCreationTime;
  FILETIME ftLastAccessTime;
  FILETIME ftLastWriteTime;
  DWORD nFileSizeHigh;
  DWORD nFileSizeLow;
  DWORD dwOID;
  TCHAR cFileName[ MAX_PATH ];
} WIN32_FIND_DATA;
```

The members of this structure provide all descriptive information about the file, either directly, or by providing a means for extracting more information (such as through the *dwOID* member).

dwFileAttributes contains the attributes of the file as described previously in Table 6.1. *ftCreationTime*, *ftLastAccessTime*, and *ftLastWriteTime* represent the times the file was created, last accessed, and last written to, respectively. *nFileSizeHigh* and *nFileSizeLow* are the high-order and low-order words of the total size of the file. The *dwOID* member contains the object identifier of the file. This means that whenever an application can get WIN32_FIND_DATA about a file, it can also get any of the CEFILEINFO data about the file with a simple call to *CeOidGetInfo*. Finally, *cFileName* is a null-terminated string containing the name of the file.

We will primarily be interested in how to use the *FindFirstFile* and *FindNextFile* functions to get WIN32_FIND_DATA information. It should be noted that Windows CE provides some additional functions for quickly accessing some of the data provided by this structure. In particular, *GetFileTime* retrieves the same information as provided by the FILETIME members of the WIN32_FIND_DATA structure. *GetFileSize* returns the size of a specified file.

In addition, there is a *SetFileTime* function to allow applications to modify the creation time, last access time, and last write time of a file.

Because of its similarity to the WIN32_FIND_DATA structure, I somewhat parenthetically mention the BY_HANDLE_FILE_INFORMATION structure. This is another data structure that contains much the same information about a file as WIN32_FIND_DATA. Given a handle to an open file, an application can get a BY_HANDLE_FILE_INFORMATION structure by calling *GetFileInformationByHandle*.

The *FindFirstFile* and *FindNextFile* Functions

The *FindFirstFile* function is used to locate a specific file or directory. It can also be used to find the first file in a specified directory.

```
FindFirstFile(lpFileName, lpFindFileData);
```

The *lpFileName* parameter contains a path and file name, or a directory name. *lpFindFileData* is used as a return value by the function. It is a pointer to a WIN32_FIND_DATA structure containing information about the located file.

If successful, *FindFirstFile* returns a *search handle*. This handle references an internal structure that is responsible for keeping track of the progress of a file search. We will see the utility of this search handle a bit later when we discuss the *FindNextFile* function. If *FindFirstFile* fails, it returns INVALID_HANDLE_VALUE.

The *lpFileName* parameter accepts wildcards. This is how you can tell *FindFirstFile* to differentiate between finding the first file in a specified directory and finding the directory itself.

For example, this line of code will try and find a directory called \MyFiles:

```
HANDLE hFile;
WIN32_FIND_DATA fd;
memset(&fd, 0, sizeof(fd));
hFile = FindFirstFile(TEXT("\\MyFiles"), &fd);
```

On the other hand, one subtle change to the *FindFirstFile* call will find the first file in the \MyFiles directory:

```
hFile = FindFirstFile(TEXT("\\MyFiles\\*"), &fd);
```

FindNextFile is used to continue a search started by *FindFirstFile*. For example, if *FindFirstFile* finds the first file in a specified directory, *FindNextFile* will attempt to find the next file in that directory. Each successive call to *FindNextFile* uses the search handle that is updated with each find operation to keep track of the search progress. The syntax of *FindNextFile* is:

```
FindNextFile(hFindFile, lpFindFileData);
```

The first parameter is the search handle returned by a previous call to *FindFirstFile*. The second parameter is the WIN32_FIND_DATA return value, just as in *FindFirstFile*.

FindNextFile returns TRUE if successful and FALSE if it fails. As with all of the file system functions, a call to *GetLastError* can be used to get additional information about why the function call failed if the return value is FALSE.

Creating and Opening Files and Directories

As under Windows NT, creating files and directories under Windows CE is done using the *CreateFile* and *CreateDirectory* functions. Under Windows CE, files are also opened using the *CreateFile* function, as we will soon see.

Creating and Opening Files

To create a file, your application calls the *CreateFile* function:

```
CreateFile(lpFileName,dwDesiredAccess,dwShareMode,
    lpSecurityAttributes, dwCreationDistribution,
    dwFlagsAndAttributes, hTemplateFile);
```

lpFileName is the null-terminated Unicode string file name of the file to be created. Long file names are supported.

dwDesiredAccess is used to indicate the access, or read-write mode, of the file. It can be any combination of the following values:

0. Specifies device query access. This allows an application to query device attributes.

GENERIC_READ. Specifies that the file is created/opened with read access.

GENERIC_WRITE. Specifies that the file is created/opened with write access.

For example, to open a file called "myfile.txt" with read-write access, an application would do the following:

```
CreateFile(TEXT("myfile.txt"),
    (GENERIC_READ|GENERIC_WRITE),...);
```

The third parameter to *CreateFile, dwShareMode,* is used to specify if and how the file can be shared. It can be a combination of one or more of the following values:

0. Indicates that the file cannot be shared

FILE_SHARED_READ. Subsequent open operations on the file will only succeed if read access is requested (via the *dwDesiredAccess* parameter).

FILE_SHARED_WRITE. Subsequent open operations on the file will only succeed if write access is requested.

Under Windows CE, file security attributes are ignored. The *lpSecurity-Attributes* parameter should therefore be set to NULL.

The *dwCreationDistribution* parameter controls how the *CreateFile* function behaves when attempting to create existing files, as well as what to do when the function tries to open a nonexistent file. This parameter can be one of the following:

CREATE_NEW. The function creates a new file. If the specified file already exists, the *CreateFile* function fails.

CREATE_ALWAYS. The function creates a new file. If the specified file already exists, it is overwritten by the *CreateFile* operation.

OPEN_EXISTING. The function opens an existing file. If the specified file does not exist, *CreateFile* fails.

OPEN_ALWAYS. The function opens an existing file. If the specified file does not already exist, it is created.

TRUNCATE_EXISTING. The function opens the file, but truncates it to zero length. The file must be opened with GENERIC_WRITE access. *CreateFile* fails if the specified file does not exist.

By taking a look at the allowed *dwCreationDistribution* values, we can see how *CreateFile* can be used to both create new files and open existing files. For example, it is common to want to open a file or have the operating system create a file of that name if it does not exist, as follows:

```
CreateFile(TEXT("myfile.txt"),
GENERIC_READ|GENERIC_WRITE, 0,
   NULL, OPEN_ALWAYS,...);
```

dwFlagsAndAttributes determines the file attributes and several operating modes. We have already discussed file attributes. The flags portion can be any combination of the following values:

FILE_FLAG_WRITE_THROUGH. Instructs Windows CE to write directly to the object store when writing to the specified file, as opposed to writing through any intermediate cache.

FILE_FLAG_RANDOM_ACCESS. The file supports random access.

Most of the flags that are supported under Windows NT are not supported under Windows CE. Also note that the SECURITY_SQOS_PRESENT flag, or any of the other values that can be used with it under Windows NT, are not supported under Windows CE.

Finally, the *hTemplateFile* parameter is ignored under Windows CE and should be set to NULL.

If *CreateFile* is successful, a handle to the open file is returned. If it fails, the return value is INVALID_HANDLE_VALUE.

Open files are closed using the *CloseHandle* function:

```
CloseHandle(hObject);
```

where *hObject* is the handle of the file to close.

Creating Directories

Creating a directory is accomplished with the *CreateDirectory* function. The *CreateDirectoryEx* function available under Windows NT is not supported in Windows CE. The *CreateDirectory* function syntax is:

```
CreateDirectory(lpPathName, lpSecurityAttributes);
```

lpPathName is a null-terminated Unicode string specifying the path of the directory to be created. The maximum allowed length of this name is the operating system–defined value MAX_PATH. The second parameter to this function is ignored, as Windows CE does not support file security attributes. *lpSecurityAttributes* therefore should be set to NULL.

If *CreateDirectory* is successful, it returns TRUE. If unsuccessful, it returns FALSE. An application can get more detailed information about why the function failed by calling *GetLastError*.

An Example

As an example, let's take a look at how the File System Explorer application creates new files and directories. These features are triggered by the New Directory and New File menu options, so the first code to look at is the command handlers in the main window procedure for these two menu options (see Figure 6.2).

The pertinent sections of the window procedure are shown below. Note that *tviCurSel* contains the currently selected tree view item TV_ITEM structure. The *lParam* member of this structure always contains the CEOID object identifier of the file or directory corresponding to the currently selected tree view item.

```
LRESULT CALLBACK WndProc(
    HWND hwnd,
    UINT message,
    WPARAM wParam,
    LPARAM lParam)
{
    CEOID oid;
    CEOIDINFO oidInfo;
```

```
TCHAR *pszFileName, *pszDirectoryName;
switch (message)
{
case WM_COMMAND:
 UINT nID;
 nID = LOWORD(wParam);
 switch(nID)
 {
 case IDC_NEWDIRECTORY:
  //Create a new directory
  oid = (CEOID)tviCurSel.lParam;
  CeOidGetInfo(oid, &oidInfo);
  if (OBJTYPE_DIRECTORY==oidInfo.wObjType)
  {
   pszFileName = NULL;
   pszDirectoryName = TEXT("Empty Folder");
  }
  else
  {
   MessageBox(NULL, TEXT("Files cannot have children"),
    TEXT("New Folder Error"),MB_OK|MB_ICONEXCLAMATION);
   return (0);
  }
  OnNew(pszFileName, pszDirectoryName, tviCurSel.hItem,
   oidInfo, TRUE);
  break;
 case IDC_NEWFILE:
  /Create a new file
  oid = (CEOID)tviCurSel.lParam;
  CeOidGetInfo(oid, &oidInfo);
  if (OBJTYPE_DIRECTORY==oidInfo.wObjType)
  {
   pszDirectoryName = oidInfo.infDirectory.szDirName;
   pszFileName = TEXT("Empty File");
  }
  else
  {
   MessageBox(NULL, TEXT("Files cannot have children"),
    TEXT("New Folder Error"),MB_OK|MB_ICONEXCLAMATION);
   return (0);
  }
  OnNew(pszFileName, pszDirectoryName,
   tviCurSel.hItem, oidInfo, FALSE);
  break;
```

In both the case of creating a new file and creating a new directory, the application first extracts the CEOIDINFO for the currently selected file or directory. A request to create a new file or directory will force the application to try and create the file or directory with the currently selected item as its parent.

Obviously, this only makes sense if the currently selected object is a directory. Files cannot contain other files. Only directories can contain other files or directories. For this reason, both the IDC_NEWDIRECTORY and IDC_NEWFILE case statement code blocks check the *wObjType* member of the object information structure. In either of these cases, if the currently selected file system object is not a directory, a warning message is displayed and the operation is aborted.

If the user is trying to create a new file or directory under an existing directory, however, the appropriate default name is assigned to *pszFileName* or *pszDirectoryName,* and the application defined *OnNew* function is called. In the case of a request to create a new directory, the value "Empty Folder" is assigned to *pszDirectory.* In the case of a new file creation request, the name "Empty File" is assigned to *pszFileName.*

The *OnNew* function contains a lot of code for adding new items to the tree view control in response to new file and directory creations. This code is left out so that we can concentrate on the parts of the function that relate directly to the file system API. Also only the part of this function which creates new files is shown. Since the section that creates new directories is very similar, it was left out for the sake of brevity.

```
BOOL OnNew(TCHAR* pszFileName,
  TCHAR* pszDirectoryName,
  HTREEITEM hParent,
  CEOIDINFO oidInfo,
  BOOL bIsDirectory)
{
  TCHAR pszFullName[MAX_PATH];
  HANDLE hFile;
  wsprintf(pszFullName, TEXT("%s\\%s"),
    pszDirectoryName, pszFileName);
  hFile = FindFirstFile(pszFullName, &fd);
  if (INVALID_HANDLE_VALUE==hFile)
  {
    /File is new
    FindClose(hFile);
    hFile = CreateFile(pszFullName,
      GENERIC_READ|GENERIC_WRITE, 0, NULL,
        CREATE_NEW, FILE_ATTRIBUTE_ARCHIVE, NULL);
  }
  else
  {
    /File already exists
    MessageBox(NULL,
      TEXT("File \"Empty File\" Already Exists"),
```

```
        TEXT("Create New File Error"),
          MB_ICONEXCLAMATION|MB_OK);
     return (FALSE);
   }
   return (TRUE);
  }
```

The arguments *pszFileName* and *pszDirectoryName* are the name of the file to be created and the parent directory name, respectively. *hParent* is the tree view item corresponding to the parent directory in the user interface. *oidInfo* is the CEOIDINFO structure containing information about the parent directory. *bIsDirectory* indicates whether a new file or a new directory is to be created by the function.

To create a directory or file, *CreateFile* must be passed the complete path name of the directory or file to be created. *OnNew*, therefore, first constructs the full path name in the variable *pszFullName*. To do this, *OnNew* only needs to concatenate the directory name contained in *pszDirectoryName* with the file name in *pszFileName*. This is the purpose of the *wsprintf* call at the beginning of the function. A "\" character is inserted between the parent directory name and the file name.

After the complete new file path name has been constructed, *OnNew* checks to see if the specified file already exists. It does so by calling *FindFirstFile*:

```
    hFile = FindFirstFile(pszFullName, &fd);
```

pszFullName contains the full path name of the file to be created. If this file does not exist, *FindFirstFile* will return INVALID_HANDLE_VALUE. Otherwise it returns the handle of the existing file.

If the file does not exist (i.e., if *hFile* equals INVALID_HANDLE_VALUE,) *OnNew* closes the search handle *hFile* and creates the new file. If the file already exists, a message to this effect is displayed for the user and the function *OnNew* returns without creating a new file.

Reading and Writing File Data

File read and write operations are closely linked to the concept of the *file pointer*. A file pointer marks the current position in a given file. Read operations read data from the file's current position. Write operations write data to the file at the position indicated by the file pointer.

Files also have an *end of file* marker. This marker indicates the last byte of data in the file. As such, the end of file marker also determines the size of the file. As file write operations increase the size of a file, they move this end of file marker. Hence there is no such thing as writing past the end of a file: files grow to accommodate the data being written to them.

Files access can be either *sequential* or *random*. Sequential access means that data is read from the file in order. Random access means that data can be read from the file in any order as determined by the application reading the file. For random access to be possible, there must be a way for applications to manually set the file pointer without requiring read or write operations to occur. We will introduce such functions later in this chapter.

NOTE
ASYNCHRONOUS FILE ACCESS

Under Windows NT, file access operations can be synchronous or asynchronous. Windows CE however does *not* support asynchronous access.

The *ReadFile* Function

Data is read from a file using the *ReadFile* function:

```
ReadFile(hFile, lpBuffer, nNumberOfBytesToRead,
    lpNumberOfBytesRead, lpOverlapped);
```

hFile is the handle of the open file from which the data is to be read. *lpBuffer* is a pointer to the data buffer which receives the data. *nNumberOfBytesToRead* specifies the number of bytes of data to read from the file. *lpNumberOfBytesRead* is a pointer to a DWORD used by *ReadFile* to return the actual number of bytes of data read. As Windows CE does not allow files to be created with the FILE_FLAG_OVERLAPPED flag, *lpOverlapped* is not used. *lpOverlapped* should be set to NULL.

ReadFile returns TRUE if the operation is successful, and FALSE if the operation fails. An application can get additional error information in this case by calling *GetLastError*.

ReadFile returns once the number of bytes specified in *nNumberOfBytesToRead* have been read, or when an error occurs. If an application specifies that more bytes be read than the file actually contains, *ReadFile* will simply read as many as it can and return the actual number of bytes read in *lpNumberOfBytesRead*.

Random Access Files

The *ReadFile* function advances the file pointer *lpNumberOfBytesRead*. This accounts for the default sequential nature of file access. To implement random file access, your applications must be able to control the position of the file pointer manually. This can be done using the *SetFilePointer* function. *SetFilePointer* can be used to move a file pointer by specifying a 64-bit number representing the number of bytes the pointer is to be moved.

The syntax of *SetFilePointer* is:

```
SetFilePointer(hFile, lDistanceToMove,
    lpDistanceToMoveHigh, dwMoveMethod);
```

hFile is the handle of the open file whose pointer is to be moved. *lDistanceToMove* specifies the low order word of the number of bytes to move the file pointer. This value can be negative, in which case the file pointer is moved backward. *lpDistanceToMoveHigh* is a pointer to the high order word of the number of bytes to move the file pointer. This parameter is also used by *SetFilePointer* to return the high order word of the new file pointer position.

The *dwMoveMethod* parameter indicates the starting point of the move operation. It can be one of the following three values:

FILE_BEGIN. The starting point is the beginning of the file. In this case, the distance to move is interpreted as the unsigned pointer location.

FILE_CURRENT. The starting point is the current file pointer position.

FILE_END. The starting point is the end of file position.

If the function succeeds, it returns the low order word of the new file pointer position. If *lpDistanceToMoveHigh* was not NULL, this parameter will return the high order word of the new position. If *SetFilePointer* fails, the return value is –1 and *lpDistanceToMoveHigh* is NULL.

Random access of Windows CE files can therefore be accomplished by first specifying FILE_FLAG_RANDOM_ACCESS as one of the *dwFlagsAndAttributes* values when creating or opening the file with *CreateFile*. *SetFilePointer* is then called to manually position the file pointer for read and write operations.

An application may also want to change the position of the end of file marker of a particular file. This is done using the *SetEndOfFile* function:

```
SetEndOfFile(hFile);
```

This functions moves the end of file marker of the file specified by the file handle *hFile* to the current file pointer position of that file. If successful, this function returns TRUE. Otherwise it returns FALSE.

For example, to move the end of file marker to the beginning of a file, an application could do this:

```
//Set file pointer to beginning of file
SetFilePointer(hMyFile, 0, 0, FILE_BEGIN);
//Now set end of file marker
SetEndOfFile(hMyFile);
```

The *WriteFile* Function

Writing data to a file in Windows CE is done with the *WriteFile* function. The syntax and use of this function is very similar to *ReadFile*:

```
WriteFile(hFile, lpBuffer, nNumberOfBytesToWrite,
    lpNumberOfBytesWritten, lpOverlapped);
```

The *WriteFile* parameters have the same meanings as the corresponding *ReadFile* parameters except for *nNumberOfBytesToWrite* and *lpNumberOfBytesWritten*. It isn't much of a stretch to realize that *nNumberOfBytesToWrite* specifies the number of bytes of data to write to the file indicated by *hFile*. Similarly, *WriteFile* returns the actual number of bytes written through the *lpNumberOfBytesWritten* parameter. As with *ReadFile*, the *lpOverlapped* parameter is ignored and should be set to NULL.

To write data to a file, the file must have been opened with GENERIC_WRITE access.

Data can be written to any position in a random access file much as data can be randomly read from a random access file. The file must be created or opened with the FILE_FLAG_RANDOM_ACCESS flag set. Then *SetFilePointer* can be used to specify the file location to which data is written.

The File System Explorer example application of this chapter demonstrates *ReadFile* and *WriteFile*, and *SetFilePointer* operations by means of its very rudimentary file editing feature.

An Example

To gain further insight into how to use the *ReadFile* and *WriteFile* functions, let's look at how the File System Explorer application implements its rudimentary file editing capabilities. See Figure 6.7 for a look at the basic file editor.

The two user operations which invoke the editor are selecting the Edit File menu option and pressing the enter key after selecting a file. Both of these operations cause the following application-defined *OnEdit* function to be called:

```
void OnEdit(HWND hwnd, OIDINFO oidInfo)
{
  if (OBJTYPE_FILE==oidInfo.wObjType)
  {
   DialogBox(ghInst, MAKEINTRESOURCE(IDD_EDITFILE),
    hwnd, (DLGPROC)EditDlgProc);
  }
  else
  {
   MessageBox(NULL, TEXT("You May Only Edit Files"),
    TEXT("Directories May Not Be Edited"),
     MB_OK|MB_ICONEXCLAMATION);
  }
}
```

The parameter *hwnd* is the parent of the dialog box which acts as the file editor. *oidInfo* is the CEOIDINFO structure containing information about the currently selected file or directory.

OnEdit checks the type of the currently selected object and displays an error message if the object is a directory. It doesn't make sense to edit a directory.

On the other hand, if the object is a file, the editor is invoked by the *DialogBox* call. All of the rudimentary file editing functionality is coded in this dialog procedure *EditDlgProc*. The dialog procedure looks like this:

```
BOOL CALLBACK EditDlgProc(
  HWND hwndDlg,
  UINT message,
  WPARAM wParam,
  LPARAM lParam)
{
  TCHAR pszText[MAX_FILE_LENGTH];
  HWND hwndEdit;
  DWORD dwBytes;
```

```
CEOID oid;
CEOIDINFO oidInfo;
switch(message)
{
case WM_INITDIALOG:
 oid = (CEOID)tviCurSel.lParam;
 CeOidGetInfo(oid, &oidInfo);
 pszText[0] = 0;
 hFile = CreateFile(oidInfo.infFile.szFileName,
  GENERIC_READ|GENERIC_WRITE, 0,
   NULL, OPEN_EXISTING, FILE_ATTRIBUTE_NORMAL,
    NULL);
 if (INVALID_HANDLE_VALUE!=hFile)
 {
  dwBytes = 0;
  ReadFile(hFile, pszText,
   oidInfo.infFile.dwLength,
    &dwBytes, NULL);
  hwndEdit = GetDlgItem(hwndDlg, IDC_FILETEXT);
  SetWindowText(hwndEdit, pszText);
  wsprintf(pszText, TEXT("Edit File %s"),
   oidInfo.infFile.szFileName);
  SetWindowText(hwndDlg, pszText);
 }
 return (TRUE);
case WM_COMMAND:
 UINT nID;
 nID = LOWORD(wParam);
 switch(nID)
 {
 case IDOK:
  //Save text to file
  DWORD nBytesToWrite;
  hwndEdit = GetDlgItem(hwndDlg, IDC_FILETEXT);
  GetWindowText(hwndEdit, pszText,
   MAX_FILE_LENGTH);
  SetFilePointer(hFile, 0, 0, FILE_BEGIN);
  nBytesToWrite = lstrlen(pszText)*sizeof(TCHAR);
  WriteFile(hFile, pszText, nBytesToWrite,
   &dwBytes, NULL);
  //Deliberate fall-through
 case IDCANCEL:
  CloseHandle(hFile);
  EndDialog(hwndDlg, nID);
  break;
 default:
  break;
 }        //End of switch(nID) statement
 return (FALSE);
default:
```

```
   return (FALSE);
   }           //End of switch(message) statement
}
```

When the dialog box is opened, the WM_INITDIALOG message handler is executed. This code gets the CEOIDINFO about the currently selected file via the global variable *tviCurSel*. As we mentioned above, this always contains the TV_ITEM of the currently selected file or directory in the tree view user interface. The file name is extracted from this CEOIDINFO data, and the application attempts to open the specified file with a *CreateFile* call.

If the file exists, *CreateFile* returns the handle of the file. This handle is stored in the global variable *hFile* so that the rest of the dialog procedure has access to it. The contents of the file are read with the *ReadFile* call:

```
ReadFile(hFile, pszText, oidInfo.infFile.dwLength,
   &dwBytes, NULL);
```

The number of bytes that *ReadFile* attempts to read is equal to the length of the file. This is specified by *oidInfo.infFile.dwLength*. The file data is read into the string *pszText*.

Next, the contents of the file are placed in the dialog box edit control by the first *SetWindowText* call:

```
SetWindowText(hwndEdit, pszText);
```

Finally, the dialog box caption is changed to show the name of the file being edited.

The FILESYS.EXE user is now free to edit the file by typing text into the edit control.

To save the new text into the file, the user presses the Save button. This action invokes the IDOK command handler in the *EditDlgProc* dialog procedure. This handler code does exactly the opposite of the WM_INITDIALOG code. The contents of the editor are copied into *pszText* by the *GetWindowText* call. Next, the file pointer is set back to the beginning of the file, and the text is written to the file via *WriteFile*.

Execution then falls through to the IDCANCEL handler, which closes the file and the dialog box. This is the same code that is executed when the user presses the Cancel button.

Copying and Renaming Files and Directories

Files and directories on Windows CE–based devices, much like their counterparts on Windows NT, are often used by users of the devices to organize data and documents. Let's say that you are writing a specification (on your Handheld PC, of course!) for a new suite of Windows CE applications. This specification might consist of several files, such as functional and design specifications for each application in the suite.

If you are like most of us, the organization of this specification will change as your understanding of the required behavior of the applications you are designing evolves. Therefore, the locations and names of the files that make up your application suite specification are unlikely to be the same when the specification is complete as they were when the files were created.

Copying files and directories, renaming them, and moving them around in a directory tree are all very common file operations. Windows CE supports these operations with the *CopyFile* and *MoveFile* functions. The *MoveFileEx* function found in Windows NT is not supported under Windows CE.

The *CopyFile* Function

Copying a file in Windows CE simply requires that an application know the name of the file to be copied and the name of the file to which it is to be copied:

```
CopyFile(lpExistingFileName, lpNewFileName, bFailIfExist);
```

The *lpExistingFileName* parameter contains the null-terminated string name of the file to be copied. *lpNewFileName* is the name of the file to which *CopyFile* copies the original file.

bFailIfExist tells *CopyFile* what to do if a file named *lpNewFileName* already exists. If this parameter is TRUE and the new file already exists, *CopyFile* fails and returns FALSE. If *bFailIfExist* is FALSE in this same scenario, *CopyFile* does not fail. In this case it overwrites the existing file named *lpNewFileName*.

Another effect of copying a file is that all of the attributes (FILE_ATTRIBUTE_HIDDEN, etc.) of the file are copied to the new file.

The *MoveFile* Function

At first glance, the *MoveFile* function seems to have been inappropriately named. *MoveFile* actually *renames* files and directories in the Windows CE file system. It might seem that *RenameFile* would be a more accurate name for this function.

In the case of renaming files, that might be correct. But consider the case of renaming a directory. Let's take the example of a Windows CE directory called MyFiles. When an application renames this directory to MyOldFiles, for example, all of the *children* of this directory are renamed accordingly as well. More specifically, all files and subdirectories that MyFiles contains have their path names changed to reflect the fact that MyFiles has changed to MyOldFiles (Figure 6.9). From this point of view, it's as if the *MoveFile* operation physically moved all the children of MyFiles to a new directory called MyOldFiles.

The syntax of the *MoveFile* function is:

```
MoveFile(lpExistingFileName, lpNewFileName);
```

The *lpExistingFileName* and *lpNewFilename* parameters are the same as in the *CopyFile* function: *lpExistingFileName* is the name of the file or directory to be renamed, and *lpNewFileName* is the name to which the file or directory is renamed.

If *MoveFile* is successful, it returns TRUE. If the function fails, it returns FALSE. In that case, an application can call *GetLastError* to get more

```
Directory structure before MoveFile (showing full path names for each
file and directory):

\MyFiles  →     \MyFiles\file1.txt
                \MyFiles\file2.txt
                \MyFiles\SavedFiles  →  \MyFiles\SavedFiles\work.txt
                                        \MyFiles\SavedFiles\picture.bmp


Directory structure after MoveFile (showing full path names for each
file and directory):

\MyOldFiles  →  \MyOldFiles\file1.txt
                \MyOldFiles\file2.txt
                MyOldFiles\SavedFiles  →\MyOldFiles\SavedFiles\work.txt
                                        \MyOldFiles\SavedFiles\picture.bmp
```

Figure 6.9 Effect of renaming a directory on its children.

information about what went wrong. For example, if an application attempts to rename a file to the name of a file that already exists, *GetLastError* would return ERROR_ALREADY_EXISTS.

Deleting Files and Directories

Deleting a file in Windows CE is a simple matter of calling *DeleteFile*:

```
DeleteFile(lpFileName);
```

Your application calls this function by passing the full path name of the file to be deleted in the *lpFileName* parameter.

If the file is deleted, *DeleteFile* returns TRUE. Otherwise, it will return FALSE, in which case you can call *GetLastError* for more information.

Similarly, directories are deleted using *RemoveDirectory*:

```
RemoveDirectory(lpPathName);
```

lpPathName is the full path name of the directory to be removed. *RemoveDirectory* has the same return values as *DeleteFile*.

RemoveDirectory will fail if an application attempts to delete a directory that is not empty. There is no parameter to force deletion of an empty directory, or to do recursive deletion of an entire directory tree. Such functionality, if required by an application, must be implemented by the application developer. The File System Explorer sample application shows how this is done with its implementation of the *OnDelete* function.

Flash Cards and Persistent Storage

Flash memory cards provide a means for Windows CE–based devices to expand the amount of RAM available. A flash card is a type of *mountable file system*. Both Handheld PCs and Palm-size PCs are equipped to use flash cards. Flash cards can be used to store files just like regular RAM.

Flash cards are assigned object identifiers just like files or directories. We will see some examples of how these identifiers are used in the next section.

Flash cards should include a \My Documents folder. Many of the mountable file system API functions will default to such a folder to perform searches and the like.

To the Windows CE device, a flash card looks like part of the file system. A flash card installed on a Palm-size PC or Handheld PC is assigned the folder name Storage Card by the operating system. Files and directories are created and accessed just as they are in standard RAM using the file system API. The only difference is that the path names of flash card files and directories begin with Storage Card.

For example, to create a directory called "FlashDocs" on a Palm-size PC storage card, an application would simply call *CreateDirectory*:

```
CreateDirectory(TEXT("\\Storage Card\\FlashDocs"), NULL);
```

Flash Card APIs

There are some additional functions provided by Windows CE for enumerating flash cards and files on flash cards. Use of these functions is very similar to their file system API counterparts.

Enumerating Flash Cards

The first set of flash card API functions is used to enumerate flash cards or other mountable file systems attached to a device.

The first of these functions is *FindFirstFlashCard*. This function is used to find the first flash card (or other mountable file system) on a device:

```
FindFirstFlashCard(lpFindFlashData);
```

The only parameter to this function is a pointer to a WIN32_FIND_DATA structure. This function is analogous to *FindFirstFile*. The difference is that instead of returning WIN32_FIND_DATA information about the first specified file or directory, it returns information about the first flash card it finds.

The most important piece of information *FindFirstFlashCard* returns is the object identifier of the flash card. This value is returned in the *dwOID* member of the *lpFindFlashData* parameter.

Also like *FindFirstFile*, *FindFirstFlashCard* returns a search handle that can be used to perform searches for additional flash cards. Additional flash cards can be found with subsequent calls to *FindNextFlashCard*:

```
FindNextFlashCard(hFlashCard, lpFindFlashData);
```

hFlashCard is the search handle returned by *FindFirstFlashCard*. *lpFind-FlashData* is a WIN32_FIND_DATA structure pointer containing information about the next flash card.

Note that it is not common for a Windows CE–based device to contain more than one flash card.

Flash card search handles, like file search handles, are closed with the *FindClose* function.

Searching for Flash Card Files

The second set of flash card API functions is used to enumerate files and directories stored on flash cards.

FindFirstProjectFile is the same as *FindFirstFile* except that it can be made to look for files on a specified mountable file system:

```
FindFirstProjectFile(lpFileName, lpFindFileData,
    dwOidFlash, lpszProj);
```

The first two parameters of this function are the same as in *FindFirstFile*. They contain the file or directory name to search for and the returned WIN32_FIND_DATA, respectively.

dwOidFlash identifies the storage card to search on. This value is obtained by a previous call to *FindFirstFlashCard* or *FindNextFlashCard*. This parameter can be set to zero, in which case the main device file system is searched instead of a mountable file system. *FindFirstProjectFile* can thus be used just like *FindFirstFile* on devices that include mountable file systems. In fact, it is recommended that on devices such as the Palm-size PC, *FindFirstProjectFile* be used exclusively.

The final parameter, *lpszProj*, indicates the folder to start the search in. If NULL, the search starts with the \My Documents folder.

FindFirstProjectFile returns a search handle, just like *FindFirstFile*. This search handle is used to perform subsequent searches with the *Find-NextProjectFile* function:

```
FindNextProjectFile(hHandle, lpFindProjData);
```

The parameters and behavior of this function are the same as *Find-NextFile*.

Concluding Remarks

That's it for the Windows CE file system. You should now be able to add file support to your Windows CE applications in order to store and retrieve data. But more often you will want to store and organize information in a more structured format than a simple flat data file. For this purpose, Windows CE provides a simple database technology. Windows CE databases are the subject of the next chapter.

CHAPTER 7

Windows CE Databases

Long before Microsoft commanded the world of personal computing, another large multinational corporation in a northwestern state far colder and wetter than Washington had its own monopoly on the market for personal information management products. Every time the need arose to record a new phone number, address, or name, or whenever a quick reminder or note had to be jotted down for future reference, millions of people across the country grabbed a pen and wrote this information in (at least in my case) marginally legible handwriting on a one-and-a-half-by-one-inch yellow square piece of sticky paper.

Over time (again in my case, at least), these little pieces of paper were stuck up all over computer monitors, to the inside covers of reference books, kitchen counters, the home office desk; particularly important contacts were even stuck to the back of credit cards in wallets for easy later retrieval. This data storage model naturally led to frequent frantic searches through sock drawers and the front of the refrigerator door for meeting times or important phone numbers. It was somewhat inefficient, but business and our lives managed to move on with few mishaps.

Fortunately, Microsoft and other companies (notably, 3Com Corporation, with its line of PalmPilot organizers) have made all of our lives easier with the introduction of personal information management devices to help keep track of phone numbers, appointments, to-do lists, and the like in one convenient place. At the tap of a stylus on a touch screen, we can now retrieve the phone numbers of friends and coworkers. With a few simple key or stylus strokes, we can tell these devices to alert us days in advance of impending birthdays and anniversaries. The persistent storage capabilities of Windows CE databases make many of these advances possible.

AFTER COMPLETING THIS CHAPTER YOU WILL KNOW HOW TO . . .

Design databases

Create and delete databases

Open and close databases

Add records to and remove them from databases

Read and write database records

Sort databases

Perform database searches

Enumerate databases

Use database notifications

Use the contacts database API

The Phone List Application

To illustrate the features of Windows CE databases and the Windows CE database application programming interface functions, we will look at the example of a phone list database application. This application maintains a database of employee names, phone numbers, and department numbers. It displays the database contents in a user interface based on a simple list view control, where each list view column represents a particular database record property. The main application window is shown in Figure 7.1.

This application will give you a feel for how to write applications that can add and delete database records, sort a database, and perform

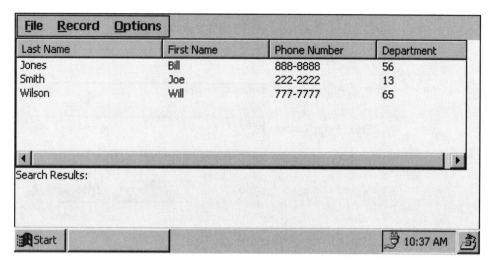

Figure 7.1   The phone list application.

database searches. It can also very easily be expanded into a full-fledged contacts or address book application by adding the appropriate properties to the database records. And you can customize the user interface to suit different needs.

The complete source code for the phone list application can be found on the companion CD in the directory \Samples\dbase. The application that is built by the project files is called DBASE.EXE.

Adding and Removing Phone List Database Records

Database entries are added or removed by choosing the appropriate option from the Record menu (Figure 7.2). This menu contains the Add, Delete, and Clear Database options.

For example, to add a new record to the phone list database, a user selects the Add option from the Record menu. When this menu item is

File	Record	Options				
Last N	Add		First Name	Phone Number	Department
Jones	Delete		Bill	888-8888	56
Smith			Joe	222-2222	13
Wilson	Clear Database		Will	777-7777	65

Figure 7.2   The phone list application Record menu.

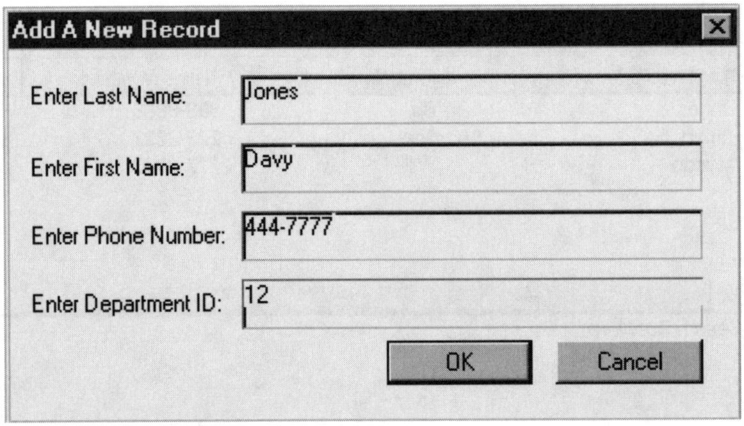

Add A New Record   ☒

    Enter Last Name: Jones

    Enter First Name: Davy

    Enter Phone Number: 444-7777

    Enter Department ID: 12

                              OK   Cancel

Figure 7.3   The Add A New Record dialog box.

selected, the dialog box shown in Figure 7.3 is displayed. This dialog box allows the user to enter the details of the record to be added to the database. Each text entry field in this dialog corresponds to one of the phone list database record properties.

After all of the properties have been entered, pressing the OK button adds the new record to the phone list database and refreshes the main application window display so that the new record is shown.

To delete a phone list database record, a user simply needs to select the record to be deleted in the main window and select the Delete option from the Record menu. To delete all database records at once, simply select the Clear Database option from the Record menu.

Sorting Phone List Database Records

The phone list application allows users to sort the database by any of the database record properties. Sorting the database by a particular property is done by tapping the column header of the corresponding record property. For example, to sort the database by phone number, the user only needs to tap the phone number column header (Figure 7.4).

File	Record	Options		
Last Name		First Name	Phone Number	Department
Smith		Joe	222-2222	13
Wilson		Will	777-7777	65
Jones		Bill	888-8888	56

Figure 7.4   Sorting the phone list database by phone number.

Searching for Records in the Phone List Database

Database applications, such as phone lists or other personal contacts, are primarily used to look up information pertaining to one or more of the records in the corresponding application database. Users of a phone list application, for example, will often want to look up the phone number of a specific person in the database.

The phone list application provides basic record search capabilities. A search is invoked by selecting the Seek option from the Options menu in the main application window. The Options menu is shown in Figure 7.5. Selecting the Seek option displays the dialog box shown in Figure 7.6.

This dialog lets the user enter a record property value in the text entry field. The record property that this corresponds to (e.g., first name, last name, etc.) depends on the property by which the database is currently sorted. For example, if the phone list database is sorted by last name, the seek record dialog box assumes that the user will enter a last name. This is emphasized by the wording of the caption above the edit field. Entering a last name and pressing the OK button in this case makes the application search the phone list database for a record containing the specified last name.

File	Record	Options		
Last Name		Seek...	Phone Number	Department
Jones		Database Memory...	888-8888	56
Smith		Joe	222-2222	13
Wilson		Will	777-7777	65

Figure 7.5   The phone list application Options menu.

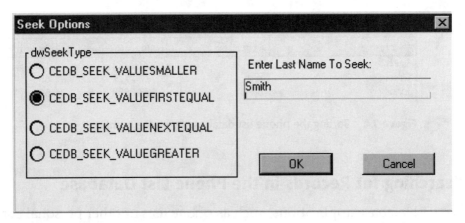

Figure 7.6   The Seek Record dialog box.

The set of radio buttons on the left side of the dialog with the very confusing labels indicate the type of search to perform. As you read the rest of this chapter, you will see that these button labels correspond to one of the parameters of the Windows CE database search function. After reading about this function, you will see that this dialog box is useful for allowing you to see the effect of passing different parameter values to the search function.

For now, from the point of view of highlighting the basic database features provided by Windows CE, it is sufficient to say that these radio buttons control how the search value entered by the user is compared to the corresponding record property for each record in the database.

For example, let's say that a user wants to search the phone list database for the first record with a last name of Smith. The user must first make sure that the database is sorted by last name. As described above, this is done by tapping the Last Name column header.

Next, the user chooses the Seek menu option from the Options menu. In the dialog box that appears, the user types "Smith" in the edit field. The CEDB_SEEK_VALUEFIRSTEQUAL radio button is selected to tell the application to search for the first record containing a last name of Smith (see Figure 7.6). When the user presses the OK button, the phone list application searches for the requested record. If the record is found, the results of the search are displayed in the Search Results field at the bottom of the main application screen as shown in Figure 7.7.

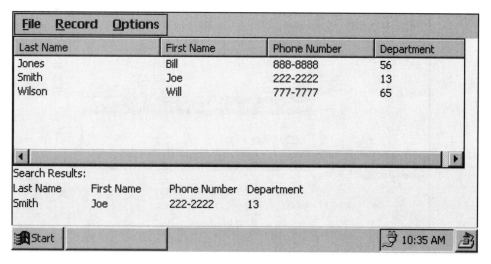

Figure 7.7   The result of a successful record search.

Determining the Size of the Phone List Database

The final interesting feature of the phone list application is that it allows the user to determine how much object store memory is being used by the phone list database. This feature is invoked by selecting the Database Memory option from the Options menu.

Selecting the Database Memory menu item displays the dialog box shown in Figure 7.8. This dialog simply reports the total number of bytes consumed by the phone list database and the records it contains.

Programming Windows CE Databases

If you are familiar with writing database applications for relational databases, you will find the Windows CE database model very different. Databases under Windows CE do not support any form of structured query language, and provide none of the relational data manipulation techniques such as table joins. Windows CE databases are simply non-hierarchical collections of an arbitrary number of *records*, each of which contains one or more data *properties*. Properties can be the integer, Unicode string, FILETIME, or blob (byte array) data.

As with any object stored in the Windows CE object store, every database and database record is assigned a unique object identifier of type

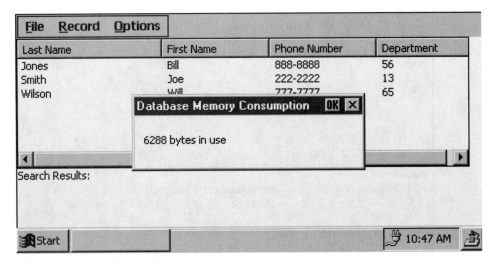

Figure 7.8   The phone list Database Memory Consumption dialog.

CEOID by the Windows CE operating system. This object identifier can be used, for example, when searching for database records or to identify records to delete from a database.

Another important part of a Windows CE database is the *current record pointer*. This is also sometimes called the *seek pointer*. This pointer indicates the record to be read by the next database read operation. The current record is therefore defined to mean the record currently pointed to by the seek pointer. As an application reads records in a database, the current record pointer (or seek pointer) can be thought of as marking the current record position. Seeking and reading records in the database can move the seek pointer position. These operations are discussed in detail later.

Windows CE provides a database application programming interface for creating and managing databases on Windows CE devices. This API provides functionality for the following database operations:

- Creating and deleting databases
- Adding and deleting database records
- Sorting records in a database
- Searching for records in a database
- Enumerating the databases on a Windows CE device

What's All This SQLing I Hear?

The database technology provided with the Windows CE operating system is significantly simpler than the full relational or object-oriented databases that you might be used to programming with in the Windows NT or Windows 98 environments. The Windows CE database technology was originally designed to support basic personal information management (PIM) applications.

The Windows CE database technology is not a relation or object-oriented database. It also does not support Structured Query Language (SQL), the lingua franca of database programmers all over the world. As such, the Windows CE database model is perfectly adequate for relatively simple databases, such as contact lists and collections of e-mail messages. But application developers who need database schema more complex than the simple record-based model of the default Windows CE database have until recently been disappointed. And performing complex searches and queries has been practically impossible due to the lack of SQL.

As Windows CE has matured from its first incarnation over two years ago, so has the level of complexity of software being written for the operating system. Various companies are designing new Windows CE–based consumer and business products, many with database requirements that exceed the capabilities of the basic Windows CE database technology.

Fortunately for these applications, database vendors have recently begun porting their database technologies to Windows CE. Relational as well as object-oriented database solutions are now available from a number of database companies. Oracle, Sybase, and Neoworks Corporations, to name a few, have all begun supporting Windows CE versions of their database software. It is, therefore, now possible to take advantage of traditional database technology, including the power of SQL, when writing software for Windows CE.

Additionally, the Microsoft Foundation Classes library for Windows CE supports Data Access Objects (DAO), providing a SQL-based interface to the Windows CE database technology.

This book, however, will only cover programming for the Windows CE database. Complete coverage of SQL programming and relation and objected-oriented databases is left to the vast number of database programming books on the market today.

For each of the functions in the database API, there is a corresponding function in the Remote Application Programming Interface, or RAPI. RAPI is a part of Windows CE that allows applications on a desktop PC, called the RAPI client, to make function calls on a Windows CE device, the RAPI server. RAPI is covered later in Chapter 15.

Square PEGs in Round Holes

From time to time as you read the Windows CE on-line documentation, you will see references to things like PEGOID when you would expect CEOID, or function names like *PegOpenDatabase* when you would swear we've been talking endlessly about *CeOpenDatabase*. What is this all about?

In Windows CE versions 1.0 and earlier, all of the database types and functions started with *Peg*, instead of *Ce*. This is a leftover from the code name for Windows CE, which was Pegasus. As Windows CE matured, Microsoft realized that function names like *CeOpenDatabase* made infinitely more sense to most software developers than *PegOpenDatabase*. They therefore made the decision (usually considered anathema in most circles) to change the names of the database types and APIs.

This of course left a backward compatibility issue. So in order to make everyone's Windows CE 1.0 database applications compatible with later versions of the operating system, the old Pegasus names are defined to the new names in the public header file WNDBASE.H:

```
#define PEGPROPID          CEPROPID
*.
*.
*.
#define PegOpenDatabase    CeOpenDatabase
etc.
```

In this way, applications written for older versions of Windows CE can be ported to new versions. Any references to the Peg-prefixed symbols get replaced with the Ce-prefixed versions, and the applications will compile and link without complaints.

The Database Design

When designing any database, it is always a good idea to first design the database schema. The database schema is the description of the database and the kinds of information it contains. In our example, this simply means describing what properties each of the phone list records will contain, including the data type of each of the properties. If applicable, you would also define the acceptable range of values that each record property can be assigned. In traditional relational database design, the schema would be more complex, including descriptions of the various relational tables that make up the database.

Taking the time up front to do this design step can save you from rewriting the database definition and management code in your applications because you overlooked an important piece of information required by your application.

The phone list database consists of records that contain these four properties: employee last name, first name, phone number, and department number (Table 7.1). We will allow users of the phone list application to sort the records in the phone list on any of these four properties.

Internal Representation of Record Properties

It is one thing to understand the format of a Windows CE database record in the abstract. It is quite another to understand how Windows CE itself think of records and the properties that they contain.

Windows CE treats each database record as a collection of one or more properties, each of which is of type CEPROPVAL. The definition of the CEPROPVAL structure is:

```
typedef struct _CEPROPVAL
{
  CEPROPID propid;
  WORD wLenData;
  WORD wFlags;
  CEVALUNION val;
} CEPROPVAL;
```

The *propid* member is of type CEPROPID, which is defined as a LONG. The low word of *propid* identifies the data type of the property. The high word is an application-defined index. Typically this index is

Table 7.1 Phone List Database Record Definition

PROPERTY	DATA TYPE
Last Name	LPWSTR
First Name	LPWSTR
Phone Number	LPWSTR
Department Number	short

Table 7.2   CEPROPID Data Type Specifiers

VALUE	DATA TYPE
CEVT_BLOB	A CEBLOB structure
CEVT_FILETIME	A FILETIME structure
CEVT_I2	A 16-bit signed integer
CEVT_I4	A 32-bit signed integer
CEVT_LPWSTR	A null-terminated Unicode string
CEVT_UI2	A 16-bit unsigned integer
CEVT_UI4	A 32-bit unsigned integer

used to represent the zero-based index of the property in the record. The low word must be one of the values listed in Table 7.2.

As an example, the phone list application defines the property identifiers of the phone list database record properties in this way:

```
//First define the indices of the properties within the record
#define PL_LASTNAME_INDEX    0
#define PL_FIRSTNAME_INDEX   1
#define PL_PHONENUMBER_INDEX 2
#define PL_DEPT_INDEX        3*
//Next define the CEPROPID values of the record properties
#define PL_LASTNAME \
  (MAKELONG(CEVT_LPWSTR,PL_LASTNAME_INDEX))
#define PL_FIRSTNAME \*
  (MAKELONG(CEVT_LPWSTR, PL_FIRSTNAME_INDEX))
#define PL_PHONENUMBER \
  (MAKELONG(CEVT_LPWSTR,PL_PHONENUMBER_INDEX))
#define PL_DEPT \
  (MAKELONG(CEVT_I2, PL_DEPT_INDEX))
```

The second member of the CEPROPVAL structure, *wLenData*, is not used. The *wFlags* member is used to define a set of special property flags. This member is typically set to 0. We will discuss the other values of this member and their meanings later when discussing reading and writing database records.

The most interesting of the CEPROPVAL members is the *val* member. As the name indicates, this member contains the actual data associated with the particular record property. This member is of type CEVALUNION, a union defined as follows:

```
typedef union _CEVALUNION
{
  short iVal;
  USHORT uiVal;
  long lVal;
  ULONG ulVal;
  FILETIME filetime;
  LPWSTR lpwstr;
  CEBLOB blob;
} CEVALUNION;
```

Each of the members of this union corresponds to one of the data type identifiers of the *propid* member of the CEPROPVAL structure (see Table 7.2). The member of this union that you would use when setting the value of a particular record property would thus depend on the data type specified in that property's property identifier. For example, to set the first name property of a phone list database record, the phone list application would do the following:

```
CEPROPVAL cepvFirstName;
cepvFirstName.propid = PL_FIRSTNAME;
cepvFirstName.val.lpwstr = TEXT("Some Name");
```

Or to set the department number property:

```
CEPROPVAL cepvDeptNum;
cepvDeptNum.propid = PL_DEPT;
cepvDeptNum.val.iVal = 12; //i.e., the appropriate dept number
```

These examples are meant only to demonstrate the use of the CEPROPVAL *val* member. As we'll see later, applications typically define an array of CEPROPVAL structures to represent the entire record to be read or written.

Creating the Database

Windows CE databases are created using the *CeCreateDatabase* function. The syntax of *CeCreateDatabase* is:

```
CeCreateDatabase(lpszName, dwDbaseType, wNumSortOrder,
  rgSortSpecs);
```

The first parameter is the Unicode string name of the database to be created. This name can be up to 32 characters long (including the null terminator). Database names that exceed this limit are truncated. The next parameter is the database type identifier. This value is defined by the application to distinguish one type of database from another. For example, let's say that an application needs to manage the phone list databases for three different companies, as well as the payroll databases for those same companies. This application could define the following database types:

```
#define DB_TYPE_PHONE_LIST   0
#define DB_TYPE_PAYROLL      1
```

Each of the phone list databases could be created with a database type identifier DB_TYPE_PHONE_LIST, and the payroll databases could be created with type identifier DB_TYPE_PAYROLL. The application could then use the database type identifier to distinguish between the different types of databases, for example when enumerating all databases on a Windows CE device.

The *wNumSortOrder* indicates the number of sort orders allowed for the database. This is a fancy way of saying how many record properties the database can use as sort keys. The final parameter is an array of SORTORDERSPEC structures defined in more detail below.

The *CeCreateDatabase* function returns the object identifier of the database if the creation is successful. If unsuccessful, *CeCreateDatabase* returns zero.

If we can create a database, we must also be able to delete it. To delete a database, simply call *CeDeleteDatabase*. This function takes one parameter, the object identifier of the database to be deleted.

Sorting and the SORTORDERSPEC

Applications sort databases by specifying up to four *sort orders*. A sort order specifies which property in each database record is to be used as the sorting key, and the order (ascending, descending, etc.) in which the database records are to be sorted when the corresponding property is used as the sorting key. This information can be provided to the database in one of two ways. The first is to pass this sort order information to the database when it is created via the last argument to the *CeCreateDatabase* function, *rgSortSpecs*. The second is to use the *CeSetDatabaseInfo* function and specify the sort orders in a CEDBASEINFO structure. To use either of these techniques, we must first understand how a sort order is represented in Windows CE.

A sort order is defined using the SORTORDERSPEC structure, which is defined as:

```
typedef struct _SORTORDERSPEC
{
  CEPROPID propid;
  DWORD dwFlags;
} SORTORDERSPEC;
```

The first member of this structure is the property identifier of a particular record property. The second member contains sort order flags. These flags define, for example, whether records are sorted in ascending or descending order.

As an example, let's assume that we want to be able to sort the phone list database by last name in ascending order, and at other times to sort by department number in descending order. We would therefore need to define two SORTORDERSPEC structures to convey this information:

```
SORTORDERSPEC sos[2];
sos[0].propid = PL_LASTNAME;   //Specify the last name
                //property id
sos[0].dwFlags = 0;        //0 indicates ascending order
sos[1].propid = PL_DEPT;     //Specify the deparment number
                //property id
sos[1].dwFlags = CEDB_SORT_DESCENDING; //Descending sort order
```

Note the value of 0 for the *dwFlags* member of *sos*[0] to indicate ascending sort order. I point this out to save you the same amount of time I wasted searching in vain for a definition of CEDB_SORT_ASCENDING in the Windows CE header files.

Now that we understand how to specify a sort order, we are ready to discuss the two techniques for supplying the database with our sort order information. The first is to pass the array of SORTORDERSPEC structures that you create as the *rgSortSpecs* parameter of the *CeCreateDatabase* function. This would seem to imply that once a database is created, an application has no control over redefining the sort order information associated with that database. This is not the case, however. The second technique for specifying sort orders is with the *CeSetDatabaseInfo* function. The syntax of this function is:

```
CeSetDatabaseInfo(oidDbase, pNewInfo);
```

The first parameter of *CeSetDatabaseInfo* is the object identifier of an open database. The second parameter is a pointer to a CEDBASEINFO structure. This structure is defined as:

```
typedef struct _CEDBASEINFO
{
  DWORD dwFlags;
  WCHAR szDbaseName[CEDB_MAXDBASENAMELEN];
  DWORD dwDbaseType;
  WORD wNumRecords;
  WORD wNumSortOrder;
  DWORD dwSize;
  FILETIME ftLastModified;
  SORTORDERSPEC rgSortSpecs[CEDB_MAXSORTORDER];
} CEDBASEINFO;
```

szDbaseName and *dwDbaseType* are the name and application-defined database type identifier respectively. *dwSize* is used by *CeSetDatabaseInfo* to return the number of bytes of data stored in the database. *ftLastModified* is used to update the time the database was last modified. The *wNumRecords* field is not used.

That leaves *dwFlags*, *wNumSortOrder*, and *rgSortSpecs*. *wNumSortOrder* specifies the new total number of sort orders associated with the database. Remember, Windows CE databases only support up to four sort orders. *rgSortSpecs* is our trusty array of SORTORDERSPEC structures. If you originally created the database with one set of sort orders, you can specify totally different sort orders here.

Finally, the *dwFlags* member is used to indicate to *CeSetDatabaseInfo* which of the other CEDBASEINFO structure members are valid, that is, which characteristics of the database are to be changed by the *CeSetDatabaseInfo* call. *dwFlags* can be one of the four values given in Table 7.3.

 It should be noted here that using *CeSetDatabaseInfo* to change the sort order of a database can be a very slow operation for Windows CE to perform, especially if the database being modified contains a large number of records. It is therefore not generally recommended that this be done. The sort order requirements for a particular database should

Table 7.3 CEDBASEINFO *dwFlags* Member Values

VALUE	MEANING
CEDB_VALIDMODTIME	ftLastModified member is valid
CEDB_VALIDNAME	szDbaseName member is valid
CEDB_VALIDTYPE	dwDbaseType member is valid
CEDB_VALIDSORTSPEC	rgSortSpecs member is valid

instead be carefully considered and defined during the application design phase. The sort orders can then be set once and for all when the database is created.

Careful readers who have suffered through this laborious account of how and when to define database sort orders will have noticed that a huge piece of the sorting story is still missing. We have yet to discuss how a Windows CE database is told on which of the properties associated with the various sort orders the database is to be sorted. This is done, mercifully simply, by simply opening the database.

Opening and Closing the Database

Not surprisingly, the function that is used to open a Windows CE database is called *CeOpenDatabase*:

```
CeOpenDatabase(poid, lpszName, propid, dwFlags, hwndNotify);
```

The *poid* argument is the object identifier of the database to open. Alternatively (and more commonly), you will open a database by name. This is done by setting the *poid* argument to zero, and supplying the name of the database to open in the *lpszName* argument. If a database is opened in this way, Windows CE will return the object identifier of the database via the *poid* argument.

The *propid* argument is a CEPROPVAL that specifies which sort order to use when sorting the database. *dwFlags* can be set to CEDB_AUTOINCREMENT, or to zero. If set to CEDB_AUTOINCREMENT, the database record pointer is incremented each time a record is read from the database. If zero, the record pointer is not incremented.

The *hwndNotify* parameter can be used to specify the window to which database notifications are sent. It can be NULL if you are not interested in receiving such notifications. Database notifications are discussed later in the chapter.

CeOpenDatabase returns a handle to the opened database if successful. Otherwise it returns the error code INVALID_HANDLE_VALUE.

To close a database, use the function *CloseHandle*, passing the handle to the open database as the *hObject* parameter.

From the point of view of database sorting, the *propid* argument to *CeOpenDatabase* gets all the glory. An application specifies how the database is sorted simply by calling *CeOpenDatabase* with the desired sorting property specified in the *propid* parameter. For example, to sort the records in the phone list database by first name, our application simply needs to open the database as follows:

```
CEOID ceoidDBase=0;  //0 because we will open the database
            //by name
CeOpenDatabase(ceoidDBase, TEXT("PhoneList"), PL_FIRSTNAME,
   CEDB_AUTOINCREMENT, NULL);
```

If the application already has the database open when it wants to resort it on a new key, it must first close the database with *CloseHandle* before reopening it.

Writing an *OpenDatabase* Function

You may often find it convenient to combine the processes of creating and opening a database into one function. Consider the following *OpenDatabase* function:

```
HANDLE OpenDatabase(
   LPWSTR lpszName,    /* Database name */
   CEPROPID cepropidSort, /* Sort property */
   DWORD dwFlags,      /*CEDB_AUTOINCREMENT,etc.*/
   HWND hwndNotify,
   CEOID* pceoid)      /*CEOID of opened database*/
{
   HANDLE hdb;
   *pceoid = 0;
   hdb = CeOpenDatabase(pceoid, lpszName,
    cepropidSort, dwFlags, hwndNotify);
   if (INVALID_HANDLE_VALUE==hdb)
   {
    SORTORDERSPEC sos[4];
    sos[0].propid = PL_LASTNAME;
    sos[0].dwFlags = 0;
    sos[1].propid = PL_FIRSTNAME;
    sos[1].dwFlags = 0;
    sos[2].propid = PL_PHONENUMBER;
    sos[2].dwFlags = 0;
    sos[3].propid = PL_DEPT;
    sos[3].dwFlags = 0;
    ceoidDBase = CeCreateDatabase(szDBaseName,0, 4, sos);
    hdb = CeOpenDatabase(pceoid, NULL,cepropidSort,
     CEDB_AUTOINCREMENT, hwndNotify);
   }
   return (hdb);
}
```

One advantage of such a function is that once the function is written, the application programmer can think of creating and opening the database as the same operation. Instead of having to consider whether or not the database exists, the programmer can simply call this *Open-Database* function. If it happens to be the first time that the database is being accessed and it doesn't yet exist, this function will create the database.

Writing and Reading Database Records

We have seen how to create, open, close, and sort the records in a database. But how do the records get into the database to begin with? And how are the records retrieved by an application that needs to use the information that these records contain?

Writing records to a database requires our old friend the CEPROPVAL structure and the *CeWriteRecordProps* function. Basically, an application fills an array of CEPROPVALs with the property information for the record, and then calls *CeWriteRecordProps* to actually write the record to the database. For example, to write a hypothetical record to the phone list database, the phone list application might do something like this:

```
CEPROPVAL cePropVal[4];
//Set the last name
cePropVal[PL_LASTNAME_INDEX].propid = PL_LASTNAME;
cePropVal[PL_LASTNAME_INDEX].val.lpwstr = TEXT("Rubble");
//Set the first name
cePropVal[PL_FIRSTNAME_INDEX].propid = PL_FIRSTNAME;
cePropVal[PL_FIRSTNAME_INDEX].val.lpwstr = TEXT("Barney");
//Set the phone number
cePropVal[PL_PHONENUMBER_INDEX].propid = PL_PHONENUMBER;
cePropVal[PL_PHONENUMBER_INDEX].val.lpwstr = TEXT("888-8888");
//Set the department id
cePropVal[PL_DEPT_INDEX].propid = PL_DEPT;
cePropVal[PL_DEPT_INDEX].val.iVal = 12;
CeWriteRecordProps(hDBase, 0, 4, cePropVal);
```

The first argument of the *CeWriteRecordProps* function is the handle of the open database to be written to. The second argument is of type CEOID and can contain the object identifier of an existing record to be written over, or zero to indicate that a new record with the given properties is to be added to the database. A database record can thus be modified by calling *CeWriteRecordProps* and passing the object identi-

fier of this record in the second parameter. The third parameter indicates the number of properties contained in the fourth parameter,
which is the array of CEPROPVALs containing the data to be written
to the database. *CeWriteRecordProps* returns the object identifier of the
record that was written.

The *wFlags* member of any of the CEPROPVAL structures can either be
zero or CEDB_PROPDELETE. If CEDB_PROPDELETE, the write operation deletes the property from the record. In this way *CeWriteRecord-
Props* can remove selected properties from existing database records.

Reading a record from the database requires *CeReadRecordProps*. This
function reads and returns the record as one big block of bytes that
actually contains a set of CEPROPVAL structures, one per record property. Once the record data is read, it is the responsibility of your application to unpack the data array, breaking it down into the constituent
properties.

The *CeReadRecordProps* function has the following definition:

```
CeReadRecordProps(hDBase, dwFlags, lpcPropID, rgPropID,
    lplpBuffer, lpcbBuffer);
```

The first argument is the handle to the open database. *dwFlags* can either be zero or CEDB_ALLOWREALLOC. Applications will usually
use this value, indicating that *CeReadRecordProps* has permission to re-
allocate the data buffer *lplpBuffer* if it doesn't contain enough space to
hold all of the record data. *lpcPropID* is an LPWORD indicating the
number of properties to be retrieved. *rgPropID* is an array of CE-
PROPID values that tells the function which record properties to read.

CeReadRecordProps can thus be used to read any or all of the properties
in a given database record. To read all properties, set *lpcPropID* to zero
and *rgPropID* to NULL. If these two parameters are used in this way,
lpcPropID contains the number of properties read once the function
returns.

After the function executes, *lplpBuffer* contains the record property
data and *lpcbBuffer* contains the total number of bytes in the buffer. If
CeReadRecordProps succeeds, it return the object identifier of the record
that was read. If it fails, it will return zero, in which case you can call
GetLastError to get more detailed information about what went wrong.

It is possible that a property specified in the *rgPropID* array does not
exist in the record retrieved by *CeReadRecordProps*. For example, an

application might accidentally specify an invalid property identifier, or specify a property that has been previously deleted from the record. In these cases, the *wFlags* parameter of the CEPROPVAL structure extracted from *lplpBuffer* for that property will be set to CEDB_PROP-NOTFOUND.

At this point, all that is left to do is to convert the data array returned by *CeReadRecordProps* into the property data. Since *lpcPropID* contains the number of properties contained by the record data buffer, the simplest way to do this is to cast the data buffer into an array of CEPROP-VAL structures and iterate on each property as follows:

```
WORD cProps = 0;
LPBYTE pBuf=NULL;
DWORD cbByte = 0;
PCEPROPVAL pVals;
CEOID oid;
int i;
//hDBase is a handle to the (previously opened) database
oid = CeReadRecordProps(hDBase, CEDB_ALLOWREALLOC, &cProps,
  NULL, &pBuf, &cbByte);
//Unpack all of the record properties
pVals = (PCEPROPVAL)pBuf;
for (i=0; i<cProps; i++)
{
  switch(HIWORD(pVals[i].propid))
  {
   case PL_LASTNAME_INDEX:
   /* pVals[i].val.lpwstr contains the last name property
     value: The application needs to do something with it.
    */
   break;
   case PL_FIRSTNAME_INDEX:
   /* pVals[i].val.lpwstr contains the first name property */
   break;
   case PL_PHONENUMBER_INDEX:
   /* pVals[i].val.lpwstr contains the phone number
     property
    */
   break;
   case PL_DEPT_INDEX:
   /* pVals[i].val.iVal contains the dept number property */
   break;
   default:
   break;
  }           //End of switch statement*
}           //End of for (i=0; i<cProps; i++) loop
LocalFree(pBuf);
```

The LPBYTE array of raw record data is cast to an array of CEPROP-VAL structures (the *pVals* variable). The for loop that follows then executes once for each property that was read from the current record by the *CeReadRecordProps* call. The switch statement checks the application-defined index of the current property in the *pVals* array, and extracts the value of that record accordingly (recall that the high word of each *propid* member of a CEPROPVAL contains the application-defined index of a particular property). The *val* members of the individual CEPROPVALs can be assigned to other variables as needed, or, as we will show later, used to construct a database record structure that is used by the application to more clearly represent the data. Notice that we free (using *LocalFree*) the data buffer returned by *CeRead-RecordProps* after using it. This needs to be done whether or not the read operation was successful, as *CeReadRecordProps* might allocate memory in any attempt to read a database record.

Deleting Database Records

Finally, we need to describe how to delete database records. Deleting records from a Windows CE database is done with the *CeDeleteRecord* function:

```
CeDeleteRecord(hDatabase, oidRecord);
```

hDatabase is the handle of the open database from which the record is to be removed. *oidRecord* is the CEOID identifying the record to delete.

CeDeleteRecord returns TRUE if the specified record is successfully deleted from the database. Otherwise the function returns FALSE. In this case, an application can call *GetLastError* for more information about why the delete operation failed.

Managing Records More Cleanly

The preceding examples of how to write and read database records leave something to be desired. In both cases, you might have been left with the impression that Windows CE database applications only work with record data in raw binary form. While it is true that the *CeReadRecordProps* always return an LPBYTE array of data, and *CeWriteRecordProps* always writes record information as a collection of somewhat cumbersome CEPROPVAL structures, it is possible to write your applications in such a way that the rest of your application can treat database records in a more natural form. Specifically, your application can define a structure that is used to represent the more abstract notion of records in your database.

For example, in the case of the phone list application, it seems natural to represent an entry in the phone list with a structure like this:

```
typedef struct _PhoneRecord
{
   TCHAR lpszLastName[MAX_NAME_LENGTH];
   TCHAR lpszFirstName[MAX_NAME_LENGTH];
   TCHAR lpszPhoneNumber[MAX_NAME_LENGTH];*
   int nDept;
}PHONERECORD, *LPPHONERECORD;
```

No CEPROPVALSs, CEOIDs, or other abstract database concepts here. A phone record is just a collection of values of C data types that we know and love. When users enter new records through the application's user interface, the application code can assign the values entered into the appropriate fields of an instance of this clear-cut data type. The mechanics of turning the elements of this structure into the form required in order to write the record to the database can be left to the inner workings of one simple *ReadRecord* function:

```
CEOID ReadRecord(LPPHONERECORD lppr)
{
   WORD cProps = 0;
   LPBYTE pBuf=NULL;*
   DWORD cbByte = 0;*
   PCEPROPVAL pVals;*
   CEOID oid;
   int i;
   oid = CeReadRecordProps(hDBase, CEDB_ALLOWREALLOC,
    &cProps, NULL,&pBuf, &cbByte);
   pVals = (PCEPROPVAL)pBuf;
   for (i=0; i<cProps; i++)
   {
    switch(HIWORD(pVals[i].propid))
    {
     case PL_LASTNAME_INDEX:
      lstrcpy(lppr->lpszLastName,
       pVals[i].val.lpwstr);
      break;
     case PL_FIRSTNAME_INDEX:
      lstrcpy(lppr->lpszFirstName,
       pVals[i].val.lpwstr);
      break;
     case PL_PHONENUMBER_INDEX:
      lstrcpy(lppr->lpszPhoneNumber,
       pVals[i].val.lpwstr);
```

```
      break;
    case PL_DEPT_INDEX:
      lppr->nDept = pVals[i].val.iVal;
      break;
    default:
      break;
    }          //End of switch statement
  }            //End of for (i=0; i<cProps; i++) loop
  LocalFree(pBuf);
  return (oid);
}
```

Writing phone list records can be abstracted in much the same way with *WriteRecord*:

```
CEOID WriteRecord(LPPHONERECORD lppr)
{
  CEPROPVAL cePropVal[PROPERTY_COUNT];
  CEOID ceoid;
  HANDLE hBase;
  WORD wCurrent = 0;
  hDBase = OpenPhoneDatabase(szDBaseName, 0,
   CEDB_AUTOINCREMENT, NULL, &ceoidDBase);
  memset(&cePropVal, 0, sizeof(CEPROPVAL)*PROPERTY_COUNT);
  cePropVal[wCurrent].propid = PL_LASTNAME;
  cePropVal[wCurrent++].val.lpwstr = lppr->lpszLastName;
  cePropVal[wCurrent].propid = PL_FIRSTNAME;
  cePropVal[wCurrent++].val.lpwstr = lppr->lpszFirstName;
  cePropVal[wCurrent].propid = PL_PHONENUMBER;
  cePropVal[wCurrent++].val.lpwstr = lppr->lpszPhoneNumber;
  cePropVal[wCurrent].propid = PL_DEPT;
  cePropVal[wCurrent++].val.iVal = lppr->nDept;
  ceoid = CeWriteRecordProps(hDBase, 0, wCurrent,
   cePropVal);
  CloseHandle(hDBase);    /Close the database
  return (ceoid);
}
```

The rest of the application can now treat phone list data in the way that you would normally model the concept of a record, as a standard C structure.

Searching for Records

The function used for searching for records is *CeSeekDatabase*:

```
CeSeekDatabase(hDatabase, dwSeekType, dwValue, lpdwIndex);
```

hDatabase is a handle to the open database. *dwSeekType* is a DWORD that indicates to the function what kind of database search to perform. It also defines where the database current record pointer is positioned at the end of the seek operation. *lpdwIndex*, the last parameter, is a pointer to a DWORD that *CeSeekDatabase* uses to return the 0-based index of the record that was found by the seek operation. *dwValue* has different meanings depending on the value of *dwSeekType*.

Before looking at the *dwSeekType* parameter more closely, it is important to point out some characteristics of the seek operation. First, *CeSeekDatabase* searches a database in the order specified by the current sort order. Second, a seek can only be performed on a sorted property value. This means that if you are calling *CeSeekDatabase* to search for some record by value, the value specified in the *dwValue* parameter will only be compared to the database property values that correspond to the current sort order property. Recall these points when tracking down bugs in your database searching code. Programmers just starting to use Windows CE databases make the common mistake of searching for a record containing a particular property when the database is sorted on a different property.

dwSeekType can be one of the following values:

- CEDB_SEEK_CEOID
- CEDB_SEEK_VALUESMALLER
- CEDB_SEEK_VALUEFIRSTEQUAL
- CEDB_SEEK_VALUENEXTEQUAL
- CEDB_SEEK_VALUEGREATER
- CEDB_SEEK_BEGINNING
- CEDB_SEEK_CURRENT
- CEDB_SEEK_END

CEDB_SEEK_CEOID implies that *dwValue* is the object identifier of the record to seek in the database. At first glance, this case might not appear to be particularly useful. If an application already knows the object identifier of the record it is seeking, why would a seek even need to be done? It is important to keep in mind that *CeSeekDatabase* repositions the current record pointer, which indicates which record will be read from the database by the next read operation. So, if the phone list application wanted to read the properties of the record with an object identifier defined as *ceoid*, the application would first have to seek to that record, and then read the record from the database:

```
WORD cProps = 0;
LPBYTE pBuf = NULL;
DWORD cbByte = 0;
if (CeSeekDatabase(hDBase, CEDB_SEEK_CEOID, (DWORD)ceoid,
    &nIndex))
{
  CeReadRecordProps(hBase, CEDB_ALLOWREALLOC, &cProps, NULL,
    &pBuf,&cbByte);
}
```

Calling *CeSeekDatabase* alone will simply point the current record pointer at the record of interest.

The next four *dwSeekType* values indicate that *dwValue* is a pointer to a CEPROPVAL structure that contains the property value for which to seek. CEDB_SEEK_VALUESMALLER says to search the database for the largest value that is smaller than the given value. CEDB_SEEK_VALUEFIRSTEQUAL tells *CeSeekDatabase* to search until it finds the first value equal to that indicated by *dwValue*. CEDB_SEEK_VALUENEXTEQUAL seeks one record forward from the current record position and checks if the property value of that record equals that of *dwValue*. CEDB_SEEK_VALUEGREATER seeks until a record with current sort order property equal to or greater than that of *dwValue* is found. If *CeSeekDatabase* fails with any of these four *dwSeek-Type* values, the function returns zero and leaves the current record pointer at the end of the database.

If you know the index of the record you are seeking in the database, the CEDB_SEEK_BEGINNING option is the one to use. For example, the user interface of the phone list application displays the phone database, sorted by the current sort order, in a list view control. It is convenient to locate the database record corresponding to the current list view selection by 0-based index. Specifying CEDB_SEEK_BEGIN-NING for *dwSeekType* implies that *dwValue* is the number of records to seek, that is, the zero-based index of the database record in the current sort order to be retrieved.

CEDB_SEEK_CURRENT moves the current record pointer forward or backward from the current record position the number of records specified by *dwValue*. If *dwValue* is positive, *CeSeekDatabase* seeks forward. The search is backward if *dwValue* is negative. CEDB_SEEK_

END is similar, except that it always seeks backward from the end of the database. It moves the current record pointer backward the number of records specified in *dwValue*.

In any of the above cases, if *CeSeekDatabase* is successful, it returns the object identifier of the record pointed to by the current record pointer.

The phone list application's Seek menu option brings up a dialog box that allows you to experiment with the *CeSeekDatabase* function. It allows you to specify various *dwSeekType* parameter values as well as property values for which to search. The application then displays the record found in the application window in the Search Results field. In the interest of keeping the phone list application to a reasonable size, this feature only allows you to specify *dwSeekType* values that perform database seeks by value.

Database Enumeration

Suppose you wanted to create a list of all the databases currently contained in the object store of a Windows CE device. Or perhaps you need to determine how much object store memory is being used by all the phone list databases available to a phone list management application. In this section we introduce the concept of *database enumeration*. Database enumeration allows applications to find all databases in the object store, or to find a subset of those databases as defined by a particular database type identifier.

Back when we discussed creating Windows CE databases, we introduced the concept of a database type identifier. This was the application-defined index that was passed as the *dwDbaseType* parameter of *CeCreateDatabase*. This index is used to identify all databases of a particular type. This type index is very important to database enumeration operations.

Database enumeration is done with two functions: *CeFindFirstDatabase* and *CeFindNextDatabase*. The enumeration process starts with a call to *CeFindFirstDatabase* to open an *enumeration context* for the type of database to be enumerated. The enumeration context is a handle through which the operating system can reference all databases with a particular database type identifier. *CeFindNextDatabase* is then called repeatedly to get the object identifier of each database of that type. These functions are analogous to the file system functions *FindFirstFile* and *FindNextFile*.

The function *CeFindFirstDatabase* takes the form:

```
CeFindFirstDatabase(dwDbaseType);
```

The *dwDbaseType* parameter is the database type identifier of interest. This can be any application-defined database type. Note, however, that if you specify zero for *dwDbaseType*, an enumeration context for *all* databases in the object store is returned. If successful, *CeFindFirstDatabase* returns an enumeration context for this database type. If the function fails, it returns INVALID_HANDLE_VALUE.

CeFindNextDatabase looks like this:

```
CeFindNextDatabase(hEnum);
```

hEnum is the enumeration context returned by the *CeFindFirstDatabase* call. This function returns the object identifier of the next enumerated database, or zero if the function fails.

Database enumeration can be used to perform a number of operations in your applications. For example, if you wanted to delete all databases of a particular type, *CeFindNextDatabase* could be used to get the object identifier of each database of that type, and *CeDeleteDatabase* would then delete each of the databases.

At other times, you may wish to determine a particular set of attributes for each database of some type. An example might be getting the name of every database in the object store. Such features would be implemented using the *CeOidGetInfo* function. As an example, let's take a look at how you might get the total amount of memory in bytes in use by databases on a Windows CE device.

```
CEOID oidTemp;
CEOIDINFO oidInfo;
HANDLE hEnum;
DWORD dwBytes;
TCHAR pszText[129];
hEnum = CeFindFirstDatabase(0);
if (INVALID_HANDLE_VALUE!=hEnum)
{
  dwBytes = 0;
  while (oidTemp = CeFindNextDatabase(hEnum))
  {
   CeOidGetInfo(oidTemp, &oidInfo);
   dwBytes += oidInfo.infDatabase.dwSize;
```

```
        }
        CloseHandle(hEnum);
        wsprintf(pszText, TEXT("%ld bytes in use"), dwBytes);
        MessageBox(NULL, pszText,
          TEXT("Database Memory Consumption"), MB_OK);
    }
    else
    {
        MessageBox(NULL, TEXT("Invalid Enumeration Context"),
          TEXT("Enumeration Error"), MB_OK|MB_ICONEXCLAMATION);
    }
```

This sample opens an enumeration context into all of the databases in the object store of the device on which the code is executed by calling *CeFindFirstDatabase* with *dwDbaseType* argument of zero. *CeOidGetInfo* is then called for each database. A running byte count is updated using the size of each enumerated database. The database size is found in the *dwSize* member of the CEDBASEINFO structure returned as part of *oidInfo*. The total byte count is then displayed in a message dialog box.

Database Notifications

The last Windows CE database topic that needs to be covered is database notifications. In all of our examples we have passed NULL to the *hwndNotify* argument of *CeOpenDatabase*. However, this parameter can be used to specify a window that receives notifications whenever another thread of execution modifies the particular database before the thread that opened the database closes it. If the *hwndNotify* parameter is NULL, the thread opening the database is indicating it is not interested in receiving any such notifications.

There are three notifications that can be sent to the *hwndNotify* window. Although called notifications, they are actually Windows CE messages that are posted to the *hwndNotify* window. To respond to them, then, your application needs to include handlers for the ones you are interested in *hwndNotify*'s window procedure. The descriptions of the three notifications (messages) are given in Table 7.4.

The Contacts Database

Perhaps you will recognize this scenario from your college years. (It comes directly from mine.) It's the next to last week of one of your

Table 7.4 Database Notifications

NOTIFICATION NAME	MEANING	WPARAM	LPARAM
DB_CEOID_CHANGED	Object modified	CEOID of	CEOID of modified object modified object's parent
DB_CEOID_CREATED	Object created	CEOID of new object	CEOID of new object's parent
DB_CEOID_RECORD_DELETED	Record deleted	CEOID of deleted	CEOID of Object deleted object's parent

more grueling calculus courses. You've spent the entire time learning how to manually integrate impossibly complex functions that you are convinced you will never encounter in the "real world," using techniques such as the Laplace Transform and integration by parts. Then, almost as an afterthought, your calculus professor makes a brief foray into the subject of how to use an integral table. The chorus of grief is as varied as the students in the classroom, but can be paraphrased something like this: "You mean to tell me we've suffered through this integration business and could have used a cookbook all along?" Prepare for a trip down memory lane. I am about to pull the same thing on you now.

Windows CE provides a predefined database of its own for storing phone number and other personal and business contact information. A number of the applications that are traditionally supplied with Windows CE–based devices use this database. It therefore lives in the Windows CE operating system for all application developers to use. The *contacts database* stores many more useful properties than our phone list database example above. And it provides a complete application programming interface for performing such operations as adding, removing, and modifying information in the database. Given that this rich functionality exists in the operating system for free, why did I just painstakingly guide you through all of the mechanics of programming generic Windows CE databases?

The contacts database is just one example of the type of database that a typical Windows CE application may need to use. Much as an integral table cannot contain all of the cases an engineer might encounter in practice, the built-in features of an operating system like Windows CE cannot anticipate every application that it will be asked to support. It is therefore crucial to have a well-established understanding of the fundamental capabilities of Windows CE in order to confidently approach any new programming challenge.

Applying the experience of our generic phone list application makes understanding the design and features of the contacts database a straightforward task. Since we have successfully explored the mechanics of generic Windows CE databases, the next sections will only briefly cover the highlights of the contacts database. To extend the classroom metaphor, the full details of using the contacts database are left to the student as an exercise!

NOTE
━━━━━ LINK WITH **ADDRSTOR.LIB**

To use the contacts database, your applications must link with **ADDRSTOR.LIB** and include the file **ADDRSTOR.H**.

Address Cards

Windows CE models the concept of a contact as *address cards*. This name is supposedly meant to conjure up the image of cards in a Rolodex. The address card is implemented as a structure with the following definition:

```
typedef struct _AddressCard
{
  SYSTEMTIME stBirthday;
  SYSTEMTIME stAnniversary;
  TCHAR *pszBusinessFax;
  TCHAR *pszCompany;
  TCHAR *pszDepartment;
  TCHAR *pszEmail;
  TCHAR *pszMobilePhone;
  TCHAR *pszOfficeLocation;
  TCHAR *pszPager;
  TCHAR *pszWorkPhone;
  TCHAR *pszTitle;
  / Other properties such as name, address, fax number, etc.
} AddressCard;
```

This structure is the contacts database analog of the PHONERECORD structure in our phone list database example. Each member of the AddressCard structure represents one of the properties in a particular contacts database record.

The properties of address card records are identified by *property tags*. The concept of property tags comes from the Microsoft Messaging Application Programming Interface (MAPI). In reality, though, a property tag is nothing more than a property identifier like PL_LAST-NAME, PL_FIRSTNAME, PL_PHONENUMBER, and PL_DEPT in the phone list application. The property tags for the contacts database all have names of the form HHPR_*. For example, the birthday property has a property identifier HHPR_BIRTHDAY. These identifiers are used to specify the properties that are to be read from or written to records in the contacts database, as we will see a bit later.

Contacts Database Functions

The *ReadRecord* and *WriteRecord* functions in the phone list application were written as function wrappers that hide the internal details of the record data stored in the phone list database. In the same way, the contacts database functions work with AddressCards to allow the application programmer to think of contact information in a more natural way.

For example, to add a new record to the contacts database, an application calls *AddAddressCard*:

```
AddAddressCard(pac, poidCard, pindex);
```

pac is a pointer to the AddressCard structure that contains the contact information to be added to the contacts database. *poidCard* is a pointer to a CEOID that is used by *AddAddressCard* to return the object identifier of the new record if it is successfully added to the contacts database. *pindex* is also a return value indicating the position index of the new record in the database.

In the phone list application example, *WriteRecord* always added a new phone list record that contained data for every property in the record. *AddAddressCard* is more generic in that it allows applications to add records with any subset of AddressCard properties. For this to work, an application must specify which properties are valid for the AddressCard to be added. This is done using the *SetMask* function:

```
SetMask(pac, hhProp);
```

pac is again a pointer to an AddressCard structure. *hhProp* is any of the property tags defined for the contacts database. For example, to add an address card in which only the company and department fields are valid, an application would do the following:

```
AddressCard ac;
CEOID ceoid;
int nIndex;
memset(&ac, 0, sizeof(AddressCard));
ac.pszCompany = TEXT("Acme Widgets");
ac.pszDepartment = TEXT("Bean Counting");
SetMask(&ac, HHPR_COMPANY_NAME);
SetMask(&ac, HHPR_DEPARTMENT_NAME);
/Now we can add the card
AddAddressCard(&ac, &ceoid, &nIndex);*
```

If all AddressCard properties are valid and are to be written to the database record, your application does not have to call *SetMask* for every property. Simply passing zero in the *hhProp* argument tells *SetMask* that all AddressCard properties are valid.

From our understanding of Windows CE databases, we can figure out what is going on inside *AddAddressCard*. *AddAddressCard* uses the mask prepared by the *SetMask* calls to know which values to extract from the AddressCard structure and which property identifiers to use to build up a CEPROPVAL array. As with any Windows CE database, all data read and write transactions ultimately boil down to reading and writing collections of CEPROPVAL structures.

Reading AddressCards is done with the *OpenAddressCard* function:

```
OpenAddressCard(oidCard, pac, uFlags);
```

oidCard is the object identifier of the record to be read. *pac* is a pointer to an AddressCard structure into which *OpenAddressCard* places the contacts properties read from the specified record. *uFlags* can be either OAC_ALLOCATE or zero. OAC_ALLOCATE says that separate memory is allocated for each string property, and the strings are copied from the object store into the particular AddressCard fields. If an application needs to modify the properties in a record, this value must be set.

If *uFlags* is zero, memory is not allocated for the string properties, and the TCHAR* members of the AddressCard record returned by *OpenAddressCard* simply point to the string data in the database. This is the technique to use when the particular AddressCard record is not going to be modified by the application, but simply displayed in the application's user interface. Applications can also use the *GetAddressCardProperties* function to read records from the contacts database.

The Complete Contacts Database API

The contacts database API provides functions for opening and closing the contacts database, as well as reading, writing and modifying AddressCards. In addition, you can use the API to sort the database on the various AddressCard properties and enumerate AddressCards. The complete contacts database API is given in Table 7.5.

Concluding Remarks

In this chapter we introduced the various aspects of programming Windows CE databases. You should now be comfortable creating databases and managing database records from your Windows CE applications. We specifically covered the topics of reading and writing database records, sorting databases, and searching for specific records in a database. The subjects of database notifications and database enumeration were also discussed.

The chapter also provided a brief introduction to the Windows CE contacts database and the contacts database API. This database, which is provided as part of the Windows CE operating system, may often come in handy when you write applications such as address books.

We continue our coverage of Windows CE persistent storage in Chapter 8 with a look at the Windows CE registry.

Table 7.5   The Contacts Database API

FUNCTION	PURPOSE
AddAddressCard	Adds an address card to the contacts database.
CloseAddressBook	Closes the contacts database.
CreateAddressBook	Creates the contacts database if it does not already exist.
DeleteAddressCard	Deletes the specified address card from the contacts database.
FreeAddressCard	Frees memory associated with an address card.
GetAddressCardIndex	Returns the position index of the specified address card in the contacts database.
GetAddressCardOid	Retrieves the object identifier of the address card as specified by its position index.
GetAddressCardProperties	Gets the properties of an address card.
GetColumnProperties	Retrieves the property tags corresponding to the columns by which the contacts database can be sorted.
GetMatchingEntry	Searches the contacts database for an address card with a name property containing the specified search string.
GetNumberOfAddressCards	Returns the number of address cards in the contacts database.
GetPropertyDataStruct	Retrieves a PropertyDataStruct for a specified contacts database property.
GetSortOrder	Returns the current contacts database sort order.
ModifyAddressCard	Changes the contents of an address card.
OpenAddressBook	Opens the contacts database if it exists.
RecountCards	Counts the number of address cards. This is necessary if another application modifies the contacts database while your application has it open.
SetColumnProperties	Specifies the properties on which the contacts database can be sorted.
SetMask	Specifies which properties are assigned in an address card.
SetSortOrder	Sets the contacts database sort order.

CHAPTER 8

Using the Windows CE Registry

T hus far in our investigation of Windows CE persistent storage, we have considered two mechanisms typically used for storing large amounts of data. The Windows CE file system is a useful way to store large amounts of data, such as documents, in a hierarchical directory structure. Windows CE databases are useful for storing and managing large numbers of data records such as phone list or contact information.

But what if your application has the need for small amounts of persistent storage? It would be overkill to create an entire database or directory structure just to keep track of a few numbers or strings.

Additionally, a particular database or file format is generally intended for use by the application that creates it. Applications generally are not prevented from accessing data in files or databases created by other applications. But to do so requires knowledge of a specific file format or database record design.

The Windows CE registry provides a generic mechanism for storing persistent information that is intended to be available on a system-wide basis. The registry has a simple hierarchical structure, and provides an application programming interface that makes it easy for any application on a Windows CE device to find information available to the entire system.

One of the most familiar examples is the use of the registry by Microsoft's Component Object Model (COM) technology. COM uses the registry as a way to, among other things, make information about COM objects available to all interested parties.

AFTER COMPLETING THIS CHAPTER YOU WILL KNOW HOW TO . . .

Program the Windows CE registry

Use the Remote Registry Editor

Registry Basics

Although it is part of the Windows CE object store, the registry is different from the Windows CE file system and databases. The registry does not store data as objects with unique object identifiers. The registry functions do not access data in the registry via a particular CEOID associated with a registry entry. The only similarity between the registry and these other two object store entities is that they are all used to store persistent data in object store RAM.

The Windows CE registry is organized as a hierarchical set of *keys*, *subkeys*, and *values*. Keys and subkeys are the registry analog of directories in the Windows CE file system. Keys can contain one or more subkeys. Keys and subkeys can contain one or more values, which are used to store the actual data contained in the registry.

Much as Windows CE databases can be assigned an application-specific database type, registry keys can be given a *class name*. Such a class name can be used to provide further distinction between registry keys.

At the root of the Windows CE registry hierarchy are three *primary keys*: HKEY_LOCAL_MACHINE, HKEY_CLASSES_ROOT, and HKEY_CURRENT_USER. Every registry subkey and value falls under one of these three primary keys.

Just as Windows CE represents files and databases as handles, there is also a handle data type for registry keys called HKEY. Many of the registry functions identify the key or subkey on which they are to operate by means of an HKEY handle.

The Windows CE registry can be used to store data of the following types: binary, DWORD, null-terminated Unicode string, Unicode symbolic link, or resource. The various registry functions refer to these data types by the symbols shown in Table 8.1. We'll see these data type values in the context of the various registry functions later.

Viewing the Windows CE Registry

The Remote Object Viewer allows you to view files and databases on a Windows CE device or in the emulation environment; similarly, the Windows CE Toolkit provides a Remote Registry Editor, which allows you to explore the registry in the emulation environment or on an actual Windows CE device. It also allows you to create, delete, and modify registry subkeys and values.

Table 8.1   Registry API Data Type Symbols

SYMBOL	MEANING
REG_BINARY	Binary data.
REG_DWORD	A 32-bit number.
REG_DWORD_LITTLE_ENDIAN	A 32-bit number in little endian format, i.e., the most significant byte of each word is the high-order byte.
REG_DWORD_BIG_ENDIAN	A 32-bit number in big endian format, i.e., the most significant byte of each word is the low-order byte.
REG_EXPAND_SZ	A null-terminated Unicode string that contains unexpanded references to environment variables, such as %PATH%.
REG_SZ	A null-terminated Unicode string.
REG_MULTI_SZ	An array of null-terminated Unicode strings. The array itself is terminated by two null characters.
REG_LINK	A Unicode symbolic link.
REG_RESOURCE_LIST	A device driver resource list.
REG_NONE	No defined data type.

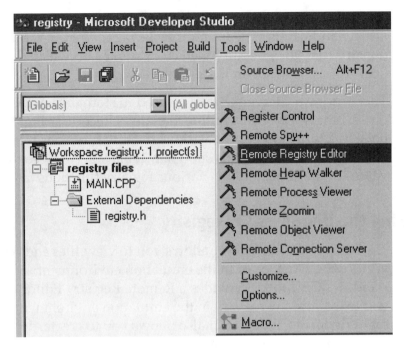

Figure 8.1   Opening the Remote Registry Editor.

You access the remote Registry Editor by choosing the Remote Registry Editor menu option from the Tools menu in the Microsoft Developer Studio development environment (Figure 8.1).

The Remote Registry Editor looks and works much like the Windows NT Registry Editor called regedit. In fact, the remote Registry Editor has all of the functionality of regedit and more.

When the Remote Registry Editor first appears, it contains two tree view nodes in the left-hand pane, labeled My Computer and My Emulation (Figure 8.2). The My Computer item is the root of all of the registry keys on the Windows NT machine on which you are running Microsoft Developer Studio. You can browse these keys and delete, add, or modify subkeys and values just as you would with regedit. Any changes that you make to the registry keys under My Computer are made in the registry of your Windows NT host machine.

The My Emulation tree view node is the root of all the registry keys contained by your Windows CE emulation object store. You can therefore make any modifications you like to your emulation registry by editing the subkeys and values under My Emulation.

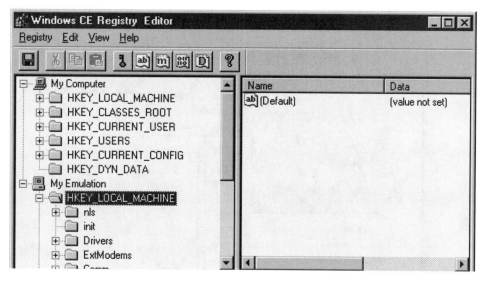

Figure 8.2 The Remote Registry Editor.

The Remote Registry Editor makes it easy for you to modify the Windows CE emulation registry manually. You will very often find yourself wanting to modify the registry in this way, particularly when debugging applications that use the registry. It would be a bit tedious if you could only edit the registry programmatically.

Adding and Removing Subkeys

You add and remove registry subkeys via the Remote Registry Editor just as you would with regedit on Windows NT.

For example, let's say you want to add a subkey called Applications under the My Emulation\HKEY_LOCAL_MACHINE key that is shown in Figure 8.2. To do this, expand the My Emulation node, and then expand the HKEY_LOCAL_MACHINE node. To add the Applications subkey, tap the HKEY_LOCAL_MACHINE key icon so that it is selected, and then select the New Key menu option from the Edit menu as shown in Figure 8.3.

As a result of this operation, the New Key dialog box shown in Figure 8.4 appears. Type "Applications", the name of the new subkey, in the edit field in this dialog box and press OK. The new subkey is then created under the HKEY_LOCAL_MACHINE key as shown in Figure 8.5.

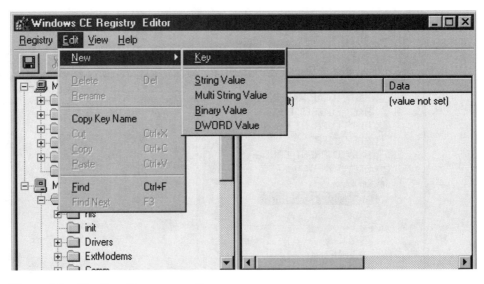

Figure 8.3 The New Key menu option.

To delete a subkey, simply tap on the subkey icon and choose the Delete option from the Remote Registry Editor Edit menu. Alternatively, pressing the Delete key will also delete the selected subkey.

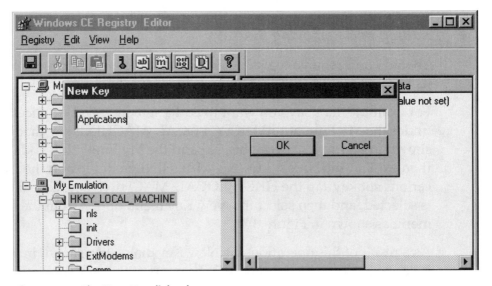

Figure 8.4 The New Key dialog box.

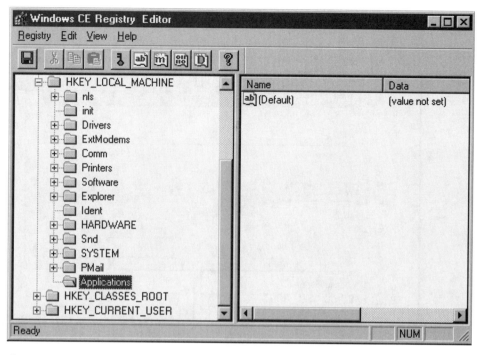

Figure 8.5 The newly created Applications subkey.

Adding and Removing Subkey Values

Registry values are added to the registry (for either Windows NT or CE emulation) in much the same way as subkeys are added. Instead of selecting the New Key menu option, you choose one of the other four New menu options (see Figure 8.3). Each of these options specifies that you want to create a value under the currently selected registry subkey. The data type of the new value is the type specified by the selected menu option.

For example, if you want to add a DWORD value called AppCount to the Applications subkey we created in the previous section, select the Applications and then select the New DWORD Value menu option from the Edit menu. The dialog box shown in Figure 8.6 will appear. Type the name of the new value and the initial value it contains in the corresponding text fields as shown. Press the OK button, and the new value appears in the right-hand pane of the Remote Registry Editor as shown in Figure 8.7.

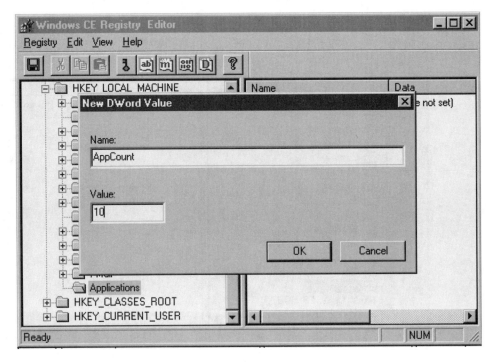

Figure 8.6   The new DWORD value dialog box.

Like registry subkeys, registry values are deleted by selecting the particular value and then choosing the Delete menu option from the Edit menu. Alternatively, pressing the Delete key will also delete the selected value.

The Remote Registry Editor also contains menu options for copying and renaming subkeys and values, as well as for generating registry files from the contents of the registry.

A Note on Registry Function Return Values

The various Windows CE registry API functions return ERROR_SUCCESS if they succeed. If a particular function fails, you might expect to call *GetLastError* in order to get additional clues as to why your function call failed.

Unfortunately, the registry functions do not set the current error code on failure with a call to *SetLastError*. Therefore, calling *GetLastError* tells you nothing in these cases.

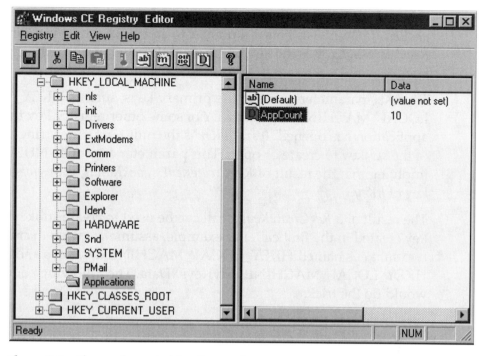

Figure 8.7 The newly created AppCount value.

The possible error return values are those defined in WINERROR.H. You can use the *FormatMessage* function with the FORMAT_MES-SAGE_FROM_SYSTEM flag set in the *dwFlags* parameter to get the message text of the error.

Alternatively, you can use my preferred (and quicker) method: Keep WINERROR.H open in your editor while debugging your registry calls and search for the error codes manually!

Creating and Opening Registry Keys

The Windows CE registry API provides functions for both creating new registry keys and opening existing keys.

An application creates a registry key with *RegCreateKeyEx*. This function will create a new key in the registry if the specified key does not exist. If the key already exists, *RegCreateKeyEx* opens the key.

```
RegCreateKeyEx(hKey, lpszSubKey, Reserved, lpszClass,
   dwOptions, samDesired, lpSecurityAttributes,
   phkResult, lpdwDisposition);
```

It is easiest to discuss this function if we start by describing the *phkResult* parameter. This is a pointer to an HKEY, which is returned by *RegCreateKeyEx*. It is the key of the newly created or opened registry key.

The *hKey* parameter is one of the primary keys, such as HKEY_ LOCAL_MACHINE, or the HKEY of some other registry key that the application has opened. *lpszSubKey* is the null-terminate string name of the subkey to create or open. This parameter cannot be NULL, implying that the result of *RegCreateKeyEx*, *phkResult*, is always a sub-key of *hKey*.

The result of a *RegCreateKeyEx* call can be used to create subkeys of the key created in the first call. For example, assume we wish to create the two subkeys named HKEY_LOCAL_MACHINE\MyKeys and HKEY_LOCAL_MACHINE\MyKeys\Data. The following code would do the trick:

```
HKEY hMyKeys, hData;
//Create HKEY_LOCAL_MACHINE\MyKeys
RegCreateKeyEx(
  HKEY_LOCAL_MACHINE, //Primary key
  TEXT("MyKeys"),    //Subkey Name
  ...,            //Parameters we've
          //yet to discuss
  &hMyKeys,       //i.e., phkResult
  ...);
//Using previous result, create the key
//HKEY_LOCAL_MACHINE\MyKeys\Data
RegCreateKeyEx(
  hMyKeys,       //HKEY_LOCAL_MACHINE\MyKeys
  TEXT("Data"),    //Data subbkey
  ...,
  &hData,        //Handle to Data subkey
  ...);
```

The *Reserved* parameter of *RegCreateKeyEx* is just that, reserved for future use by Windows CE. This parameter must be set to zero.

lpszClassName is a null-terminated string containing the class of the key to be opened or created. If you are not interested in assigning a class name, this parameter can be NULL.

The parameters *dwOptions*, *samDesired*, and *lpSecurityAttributes* are ignored. *dwOptions* and *samDesired* should be zero, and *lpSecurityAttributes* should be NULL.

The final parameter, *lpdwDisposition*, is a DWORD pointer used as a return value which specifies whether the function created a new key or simply opened an existing key. The possible values returned are REG_CREATED_NEW_KEY and REG_OPENED_EXISTING_KEY.

Existing registry keys can alternatively be opened using *RegOpenKeyEx*:

```
RegOpenKeyEx(hKey, lpszSubKey, ulOptions, samDesired,
  phkResult);
```

As with *RegCreateKeyEx*, *hKey*, and *lpszSubKey* are the key and subkey of the key to open. In the case of *RegOpenKeyEx*, however, *lpszSubKey* can be NULL. *ulOptions* and *samDesired* are reserved and must be zero. *phkResult* is the same as in *RegCreateKeyEx*. It returns a handle to the opened key if *RegOpenKeyEx* is successful.

Reading and Writing Registry Values

The real data stored by the Windows CE registry is kept in the various *values* contained in each registry key. As described above, registry values can store data of a variety of types, making registry storage very flexible.

A registry key value is like a data slot. Each key can have one or more values for storing information. An application can read and write data from existing registry values, or it can create new values for its purposes. In either case, the application uses *RegSetValueEx*. This function assigns data to a specified registry value. If the value does not exist, it is created. The syntax of *RegSetValueEx* is:

```
RegSetValueEx(hKey, lpszValueName, Reserved, dwType,
  lpData, cbData);
```

hKey is the key that contains the value to which data is assigned. *lpszValueName* is the null-terminated Unicode string name of the value to set. *Reserved*, again, is reserved for later versions of Windows CE and as such must be set to zero. *dwType* is one of the data type specifiers. It tells *RegSetValueEx* what type of data is being placed in the registry value. *lpData* is a constant BYTE pointer containing the data to be assigned to the value. *cbData* contains the size, or length in bytes, of the data in *lpData*.

As an example, let's say that we wish to create a registry key under the HKEY_LOCAL_MACHINE primary key called "Test." We then wish to create 20 values in that key named Value0, Value1, and so on up to Value19. Additionally, we want to assign each of these values the DWORD integer corresponding to the number in the value name. For example, the number in Value0 will be 0 and the number in Value1 will be 1.

To accomplish this, our application would do the following:

```
HKEY hKeyTest;
DWORD dwDisp, dwSize;
TCHAR pszValue[MAX_STRING_LENGTH];
int i;
if (ERROR_SUCCESS != RegCreateKeyEx(HKEY_LOCAL_MACHINE,
    TEXT("Test"), NULL, NULL, 0, 0,
     NULL, &hKeyTest, &dwDisp))
{
   MessageBox(NULL, TEXT("Could Not Create Key"),
    TEXT("Registry Error"), MB_ICONEXCLAMATION|MB_OK);
}
else
{
   for (i=0; i<20; i++)
   {
   dwSize = sizeof(DWORD);
   wsprintf(pszValue, TEXT("Value%d"), i);
   if (ERROR_SUCCESS != RegSetValueEx(hKeyTest,
    pszValue, NULL, REG_DWORD, (CONST BYTE*)&i,
     dwSize))
   {
    MessageBox(NULL, TEXT("Could Not Set Value"),
     pszValue, MB_ICONEXCLAMATION|MB_OK);
   }
   }    //End of for i loop
}
```

The first thing we do is attempt to create the HKEY_LOCAL_MACHINE\Test registry key. If this *RegCreateKeyEx* call fails, we display a message box to that effect. If the create was successful, we proceed to the for loop, which sets the 20 registry values. *RegSetValueEx* creates each of the registry values if they don't already exist in the registry. The *RegSetValueEx* call passes REG_DWORD as the *dwType* parameter, indicating that the value to be written is a DWORD. The name of each registry value is constructed with the *wsprintf* call.

Reading a registry value is done with the function *RegQueryValueEx*:

```
RegQueryValueEx(hKey, lpszValueName, lpReserved,
  lpType, lpData, lpcbData);
```

hKey and *lpszValueName* have the same meaning as in *RegSetValueEx*. *lpReserved* is a reserved DWORD pointer and must be NULL. *lpType* is a DWORD pointer that contains the registry value's data type. *lpData* is a BYTE pointer in which the function returns the value data. *lpcbData* is a DWORD pointer that contains the length in bytes of the data to be read from the registry value.

The *lpcbData* parameter deserves some illumination. Otherwise it will haunt your every registry query. You must assign the number of bytes to be read from the particular registry value to the DWORD pointed to by the *lpcbData* parameter. So far so good. But *RegQueryValueEx* uses this parameter as a return value as well. It returns the actual number of bytes read from the registry key, which may indeed be different from the number you said to read. For example, you may expect a string you are querying to be 50 bytes long. If the string is really 15 bytes long, *RegQueryValueEx* will return 15 in *lpcbData*.

This still sounds OK? Well, maybe, until you try using *RegQueryValueEx* to read multiple registry keys in a loop *and do not reassign lpcsData to the number of bytes you want to read for each query.*

Let's look at the following example:

```
int i;
DWORD dwSize;
DWORD dwType;
TCHAR pszText[128];
dwSize = 128;
dwType = REG_SZ;
for (i=0; i<5; I++)
{
  wsprintf(pszText, TEXT("Value%ld"), i);
  RegQueryValueEx(
   hKeyTest,
   pszValue,
   NULL,
   &dwType,
   (LPBYTE)pszText,
   &dwSize);
  //Do something with dwValue
}
```

You expect this code to read five Unicode strings of length 128 bytes from five registry values named Value0 through Value4.

But what if any of the actual strings is less than 128 bytes long? *Reg-QueryValueEx* will return the real length of that string in *dwSize*. The next *RegQueryValueEx* call will then say to read only as many bytes as were in the last string. At this point, you can count on all the rest of the values read to be completely unreliable. Believe me, the bugs that result from such an oversight are very difficult to track down.

The moral of this story is: Set the *lpcbData* value properly for each and every call to *RegQueryValueEx*.

The *RegQueryInfoKey* Function

There is one more registry function related to reading information about registry keys. Whereas *RegQueryValueEx* reads the actual value data from a specified registry key value, *RegQueryInfoKey* allows your application to determine the number of subkeys and values that a particular registry key contains. This becomes important when you need to iterate over a set of subkeys or values, which is the subject of the next section.

RegQueryInfoKey also does other work for you, such as determining the class name of the particular key and the length of that class name, as well as the maximum subkey, class, and value name lengths of all subkeys and values associated with the queried key.

The syntax of *RegQueryInfoKey* is:

```
RegQueryInfoKey(hKey, lpClass, lpcbClass, lpReserved,
   lpcSubkeys, lpcbMaxSubKeyLen, lpcbMaxClassLen, lpcValues,
     lpcbMaxValueNameLen, lpcbMaxValueData,
       lpcbSecurityDescriptor, lpftLastWriteTime);
```

hKey is the HKEY of the key to be queried. *lpClass* is a Unicode string buffer used by the function to return the class of *hKey*. This parameter can be NULL if your application is not interested in class name information. *lpcbClass* is a DWORD pointer used to return the length of the string returned in *lpClass*. *lpcbClass* should be NULL if *lpClass* is NULL. *lpReserved* is reserved and should be NULL.

The next parameter is *lpcSubkeys*. This is a DWORD pointer in which *RegQueryInfoKey* returns the number of subkeys contained by *hKey*. This parameter can be NULL if this information is not of interest. *lpcb-MaxSubKeyLen* returns the length in characters of the longest subkey name. For some mysterious reason, this count does *not* include the null-terminating character. Compare this with the *lpcbData* parameter of *RegQueryValueEx*, which does include the null-terminator in cases where it is used to read string values from the registry.

lpcbMaxClassLen returns the length of the longest class name of any of the subkeys contained by *hKey*. No null-terminator here, either. Both *lpcbMaxSubKeyLen* and *lpcbMaxClassLen* can be NULL.

lpcValues returns the number of values contained by the queried key. This can be NULL if you are not interested in this information. *lpcbMaxValueNameLen* returns the length of the longest value name string. This parameter can be NULL, and again, does not include the null-terminator in its string character length count.

lpcbMaxValueData and *lpcbSecurityDescriptor* are not used. They should therefore be set to NULL.

Finally, *lpftlastWriteTime* is not used and can be NULL. Under Windows NT, this parameter could be used to determine the last time a key or any of its values were changed. Windows CE, however, does not provide this feature.

A typical use of *RegQueryInfoKey* is to determine the number of subkeys and values contained by a particular registry key. To continue our example of the HKEY_LOCAL_MACHINE\Test key, let's write the code necessary to find the number of subkeys and values in this key:

```
HKEY hKeyTest;
DWORD dwSubKeys, dwValues;
RegOpenKeyEx(HKEY_LOCAL_MACHINE, TEXT("Test"),
   0, 0, &hKeyTest);
RegQueryInfoKey(hKeyTest, NULL, NULL, NULL,
   &dwSubKeys, NULL, NULL, &dwValues, NULL,
   NULL, NULL, NULL);
```

We first open the HKEY_LOCAL_MACHINE\Test registry key. The *RegQueryInfoKey* call then gets the number of subkeys in *dwSubKeys*, and the number of values in *dwValues*.

Notice all of the NULL parameter values. In this example we are not interested in the class names, class name lengths, value name lengths, and the other sundry things that this function can return. Therefore, the parameters corresponding to these pieces of information are all NULL.

Now that our applications can get subkey and value counts, they have all the information they need to iterate over subkeys and values, reading or writing data as needed. All we need to do is introduce the registry enumeration functions.

Enumerating Registry Keys and Values

Enumeration is the process of iterating over a set of registry keys or values and extracting information about each one as it is iterated.

The *RegEnumValue* Function

The first registry enumeration function is *RegEnumValue*. This function is useful, for example, inside of loops where your application wants to read the data from every value in a subkey. Given the handle to an open key, an application can use this function to iterate over all values of that key, reading their data values, without knowing the names of the values being read. In fact, *RegEnumValue* reads both the value data and value name for you.

The syntax of *RegEnumValue* is:

```
RegEnumValue(hKey, dwIndex, lpValueName,
  lpcbValueName, lpReserverd, lpType,
    lpData, lpcbData);
```

hKey is the handle of the open key whose values are being read. *dwIndex* is the index of the value to retrieve. The name of the value corresponding to *dwIndex* is returned in the *lpValueName* parameter.

lpcbValueName is a pointer to a DWORD that contains the size of the *lpValueName* buffer. This parameter requires all of the caveats pointed out with the *lpcbData* parameter of *RegQueryValueEx*. Specifically, you specify the number of bytes you think the *lpValueName* string will be, and *RegEnumValue* returns the actual length through the same parameter. Hence, you need to reset this value appropriately for every *RegEnumValue* call. To further complicate matters, when you specify a value in *lpcbValueName*, you must take into account the null-terminating character of the *lpValueName* string that will be returned. But the value of *lpcbValueName* returned by *RegEnumValue* does not contain the null-terminating character.

The *lpReserved* parameter should again be NULL. *lpType* returns the type of data in the registry value being enumerated.

lpData points to the data read from the registry value. Finally, *lpcbData* is used both to pass in the expected number of bytes to be read, and to return the actual number of bytes returned in *lpData*. The same caveats apply here as with the *lpcbData* parameter of *RegQueryValueEx*.

You use *RegEnumValue* by initially setting *dwIndex* to zero for the first call of the function, and then incrementing it for each successive *RegEnumValue* call. Let's extend our previous example. The code below shows how to read the number of values associated with the key HKEY_LOCAL_MACHINE\Test as before. It then iterates over all of the registry values and reads their contents:

```
#define MAX_STRING_LENGTH 129
HKEY hKeyTest;
DWORD dwIndex;     //Loop index
DWORD dwValueIndex; //Index of value to read
DWORD dwValues, dwSubKeys; //Number of values, subkeys
DWORD dwSize;      //Size of data returned by
           //RegEnumValue, i.e., the
           //lpcbData parameter
DWORD dwSizeValue;  //Size of the value name string
           //read, i.e., the RegEnumValue
           //lpcbValueName parameter
RegOpenKeyEx(HKEY_LOCAL_MACHINE, TEXT("Test"),
  0, 0, &hKeyText);
if (ERROR_SUCCESS == RegQueryInfoKey(hKeyTest,NULL,
  NULL, NULL, &dwSubKeys, NULL, NULL, &dwValues,
   NULL, NULL, NULL, NULL))
{
  dwValueIndex = 0; //Init to zero to read first value
  for (dwIndex=0; dwIndex<dwValues; dwIndex++)
  {
   dwSizeValue = MAX_STRING_LENGTH;
   dwSize = sizeof(DWORD);
   if (ERROR_SUCCESS==RegEnumValue(
    hKeyTest, dwKeyIndex++,pszValue,
     &dwSizeValue, NULL, &dwType,
      (LPBYTE)&dwValue, &dwSize))
   {
    //Do something with the data
    //read in dwValue
   }
  }       //End of for dwIndex loop
}         //End of if (ERROR_SUCCESS==RegQueryInfoKey)
         //statement
RegCloseKey(hKeyTest);     //Close the key
```

The first part of this example is essentially the same as in the previous example. After opening the registry key HKEY_LOCAL_MACHINE\

Test, we call *RegQueryInfoKey* to determine the number of values in the key.

The code then reads each of the registry values with a call to *RegEnum-Value*. The for loop iterates over *dwValues*, the number of registry values as determined by the *RegQueryInfoKey* call. Notice that *dwValueIndex* is initialized to zero, and then incremented with every *RegEnumValue* call. This ensures that each registry key value is read in order.

Also, *dwSizeValue* and *dwSize* are reset after every *RegEnumValue* call. Recall that the *lpcbValueName* and *lpcbData* parameters of *RegEnum-Value* are used by the function as return values, and, therefore, the values you initially set may be gone.

At the end we close the key with *RegCloseKey*:

```
RegCloseKey(hKey);
```

The *RegCloseKey* function simply closes the open registry key indicated by the *hKey* parameter.

The *RegEnumKeyEx* Function

The second registry enumeration function is *RegEnumKeyEx*. You can think of it as the subkey analog of *RegEnumValue*. Whereas *RegEnum-Value* is used to extract data and other properties from values associated with registry subkeys, *RegEnumKeyEx* extracts information about the subkeys of a specified registry key. The parameters of this function are also analogous to those for *RegEnumValue*.

```
RegEnumKeyEx(hKey, dwIndex, lpName, lpcbName, lpReserved,
    lpClass, lpcbClass, lpftLastWriteTime);
```

hKey is the key whose subkeys are being enumerated. *dwIndex* represents the index of the subkey to enumerate. *lpName* is a Unicode string buffer that will return the name of the subkey enumerated. *lpcbName* works just as it does in all the other registry functions where we've seen it. The expected size of *lpName* goes in, the real size comes out. It's up to your application to make sure it is always initialized properly. *lpReserved* is reserved and must be NULL.

RegEnumKeyEx can return registry subkey class information. The *lpClass* and *lpcbClass* parameters are used for this purpose. *lpClass* is a Unicode string pointer that contains the class name of the enumerated key when the function returns. *lpcbClass* is a pointer to a DWORD containing the length of *lpClass*. The same caveats about *lpcbName* apply to *lpcbClass*: It is used as both an input and a return parameter. If your application does not use class information, simply set *lpClass* and *lpcb-Class* to NULL.

The final parameter, *lpftLastWriteTime*, is not used under Windows CE. You can therefore set it to NULL.

RegEnumKeyEx is typically used to read through a hierarchy of registry keys and subkeys. *RegQueryInfoKey* gets the number of subkeys. Each of these subkeys is then enumerated with *RegEnumKeyEx* and *RegEnumValue*.

NOTE
▬▬ Be Careful During Key Enumeration

Your applications should not perform any operation that changes the number of sub-keys or values of a registry key while it is being enumerated. Both *RegEnumValue* and *RegEnumKeyEx* use the index of the key or value being enumerated. Changing the number of subkeys or values will throw any iterative enumeration off and lead to unexpected results.

Deleting Registry Keys and Values

The last thing to know about the registry is how to delete keys and values. The registry API provides two functions, *RegDeleteKey* and *RegDeleteValue*, for these purposes.

RegDeleteKey deletes a specified registry and all of its values. It will not delete all of the subkeys contained in the specified subkey. As with directories in the file system, your applications must iterate through the entire subkey hierarchy of a particular key in order to delete all of its subkeys and their values.

The syntax of *RegDeleteKey* is:

```
RegDeleteKey(hKey, lpSubKey);
```

hKey is the handle of an open key, or one of the three primary keys. *lp-SubKey* is the Unicode string name of the subkey to delete. This parameter cannot be NULL. As described above, *RegDeleteKey* will not delete keys that contain subkeys.

So, in order to delete our HKEY_LOCAL_MACHINE\Test subkey, we would could write the following:

```
RegDeleteKey(HKEY_LOCAL_MACHINE, TEXT("Test"));
```

But note that the following cannot be done (assume the *hKeyTest* is the open HKEY of the HKEY_LOCAL_MACHINE\Test subkey):

```
RegDeleteKey(hKeyTest, NULL);
```

Deleting a value is done with *RegDeleteValue*:

```
RegDeleteValue(hKey, lpValueName);
```

As with *RegDeleteKey*, *hKey* is one of the primary keys or a handle to an open subkey. *lpValueName* is the Unicode string name of the value to be deleted from this subkey.

The Registry Sample Application

The sample application for this chapter is nothing to write home about. It simply packages all of the examples we discussed in this chapter into a Windows CE application. All of the registry functionality it includes is done in *WinMain* before the application even hits its message loop.

The sample creates our favorite HKEY_LOCAL_MACHINE\Test subkey and twenty values. It then queries the subkey for the number of values it contains, and then enumerates each of these values, adding the registry name and value to a list box.

The application also shows how to create and enumerate nested subkeys and values. It also creates the HKEY_LOCAL_MACHINE\Test\SubKey0 and HKEY_LOCAL_ MACHINE\Test\SubKey1 subkeys. It then adds two Unicode string values to each of these subkeys. Finally, the application shows you how to read a hierarchy of nested subkey values using *RegEnumKeyEx* and *RegEnumValue*.

The user interface of this application is very basic (Figure 8.8). It has an Exit button in the main application window for terminating the application. It also includes a list box for displaying the values read by the application from the Windows CE registry.

All of the source code and the project files for building this application can be found on the companion CD in the directory \Samples\ registry.

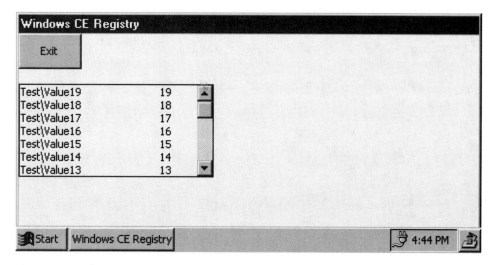

Figure 8.8 The Registry sample application.

Concluding Remarks

In Part II, we have covered how to program the various persistent storage features available under Windows CE. You can now write applications capable of taking advantage of the Windows CE file system and the registry. For more complex data storage needs, your applications can create their own custom databases.

If you stopped reading at this point, you would be well equipped to solve most Windows CE application programming problems. You know all about persistent storage now, and Part I presented the most common application user interface components. You could therefore begin writing applications capable of storing user information and interacting with users.

But most companies building Windows CE–based software and hardware hope to attract customers with features such as nontraditional user interfaces and desktop connectivity. So, up to this point, you really only have half of the Windows CE story. In the next sections we discuss more advanced user interface programming techniques, as well as the area of desktop connectivity.

PART THREE

Windows CE User Interface Programming

Microsoft has big plans for Windows CE. The company hopes to make Windows CE become for consumer electronics what Windows 98 and Windows NT have become for personal computers. The Microsoft vision puts Windows CE on everything from handheld computing devices to Internet-enabled telephones. Although you shouldn't exactly count on (let alone want) Windows CE to toast your bread in the morning, you can expect a growing number of consumer electronics companies to market devices driven by the Windows CE operating system.

Many have compared this phase of the technology revolution to the introduction of the first personal computers. To their way of thinking, the growth of handheld and mobile computing devices and the introduction of new sophisticated consumer devices is the next "paradigm shift" the computer industry has been waiting for.

Along with this wave of innovation in product and software design has come the usual army of designers. These are the folks that are tasked by companies to design the user interfaces for next generation products.

Using such nontechnical personnel who are dedicated exclusively to designing the look and feel of Windows CE applications is usually justifiable. Someone needs to constantly be interacting with a product's potential user community to try and figure out what consumers want from a particular Windows CE device or application.

A second argument usually given for hiring user interface designers goes something like this: Since many companies are designing devices intended for a consumer audience (a polite way of saying non–PC-savvy users), this new breed of Windows CE-based devices must first and foremost *not look like PCs*.

This is generally woefully interpreted to mean, "make the user interface look as different from the traditional Windows user interface as possible." Unfortunately, this often leads companies to release products with user interfaces that make their products *more difficult to use than the PC.*

While many visual improvements on the standard Windows CE interface components are indeed useful in order to more clearly convey the meaning of various user interface elements, many Windows CE user interfaces end up just as cluttered, busy, and confusing as the desktop applications they were meant to improve upon.

Furthermore, those improvements often come at enormous software development cost. One of the largest mistakes being made today by companies pursuing their fortunes through Windows CE is to adamantly insist that the wishes and visions of interface design teams be realized at any cost.

Windows CE is nothing more than a big piece of software. Like any piece of software, there are things Windows CE can do and things it can't. There are things it can do easily, and things it can be made to do with lots and lots of ugly application code. Of all the people in your organization, no one understands the strengths and limitations of Windows CE better than your software engineering staff.

Part III of this book focuses on the vast subject of implementing Windows CE user interfaces and controls that look different from the standard Windows CE model. The focus will be on features provided by Windows CE that allow application programmers to customize the look and feel of the various parts of a user interface. Like all the other chapters in this book, the chapters in this section are primarily intended for Windows CE software developers.

However, if there is one part of this book that I recommend be read by project management, application developers, and user interface designers alike, it is this one. If your entire organization understands the limits and abilities of Windows CE, more realistic user interface designs and more realistic development schedules will result. This ultimately means that you will do what so few companies so far have done: release a Windows CE–based product into the marketplace.

A final word, and then it's off the soapbox and back into programming: If you are in charge of a Windows CE development project, involve your software engineers in the user interface design process from day one. And heed their words if they say certain things can't be done; what they generally mean is that they can't be done before your competition begins shipping.

What We Will Learn

In the following chapters, we will cover the following Windows CE features for implementing a custom user interface. The order in which they are presented follows the progression of simplest feature to most complex. The features covered are:

- Owner draw controls
- Customizing the application's main window class
- The Windows CE custom draw service
- Implementing custom controls
- Window subclassing

This section also includes chapters on programming the Windows CE HTML Viewer control, and some of the Palm-size PC input techniques such as the rich ink control and the voice API.

We begin in the next chapter with a discussion of owner draw control techniques. This discussion will focus on applying these techniques to owner draw buttons.

CHAPTER 9

Owner Draw Controls and Custom Window Classes

T he easiest way to change the appearance of a Windows CE control is to make the control *owner draw*. An owner draw control is a control whose parent window, not the control itself, takes responsibility for creating the physical appearance of the control.

A number of Windows CE controls support the owner draw feature. The techniques for programming owner draw controls is the same for any supported control. This chapter therefore presents these techniques in the context of owner draw buttons.

Why Focus on Owner Draw Buttons?

Of all of the controls that can be used in Windows CE applications, push buttons are probably the most common. Buttons appear everywhere. They fill dialog boxes, letting users choose between various application feature options. Buttons are universal in providing the OK-Cancel choices for committing user input. Buttons send our e-mail and help us navigate around Web pages in Web browser software.

Given how common this control is in applications, it is no wonder that most Windows CE software vendors are interested in changing the

Other Windows CE Owner Draw Controls

The concepts presented in this chapter can be applied to more than just owner draw buttons. Several other controls in Windows CE, such as the list view control and the tab control, to mention a few, support the owner draw functionality.

For example, a tab control created with the TCS_OWNERDRAWFIXED style sends WM_DRAWITEM messages to its parent just like owner draw buttons do. The DRAWITEMSTRUCT structure passed with each message contains information about the individual tab control items. The owner window can use this information to draw the tab items any way it pleases.

The Windows CE controls that support owner draw functionality are the header control, list view control, status bar control, tab bar control, and, of course, the button control.

basic appearance of the button control to differentiate their user interfaces from those of their competitors.

Fortunately, modifying the appearance of button controls is relatively simple. Windows CE, like its Win32 desktop relatives, provides this feature with a programming technique called *owner draw buttons*. With an owner draw button, as with regular push buttons, all of the messaging behavior such as detecting stylus taps and generating WM_COMMAND messages is taken care of for you by Windows CE. But all aspects of the appearance of an owner draw button must be implemented by the owner of the button. Hence the name owner draw button.

The basic concept of owner draw buttons is one that will already be familiar to the more experienced Windows programmers who read this book. But it is presented here nonetheless for a variety of reasons.

First, organizations that are developing Windows CE–based products are almost universally consumed with a passion for making their user interfaces look like anything but a desktop PC. Therefore, it is useful to review even the most basic techniques for customizing an application's look and feel.

Second, the details of owner draw buttons may be unfamiliar to application programmers who come to Windows CE with lots of experience programming with the Microsoft Foundation Classes. This chapter, like Chapters 2 and 3, is partly motivated by a desire to familiarize such programmers with key Windows CE features at the API level.

And third, not everyone is familiar with every traditional Windows programming technique. Many Windows CE software developers come from embedded systems backgrounds. They often need to understand Windows CE programming from both a systems and an applications level. Such readers can benefit from a description of the basics.

AFTER COMPLETING THIS CHAPTER YOU WILL KNOW HOW TO . . .

Use owner draw buttons in your applications

Use Windows CE timers

Draw graphics using offscreen bitmaps

Design custom window classes

The Example Application

The example application demonstrating the concepts presented in this chapter is found in \Samples\kiosk on the companion CD. The executable is called KIOSK.EXE.

This application attempts to demonstrate what the front end of a kiosk-style Windows CE device might look like. A common example of a kiosk familiar to most people is the bank automatic teller machine. A kiosk can be described as a dedicated single-purpose device that performs one service for a user. Other examples include the computerized video catalogs that are common in many movie rental chains or those do-it-yourself photo enlargers that are making their way into photo finishing shops.

KIOSK.EXE is an example bank ATM user interface. The user's choices are represented on the screen as owner draw buttons. The main application window and the secondary window that contains the owner draw buttons are made to look different from standard Windows CE windows. This is done by customizing certain aspects of the window classes that govern these windows.

In addition to providing insight into owner draw buttons and custom window classes, this example will also provide a review of some important graphics functions of the Windows CE Graphics, Windowing, and Event Subsystem.

NOTE
THIS CHAPTER CONTAINS TWO SAMPLE APPLICATIONS

This chapter actually contains two sample applications. KIOSK.EXE is the main one, demonstrating the entire kiosk user interface. \Samples\button contains the source code for the short owner draw button example, BUTTON.EXE, shown in Figures 9.1 and 9.2.

The Anatomy of a Windows CE Control

Understanding owner draw buttons and how to use them will be easier if we first look at how Windows CE controls such as buttons are implemented.

In each of the sample applications that we have encountered in this book, we have created and registered a window class. This window class has described some of the visual aspects of the main application window, as well as the behavior of the main window by means of the window procedure assigned to the window class. In each of the sample applications, we have created just one instance of this window class. But there is nothing stopping us from using this main window's window class to create multiple instances of the window class, each with a different set of window styles, dimensions, window caption text, and the like.

Windows CE controls are used in exactly this way. Each control in a Windows CE application is just a special type of window. Windows CE controls have their own window classes, and hence, their own window procedures controlling their behavior and appearance.

Let's look at the button control class in closer detail. Deep in the implementation of the Windows CE Graphics, Windowing, and Events Subsystem (GWES) lives the implementation of the Windows CE button control class. Somewhere in the GWES code the button class is defined, and registered with a call to *RegisterClass*, just as you register your own window classes in your applications. The button class that gets registered includes a window procedure that implements all of the behavior of every button that appears in any Windows CE application.

The default appearance of buttons, a gray rectangle with text, is implemented by the button class window procedure's WM_PAINT message handler. What happens when you press or release a button is dictated by the WM_LBUTTONDOWN and WM_LBUTTONUP handling code.

When you create a button control, you specify the button class name in the *CreateWindow* (or *CreateWindowEx*) call:

```
HWND hwndButton;
hwndButton = CreateWindow(TEXT("BUTTON"), ...);
```

This tells Windows CE to create an instance of the window class identified by the Unicode string "BUTTON". All messages sent to *hwndButton* are thus handled by the window procedure identified by that window class. Hence, *hwndButton* knows how to walk and talk like a button control.

When a button needs to be repainted, the button class window procedure does all of the work. This is how Windows CE provides the default appearance and behavior of buttons and all other child or common controls.

How Owner Draw Buttons Are Different

Owner draw buttons work almost exactly like other Windows CE controls just described. The only difference is that the button control's parent window, not the button, is responsible for defining the appearance of the button.

An owner draw button behaves in all other ways like a non–owner draw button. For example, it still sends WM_COMMAND messages to its parent when pressed. The difference is that in the case of an owner draw button, the button skips its default WM_PAINT processing and instead sends its parent a WM_DRAWITEM message. The window procedure of the button's parent responds to this message by drawing the button.

The BS_OWNERDRAW Style

An application tells Windows CE that a particular button is an owner draw button by specifying the BS_OWNERDRAW style when the button is created:

```
         #define IDC_BUTTON
     HWND hwndButton;

     hwndButton = CreateWindow(TEXT("Button"),
                 TEXT("Some Caption"),
                 WS_VISIBLE|WS_CHILD|
                 BS_OWNERDRAW,
                 ...);
```

The WM_DRAWITEM Message

To Windows CE, the button *hwndButton* is like any other button except that it has the BS_OWNERDRAW style bit set. The button class window procedure checks for this style when a button is about to be painted. If this style bit is set, the default painting is skipped, and the button sends a WM_DRAWITEM message to its parent.

The WM_DRAWITEM message is sent when an owner draw button must be repainted for any reason. This includes when the button is pressed, released, or receives focus. How a window responds to the WM_DRAWITEM message completely defines how owner draw buttons appear to the user.

A window may contain more than one owner draw button. Each of these buttons may have a completely different appearance. The WM_DRAWITEM message contains information about which button is sending the message so that the parent window can execute the appropriate drawing code. Table 9.1 gives the WM_DRAWITEM message parameter details.

The *wParam* value tells the parent window which of the owner draw buttons that it contains needs to be redrawn. The DRAWITEM-STRUCT pointed to by the *lParam* contains all of the information about the control and why it must be redrawn.

Applications should return TRUE when they finish processing the WM_DRAWITEM message.

Table 9.1   The WM_DRAWITEM Message

PARAMETER	MEANING
(UINT)wParam	Command identifier of the button sending the message.
(LPDRAWITEMSTRUCT)lParam	Pointer to a DRAWITEMSTRUCT structure containing information about the control to be drawn.

The DRAWITEMSTRUCT structure is defined as:

```
typedef struct tagDRAWITEMSTRUCT
{
  UINT   CtlType;
  UINT   CtlID;
  UINT   itemID;
  UINT   itemAction;
  UINT   itemState;
  HWND   hwndItem;
  HDC    hDC;
  RECT   rcItem;
  DWORD  itemData;
} DRAWITEMSTRUCT, *PDRAWITEMSTRUCT, *LPDRAWITEMSTRUCT;
```

The first two members define the type of the control and its identifier.

The *hwndItem* member contains the window handle of the button that sent the WM_DRAWITEM message. Similarly, *hDC* is the button's device context. Any drawing operations performed to render the appearance of the button should be done in this device context.

rcItem contains the rectangular dimensions of the button in client coordinates.

The *itemData* member only has meaning with owner draw list boxes and combo boxes. It therefore has no meaning under Windows CE, which does not support owner draw list boxes or combo boxes.

The two most important members of the DRAWITEMSTRUCT are *itemAction* and *itemState*. These members describe the drawing action that must be performed and the state of the button respectively. An application uses these values to determine how to draw the owner draw button. *itemAction* can be one or more of the following values (combined by a bitwise OR):

ODA_DRAWENTIRE. The entire button must be redrawn.

ODA_FOCUS. The button has lost or gained keyboard focus (as indicated by the *itemState* value).

ODA_SELECT. The button selection status has changed (as indicated by the *itemState* value).

itemState can be one or more of the following:

ODS_CHECKED. Only used for owner draw menus; indicates the item is checked.

ODS_SELECTED. The button is selected/pressed.

ODS_GRAYED. Only used for owner draw menus; indicates the item is to be grayed.

ODS_DISABLED. The button is to be drawn as disabled.

ODS_FOCUS. The button has the keyboard focus.

Application programmers typically just use the *itemState* value to determine how to draw their own draw buttons. Since *itemAction* only indicates which of the *itemState* values to be on the lookout for, it is easiest to just test *itemState*.

An Example

How does all of this get used in practice? Let's take a simple example and demonstrate how a parent window would respond to the WM_DRAWITEM message. Assume that the parent window wants to create an owner draw button with a control identifier defined as IDC_BUTTON and the string "Press Here" as the button text. When the button is unpressed, it appears as shown in Figure 9.1. Figure 9.2 shows the button in the pressed state.

The button is created by the code shown below. *hwndMain* and *hInstance* are the application main window and application instance, respectively.

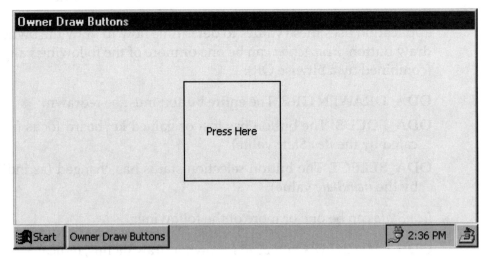

Figure 9.1   Sample owner draw button in the unpressed state.

Figure 9.2   Sample owner draw button in the pressed state.

```
#define IDC_BUTTON  1028
HWND hwndButton;
hwndButton = CreateWindow(TEXT("BUTTON"),
  TEXT("Press Here"),
  WS_VISIBLE|WS_CHILD|BS_OWNERDRAW,
  175,50,100,100,hwndMain,
  (HMENU)IDC_BUTTON,
  hInstance, NULL);
```

The WM_DRAWITEM code to implement the button appearance, which appears in the button parent window's window procedure, is shown below. Only the part of the window procedure relevant to drawing the owner draw buttons is included here.

```
LRESULT CALLBACK WndProc(HWND hwnd,
             UINT message,
             WPARAM wParam,
             LPARAM lParam)
{
  UINT nID;
  switch(message)
  {
  /* Other message handlers here... */
  case WM_DRAWITEM:
   UINT nID;
   LPDRAWITEMSTRUCT lpdis;
   nID = (UINT)wParam;
   switch (nID)
   {
   case IDC_BUTTON:
```

```
      HDC hdc;
      RECT rc;
      HBRUSH hBrushOld;
      HPEN hPenOld;
      int nModeOld;
      TCHAR pszText[129];
      lpdis = (LPDRAWITEMSTRUCT)lParam;
      rc = lpdis->rcItem;
      hdc = lpdis->hDC;
      if (lpdis->itemState & ODS_SELECTED)
      {
       //Invert the button when selected
       PatBlt(hdc, rc.left,rc.top,
         rc.right,rc.bottom, DSTINVERT);
      }
      else
      {
       //Draw the button in its unpressed state
       hPenOld = (HPEN)SelectObject(hdc,
         GetStockObject(BLACK_PEN));
       hBrushOld = (HBRUSH)SelectObject(hdc,
         GetStockObject(WHITE_BRUSH));
       nModeOld = SetBkMode(hdc, TRANSPARENT);
       Rectangle(hdc, rc.left,rc.top,
         rc.right,rc.bottom);
       GetWindowText(lpdis->hwndItem,
         pszText, 129);
       DrawText(hdc, pszText, -1, &rc,
         DT_CENTER|DT_VCENTER);
       SetBkMode(hdc, nModeOld);
       SelectObject(hdc, hBrushOld);
       SelectObject(hdc, hPenOld);
      }
      break;
     default:
      break;
     }    //End of switch(nID) block
     return (TRUE);
    /* Other message handlers here... */
     }        //End of switch(message) block
    }
```

The WM_DRAWITEM handler contains a switch statement for determining which owner draw button is responsible for sending the WM_DRAWITEM message. Although this example only contains one owner draw button, it is a good practice to put such a switch statement in your handler in case you add more owner draw buttons later.

We need to draw the IDC_BUTTON button in the pressed and unpressed states. We check to see if the button is pressed with the following test:

```
if (lpdis->itemState & ODS_SELECTED)
```

In other words, if the ODS_SELECTED flag is set in the DRAWITEM-STRUCT *itemState* member, the button is being pressed. Note that the test is not

```
if (lpdis->itemState == ODS_SELECTED)
```

Since a pressed button also has focus, the second test is too limiting, because the ODS_FOCUS flag will also be set. The *itemState* member of *lpdis* therefore is equal to ODS_SELECTED | ODS_FOCUS when the button is pressed.

If the button is pressed, we simply invert the control rectangle with a call to *PatBlt*. Whatever was drawn in the button in the unpressed state is inverted because *PatBlt* is called with the DSTINVERT.

Much more happens in the unpressed state. A black pen and white brush are selected into the button's device context, and the background mode is set to transparent so that the button surface shows through the background of any text that is drawn. The *Rectangle* call results in the white rectangle with the black outline that you see in Figure 9.1. The *Rectangle* function fills the specified rectangle with the current brush (white, in our case) and draws the rectangle outline with the current pen (in our case, black).

Next the code obtains the button text by calling *GetWindowText*, and draws it centered in the button rectangle with *DrawText*.

After the button is drawn, the original brush and pen are selected back into the device context, and the old background mode is restored.

This example gives us a high-level understanding of how to handle WM_DRAWITEM. The handler checks the command identifier of the control sending the message. It next looks at the *itemState* of the control to determine which state of the control needs to be drawn, and then performs the necessary drawing operations.

This example is a bit simplistic. Real owner draw buttons typically have much fancier graphics that are rendered by drawing custom bitmaps. The KIOSK.EXE example uses bitmaps for richer graphics in its owner draw buttons. Of course, "richer" is a very subjective term. I make absolutely no claims to artistic ability!

The Kiosk Application

At this point we are ready to present the KIOSK.EXE application. Bear in mind that it is only really a mock-up of a front-end user interface for a kiosk-style Windows CE device. It only demonstrates some owner draw buttons and other user interface customization techniques. There is no real functionality behind this application.

The idea behind the kiosk model is that a user perceives it as a dedicated single-use device, such as an automatic teller machine. It does not provide real-time stock quotes or send e-mail as well.

A kiosk user interface is supposed to be one hundred percent obvious to a user. No on-line help is required, and the user is not faced with myriad confusing user interface components to figure out.

To meet these objectives, the main application window of KIOSK.EXE is entirely blank except for the string "Tap Anywhere To Begin" scrolling continuously across the screen (Figure 9.3). What could be simpler than this? No menus, no buttons, just a black screen and very obvious instructions about how to use the application. The window doesn't even have a border or caption bar.

Figure 9.3   The Kiosk application main window.

Creating the Main Application Window

The implementation of this main window is straightforward. Here is how the window class that was used to create the main window is defined and registered. *WndProc* is the main application window's window procedure. *hInstance* is the application HINSTANCE, and *pszAppName* is the window class name.

```
WNDCLASS wndClass;
wndClass.style = 0;
wndClass.lpfnWndProc = WndProc;
wndClass.cbClsExtra = 0;
wndClass.cbWndExtra = 0;
wndClass.hInstance  = hInstance;
wndClass.hIcon     = NULL;
wndClass.hCursor   = NULL;
wndClass.hbrBackground =
   (HBRUSH)GetStockObject(BLACK_BRUSH);
wndClass.lpszMenuName = NULL;
wndClass.lpszClassName = pszAppName;
RegisterClass(&wndClass);
```

This is not much different from most of the other window class declarations that we have seen. The *hbrBackground* member of the WND-CLASS structure is set to the stock black brush. Hence the black background of any instance of this window class.

The main window then gets created:

```
HWND hwndMain;
hwndMain = CreateWindow(pszAppName,
            NULL,
            WS_VISIBLE,...);
```

The only window style that we set is WS_VISIBLE. Therefore the main window has no border and no caption bar. This is why the main application window appears as the plain black background we see in Figure 9.3.

Adding the Scrolling Text

The scrolling banner text in the main application window is implemented using a bitmap and a Windows CE *timer*.

Windows CE Timers

A timer is a device that applications can use to have Windows CE notify them that a specified interval of time has elapsed. In our case, the timer fires every 0.5 seconds. In response to this timer, the main window produces the effect of scrolling the text by repainting the bitmap in a new position.

Timers are used extensively in a wide variety of Windows CE applications. For example, calendar applications use timers to trigger the alarms that users set to remind them of scheduled appointments.

Each timer that an application creates is associated with a particular window. Windows CE notifies a window that a timer associated with it has elapsed by sending a WM_TIMER message to that window's window procedure. Alternatively, an application-defined callback function can be specified for each timer. In this case, the callback function assigned to the timer is called.

To create the timer, KIOSK.EXE calls the *SetTimer* Windows CE function:

```
SetTimer(hwnd, uIDEvent, uElapse, lpTimerFunc);
```

SetTimer returns the identifier of the new timer (i.e., *uIDEvent*) if the function succeeds. Otherwise the return value is zero.

hwnd is the window that owns the timer. Since a window can own more than one timer, Windows CE needs a way to distinguish between timers. Callers therefore specify the *uIDEvent* parameter. *uIDEvent* is a UINT identifying the timer. *uElapse* defines the *timer interval*, the number of milliseconds that elapse between WM_TIMER messages.

lpTimerFunc is a pointer to a timer callback function. This is the function that gets called by Windows CE whenever the timer interval identified by *uIDEvent* elapses. A timer callback function has the following signature:

```
VOID CALLBACK TimerProc(hwnd, uMsg, idEvent, dwTime);
```

hwnd and *idEvent* identify the window that owns the timer and the timer identifier, respectively. *idEvent* is the same as the *uIDEvent* value that is in the *SetTimer* call.

The *uMsg* parameter is always WM_TIMER for a timer callback. Given that a timer callback is always called because a timer interval has elapsed, it is anyone's guess why this parameter was added to the function definition.

dwTime gives the number of milliseconds since Windows CE was launched on the device hosting the application.

Table 9.2   The WM_TIMER Message

PARAMETER	MEANING
(UINT)wParam	Identifier of the timer whose interval elapsed, causing the WM_TIMER message to be sent.
(TIMERPROC*)lParam	Pointer to the timer callback function.

If you are like me, you might prefer to set *lpTimerFunc* to NULL. In this case, Windows CE sends a WM_TIMER message to the window that owns a timer whose *uElapse* interval has elapsed (Table 9.2). All of the information that you would get from a timer callback is available to any window procedure that handles this message. Perhaps this is why most people don't bother using timer callbacks.

If the *lpTimerFunc* parameter of *SetTimer* is NULL, *lParam* will be NULL for the corresponding WM_TIMER messages.

KIOSK.EXE creates one timer identified as IDT_SCROLL and assigns it to the main application window. The IDT_SCROLL timer fires every 0.5 seconds.

The main window responds to IDT_TIMER by scrolling the banner text. The WM_TIMER handler of the main window's window procedure looks like this:

```
case WM_TIMER:
  if (IDT_SCROLL==wParam)
  {
   //Perform scrolling
  }
  return (0);
```

A WM_TIMER handler typically checks the identity of the timer whose interval has elapsed and performs whatever action that timer was meant to trigger.

An application can destroy a timer by calling *KillTimer*:

```
KillTimer(hwnd, uIDEvent);
```

hwnd identifies the window that owns the timer to be destroyed, and *uIDEvent* is the timer identifier. If the timer specified by *uIDEvent* is successfully destroyed, *KillTimer* returns TRUE. Otherwise it returns FALSE.

Creating the Text: Offscreen Bitmaps

The text that scrolls across the kiosk application's main window is implemented as a bitmap. But you will search in vain if you try to find a bitmap resource somewhere in the project files on the companion CD that has the text "Tap Anywhere To Begin" in it.

This is because the bitmap that is used to draw the scrolling text is created programmatically. It is done using a common Windows CE graphics programming technique known as drawing an *offscreen bitmap*.

An offscreen bitmap is a bitmap like any other. The only difference, as the name implies, is that the bits that constitute the bitmap reside in some portion of program memory that is not owned by the display device. The basic idea is that an application generates the bitmap off screen, and then renders it in some device context when needed.

Note that the actual string "Tap Anywhere To Begin" is stored in a Unicode string variable called *pszText*, defined in the project file KIOSK.H. The offscreen bitmap is generated using this string. So when we say that the text scrolls across the screen, what we really mean is that the offscreen bitmap representing the string is being scrolled.

There are two primary ingredients required to create an offscreen bitmap. The first is a *memory device context*. The second is the bitmap itself.

TIP

STORING THE BANNER TEXT IN THE REGISTRY

Chapter 8 discussed the Windows CE registry as one form of persistent storage. In a complete commercial kiosk application, the scrolling banner text string would most likely be stored in the registry. This would allow the banner text to be changed without requiring the application to be recompiled.

The Memory Device Context

A memory device context is similar to a window device context. The difference is that a memory device context represents a virtual display surface. It is a display surface in memory only. Other than this important distinction, a memory device context is like any other device context.

A memory device context becomes really useful when it has a bitmap selected into it. Then any graphics function call that operates on the memory device context has the effect of producing the result of the function call on the selected bitmap.

Thus, if an application selects a bitmap into a memory device context and then draws a rectangle on that device context, the bitmap will contain that rectangle.

A memory device context is created with the function *CreateCompatibleDC*:

```
CreateCompatibleDC(hdc);
```

This function returns a memory device context with the same attributes as that specified by the parameter *hdc*.

Creating the Bitmap

The second ingredient we need in order to produce an offscreen bitmap is the bitmap object itself. For this purpose an application calls *CreateCompatibleBitmap*:

```
CreateCompatibleBitmap(hdc, nWidth, nHeight);
```

This function returns a handle to a BITMAP object (HBITMAP) *nWidth* pixels wide and *nHeight* pixels tall. The number of bits per pixel and the number of color planes of the bitmap are the same as those of the device context specified in *hdc*. A bitmap created in this way is called an offscreen bitmap.

Once a bitmap has been created in this way, it can be selected into a memory device context with a call to *SelectObject*. Any subsequent graphics operations involving that memory device context are rendered on the offscreen bitmap.

In the case of the KIOSK.EXE application, the offscreen bitmap containing the banner text is produced with the following code. *hdc* is the main application window device context. *nRight* and *nBottom* are the width and height of the main application window.

```
#define BK_COLOR (RGB(0,0,0)) //Black text background
#define TEXT_COLOR (RGB(255,255,0)) //Yellow text
HDC hdcMem;
HBITMAP hBmp;
RECT rc;
```

```
TCHAR* pszBanner[] = TEXT("Tap Anywhere To Begin");
hdcMem = CreateCompatibleDC(hdc);
hBmp = CreateCompatibleBitmap(
  hdc, nRight, nBottom);
SelectObject(hdcMem, hBmp);
SetBkColor(hdcMem, BK_COLOR);
SetTextColor(hdcMem, TEXT_COLOR);
DrawText(hdcMem, pszBanner, -1, &rc, DT_LEFT);
```

The last three statements in the example above operate on the memory device context *hdcMem*. The operations they represent are therefore rendered on the offscreen bitmap currently selected into that device context.

Making the Text Scroll

At this point, the application has the complete offscreen bitmap for displaying the kiosk banner text. Making this text scroll is now very simple.

The main application window simply draws the offscreen bitmap whenever the window gets painted. The scrolling effect is achieved by updating the location at which the bitmap is drawn. This position is updated in response to the IDT_SCROLL timer firing.

Inside the window procedure for the main window, we find this code:

```
case WM_TIMER:
  if (IDT_SCROLL==wParam)
  {
   nScrollX += 50;
   if (nScrollX > nRight)
   {
    nScrollX = -nStringWidth;
   }
   InvalidateRect(hwnd, NULL, TRUE);
  }
  return (0);
```

nStringWidth is the width of the banner text string in pixels. It is calculated at the beginning of the application with a *DrawText* call that uses DT_CALCRECT as a text drawing option.

nScrollX is an integer initialized to zero in *WinMain*. It represents the current x position in pixels of the offscreen bitmap. On every IDT_SCROLL timer tick, this value gets incremented by 50 pixels.

Once *nScrollX* exceeds *nRight*, the right edge of the main window, *nScrollX* is set to the value *-nStringWidth*. This effectively moves the offscreen bitmap off the left edge of the main window.

The *InvalidateRect* call tells Windows CE that the entire client area of the main application window must be redrawn. So, the entire window is redrawn after every IDT_SCROLL timer interval.

The main window is drawn with the WM_PAINT handler code:

```
case WM_PAINT:
  PAINTSTRUCT ps;
  hdc = BeginPaint(hwnd, &ps);
  BitBlt(hdc, nScrollX, 0, nRight, nBottom,
   hdcMem, 0,0, SRCCOPY);
  EndPaint(hwnd, &ps);
  return (0);
```

The *BitBlt* call redraws the offscreen bitmap containing the text at the new *nScrollX* x location.

Implementing the Options Window

The window that appears when a user taps the kiosk application's main window is called the options window. It is the window that the user interacts with to make various banking choices (Figure 9.4).

The options window is another example of a Windows CE user interface designed to look very little like traditional windows. The options

---

Why Not Just Use *ScrollWindowEx*?

Experienced Windows programmers might question my method of implementing scrolling text with an offscreen bitmap. Why not just draw the text once using *DrawText*, and then call *ScrollWindowEx* in response to the WM_TIMER message?

In addition to giving me an excuse to introduce the offscreen bitmap concept to programmers who may not be familiar with it, my method also makes it easier to produce the scrolling text effect.

ScrollWindowEx only scrolls pixels that appear on the window specified by the *hWnd* parameter of *ScrollWindowEx*. After the text scrolls off the right side of the main window, it re-enters the screen from the left. Producing this effect without a bitmap, which has a fixed set of bits, would require clever *DrawText* calls to draw incomplete portions of the text to make it appear to scroll back on the screen.

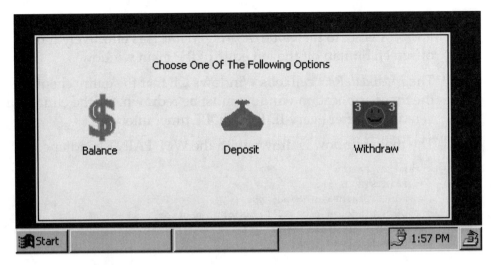

Figure 9.4 The Kiosk application options window.

window allows users to check their bank account balance, make a deposit, or withdraw cash. Of course none of this banking functionality is actually implemented by KIOSK.EXE. The point of the options window and the entire kiosk sample application is to give you insight into the Windows CE options available for implementing non-standard user interfaces.

The options window consists of three owner draw buttons, a custom window border, and some descriptive text. Like the main window, it has no title bar or window caption.

The options window class is defined and registered as follows:

```
TCHAR pszEntryClass[] = TEXT("ENTRYWINDOW");
WNDCLASS wndClassOptions;
wndClassOptions.style = 0;
wndClassOptions.lpfnWndProc = OptionsWndProc;
wndClassOptions.cbClsExtra = 0;
wndClassOptions.cbWndExtra = 0;
wndClassOptions.hInstance  = hInstance;
wndClassOptions.hIcon      = NULL;
wndClassOptions.hCursor    = NULL;
wndClassOptions.hbrBackground=
    (HBRUSH)GetStockObject(WHITE_BRUSH);
wndClassOptions.lpszMenuName = NULL;
wndClassOptions.lpszClassName= pszEntryClass;
RegisterClass(&wndClassOptions);
```

OptionsWndProc is the window procedure for the options window.

Also notice the WHITE_BRUSH background instead of the BLACK_BRUSH background defined for the main window class.

When a user taps the main application screen, an instance of this window class is created. Since the options window appears as a result of tapping the main application window, the options window *CreateWindow* call must appear in the WM_LBUTTONDOWN message handler of the main window's window procedure as shown below. Only the part of the window procedure relevant to options window creation is included here.

```
HWND hwndOptions;
int nOptionsWidth, nOptionsHeight;
LRESULT CALLBACK WndProc(
  HWND hwnd,
  UINT message,
  WPARAM wParam,
  LPARAM lParam)
{
  switch(message)
  {
  /* Other message handlers here... */
  case WM_LBUTTONDOWN:
   nOptionsWidth = (nRight-50);
   nOptionsHeight= (nBottom-50);
   KillTimer(hwndMain, IDT_SCROLL);
   hwndOptions = CreateWindow(pszEntryClass,
    NULL, WS_VISIBLE,
     20, 20, nOptionsWidth, nOptionsHeight,
      hwnd, NULL, ghInst, NULL);
   return (0);
   /* Other message handlers... */
  default:
   return (DefWindowProc(hwnd, message, wParam, lParam));
  }        //End of switch(message) statement
}
```

nRight and *nBottom* are the horizontal and vertical dimensions of the main window's bounding rectangle. *ghInst* is the globally defined application instance.

The first thing to notice in this code is the *KillTimer* call. When the options window is displayed, the text on the main application window stops scrolling. This is done by simply turning the scrolling timer IDT_SCROLL off.

The *CreateWindow* call makes an instance of the options window class that contains only the WS_VISIBLE style. Thus the window does not include the standard Windows CE border or caption bar. The window does appear to have a border, though. This is rendered by the application in response to the WM_ERASEBKGND messages that are sent to the options window.

Drawing the Options Window Border

The WM_ERASEBKGND message is similar to its more well known cousin, WM_PAINT. A WM_PAINT message is sent to a window whenever part or all of the window's client area needs to be repainted. Similarly, WM_ERASEBKGND is sent when part or all of a window's client area needs to be erased.

For example, we've probably all seen applications that have windows with interesting bitmaps as their background. These backgrounds are drawn in response to WM_ERASEBKGND messages (Table 9.3). Including the WM_ERASEBKGND message in the operating system allows applications to break the process of drawing windows into two steps. The WM_ERASEBKGND step can be used to draw the fixed parts of a window's client area display such as custom backgrounds. WM_PAINT is then used to paint the parts of the display that change, such as the text that appears on a page in a word processing application.

The value returned by a window procedure that handles the WM_ERASEBKGND is very important. Returning the wrong value can lead to very subtle bugs in an application which appear as window backgrounds being drawn incorrectly. An application should return a non-zero value if it handles the WM_ERASEBKGND mes-

Table 9.3 The WM_ERASEBKGND Message Parameters

PARAMETER	MEANING
(HDC)wParam	Device context of the window whose background is to be erased.
lParam	Not used.

sage. This tells Windows CE not to perform the default WM_ERASE-BKGND processing. Returning zero tells Windows CE that the default processing should be performed.

This is how the *hbrBackground* member of the window class definition gets used by Windows CE. If an application leaves the processing of WM_ERASEBKGND messages to Windows CE (either by returning zero in response to the message or by calling *DefWindowProc* for WM_ERASEBKGND messages), Windows CE erases the window background itself. It does so by filling the window's client area with the brush specified in the *hbrBackground* member of the window class definition for the particular window. This is how, for example, the background of the kiosk application's main window is painted black.

You can see how telling Windows CE that you erased your window background when you really didn't can cause problems. Incorrectly returning a non-zero value in response to WM_ERASEBKGND can prevent the proper background from being painted.

In the case of the options window in the kiosk application, WM_ERASEBKGND is used to draw the window border. The relevant portion of the *OptionsWndProc* window procedure is shown below:

```
LRESULT CALLBACK OptionsWndProc(
   HWND hwnd,
   UINT message,
   WPARAM wParam,
   LPARAM lParam)
{
   HDC hdc;
   UINT nID;
   RECT rc;
   switch(message)
   {
   //Other message handlers */
   //...
   case WM_ERASEBKGND:
    HBRUSH hBrushOld;
    hdc = (HDC)wParam;
    GetClientRect(hwnd, &rc);
    hBrushOld = (HBRUSH)SelectObject(hdc,
     GetStockObject(WHITE_BRUSH));
    Rectangle(hdc, rc.left, rc.top,
     rc.right, rc.bottom);
    InflateRect(&rc, -3, -3);
    Rectangle(hdc, rc.left, rc.top,
```

```
    rc.right, rc.bottom);
   SelectObject(hdc, hBrushOld);
   return (TRUE);
  default:
   return (DefWindowProc(hwnd, message, wParam, lParam));
  }    //End of switch(message) statement
 }
```

The WM_ERASEBKGND handler first extracts the HDC of the options window from the *wParam* parameter of the window procedure. Next it gets the coordinates of the options window client rectangle by calling *GetClientRect*. It then selects the stock object WHITE_BRUSH into this device context. Any subsequent graphics function calls that fill a rectangle or region will thus use white as the fill color.

The two *Rectangle* function calls result in the border being drawn. The first *Rectangle* call fills the entire client area of the options window with white. The effect of the second *Rectangle* call is to draw the black inset border. This happens for two reasons. First, the *InflateRect* call decreases the dimensions of the rectangle to be drawn. Second, the outline of a rectangle drawn by *Rectangle* is the color of the pen currently selected into the device context specified by the *hdc* parameter. Since this pen is black by default, the rectangle border is black.

Note that we have to make the first *Rectangle* call to fill the entire client area before drawing the inset border. Since the message handler code returns TRUE when it's done, the default WM_ERASEBKGND processing is skipped. If the first *Rectangle* call is not made, only the inset rectangle would ever get drawn by our WM_ERASEBKGND message handler.

Creating and Drawing the Options Buttons

We've seen how the options window is created. But what about the three owner draw buttons that the window contains?

The three owner draw buttons in the options window are created in response to the WM_CREATE message sent to *OptionsWndProc*:

```
/* Global variables and child control
   identifiers defined in kiosk.h */
#define IDC_BALANCE   1028
#define IDC_DEPOSIT   1029
#define IDC_WITHDRAW  1030
HDC hdcButtons;
```

```
HBITMAP hBmpButtons;
HWND hwndBalance;
HWND hwndDeposit;
HWND hwndWithdraw;
LRESULT CALLBACK OptionsWndProc(
  HWND hwnd,
  UINT message,
  WPARAM wParam,
  LPARAM lParam)
{
  HDC hdc;
  UINT nID;
  RECT rc;
  switch(message)
  {
  case WM_CREATE:
   hdc = GetDC(hwnd);
   hdcButtons = CreateCompatibleDC(hdc);
   hBmpButtons = LoadBitmap(ghInst,
    MAKEINTRESOURCE(IDB_BALANCE));
   SelectObject(hdcButtons, hBmpButtons);
   ReleaseDC(hwnd, hdc);
   hwndBalance = CreateWindow(TEXT("BUTTON"), NULL,
    WS_VISIBLE|WS_CHILD|BS_OWNERDRAW,
    ...,
    (HMENU)IDC_BALANCE,...);
   hwndDeposit = CreateWindow(TEXT("BUTTON"), NULL,
    WS_VISIBLE|WS_CHILD|BS_OWNERDRAW,
    ...,
    (HMENU)IDC_DEPOSIT,...);
   hwndWithdraw = CreateWindow(TEXT("BUTTON"), NULL,
    WS_VISIBLE|WS_CHILD|BS_OWNERDRAW,
    ...,
    (HMENU)IDC_WITHDRAW,...);
   return (0);
  //Other message handlers
  //...
  default:
   return (DefWindowProc(hwnd, message, wParam, lParam));
  }    //End of switch(message) statement
}
```

The WM_CREATE handler does more than just create the three owner draw buttons. It also loads the bitmap containing the button images and selects that bitmap into a global memory device context called *hdcButtons*.

The button images are stored in one bitmap as shown in Figure 9.5. Each button has a pair of 48-pixel-wide images. The first image in the

Figure 9.5 Options window button image bitmap.

pair is used to draw the button's unpressed state. The second is used to draw its pressed state.

When the options window draws the buttons in response to the various WM_DRAWITEM messages it is sent, it uses the control identifier of the button sending the WM_DRAWITEM message to determine which set of images to use from the button image bitmap.

```
#define BMP_WIDTH  48
LRESULT CALLBACK OptionsWndProc(
  HWND hwnd,
  UINT message,
  WPARAM wParam,
  LPARAM lParam)
{
  HDC hdc;
  UINT nID;
  RECT rc;
  switch(message)
  {
  //Other message handlers
  //...
  case WM_DRAWITEM:
   LPDRAWITEMSTRUCT lpdis;
   int xBmp, xBmpPressed;
   nID = (UINT)wParam;
   lpdis = (LPDRAWITEMSTRUCT)lParam;
   rc = lpdis->rcItem;
   hdc = lpdis->hDC;
   xBmp = 0;
   xBmpPressed = BMP_WIDTH;
   switch(nID)
   {
    case IDC_DEPOSIT:
     xBmp += 2*BMP_WIDTH;
     xBmpPressed += 2*BMP_WIDTH;
     break;
    case IDC_WITHDRAW:
     xBmp += 4*BMP_WIDTH;
     xBmpPressed += 4*BMP_WIDTH;
     break;
    default:
```

```
        break;
    }   //End of switch(nID) block
```

The WM_DRAWITEM handler first extracts the information it needs to draw the button bitmaps such as the device context of the button and the button's bounding rectangle. Next, it initializes the two offset variables, *xBmp* and *xBmpPressed*, to the x pixel offsets of the first unpressed and pressed button images.

The *nID* switch statement then adjusts these values to correspond to the left edge of the appropriate button bitmaps depending on which button sent the WM_DRAWITEM message.

For example, if the WM_DRAWITEM message was sent by the IDC_DEPOSIT button, *xBmp* and *xBmpPressed* are set to the values 96 and 120, respectively. These values correspond to the leftmost pixels of the images to be used to draw the pressed and unpressed states of the IDC_DEPOSIT button.

Finally, the WM_DRAWITEM handler checks the *itemState* of the button, and displays the proper image with a call to *BitBlt*:

```
/* If the button is pressed... */
if (lpdis->itemState & ODS_SELECTED)
{
  BitBlt(hdc, rc.left,rc.top,
    (rc.right-rc.left),
    (rc.bottom-rc.top),
    hdcButtons,
    xBmpPressed,0,SRCCOPY);
}
/* If the button is not pressed... */
else
{
  BitBlt(hdc, rc.left,rc.top,
    (rc.right-rc.left),
    (rc.bottom-rc.top),
    hdcButtons,
    xBmp,0,SRCCOPY);
}
return (TRUE);
```

Concluding Remarks

In this chapter, you have been introduced to some of the more common techniques for programming custom Windows CE user interfaces. But owner draw controls and offscreen bitmaps are but a few of the many ways that you can create user interfaces for your applications that are different from the Windows CE standard.

The next chapter expands on the owner draw concept with the more general subject of the Windows CE custom draw service. The custom draw service, like owner draw controls, allows you to dramatically influence the look and feel of various Windows CE controls—but with much more flexibility.

CHAPTER 10

The Windows CE Custom Draw Service

We have seen how owner draw techniques allow applications to define the appearance of various Windows CE control types. For example, by simply adding the BS_OWNERDRAW style to a button, and responding appropriately to the WM_DRAWITEM message in the parent window procedure, an application can completely redefine the look and feel of the button.

Another programming option that provides even more flexibility for modifying the appearance of Windows CE controls is the *custom draw service*.

In some ways, the custom draw service functionality is very similar to the way that owner draw controls work. With owner draw buttons, the WM_PAINT message handler in the button window procedure sends a WM_DRAWITEM message to the button's parent and skips doing the default button painting operations. Similarly, controls that support the custom draw service send WM_NOTIFY messages to their parents at various times throughout their painting process. The custom draw service is more flexible because it provides more hooks for the parent window to influence the look of the control.

The custom draw service is supported by the following Windows CE common controls, which live in COMMCTRL.DLL. It is not supported by any of the child controls.

- command bands
- header controls
- list view controls
- toolbars
- trackbar controls
- tree view controls

In this chapter, we describe how to use the custom draw service through the example of a custom trackbar control. The control that results is shown in Figure 10.1. (I did not originally set out to try and make this control look like a thermometer!) Compare this to the standard trackbar control shown in Figure 10.2. The custom drawn version of the control demonstrates quite a bit of customization. The trackbar border appears rounded, with nice drop shadowing. The thumb, which is a little black dot, looks totally different from the standard trackbar thumb. And the channel, the area that the thumb gets dragged around in, is different.

The application source code that implements this example is found in \Samples\custdraw on the companion CD. The resulting executable is

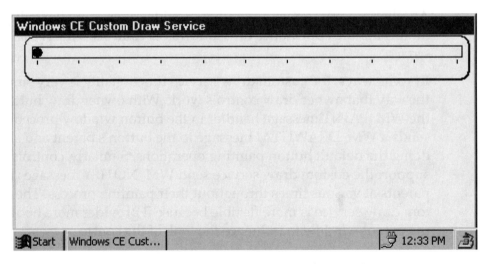

Figure 10.1 A trackbar control drawn using the custom draw service.

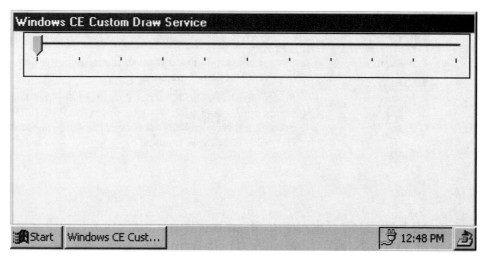

Figure 10.2   A standard trackbar control.

called CUSTDRAW.EXE. To exit the application, tap any part of the main window's client area not covered by the trackbar.

AFTER COMPLETING THIS CHAPTER YOU WILL KNOW HOW TO . . .

Use the custom draw service to customize the appearance of

Windows CE common controls

Custom Draw Notification

Windows CE controls that support the custom draw service give their parents the opportunity to customize the control drawing process at various times during the control's *paint cycle*.

The paint cycle is defined as all processing that a control (or any window, for that matter) performs in response to the WM_ERASEBKGND and WM_PAINT messages. WM_ERASEBKGND is sent to a window when the window background needs to be erased in preparation for painting. WM_PAINT is sent when a window is asked to repaint itself.

Controls using the custom draw service give their parent windows the opportunity to handle parts of the drawing process by sending the

Table 10.1 Custom Draw Service WM_NOTIFY Message Parameters

PARAMETER	MEANING
wParam	Integer containing the command identifier of the control sending the WM_NOTIFY message.
lParam	Pointer to an NMCUSTOMDRAW structure. If a tree view control sends the message, this parameter is an NMTVCUSTOMDRAW pointer. If the control is a list view control, this parameter is an NMLVCUSTOMDRAW pointer.

NM_CUSTOMDRAW notification. This notification is sent in the form of a WM_NOTIFY message. The parameters sent with the WM_NOTIFY message are described in Table 10.1.

For list view and tree view controls, the first member of the structure pointed to by *lParam* is an NMCUSTOMDRAW structure.

The NMCUSTOMDRAW structure contains information about the control and where the control is in its paint cycle:

```
typedef struct tagNMCUSTOMDRAWINFO
{
  NMHDR hdr;
  DWORD dwDrawStage;
  HDC hdc;
  RECT rc;
  DWORD dwItemSpec;
  UINT uItemState;
  LPARAM lItemlParam;
} NMCUSTOMDRAW, FAR* LPNMCUSTOMDRAW;
```

The *hdr* member of this structure is an NMHDR notify message header structure that always accompanies common control notifications. *hdc* is the device context of the control, and *rc* is supposed to contain the control's bounding rectangle. See the tip "Bogus NMCUSTOMDRAW rc Member" later in this chapter.

dwDrawStage tells your application what stage of the drawing process the custom draw control is in. This member can be one of eight values. The first four specify the state that the paint cycle of the control is in. These are referred to as *global* draw stages:

CDDS_PREPAINT. Sent before the control's WM_PAINT handler begins.

CDDS_POSTPAINT. Sent after the control's WM_PAINT processing is complete.

CDDS_PREERASE. Sent before the control's WM_ERASEBKGND handler begins. Not currently supported.

CDDS_POSTERASE. Sent after the control's WM_ERASEBKGND processing is complete. Not currently supported.

Note that CDDS_PREERASE and CDDS_POSTERASE are not currently supported.

dwDrawStage can also inform the parent window where the control is in the process of drawing individual items within the control. For example, a list view control keeps its parent apprised of the drawing progress for each list view item that is drawn. Trackbar controls tell their parents about trackbar thumb, channel, and tic mark drawing progress. The four possible values of *dwDrawStage* that convey this information are:

CDDS_ITEMPREPAINT. Sent before a control item is painted.

CDDS_ITEMPOSTPAINT. Sent after a control item is painted.

CDDS_ITEMPREERASE. Sent before a control item is erased. Not currently supported.

CDDS_ITEMPOSTERASE. Sent after a control item is erased. Not currently supported.

Note that CDDS_ITEMPREERASE and CDDS_ITEMPOSTERASE are not currently supported.

NOTE
CUSTOM DRAW NOTIFICATIONS

All custom draw service information comes to a control's parent window via the WM_NOTIFY message. This is the way that all common control notifications get to parent windows. But common controls can specify a variety of notification codes when they send WM_NOTIFY messages. This has led to the convention of referring to common control notifications, where the specific code identifies the notification.

Similarly, we will refer to custom draw notifications. Each *dwDrawStage* value specifies a particular custom draw notification. So when we say, for example, the item pre-paint notification, what is specifically meant is a WM_NOTIFY message with notification code NM_CUSTOMDRAW and an NMCUSTOMDRAW *dwDrawStage* member of CDDS_ITEMPREPAINT.

An application's response to the NM_CUSTOMDRAW notification under each of these conditions determines how the custom draw control proceeds with the paint cycle.

The *dwItemSpec* member of NMCUSTOMDRAW specifies the item number to which the notification corresponds. For example, this value would indicate the zero-based index of the particular list view control item being drawn.

For trackbar controls, three unique values are defined for the *dwItemSpec* member. These values specify what part of the trackbar control the parent window is being notified about:

TBCD_CHANNEL. Identifies the trackbar channel.

TBCD_THUMB. Identifies the trackbar thumb.

TBCD_TICS. Identifies the trackbar tic marks.

A separate NM_CUSTOMDRAW notification is sent by a control for each item in that control. This gives the parent window the chance to customize every part of the control's appearance.

For example, assume an NM_CUSTOMDRAW notification sent by a trackbar control with a *dwDrawStage* value of CDDS_ITEMPREPAINT and a *dwItemSpec* value of TBCD_TICS. This means that the trackbar control is notifying its parent that the trackbar is about to draw its tic marks.

The *uItemState* member of the NMCUSTOMDRAW structure specifies the current state of the item indicated by *dwItemSpec*. The following state identifiers can appear in this member. Not all values necessarily have meaning for all custom draw controls. For example, CDIS_CHECKED has no meaning for a trackbar, but does for a list view control that includes the LVS_EX_CHECKBOXES style:

CDIS_CHECKED. The item is checked.

CDIS_DEFAULT. The item is in its default state.

CDIS_DISABLED. The item is disabled.

CDIS_FOCUS. The item has focus.

CDIS_GRAYED. The item is grayed.

CDIS_HOT. The item is under the stylus/pointing device.

CDIS_SELECTED. The item is selected.

The final NMCUSTOMDRAW member, *lItemlParam*, contains any application-defined data that may have been previously assigned to the control item by the application.

For example, list view control items are described by LV_ITEM structures. One of the LV_ITEM members is *lParam,* which can be used by applications to associate data with items. List view items participating in an NM_CUSTOMDRAW notification would send their *lParam* data in the NMCUSTOMDRAW *lItemlParam* member.

TIP
Bogus NMCUSTOMDRAW rc Member

I have never seen a case where an NM_CUSTOMDRAW notification is sent by a control and the NMCUSTOMDRAW *rc* member had anything but garbage data in it. When implementing responses to custom draw notifications, it is more reliable to get the control's bounding rectangle yourself with a call to *GetClientRect*.

I should point out here that the Windows CE common controls that support the custom draw service do not need to be told by an application to enable their custom draw support. An application programmer might assume that some new control style must be added at creation time so that the control knows that its parent is interested in receiving custom draw notifications. But this is not the case. Controls send custom draw notifications by default. Applications decide to use the custom draw features by responding to these notifications. If the notifications are ignored by the parent window procedure, the service is effectively not used.

NOTE
Erase Notifications Currently Not Supported

None of the global or item-specific pre- or post-erase notifications are currently supported in Windows CE.

Responding to Custom Draw Notifications

An application's response to the various custom draw notifications controls the custom draw service behavior. Return values can specify how Windows CE completes a particular draw stage. They also can indicate whether or not further custom draw notifications are sent by the control.

We first list all of the defined custom draw notification return values, and then discuss some examples of their use. The values that an application can return in response to an NM_CUSTOMDRAW notification are:

CDRF_DODEFAULT. Tells the control to perform default processing for the particular draw stage.

CDRF_SKIPDEFAULT. Tells the control not to perform default processing for the particular draw stage.

CDRF_NEWFONT. Tells the control that a new font has been selected into the HDC indicated by the *hdc* member of the NMCUSTOM-DRAW structure sent with the custom draw notification.

CDRF_NOTIFYPOSTPAINT. Tells the control to send a CDDS_ITEM-POSTPAINT notification after painting an item. This is returned in response to the CDDS_ITEMPREPAINT notification.

CDRF_NOTIFYITEMDRAW. Tells the control to send all item-specific custom draw notifications. NM_CUSTOMDRAW notifications will be sent before and after items are drawn, i.e., CDDS_ITEMPREPAINT and CDDS_ITEMPOSTPAINT notifications will be sent.

CDDS_NOTIFYPOSTERASE. In theory, tells the control to send the parent window post-erase notifications. In reality, this is currently not supported.

The CDDS_NOTIFYITEMDRAW return value is in many ways the most important. An application returns this value in response to the CDDS_PREPAINT notification to request that the control send subsequent notifications for the rest of the current paint cycle.

If, on the other hand, the parent window returns CDRF_DODEFAULT in response to the CDDS_PREPAINT notification, the control will not send any more custom draw notifications for the rest of the current paint cycle.

If your application wants to use a different font to draw a control, select the desired font into the *hdc* member of the NMCUSTOMDRAW structure. You must return CDRF_NEWFONT in that case so that the control knows a new font was selected.

A typical NM_CUSTOMDRAW notification handler looks something like this:

How Are Custom Draw Notifications Ignored by Default?

If you dig through COMMCTRL.H, you'll find the definitions for the various custom draw notification return values. One of these is:

```
#define CDRF_DODEFAULT    0x00000000
```

In the typical window procedure, messages that are not handled are passed to *DefWindowProc* to let Windows CE perform default processing in response to those messages. If a parent window does not respond to custom draw notifications, *DefWindowProc* is called. For WM_NOTIFY messages containing the NM_CUSTOMDRAW notification code, *DefWindowProc* returns 0.

So, by default a control that sends a CDDS_PREPAINT notification at the beginning of its paint cycle will get back 0 if the notification is handled by *DefWindowProc*. Therefore, no more custom draw notifications get sent.

```
case WM_NOTIFY:
  LPNMHDR lpnmhdr;
  lpnmhdr = (LPNMHDR)lParam;
  switch(lpnmhdr->code)
  {
  case NM_CUSTOMDRAW:
   LPNMCUSTOMDRAW lpnmcd;
   lpnmcd = (LPNMCUSTOMDRAW)lParam;
   switch(lpnmcd->dwDrawStage)
   {
   case CDDS_PREPAINT:
    return (CDRF_NOTIFYITEMDRAW);
   case CDDS_ITEMPREPAINT:
   /* Do item-specific painting and
     return a CDRF_ value depending
     on how you want the item painting
     to proceed.
    */
   default:
    return (CDDS_DODEFAULT);
   }     //End of switch(dwDrawStage) block
  default:
   return (0);
  }     //End of switch(code) block
```

This short code sample is the parent window's WM_NOTIFY message handler. It tells the custom draw controls to send all custom draw notifications by returning CDRF_NOTIFYITEMDRAW in response to the CDDS_PREPAINT notification. The CDDS_ITEMPREPAINT handler then performs the custom drawing. The value returned when this is done depends on whether the application wants the control to continue with default item drawing or not.

A parent window can of course respond to custom draw notifications from various controls in different ways. In that case, the WM_NOTIFY handler would have to look at the *hwndFrom* or *idFrom* member of the NMHDR passed with the NMCUSTOMDRAW structure to determine which control is sending a particular notification.

Other NMCUSTOMDRAW Info Structures

Earlier we said that list view and tree view custom draw controls conveyed information about themselves in custom draw notifications with structures other than NMCUSTOMDRAW. This section describes those control-specific structures.

When list view controls and tree view controls send custom draw notifications, the *lParam* of the corresponding WM_NOTIFY message is a pointer to an NMLVCUSTOMDRAW or NMTVCUSTOMDRAW structure. These structures are identical, so we will discuss just the first. The NMLVCUSTOMDRAW structure is defined as:

```
typedef struct tagNMLVCUSTOMDRAW
{
  NMCUSTOMDRAW nmcd;
  COLORREF clrText;
  COLORREF clrTextBk;
} NMLVCUSTOMDRAW, *LPNMLVCUSTOMDRAW;
```

This structure is very similar to the NMCUSTOMDRAW structure that is sent by other custom draw controls with their custom draw notifications. In fact, the first member of the NMLVCUSTOMDRAW structure, *nmcd*, is an NMCUSTOMDRAW structure.

The NMLVCUSTOMDRAW structure contains two additional members. *clrText* is the color to be used as the foreground color when the particular list view or tree view item's text is drawn. *clrTextBk* is the item's text background color.

These values are useful if an application wants to change the text or background colors that are used when list view or tree view items are drawn. An application can assign new colors to these members and return CDRF_DODEFAULT in response to CDDS_ITEMPREPAINT notifications. The control will then paint its items with the new colors.

A Real Example

Let's look at the real CUSTDRAW.EXE example and see how the custom trackbar of Figure 10.1 is implemented.

The trackbar parent window draws the channel and thumb itself. It also responds to the TBCD_TICS item spec to draw the rounded trackbar outline. The NM_CUSTOMDRAW notification handler looks like this:

```
#define IDC_TRACKBAR  1028
case WM_NOTIFY:
  LPNMHDR lpnmhdr;
  lpnmhdr = (LPNMHDR)lParam;
  switch(lpnmhdr->code)
  {
  case NM_CUSTOMDRAW:
   LPNMCUSTOMDRAW lpnmcd;
   lpnmcd = (LPNMCUSTOMDRAW)lParam;
   /* Respond to notification if it comes
     from the trackbar control.
    */
   if (lpnmcd->hdr.idFrom==IDC_TRACKBAR)
   {
    BOOL bSel;
    bSel = (lpnmcd->uItemState==CDIS_SELECTED);
    switch(lpnmcd->dwDrawStage)
    {
     case CDDS_PREPAINT:
      return (CDRF_NOTIFYITEMDRAW);
     case CDDS_ITEMPREPAINT:
      return (OnDrawTrackbar(
       lpnmcd->hdr.hwndFrom,
       lpnmcd->hdc,
       lpnmcd->dwItemSpec,
       bSel);
     default:
      return (CDRF_DODEFAULT);
    }        //End of switch(dwDrawStage) block
   }         //End of if (hwndTB) block
  default:
   return (0);
  }          //End of switch(lpnmhdr->code) block
```

The trackbar control's parent window tests to see if the NM_CUSTOMDRAW notification is sent by the trackbar. This is done by comparing the trackbar command identifier IDC_TRACKBAR to the NMHDR *idFrom* value:

```
if (lpnmcd->hdr.idFrom==IDC_TRACKBAR)
```

The next thing the code does is obtain the current item state. If you run the CUSTDRAW.EXE application and press the trackbar thumb, the black dot changes to gray. In order to do this, the application needs to know if the thumb is selected.

After that, the code proceeds as in the general NM_CUSTOMDRAW notification handler presented earlier. It returns CDRF_NOTIFYITEM-DRAW in response to the CDDS_PREPAINT notification. This ensures that the trackbar control sends further paint cycle notifications. In response to the individual CDDS_ITEMPREPAINT notifications, the code performs the custom trackbar drawing operations as implemented by the application function *OnDrawTrackbar*:

```
int OnDrawTrackbar(HWND hwnd,
  HDC hdc,
  DWORD dwItemSpec,
  BOOL bSelected)
{
  HBRUSH hBrushOld;
  RECT rc, rcChannel;
  int nRes;
  int nHeight, nCenter;
  /* Calculate the custom channel RECT */
  GetClientRect(hwnd, &rc);
  nHeight = (rc.bottom-rc.top);
  nCenter = rc.top+nHeight/2;
  SendMessage(hwnd, TBM_GETCHANNELRECT, 0,
    (LPARAM)&rcChannel);
  rcChannel.top = nCenter-12;
  rcChannel.bottom = rcChannel.top+12;
  switch(dwItemSpec)
  {
  case TBCD_THUMB:
    SendMessage(hwnd, TBM_GETTHUMBRECT, 0, (LPARAM)&rc);
    rc.top = rcChannel.top+1;
    rc.bottom = rcChannel.bottom-1;
    if (!bSelected)
    {
      hBrushOld = (HBRUSH)SelectObject(hdc,
        GetStockObject(BLACK_BRUSH));
    }
    else
    {
      hBrushOld = (HBRUSH)SelectObject(hdc,
        GetStockObject(LTGRAY_BRUSH));
    }
    RoundRect(hdc, rc.left, rc.top,
     rc.right, rc.bottom, 20, 20);
    nRes = CDRF_SKIPDEFAULT;
```

```
     break;
   case TBCD_CHANNEL:
    hBrushOld = (HBRUSH)SelectObject(hdc,
     GetStockObject(WHITE_BRUSH));
    Rectangle(hdc, rcChannel.left, rcChannel.top,
     rcChannel.right, rcChannel.bottom);
    nRes = CDRF_SKIPDEFAULT;
    break;
   case TBCD_TICS:
    /* Tic marks get drawn first. Therefore draw the
       entire control outline here, so that it doesn't
       wipe out any subsequent painting.
     */
    GetClientRect(hwnd, &rc);
    //First draw a black filled round rectangle
    hBrushOld = (HBRUSH)SelectObject(hdc,
     GetStockObject(BLACK_BRUSH));
    RoundRect(hdc, rc.left, rc.top,
     rc.right, rc.bottom, 20, 20);
    /* Next inset the rectangle slightly, and fill
       it with white to leave behind the black
       "drop shadow" outline.
     */
    SelectObject(hdc,GetStockObject(WHITE_BRUSH));
    rc.bottom--;
    rc.right--;
    RoundRect(hdc, rc.left, rc.top,
     rc.right, rc.bottom, 20, 20);
    nRes = CDRF_DODEFAULT;
    break;
   }   //End of switch(dwItemSpec) statement
   SelectObject(hdc, hBrushOld);
   return (nRes);
 }
```

This function is responsible for drawing all of the trackbar control components. As parameters it takes the control HWND and HDC. It also takes the NMCUSTOMDRAW *dwItemSpec* value to specify which part of the control is to be drawn. Finally, it takes a BOOL indicating if the part of the control specified in the *dwItemSpec* parameter is selected.

The first six lines of this function determine the vertical center of the control's bounding rectangle and calculate a new channel rectangle, 24 pixels high and centered around that vertical center point.

The real fun begins with the *dwItemSpec* switch statement. For each of the three trackbar components (thumb, channel, and tic marks), drawing code is implemented to customize the appearance of the control.

The thumb is drawn as a small circle inside the trackbar channel. The color of the thumb depends on whether or not the thumb is pressed. After the thumb is drawn, *OnDrawTrackbar* (and hence the NM_CUSTOMDRAW notification) returns CDRF_SKIPDEFAULT. Since the application has customized the appearance of the thumb, it needs to prevent the control from drawing the default thumb.

The channel is drawn as a white rectangle of dimensions determined at the beginning of the function. This also returns CDRF_SKIPDEFAULT.

The most interesting case is the TBCD_TICS case. We wanted the trackbar to have a rounded border with a thin black outline. *OnDrawTrackbar* draws this outline here because trackbar tic marks are drawn before the thumb and channel. Since drawing the rounded outlines is done with calls to the Windows CE function *RoundRect*, anything inside the specified rectangle dimensions will be drawn over. Therefore, drawing the outline during the tic mark pre-paint notification doesn't erase the custom thumb or channel.

Notice how the application returns CDRF_DODEFAULT after the TBCD_TICS draw processing. The application only drew the control outline here, not the tic marks. To force the control to draw the standard tic marks, CDRF_DODEFAULT is returned.

Concluding Remarks

In this and the previous chapter, we have looked at how to take advantage of the features that Windows CE provides for customizing the appearance of various control classes. But owner draw and custom draw controls only allow your applications to modify the appearance of certain controls. What if you want to design and implement a completely new Windows CE control from scratch? You may not want to be limited to the customization hooks provided by owner draw and custom draw controls.

The next chapter shows you how to implement custom controls in Windows CE. Custom control programming techniques allow you to define completely new controls from scratch. With custom controls, you take complete control of the appearance and even the behavior of the controls you design. As you will see, custom controls provide for great flexibility in Windows CE user interface design.

CHAPTER 11

Designing Windows CE Custom Controls

Windows CE provides a lot of flexibility in designing user interfaces for applications. The child controls and common controls give programmers and designers a wide selection of user input and data presentation options. When the standard controls are not sufficient, Windows CE features such as owner draw buttons and the custom draw service provide ways to customize many of the more commonly used controls.

But sometimes even these options are not flexible enough to implement applications whose user interfaces deviate significantly from the standard Windows CE look and feel. In such cases, application programmers may be compelled to write user interface components from scratch. A *custom control* is any control used in an application that is not part of the Window CE operating system.[1]

A custom control is in many ways like any of the standard Windows CE child or common controls. Like the controls supplied with the Windows CE operating system, custom controls are child windows used in

[1] This definition would imply that other types of controls completely defined by an application programmer, such as ActiveX controls, are custom controls. While technically this is true, this chapter only describes custom controls as they are traditionally defined. Specifically this means any custom HWND-based control whose interface to a client application is the Win32 API.

applications to perform functions like displaying data, editing text, or responding to stylus taps in various ways. Your applications create custom controls by calling *CreateWindow* or *CreateWindowEx*, and respond to WM_COMMAND or WM_NOTIFY messages generated by the controls.

The big difference between the standard Windows CE controls and custom controls is that as the applications programmer, you design and implement the control. All aspects of the appearance of the control and its behavior are implemented by you to satisfy some special user interface needs not satisfied by any of the standard controls that come with Windows CE.

This points out the biggest benefit of using custom controls: As the control programmer, you have complete control over every aspect of the control's appearance and behavior.

In this chapter we will look at how to implement custom controls by implementing a simple custom control in a Windows CE dynamic link library.

AFTER COMPLETING THIS CHAPTER YOU WILL KNOW HOW TO . . .

Statically or dynamically link with a dynamic link library

Implement a dynamic link library

Design and implement a custom control as a dynamic link library

The Example Custom Control

Rather than focus on writing fancy control features and graphical appearance, this chapter concentrates on the framework required to implement a custom control. Therefore the custom control implemented in this chapter will look very familiar. We implement the standard button from scratch, and add some new custom control styles in the process.

Yes, this is pretty boring from the point of view of learning how to create user interface components that look nothing like Windows CE. But the aspects of implementing custom controls requiring the most attention are issues such as supporting control-specific styles and responding to window messages. Also more worth our time is how to package custom controls for the most convenient use by applications.

The custom button defines three styles that are specific to this custom control. These styles are detailed in Table 11.1. Some examples of custom buttons with the various styles are shown in Figures 11.1 and 11.2.

The complete source code for the custom control and the client application that uses the control can be found under \Samples\custom on the companion CD. The workspace (.dsw) file is under the \Samples\custom\control subdirectory and is called control.dsw. This workspace contains the project for the custom control, CONTROL.DLL, as well as the client application, CUSTOM.EXE.

Packaging a Custom Control as a Dynamic Link Library

The first thing to think about when implementing a Windows CE custom control is *not* how to make the control green. Programming the various appearance and behavioral aspects of the control comes second.

Your first concern as a custom control developer should be how to package the control. Your decision to implement a custom control was probably motivated by the specific requirements of one Windows CE application. But if designed properly, your control may find use in a number of different applications. You may even be able to sell it to other software developers.

Table 11.1 Custom Button Control Styles

STYLE	MEANING
CBTN_PUSH	Creates a custom button that acts like a standard Windows CE push-button control.
CBTN_TOGGLE	Creates a custom button that toggles, much like a check box. The button stays pressed when tapped. It must be tapped again to unpress it.
CBTN_LARGEFONT	Tells the control to draw button text with 18 point Times New Roman font. Without this style, the font used is 12 point Times New Roman.

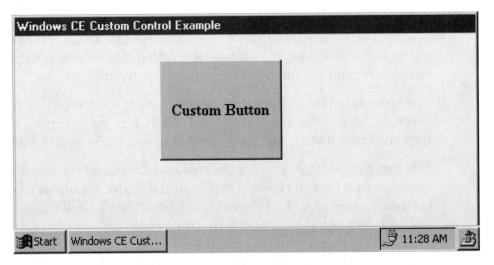

Figure 11.1 A custom button with the CBTN_PUSH style.

If a custom control is implemented inside an application that uses it, it is very hard for another application to use. Therefore, it is highly recommended that any custom control be implemented in a dynamic link library, or DLL. The control is thus packaged as a stand-alone module that can be used by any number of applications.

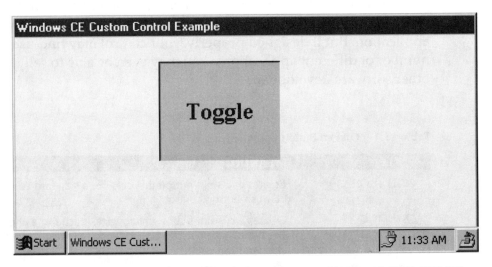

Figure 11.2 A custom button control with the CBTN_LARGEFONT and CBTN_TOGGLE styles in the pressed state.

DLL Basics

There are numerous resources that explore the details of dynamic link libraries in far more depth than can be covered here. This chapter will, however, highlight the main points of DLL programming and point out some of the benefits of using DLLs.

A dynamic link library is very similar to an executable application. A DLL can contain data, resources, and executable code just like an .EXE file. But a DLL is not a program. It is not run like an application. Applications load DLLs and use the data and resources they contain or call functions implemented inside the DLL. Dynamic link libraries are often called *application extensions* because they only become useful within the context of a running application.

Another important feature of dynamic link libraries relates to how functions in the DLL are linked to an application that uses them. Applications can link either *statically* or *dynamically* with the functions in a DLL.

When a DLL is loaded by an application, it technically means that a copy of the DLL is placed in the program memory of the application. The DLL and the application share the same address space. This is why more than one application can use the same DLL at the same time. For example, more than one Windows CE application written using MFC can run at the same time because each application has its own copy of the MFC DLL.

Static Linking

When you compile and link a dynamic link library, the DLL gets created as a file with the extension .DLL. Another file, called the *import library*, is also created with the extension .LIB. This file contains one or more *import records*, one for each function exported by the dynamic link library. Each import record contains the name of the DLL that contains the code implementing the function. It also contains either the name of the function or its *ordinal number*, or both. The ordinal number is simply a number that uniquely identifies a function in a DLL.

When an application statically links with a DLL, it means that the application links with the corresponding import library at link time. The information from the import records corresponding to any DLL functions referenced by the application get copied into the application's .EXE file.

When the application runs, Windows CE looks for any dynamic links in the .EXE file. Windows CE loads any DLLs referenced in these links that are not already loaded and resolves the import record function reference to the actual address of the function in the DLL. Hence, whenever the application calls a function in a DLL with which it was linked, it can call into the proper function code at run-time.

Dynamic Linking

One disadvantage of static linking is that when an application that statically links with a DLL starts executing, the DLL is loaded as well—even if the application only calls one function in that DLL, and that very rarely. So the DLL takes up room in the application's address space even when it is not in use. This can become problematic if an application uses many DLLs, especially in Windows CE environments where memory is often in short supply.

Dynamic linking offers an alternative. With dynamic linking, an application does not link with the DLL's import library. No import records are copied into the executable, and no dynamic links are established. And if there are no dynamic links in the executable file, no DLLs get loaded when the application begins execution.

Instead, with dynamic linking the application is responsible for loading any DLLs that it uses. Furthermore, the application must determine the address of any function it needs to call, get a pointer to the function, and call the function by de-referencing the pointer. Finally, the application must unload the DLL when it is done using it, in the same way that it frees up resources like fonts or bitmaps.

The benefit of using dynamic linking is that an application can control when a particular DLL is loaded. The application can also better manage its memory resources by deleting DLLs from memory when they are not in use.

Dynamic linking obviously means more work for the application programmer. With static linking, as long as you include the appropriate DLL header files and link with the import library, you can make calls to DLL functions as you would call any other function. Dynamic linking forces the application programmer to load DLLs, get function pointers, and free DLLs.

Let's look at the dynamic linking steps in more detail. An application loads a dynamic link library by calling the Windows CE function *Load-Library*:

```
LoadLibrary(lpLibFileName);
```

lpLibFileName is the null-terminated Unicode string name of the DLL to load. A search path to the DLL name cannot be specified. You must therefore either give the full path name of the DLL to be loaded or depend on Windows CE to find the DLL. If you choose the latter alternative, Windows CE will first look in the root directory of the storage card attached to the device, if any. If there is no such card, or the DLL is not found in the card's root directory, Windows CE proceeds by looking in the \Windows directory. Finally, if that fails, it searches the device's root directory.

If the DLL is found, *LoadLibrary* returns a handle to the DLL as an HINSTANCE. If it fails, the function returns NULL.

Note that *LoadLibrary* can be used to load any Windows CE module (.EXE or .DLL). It is most commonly used for DLLs, though.

When an application is done with a DLL, it calls *FreeLibrary*:

```
FreeLibrary(hLibModule);
```

hLibModule is the DLL instance handle returned by the previous *Load-Library* call.

Note that calling *FreeLibrary* does not necessarily mean that the specified module is removed from the process memory. In multithreaded applications, *LoadLibrary* can be called by one or more threads in a process, incrementing the module's *reference count. FreeLibrary* decrements this reference count for the specified module and only removes it from memory once its usage count goes to zero.

Finally, to get a pointer to an exported DLL function, an application uses *GetProcAddress*:

```
GetProcAddress(hModule, lpProcName);
```

hModule is the instance handle of the DLL containing the function of interest. *lpProcName* is the Unicode string name of the function. *GetProcAddress* returns a pointer to the requested function.

We will see an example of how to dynamically link with a DLL a little later in this chapter.

Exporting DLL Functions

The discussion above made references to *exported* DLL functions. A function must be exported by a DLL in order for it to be available to applications or other DLLs.

A dynamic link library can export a function using any one of the following techniques:

- Using the /EXPORT linker option

- Defining functions to be exported with the __declspec(dllexport) modifier

- Specifying the functions to be exported in a module definition file

A module definition file name uses the .DEF extension.

Let's look at an example of a DLL module definition file. The custom button control DLL of this chapter exports the function *InitCustomButton* via this module definition file:

```
LIBRARY    CONTROL.DLL
EXPORTS

    InitCustomButton    @1
```

The first line of the file assigns the name "CONTROL.DLL" to the DLL. The EXPORTS keyword says that the functions that follow are to be exported. Specifically, these are the functions for which import records are included in the import library that is generated when the DLL is linked. The @ sign specifies the ordinal number to assign to the corresponding function in the import record. If an ordinal number is not specified in the .DEF file, one is assigned by the linker.

Any application that appropriately links with CONTROL.DLL, either statically or dynamically, can now call the function *InitCustomButton*.

The DLL Entry Point

When a Windows CE application starts running, a little piece of startup code added to the beginning of the .EXE file by the linker calls a function known as the application *entry point*. This function is called *WinMain*. It is the function that application programmers think of as the starting point of their applications.

Dynamic link libraries also have an entry point. At various times, such as when a DLL is initially loaded by Windows CE, the operating system calls the function *DllMain*. The signature of *DllMain* is:

```
BOOL WINAPI DllMain(hinstDLL,
    fdwReason, lpvReserved);
```

The WINAPI modifier is simply defined as __stdcall in the Windows CE header files.

hinstDLL contains the instance handle of the DLL for which *DllMain* is being called. *fdwReason* and *lpvReserved* can take on various values depending on why *DllMain* is being called. These values and when they are passed to *DllMain* are described in Tables 11.2 and 11.3.

NOTE

CHANGING THE DLL ENTRY POINT FUNCTION NAME

You can freely change the entry point function name on a DLL-by-DLL basis. Simply use the /entry linker flag when linking the particular DLL. For example, many programmers like to use the name *DllEntryPoint* for their DLLs. To do so, add the following to the Project Options under the Link tab of the corresponding Microsoft Developer Studio project settings:

```
/entry:"DllEntryPoint"
```

Of course this new name must then be used in the entry point function implementation.

The value returned by *DllMain* is ignored except when the *fdwReason* parameter is DLL_PROCESS_ATTACH. In this case, *DllMain* should return TRUE if the DLL initialization succeeds and FALSE if it fails.

Table 11.2 DllMain fdwReason Parameter Values

VALUE	MEANING
DLL_PROCESS_ATTACH	DLL is being loaded for the first time by an application.
DLL_PROCESS_DETACH	DLL is being detached from the process that uses it. This happens when the process terminates or a *FreeLibrary* call has forced the DLL usage count to 0.
DLL_THREAD_ATTACH	A new thread has been created in the calling process.
DLL_THREAD_DETACH	A thread has been terminated in the calling process.

Table 11.3 DllMain lpvReserved Parameter Values

VALUE	MEANING
NULL	If *fdwReason* is DLL_PROCESS_ATTACH, this means that *DllMain* was called as a result of a dynamic *LoadLibrary* call.
	If *fdwReason* is DLL_PROCESS_DETACH, this means that *DllMain* was called as a result of a dynamic *FreeLibrary* call that reduced the DLL reference count to 0.
Non-NULL	If *fdwReason* is DLL_PROCESS_ATTACH, this means that *DllMain* was called as a result of a static DLL load when the process started.
	If *fdwReason* is DLL_PROCESS_DETACH, this means that *DllMain* was called as a result of process termination.

DLL Benefits

There are numerous reasons for using dynamic link libraries. The most important reasons include:

Maintainability. Applications are broken down into a number of components, each of which is easier to maintain than a larger monolithic application.

Reusability. Functions and resources exported by a DLL are more easily used by multiple applications.

Memory management. Applications have more direct control over memory usage if they choose when to load and free DLLs.

Initializing the DLL in the Client Application

Before we explore the details of programming our custom control DLL, let's look at how the client application initializes the DLL. This provides a real example of how to dynamically link an application with a DLL.

To use our custom button control, an application must do two things. It must first link with the dynamic link library that implements the control. As discussed above, this can be done either statically or dynamically. Next, the application must call the appropriate function to register the custom control window class.

The client application CUSTOM.EXE dynamically links with the custom control library CONTROL.DLL. The code below comes from the

WinMain function found on the companion CD in the file
\Samples\custom\main.cpp. *hInstDLL* is an HINSTANCE defined in
the file \Samples\custom\custom.h.

The DLL initialization function called *InitCustomButton* is described in
detail in the next section.

```
#include <control.h>
typedef void (*LPINITCUSTOMBUTTON)();
LPINITCUSTOMBUTTON lpicb;
HINSTANCE hInstDLL;
HWND hwndExit;
int WINAPI WinMain(HINSTANCE hInstance,
  HINSTANCE hPrevInstance,
  LPTSTR lpCmdLine,
  int nCmdShow)
{
  MSG msg;
  WNDCLASS wndClass;
  /* Save application instance in ghInst for
    possible use by other functions, such as
    the main window's window procedure.
   */
  ghInst = hInstance;
  /* We are dynamically linking with control.dll.
    The application must therefore load the DLL
    and get the address of all exported functions
    that it wishes to call.
   */
  hInstDLL = LoadLibrary(TEXT("control.dll"));
  if (hInstDLL)
  {
   lpicb = (LPINITCUSTOMBUTTON)GetProcAddress(
    hInstDLL, TEXT("InitCustomButton"));
   /* Call the custom control initialization function
     by dereferencing the function pointer extracted by
     the previous line of code.
    */
   (*lpicb)();
  }
  else
  {
   MessageBox(NULL, TEXT("Could not load DLL"),
    TEXT("Custom Control Sample Error"),
    MB_ICONEXCLAMATION|MB_OK);
  }
  /* Application code which registers the application
    main window class, creates the main window, etc.
    not shown
```

```
  */
  hwndExit = CreateWindow(
    CUSTOMBUTTON,
    TEXT("Exit"),
    WS_VISIBLE|WS_CHILD|CBTN_LARGEFONT,
    0,0,100,100,
    hwndMain,
    (HMENU)IDC_EXIT,
    hInstance,
    NULL);
  /* Etc. etc. */
}
```

The first interesting thing in this code sample is the *LoadLibrary* call.
This function loads the dynamic link library CONTROL.DLL into the
client application's address space. *hInstDLL* contains an instance handle of this DLL.

Next, the client application gets the address of the exported DLL function *InitCustomButton*. It does this by calling *GetProcAddress*:

```
lpicb = (LPINITCUSTOMBUTTON)GetProcAddress(
  hInstDLL, TEXT("InitCustomButton"));
```

lpicb is declared as type LPINITCUSTOMBUTTON. This type is defined by the client application as an alias for pointers to functions with
the same signature as *InitCustomButton*. Therefore, after the *GetProcAddress* call, *lpicb* contains a pointer to the *InitCustomButton* function. The
application then initializes the custom button control by calling this
function by simply de-referencing this function pointer.

After that, the application is free to create instances of the custom button control by calling *CreateWindow* with the CUSTOMBUTTON window class name. The CUSTOMBUTTON symbol is defined in the
header file CONTROL.H. We will see this definition a little later.

From the point of view of the client application, that's it. The application can now send window messages or any custom messages defined
by the control to *hwndExit*. The application can also respond to notifications or messages (such as WM_COMMAND) that the button may
send it.

Implementing the Custom Button Control

We now focus our attention on the details of the custom control DLL
implementation.

The *InitCustomButton* Function

The first part of the custom button control implementation we will look at is the *InitCustomButton* function. This is the exported function that client applications call to register the control window class. This function also initializes the two fonts used by the control, but this part of the function is left out for brevity.

```
void InitCustomButton()
{
  WNDCLASS wndClass;
  wndClass.style       = 0;
  wndClass.lpfnWndProc = ControlWndProc;
  wndClass.cbClsExtra  = 0;
  wndClass.cbWndExtra  = 8;
  wndClass.hInstance   = NULL;
  wndClass.hIcon       = NULL;
  wndClass.hCursor     = NULL;
  wndClass.hbrBackground = (HBRUSH)(COLOR_WINDOW+1);
  wndClass.lpszMenuName = NULL;
  wndClass.lpszClassName = CUSTOMBUTTON;
  RegisterClass(&wndClass);
  /* This function also goes on to create the
     two fonts used by the DLL.
   */
}
```

ControlWndProc is the window procedure of the custom button control. We will discuss this function later. Also notice that the *cbWndExtra* member of the WNDCLASS structure is 8. This means that every custom button HWND carries around 8 extra bytes. We will see how these bytes are used later as well.

The header file associated with the custom control DLL, CONTROL.H, includes the following definition:

```
#define CUSTOMBUTTON (TEXT("CUSTOMBUTTON"))
```

This defines the window class name for the control. This name gets assigned to the *lpszClassName* member of the WNDCLASS structure.

Note that since all window classes are global under Windows CE, the *hInstance* member of the window class structure can be set to NULL.

NOTE

A Custom Control Class Can Be Registered in DllMain

Your custom control implementations can do all of the control window class registration in *DllMain* in response to the DLL_PROCESS_ATTACH event. This would eliminate the need for implementing an initialization function. Applications would have one less function to call as well. This chapter chooses to implement the initialization function to more fully demonstrate dynamic linking, and the way *GetProcAddress* is used to obtain pointers to exported functions.

Custom Button Control Styles

The custom button control supports three control styles: CBTN_PUSH, CBTN_TOGGLE, and CBTN_LARGEFONT. Refer to Table 11.1 at the beginning of the chapter for a description of these styles.

In Windows CE, control styles generally occupy the low word of the 32-bit integer that defines the control window styles. The high word is used for the window styles such as WS_CHILD or WS_VISIBLE.

The custom control header file CONTROL.H thus defines the three control styles as the following 16-bit integers:

```
#define CBTN_PUSH      0x0000
#define CBTN_TOGGLE    0x0001
#define CBTN_LARGEFONT 0x0002
```

Assigning CBTN_PUSH a value of zero means that this style is the default custom button control style. Each of the other styles is assigned a unique bit of a 16-bit integer.

An instance of the custom button control class often needs to test one or more of these style bits to see if it is set. Determining if a particular button is toggle style, for instance, requires that the custom control code check for the CBTN_TOGGLE bit.

A window can check its styles by calling the Windows CE *GetWindowLong* function. The function extracts a particular 32-bit integer value that is stored with the window:

```
GetWindowLong(hWnd, nIndex);
```

hWnd specifies the window, and *nIndex* is a value specifying which 32-bit value to retrieve. This parameter can be any one of the values shown in Table 11.4.

As an example, an application can check to see if an instance of the custom button control class has the CBTN_LARGEFONT style with the following code:

```
HWND hwndButton;   //The custom button control HWND
DWORD dwStyle;

dwStyle = GetWindowLong(
  hwndButton,
  GWL_STYLE);
if (dwStyle & CBTN_LARGEFONT)
{
  //Do something
}
```

GetWindowLong has a counterpart, *SetWindowLong*, which can be used to set any of the values described in Table 11.4.

```
SetWindowLong(hWnd, nIndex, dwNewLong);
```

This function sets the window value indicated by *nIndex* to the value specified by *dwNewLong*. The previous value that the window stored for that index is returned by the function.

NOTE
UNSUPPORTED INDICES

Under Windows CE, *GetWindowLong* and *SetWindowLong* do not support the GWL_HINSTANCE, GWL_HWNDPARENT, or GWL_USERDATA indices.

Table 11.4 GetWindowLong and SetWindowLong Index Values

VALUE	MEANING
GWL_EXSTYLE	Retrieves/sets the window extended style.
GWL_STYLE	Retrieves/sets the window style.
GWL_WNDPROC	Retrieves/sets the window procedure.
GWL_ID	Retrieves/sets the window identifier.
DWL_DLGPROC	Retrieves/sets the dialog procedure for a specified dialog box.
DWL_MSGRESULT	Retrieves/sets the return value of a message processed in the dialog box procedure.
DWL_USER	Retrieves/sets an application-specific 32-bit value associated with the specified dialog box.

Performing a Window Brain Transplant: Window Subclassing

The Windows CE functions *GetWindowLong* and *SetWindowLong* provide some very powerful possibilities when used with the GWL_WNDPROC index. With these functions, an application can *subclass* any Windows CE window.

Window subclassing in this sense means replacing the window procedure of a window with a different window procedure. With this technique, an application can give custom behavior to a window on the fly.

This becomes most significant when subclassing Windows CE controls. Subclassing a control lets you take full advantage of the default functionality of the control while adding custom behavior only where needed.

To subclass a control or any other window, you write a window procedure for that control which contains your custom responses to the various Windows CE messages you wish to override. You then make the control use this window procedure by calling *SetWindowLong*:

```
LRESULT CALLBACK myWndProc(HWND hwnd,
  UINT message.
  WPARAM wParam,
  LPARAM lParam);
HWND hwndControl;
WNDPROC wndProcOld;
wndProcOld = (WNDPROC)SetWindowLong(
  hwndControl, GWL_WNDPROC, (LONG)myWndProc);
```

In one step, *SetWindowLong* changes the window procedure to be used by the control *hwndControl* and stores the original control window procedure in *wndProcOld*.

Using Extra Window Words to Maintain the State of the Control

So far we have ignored the significance of the following line of code that is executed when initializing the custom button control's window class:

```
wndClass.cbWndExtra = 8;
```

As discussed back in Chapter 2, this statement means that every instance of the window class will contain eight extra bytes, or two 32-bit values. An application can use these values to store information about an instance of the window class.

Saving the old window procedure makes it easy for your custom window procedure to implement the original default behavior for messages you do not want to override. This is done by calling *CallWindowProc*:

```
CallWindowProc(wndprcPrev, hwnd, uMsg, wParam, lParam);
```

This function passes handling of the message *uMsg* to the window procedure specified by *wndprcPrev*. In other words, *CallWindowProc* allows an application to directly call into a specified window procedure.

As an example, let's say that you only wish to customize the stylus tap logic for a list box control. You could write the custom list box window procedure as follows. *ListWndProcOld* is the original list box window procedure extracted by a call to *SetWindowLong* like the one shown above.

```
LRESULT CALLBACK myWndProc(
  HWND hwnd,
  UINT message.
  WPARAM wParam,
  LPARAM lParam)
{
  switch(message)
  {
   case WM_LBUTTONDOWN:
    //Custom logic here
    return (0);
   default:
    return (CallWindowProc(ListWndProcOld,
     hwnd, message, wParam, lParam));
   }
 }
```

These extra words are accessed using *GetWindowLong* and *SetWindowLong*. Instead of using one of the predefined indices in Table 11.4, the application references a particular 32-bit value by its zero-based offset. Since the number of bytes defined by *cbWndExtra* must be a multiple of four, and each extra word is 4 bytes, the index of the first word is 0, the second is 4, and so on.

For example, to access the second of these extra window words, an application would do this:

```
DWORD dwVal;
dwVal = GetWindowLong(hwndControl, 4);
```

The custom button control implementation uses the two extra words it defines to keep information about the state of each instance of the control class. CONTROL.H defines the following two indices:

```
#define GWL_BUTTONINVERT   0
#define GWL_BUTTONFONT     4
```

These are the indices used to access the first and second extra window words, respectively, defined by the custom button control's window class.

The first extra window word keeps track of whether the particular button is currently painted in the inverted state. This information is used by the control's window procedure, for example, to determine which state to repaint a toggle-style control in when a user taps it.

The second word stores the font handle of the font used to draw the button text.

As an example of how this state information is used, let's look at the processing that occurs when a custom button control is created. The following code comes from the control window procedure's WM_CREATE handler. *hwnd* is the HWND of the control, and *lpcs* is a pointer to the CREATESTRUCT. *hFont12Pt* and *hFont18Pt* are the handles to the two fonts available to the control:

```
if (lpcs->style & CBTN_LARGEFONT)
{
  SetWindowLong(
    hwnd,
    GWL_BUTTONFONT,
    (LONG)hFont18Pt
    );
}
else
{
  SetWindowLong(
    hwnd,
    GWL_BUTTONFONT,
    (LONG)hFont12Pt
    );
}
return (TRUE);
```

When an instance of the control is created, the appropriate font is assigned depending on whether the CBTN_LARGEFONT style bit is set.

The control then uses this font when painting itself. The WM_PAINT handler code contains the following line for selecting the font into the control's device context. *hwnd* is the window handle of the control:

```
hFontOld = (HFONT)SelectObject(hdc,
    (HFONT)GetWindowLong(hwnd, GWL_BUTTONFONT));
```

Any text drawn inside the control is thus in the correct font.

Handling Button Presses

Probably the most interesting code in the custom button control implementation is the stylus handling logic. The custom button control class supports the CBTN_PUSH and CBTN_TOGGLE styles, and the stylus code must implement the appropriate behavior for both.

To make it easier for the control source code to determine which of these styles is assigned to a particular button, the CONTROL.H header file defines the following macro:

```
#define IsToggleStyle(hwnd) \
   ((GetWindowLong(hwnd, GWL_STYLE) & CBTN_TOGGLE) \
   ? TRUE : FALSE)
```

The control also uses the first extra window word, indexed by GWL_BUTTONINVERT, to keep track of whether a button instance is in the pressed or unpressed state.

CBTN_PUSH Style Custom Button Controls

Buttons with the CBTN_PUSH style act like regular Windows CE button controls. When pressed, they are painted in the pressed state. Once released, they are repainted in the unpressed state. Also, if a user presses the button and drags the stylus on and off the button without releasing the button, the button changes between the pressed and unpressed states.

When a user presses a CBTN_PUSH-style button, the following WM_LBUTTONDOWN handler code is invoked:

```
SetCapture(hwnd);
SetWindowLong(hwnd, GWL_BUTTONINVERT, (LONG)TRUE);
```

The stylus capture is assigned to the button control window. This forces all subsequent stylus input to be passed to the control. Next, the

GWL_BUTTONINVERT extra window word is set to TRUE. This state
information will be used during WM_PAINT handling to determine
which state to paint the button in. Specifically, the WM_PAINT handler includes the following code. *hwnd* is the HWND of the control,
and *hdc* is the control's device context:

```
RECT rc;
BOOL bInvert;
GetClientRect(hwnd, &rc);
bInvert = (BOOL)GetWindowLong(hwnd, GWL_BUTTONINVERT);
if (bInvert)
{
  DrawEdge(hdc, &rc, EDGE_SUNKEN,
    BF_SOFT|BF_RECT);
}
else
{
  DrawEdge(hdc, &rc, EDGE_RAISED,
    BF_SOFT|BF_RECT);
}
```

In the pressed state the control is drawn with a sunken edge. In the
unpressed state, it is drawn in the raised state.

When the user releases the button, the WM_LBUTTONUP code shown
in Figure 11.3 is invoked.

Capture is released from the control HWND. The GWL_BUTTONIN-
VERT window word is set to FALSE so that the button is drawn in the
unpressed state during the next paint cycle.

The rest of the WM_LBUTTONUP code determines whether the stylus
was in the button when it was released. If so, the button sends a
WM_COMMAND message to its parent window. WM_COMMAND
messages are not sent if a user presses a button and then drags the stylus off of it without releasing the button.

The *PtInRect* call determines if the stylus point is in the control's
bounding rectangle. Also note the use of the GWL_ID index in the call
to *GetWindowLong*. This extracts the control identifier of the custom
button, which must be sent with the WM_COMMAND message.

Finally, the control must handle stylus move messages. The
WM_MOUSEMOVE handler implementation is:

```
RECT rc;
BOOL bInvert;
if (GetCapture()==hwnd)
```

```
  {
    GetClientRect(hwnd, &rc);
    bInvert = (PtInRect(&rc, pt)) ? TRUE : FALSE;
    if (!IsToggleStyle(hwnd))
    {
      SetWindowLong(hwnd, GWL_BUTTONINVERT, (LONG)bInvert);
    }
  }
```

If the control does not have stylus capture, the WM_MOUSEMOVE handler does nothing. This means that if the stylus moves when a button is not pressed, nothing needs to be done.

Otherwise, the code simply toggles the GWL_BUTTONINVERT state depending on whether the stylus is dragged into or out of the pressed button. When the button is repainted, its appearance will alternate between the pressed and unpressed states.

CBTN_TOGGLE Style Custom Button Controls

There are only minor differences in the stylus handling for CBTN_TOGGLE-style buttons. The basic difference is determining when to change the GWL_BUTTONINVERT state so that the button remains pressed until tapped again.

```
HWND hwndParent;
RECT rc;
GetClientRect(hwnd, &rc);
ReleaseCapture();
if (!IsToggleStyle(hwnd))
{
  SetWindowLong(hwnd, GWL_BUTTONINVERT, (LONG)FALSE);
}
  /* Send a WM_COMMAND to the parent if
    stylus went up in the control.
  */
if (PtInRect(&rc, pt))
{
  InvalidateRect(hwnd, NULL, TRUE);
  hwndParent = GetParent(hwnd);
  SendMessage(
   hwndParent,
   WM_COMMAND,
   MAKEWPARAM((WORD)GetWindowLong(hwnd, GWL_ID), 0),
    (LPARAM)hwnd);
}
```

Figure 11.3   Custom button control WM_LBUTTONUP message handling code.

The WM_LBUTTONDOWN code for CBTN_TOGGLE-style controls looks like this:

```
BOOL bInvert;
SetCapture(hwnd);
bInvert = (BOOL)GetWindowLong(hwnd, GWL_BUTTONINVERT);
SetWindowLong(hwnd,
  GWL_BUTTONINVERT, (LONG)(!bInvert));
```

Whereas the CBTN_PUSH style controls always set the GWL_BUT-TONINVERT state to TRUE on a stylus tap, the CBTN_TOGGLE buttons toggle this state.

If you refer to the WM_LBUTTONUP code in Figure 11.3, you will see only one difference between CBTN_TOGGLE and CBTN_PUSH controls. The difference is these lines, which force toggle-style buttons to set the invert state extra window word to FALSE:

```
if (!IsToggleStyle(hwnd))
{
  SetWindowLong(hwnd, GWL_BUTTONINVERT, (LONG)FALSE);
}
```

In other words, when the user releases a CBTN_TOGGLE-style button, the toggle state does not change. In this way, a pressed button stays pressed and an unpressed button stays unpressed. The toggle state does not change until the button is pressed again, as shown by the WM_LBUTTONDOWN code above.

Similarly, CBTN_TOGGLE-style buttons do not change state when the stylus moves across them. These lines in the WM_MOUSEMOVE code ensure this:

```
if (!IsToggleStyle(hwnd))
{
  SetWindowLong(hwnd, GWL_BUTTONINVERT, (LONG)bInvert);
}
```

The Complete Sample Application

The complete source code for the custom button control DLL and the client application are included on the companion CD. The directory \Samples\custom contains the client application source code. The directory \Samples\control contains the source code for the custom control DLL, as well as the Microsoft Developer Studio workspace file for both of these components.

Concluding Remarks

In Chapters 9, 10, and 11, we have discussed some of the features provided by Windows CE for designing custom application user interfaces. Owner draw controls let you take over the control painting process in your application code. The custom draw service is similar, but provides more flexibility by giving your application the opportunity to intercede at specific times in the control's paint cycle.

There may be occasions when even more customization is required. For these jobs you can implement complete new controls from scratch using the custom control programming techniques you have just read about.

As you gain experience using these programming techniques, you will come to appreciate the flexibility that Windows CE offers for designing custom user interfaces for your applications.

The next two chapters discuss some additional Windows CE user interface features. Chapter 12 introduces the HTML Viewer control. Chapter 13 describes how to program some of the user interface features specific to the Palm-size PC platform.

CHAPTER 12

The HTML Viewer Control

T he advent of the Internet and the World Wide Web have led to dramatic changes in the basic functionality of computer operating systems. Microsoft's Win32-based operating systems are no exception. Windows NT, Windows 98, and Windows CE are all very comfortable with providing users with the ability to browse the Internet and display data in all of the various new formats that this medium has generated.

Applications such as Pocket Internet Explorer, the Microsoft Windows CE Web browser, can display hypertext markup language (HTML) documents containing formatted text and images just like their desktop Web browser counterparts.

HyperText Markup Language, or HTML, has always been an important part of the Internet. One of the simplest ways to display HTML in Windows CE applications is with the HTML viewer control provided with Windows CE. This control is in fact used by Pocket Internet Explorer for viewing HTML pages. As we will see, adding HTML rendering capabilities to your Windows CE applications can be easily done with the HTML viewer control.

AFTER COMPLETING THIS CHAPTER YOU WILL KNOW HOW TO . . .

Use the HTML viewer control to display HTML documents

Overview of the HTML Viewer Control

The Windows CE HTML viewer control is not a child control. Therefore it is not part of the Graphics, Windowing, and Event Subsystem. Nor is it part of COMMCTRL.DLL. That means it does not get loaded along with the tree view and trackbar controls when you call *InitCommonControls*.

The HTML viewer control resides in its very own dynamic link library, called HTMLVIEW.DLL. To use the control, applications must either explicitly link with the DLL's import library, HTMLVIEW.LIB, or dynamically link with HTMLVIEW.DLL by loading the DLL at runtime.

Next, before using the HTML viewer control, applications must initialize it by calling *InitHTMLControl*. This is a function, exported by HTMLVIEW.DLL, that is responsible for registering the control's window class. After calling *InitHTMLControl*, applications are free to create instances of the control. In these respects, the design of this control closely resembles the custom control we designed in the previous chapter.

Control Features

The HTML viewer control provides very basic (and I mean *very* basic) functionality for viewing HTML documents. As we will soon see, the control leaves many of the details of navigating between HTML links, displaying images, and playing sounds to the application that contains the control.

First and foremost, it is important to keep in mind that the control is only an HTML viewer. It does not provide HTML editing capabilities.

Next, the HTML viewer control interprets HTML and displays data in the correct format. The control understands all the standard HTML

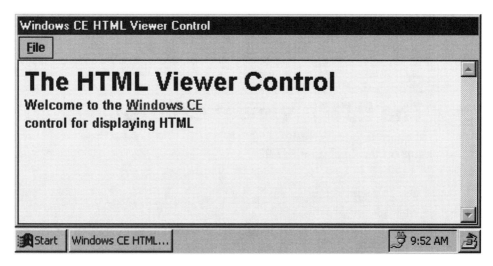

Figure 12.1 The HTML viewer control at work.

tags, and displays text in the correct sizes and styles based on those tags.

As an example, Figure 12.1 shows the HTML viewer control's rendering of the following HTML file:

```
<h1>The HTML Viewer Control</h1>
<h4>Welcome to the <a href="\Windows\wince.htm">Windows
  CE</a></h4>
<h4>control for displaying HTML</h4>
```

The only work the application had to do was send the HTML text to the control. The HTML viewer control takes care of the rest.

The situation is not quite so pleasant in the case of images or sound references in an HTML document. For example, the HTML viewer control does not automatically render GIF files referenced in a document. Nor does it automatically play sound files.

If we add a line to the top of the sample HTML file referencing an inline GIF image, the HTML viewer control displays the file as shown in Figure 12.2:

```
<IMG SRC="\Windows\home.gif">
<h1>The HTML Viewer Control</h1>
<h4>Welcome to the <a href="\Windows\wince.htm">Windows  CE</a> </h4>
<h4>control for displaying HTML</h4>
```

The HTML viewer control only sends a notification to its parent window when it reads a reference to an image from an HTML file. It is the

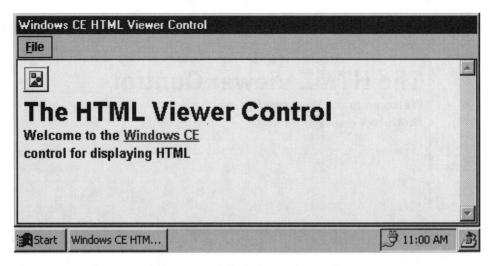

Figure 12.2 The HTML Viewer Control displaying an image.

responsibility of the application to then convert the image file to a Windows CE bitmap. The application must then send the appropriate message to the control telling it to display the bitmap representation of the original image file.

The HTML viewer control will also notify its parent when a user has tapped on a hypertext link. It is again, however, the application's responsibility to follow the link. That is, the application must respond to this notification by loading the referenced file and telling the HTML viewer control to display it.

At first this seems like a major limitation of the control. But it does make sense for the application, not the control, to do this work. A particular instance of the HTML viewer control has no idea if the HTML documents it is being asked to render are stored locally on the Windows CE device or are coming from a live Internet connection. The application has all of this context information and should therefore be responsible for supplying the data to the control in the correct form.

NOTE

THE NAMES SHOULD HAVE BEEN CHANGED TO PROTECT THE INNOCENT

You will notice that all of the HTML viewer control message names begin with DTM_. This is somewhat confusing, because the message names for the date time picker control start with DTM_ as well.

The Sample Application

Our discussion of the HTML viewer control is motivated by the sample application HTML.EXE. This application, which can be found in \Samples\html on the companion CD, illustrates many of the features provided by the HTML viewer control.

HTML.EXE implements a basic HTML file viewer. It allows a user to view any HTML file on the file system of a Windows CE device (or the emulation file system if run in the emulator). Two simple HTML files, sample.htm and wince.htm, are provided. These files must be placed in the device or emulator file system under the \Windows directory. See the section on "Viewing the Windows CE Object Store" in the introduction to Part II for a description of how to transfer files using the Remote Object Viewer.

The main application window was shown in Figure 12.1. When the application first starts, there is no HTML displayed, however. Users can display files by opening them with the Open option of the File menu. Choosing this option presents the user with a standard File Open dialog shown in Figure 12.3. Using this interface, the user can search the file system for a particular HTML file. Selecting the file and pressing the OK button causes the application to display the contents of the selected file.

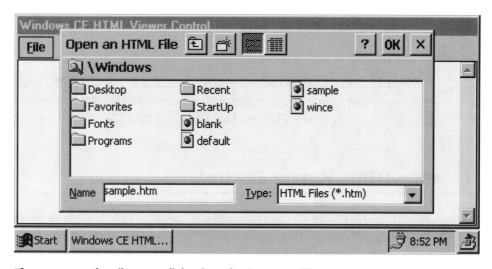

Figure 12.3 The File Open dialog for selecting HTML files.

Preparing to Use the HTML Viewer Control

As mentioned earlier, an application must initialize the HTMLVIEW. DLL module before instances of the HTML viewer control can be created and used. Applications can link with HTMLVIEW.DLL dynamically, or they can link with HTMLVIEW.LIB to avoid loading the DLL at run-time.

To make the application a little less complicated, HTML.EXE links with the import library. It can therefore call *InitHTMLControl* directly. The only thing that must be done that we have not yet mentioned is that the application must include the file HTMLCTRL.H. This is the header file that defines all of the messages and notifications which the HTML viewer control can send, as well as the function *InitHTMLControl*.

InitHTMLControl must be called in order to register the window class that defines the HTML viewer control. This step is analogous to calling *InitCommonControls* before using COMMCTRL.DLL.

HTML.EXE calls *InitHTMLControl* in *WinMain*:

```
#include <htmlctrl.h>
int WINAPI WinMain(HINSTANCE hInstance,
  HINSTANCE hPrevInstance,
  LPTSTR lpCmdLine,
  int nCmdShow)
{
  /* Other application code */
  ...
  InitHTMLControl(hInstance);
  ...
}
```

InitHTMLControl takes only one argument: the HINSTANCE of the application that is using the control. It returns TRUE if the window class is registered properly. Otherwise it returns FALSE.

Creating HTML Viewer Controls

You are now ready to create instances of the HTML viewer control. This step is done with *CreateWindow* or *CreateWindowEx*, just as when creating any other Windows CE control. The only thing left to know is the name of the window class to use.

The HTML viewer control window class is called DISPLAYCLASS. That's an obvious one, isn't it? To create a control with a control identifier defined as IDC_HTML and whose parent is *hwndParent*, an application would do this:

```
HWND hwndHTML;
hwndHTML = CreateWindow(
  TEXT("DISPLAYCLASS"), NULL,
  WS_CHILD|WS_VISIBLE|WS_BORDER,
  0,0,100,100, //i.e., some dimensions
  hwndParent, (HMENU)IDC_HTML,
  hInstance, NULL);
```

The control, referred to by *hwndHTML*, is now ready to display HTML data.

NOTE
HTML VIEWER CONTROL STYLES

Unlike most of the other Windows CE controls, the HTML viewer control defines no control-specific styles or extended styles to allow programmers to customize the control's appearance or behavior.

Displaying HTML Formatted Text

As an HTML viewer, the HTML viewer control must provide a way for applications to give it HTML text to display.

Text is inserted into the control by sending either the message DTM_ADDTEXT or DTM_ADDTEXTW. DTM_ADDTEXT is for adding non-Unicode text. DTM_ADDTEXTW is the Unicode version.

HTML.EXE uses DTM_ADDTEXT because it assumes that the files it reads are saved as ANSI text, not Unicode.

As the name of these two messages implies, they add text to the specified control. So if there is already text in an HTML viewer control before an application sends one of these messages, the text is added to the bottom of the control's client area. The message does not cause the control to clear its contents before the new text is displayed.

In order to display text by itself, you must first remove the current contents of the control. The easiest way to do this is to send a WM_SETTEXT message to the control with a NULL text string:

```
SendMessage(hwndHTML, WM_SETTEXT, 0, NULL);
```

Closely related to these ADDTEXT messages is the message DTM_ENDOFSOURCE. An application sends this message to an HTML viewer control to tell it that the application is done sending text. Both parameters to this message, *wParam* and *lParam*, are zero.

NOTE
Do You Really Need DTM_ENDOFSOURCE?

It appears that not sending DTM_ENDOFSOURCE has no negative side effects.

An Example

The sample application HTML.EXE allows users to pick the HTML file to display using a File Open dialog. Once a file is specified, the application must read the HTML text from the file and send it to the HTML viewer control using the DTM_ADDTEXT message.

The function that HTML.EXE uses to load an HTML file is called *Link-ToFile*. (This name will make more sense a bit later when we see that the application uses the same function for following hyperlinks.)

```
void LinkToFile(TCHAR* pszFilename)
{
  DWORD dwSize, dwBytes;
  LPSTR lpszBuf;
  WIN32_FIND_DATA fd;
  CEOIDINFO oidInfo;
  //Clear the control
  SendMessage(hwndHTML, WM_SETTEXT, 0, NULL);
  hFile = FindFirstFile(pszFilename, &fd);
  if (INVALID_HANDLE_VALUE!=hFile)
  {
   CeOidGetInfo(fd.dwOID, &oidInfo);
   dwSize = oidInfo.infFile.dwLength+1;
   FindClose(hFile);
  }
  hFile = CreateFile(pszFilename,
   GENERIC_READ, 0,
   NULL, OPEN_EXISTING,
   FILE_ATTRIBUTE_NORMAL, NULL);
  lpszBuf = (LPSTR)LocalAlloc(LPTR, dwSize+1);
  lpszBuf[dwSize] = 0; //Add NULL terminator
  ReadFile(hFile, lpszBuf, dwSize, &dwBytes, NULL);
  SendMessage(hwndHTML, DTM_ADDTEXT,
   (WPARAM)FALSE, (LPARAM)lpszBuf);
```

```
    SendMessage(hwndHTML, DTM_ENDOFSOURCE, 0, 0);
    CloseHandle(hFile);
}
```

hwndHTML is the window handle of the HTML viewer control. It is defined as a global variable so that the entire application can reference it. *LinkToFile* looks formidable, but it is actually quite straightforward.

First it searches the file system for the file specified by the parameter *pszFilename*. The application already knows the name of the file to display because the user selected a file from the File Open dialog. But the application calls *FindFirstFile* in order to get the object identifier of the selected file. It can then get the size of the file with the *CeOidGetInfo* call, which it needs to allocate space for the file contents. The function then opens the file with the appropriate call to *CreateFile*.

Next, *LinkToFile* allocates enough space in the buffer *lpszBuf* to hold the contents of the entire file by calling *LocalAlloc*. It knows the size it needs to allocate because previously the function determined the byte size of the file. Once the *lpszBuf* is allocated, *ReadFile* fills the buffer with the contents of the file *pszFilename*.

Finally, *LinkToFile* sends a DTM_ADDTEXT message to display the HTML text it just read in the HTML viewer control:

```
    SendMessage(hwndHTML, DTM_ADDTEXT,
        (WPARAM)FALSE, (LPARAM)lpszBuf);
```

As noted in Table 12.1, the FALSE *wParam* parameter tells the control to treat the contents of *lpszBuf* as HTML formatted text.

Handling Hyperlinks

The Windows CE HTML viewer control provides some built-in support for hyperlinks in HTML formatted text. The control knows how

Table 12.1 The DTM_ADDTEXT/DTM_ADDTEXTW Messages

PARAMETER	MEANING
(BOOL)wParam	Indicates the type of text to add. If TRUE, the control treats the text as plain text. If FALSE, the control treats the text as HTML formatted text.
(LPSTR)lParam or (LPWSTR)lParam	Pointer to the string to be added. String is ANSI for DTM_ADDTEXT, Unicode for DTM_ADDTEXTW.

to recognize anchor tags. The text corresponding to an anchor is automatically formatted when the HTML viewer control displays the text. Specifically, the text color is changed to blue and the text is underlined.

The HTML viewer control also notifies its parent window whenever a user taps on such a link on the display screen. All of the logic for determining where the stylus taps the screen and decides if that point corresponds to a link is implemented in the viewer control's window procedure.

On the other hand, an application that uses an HTML viewer control is responsible for responding to the fact that a user tapped on a hyperlink. If the link points to another file, the application must load and display it.

The HTML viewer control sends notifications to its parent window when events such as a hyperlink tap occur. These notifications are sent in the form of WM_NOTIFY messages. This is exactly the same notification mechanism used by the Windows CE common controls.

The notification that is sent when a hyperlink is tapped is NM_HOTSPOT. This notification is also sent in response to the user submitting a form, a subject we will not be covering here. The *lParam* sent with this notification is a pointer to an NM_HTMLVIEW structure, In fact, many of the notifications sent by the HTML viewer control pass such a structure.

NM_HTMLVIEW is defined as:

```
typedef struct tagNM_HTMLVIEW
{
  NMHDR hdr;
  LPSTR szTarget;
  LPSTR szData;
  DWORD dwCookie;
} NM_HTMLVIEW;
```

The first member, as with any control notification, is an NMHDR structure.

szTarget contains a NULL-terminated string whose meaning depends on the notification being sent. For example, in the case of the NM_HOTSPOT notification, *szTarget* contains the string that follows the HREF field in the line of HTML text defining the link.

For example, consider again the situation illustrated in Figure 12.1 and the sample HTML file that produced that display. If a user taps the "Windows CE" link in that case, the HTML viewer control that contains the text sends an NM_HOTSPOT notification. The *szTarget* member of the NM_HTMLVIEW structure that is sent with this notification will contains the string "\Windows\wince.htm."

szData and *dwCookie* contain data specific to the particular notification being sent. For example, in the case of an NM_HOTSPOT, *szData* contains the query data sent with a form POST submission. The *dwCookie* value is not used by NM_HOTSPOT.

An Example: How HTML.EXE Follows Links

Now let's see how to respond to the NM_HOTSPOT notification in a real example.

If you run the HTML.EXE sample application, you will see that it properly follows hyperlinks. As long as the links refer to HTML files that are in the emulator file system or the file system of the Windows CE device running the application, everything works fine.

This behavior is implemented by responding to the NM_HOTSPOT notification described above. The relevant part of main application window's window procedure is given below:

```
LRESULT CALLBACK WndProc(
  HWND hwnd,
  UINT message,
  WPARAM wParam,
  LPARAM lParam)
{
  UINT nID;
  int nLen;
  TCHAR* pszFilename;
  switch(message)
  {
  case WM_NOTIFY:
   NM_HTMLVIEW* lpnm;
   lpnm = (NM_HTMLVIEW*)lParam;
   switch(lpnm->hdr.code)
   {
   case NM_HOTSPOT:
    nLen = strlen(lpnm->szTarget);
    pszFilename = (TCHAR*)LocalAlloc(LPTR,
```

```
     sizeof(TCHAR)*nLen);
    AnsiToWide(lpnm->szTarget, pszFilename);
    LinkToFile(pszFilename);
    LocalFree(pszFilename);
    break;
   default:
    break;
  }       //End of switch(lpnm->hdr.code) block
  return (0);
  /* Other message handler code */
  ...
  default:
   return (DefWindowProc(hwnd, message, wParam, lParam));
  }       //End of switch(message) block
}
```

The NM_HOTSPOT notification handler first extracts the string containing the HREF hyperlink text from the *szTarget* member of the NM_HTMLVIEW structure. HTML.EXE assumes that this contains the file name of an HTML document. *LocalAlloc* is called to allocate enough space in the buffer *pszFilename* to hold the file name.

Then all that is left to do is open, read, and display the contents of the file. This is exactly what the *LinkToFile* function does, so the NM_HOTSPOT notification handler simply needs to call this function. The HTML viewer control responds by displaying the new HTML file.

An important step of the process was skipped, however. The purpose of these two lines of code is not obvious:

```
pszFilename = (TCHAR*)LocalAlloc(LPTR,
   sizeof(TCHAR)*nLen);
AnsiToWide(lpnm->szTarget, pszFilename);
```

The HTML files read by HTML.EXE are assumed to be ANSI text. But the file system API functions called by *LinkToFile* require Unicode file names. Therefore the ANSI string contained by *lpnm->szTarget* (the link file name) must be converted to Unicode.

Each Unicode character requires two bytes (the size of a TCHAR), and there are *nLen* characters in the file name string. So *LocalAlloc* allocates enough bytes to accommodate the Unicode representation of the string *lpnm->szTaget*.

AnsiToWide is an application-defined function that converts ANSI strings to Unicode:

```
void AnsiToWide(LPSTR lpStr, TCHAR* lpTChar)
{
```

```
    while(*lpTChar++ = *lpStr++);
}
```

This is a variation of the classic one-line string copy function.[1] As long as the two string arguments are NULL-terminated, this function copies the ANSI string in *lpStr* to the Unicode string *lpTChar*. Since the ++ operator increments a pointer variable by the size of the type it points to, incrementing *lpTChar* leaves two bytes per character.

Displaying Inline Images

The HTML viewer control provides limited support to displaying images referenced in HTML formatted text. The control sends a notification to its parent window when it encounters an IMG reference in HTML text, but makes no attempt to render the image. As with moving among hyperlinks, this is the responsibility of the application.

An example of including an inline image in an HTML file is:

```
<IMG SRC="image.gif">
```

When an HTML viewer control encounters such a tag, for example while responding to a DTM_ADDTEXT message, it alerts its parent that an image needs to be loaded by sending an NM_INLINE_IMAGE notification.

As with the NM_HOTSPOT notification, the control sends an NM_HTMLVIEW structure in the *lParam* of the WM_NOTIFY message.

The *szTarget* member of this structure contains the text following the SRC parameter in the HTML text. In the example above, *szTarget* would contain the string "image.gif."

In the case of NM_INLINE_IMAGE notifications, the *szData* member of the NM_HTMLVIEW structure is not used. But the *dwCookie* value is. It contains a value that must be passed to the DTM_SETIMAGE message described a little later.

The basic idea to take away from this discussion is that the HTML viewer control only notifies its parent window that a reference to an image has been detected. It is up to the application to load and display

---

[1]For a more complete explanation of how this function works, see B. Stroustrup, *The C++ Programming Language*, 2nd Ed. (Addison-Wesley, 1991), pp. 92-93.

the image. But the application gets a little help in this from the
DTM_SETIMAGE message.

The DTM_SETIMAGE Message

An application tells an HTML viewer control how to display an inline
image by sending the control a DTM_SETIMAGE message. This message associates an inline image with a bitmap sent with the message.
In other words, after responding to this message, the HTML viewer
control displays the specified bitmap in place of the inline image. The
parameters for DTM_SETIMAGE are described in Table 12.2.

The application must specify the various attributes of the bitmap to be
used for the inline image. This information is specified in an
INLINEIMAGEINFO structure:

```
typedef struct tagINLINEIMAGEINFO
{
    DWORD dwCookie;
    int iOrigHeight;
    int iOrigWidth;
    HBITMAP hbm;
    BOOL bOwnBitmap;
} INLINEIMAGEINFO, *LPINLINEIMAGEINFO;
```

The *dwCookie* member of this structure is the same value sent by the
control in its NM_INLINE_IMAGE notification. *iOrigHeight* and *iOrigWidth* specify the height and width of the bitmap. The bitmap itself is
contained in the *hbm* member.

Finally, *bOwnBitmap* specifies who is responsible for destroying the
bitmap resource once it has been displayed. If this member is TRUE,
the HTML viewer control must free the resource. If *bOwnBitmap* is
FALSE, the application is telling the control that the application will
handle destroying the bitmap.

Related to the DTM_SETIMAGE message is DTM_IMAGEFAIL. An
application sends this message to an HTML viewer control to indicate

Table 12.2 The DTM_SETIMAGE Message

PARAMETER	MEANING
wParam	Not used.
(LPINLINEIMAGEINFO)lParam	Pointer to an INLINEIMAGEINFO structure that defines the bitmap to use.

that the image specified in an NM_INLINE_IMAGE notification could not be loaded. The control responds by displaying the default "broken image" bitmap for that inline image.

All of this means, of course, that an application that wishes to properly display inline images in an HTML viewer control must have a way of converting the image data in a particular image file into a Windows CE bitmap resource. The NM_INLINE_IMAGE notification tells the application that an inline image has been detected. It does not convert the referenced image file into the required Windows CE bitmap resource.

HTML Viewer Control Messages and Notifications

The HTML viewer control supports many more messages and notifications than those we have detailed. The examples in this chapter should provide enough insight into the use of the HTML viewer to make using the rest of the control features easy.

A complete list of messages and notifications associated with the HTML viewer control are given in Tables 12.3 and 12.4.

Table 12.3 HTML Viewer Control Messages

MESSAGE	BEHAVIOR
DTM_ADDTEXT	Adds the specified ANSI text to the control. The *wParam* indicates if the text is plain or HTML formatted text.
DTM_ADDTEXTW	Unicode version of DTM_ADDTEXT.
DTM_ANCHOR	Tells the control to jump to the specified anchor.
DTM_ANCHORW	Unicode version of DTM_ANCHOR.
DTM_ENABLESHRINK	Toggles the control image shrink mode. The control shrinks images to make the HTML document fit the control window.
DTM_ENDOFSOURCE	Tells the control that the application is done adding text to the control.
DTM_IMAGEFAIL	Used to inform the control that the specified image could not be loaded.
DTM_SETIMAGE	Associates the specified bitmap with an inline image.
DTM_SELECTALL	Selects (highlights) all text displayed in the control.

Table 12.4 HTML Viewer Control Notifications

NOTIFICATION	MEANING
NM_BASE	Sent by the control when it encounters a BASE tag in HTML text.
NM_CONTEXTMENU	Sent by the control when the user taps the client area of the control while pressing the Alt key.
NM_HOTSPOT	Sent by the control when a user taps a hyperlink or submits a form.
NM_INLINE_IMAGE	Sent by the control to tell the application that an image needs to be loaded.
NM_INLINE_SOUND	Sent by the control to tell the application that a sound file needs to be loaded.
NM_META	Sent by the control when it encounters a META tag in HTML text. Notification includes the HTTP-EQUIV and CONTENT parameters of this tag.
NM_TITLE	Sent by the control when it encounters a TITLE tag in HTML text. Notification includes the document title.

Palm-size PC Input Techniques

T raditional computing devices such as personal computers get a large amount of their user input from a keyboard. Composing e-mail, writing documents in a word processor, or even simply entering a password typically requires keyboard input.

But Windows CE-based devices are not required to have a keyboard. For example, users of Palm-size PCs are very comfortable using these devices without a keyboard. Despite the presence of a software keyboard that can be invoked at any time, the majority of user input gets to a Palm-size PC via the stylus, navigation buttons, or even voice.

AFTER COMPLETING THIS CHAPTER YOU WILL KNOW HOW TO . . .

Use the rich ink control

Program Palm-size PC navigation buttons

Use the voice recorder control

This chapter also introduces the Palm-size PC emulation environment for the first time. If you have installed the Palm-size PC SDK, you are

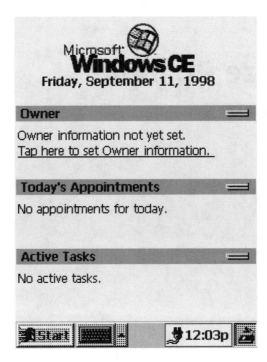

Owner

Owner information not yet set.
Tap here to set Owner information.

Today's Appointments

No appointments for today.

Active Tasks

No active tasks.

Figure 13.1 The Palm-size PC emulation environment.

able to build applications for the Palm-size PC target. The Palm-size PC emulation environment is shown in Figure 13.1.

The Rich Ink Control

To get our feet wet, we begin this chapter with a discussion of the rich ink control. This control is the easiest way for a Palm-size PC application to provide rudimentary stylus input capability.

As usual, our discussion is motivated by a simple sample application. INK.EXE is the application that results from building the project in the \Samples\ink directory on the companion CD. This application allows users to enter inking input and save such input to files in the object store. It also gives users the option of opening and displaying such files. Figure 13.2 shows the INK.EXE application in action.

The application allows users to save inking input to files with the .ink extension. This feature is implemented using the Save As common dialog. (Refer to Chapter 3 for an overview of programming the Windows

Figure 13.2   Using the rich ink control.

CE common dialogs.) Users invoke the save feature by selecting the Save Ink File option from the File menu, as shown in Figure 13.3.

Invoking this menu option displays the Save As dialog, which lets the user specify the name and location of the file in which to save the inking data. Figure 13.4 shows the Save As dialog as it appears after the Create In button has been pressed. By default, INK.EXE saves files in a directory called \MyDocuments\InkFiles.

The Open Ink File option of the File menu lets the user open and display an existing .ink file. This option displays an Open File common dialog to allow the user to choose which .ink file to open.

Rich Ink Control Features

The rich ink control is actually implemented as an edit control that includes inking support. A user can type into a rich ink control using the Palm-size PC soft keyboard to enter regular text, as shown in Figure 13.5.

Figure 13.3 The Save Ink File menu option.

The rich ink control also includes a command bar containing a menu of options. This command bar can be shown by pressing the large Restore button that appears at the bottom right of the control's client area. Pressing the Restore button when the command bar is visible hides the command bar.

This command bar can also be hidden or shown programmatically by your application, as we will discuss later.

The menu contained by this command bar provides various options for customizing the rich ink control. For example, one of the options on the Edit menu is called Format. Choosing this option invokes the dialog box shown in Figure 13.7. This dialog allows the user to specify various options related to the color and size of the pen used for inking.

Programming the Rich Ink Control

Programming the rich ink control is fairly simple. The simplicity comes from the fact that the control supports no custom styles, and

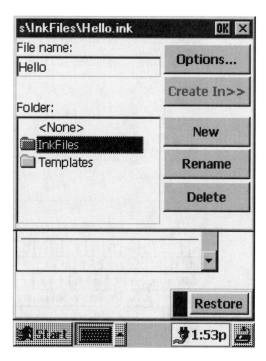

Figure 13.4 Saving an inking input file.

there are only five rich ink control messages. These messages are detailed in Table 13.1 on page 336. The remainder of this section describes how to use each of the messages.

IM_REINIT DOES NOT EXIST

The Palm-size PC SDK on-line documentation incorrectly identifies a message called IM_REINIT for erasing the contents of a rich ink control. This message is not defined in any of the Windows CE header files. The real message is called IM_CLEARALL.

Initializing and Creating the Rich Ink Control

Like the HTML viewer control, the rich ink control lives in its own DLL. This DLL is called INKX.DLL. The header file defining the rich ink control messages and exported functions is RICHINK.H.

Before an application can create instances of the rich ink control, it must first load INKX.DLL and then call the exported function *InitInkX*.

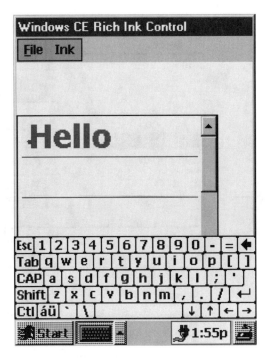

Figure 13.5 Entering text from the soft keyboard.

If the DLL is implicitly linked, it is not necessary for the application to load it. See Chapter 11 for background on explicit and implicit linking of DLLs.

InitInkX is responsible for registering the rich ink control window class. The control's window class name is defined by the symbol WC_INKX in the header file RICHINK.H. After calling *InitInkX*, an application can create rich ink controls.

For example, the sample application INK.EXE includes the following code in its *WinMain* function to create the rich ink control that it uses:

```
#define IDC_INK    1028
HWND hwndInk;
#include <richink.h>
int WINAPI WinMain(HINSTANCE hInstance,
  HINSTANCE hPrevInstance,
  LPTSTR lpCmdLine,
  int nCmdShow)
{
    /* Other application initialization code */
```

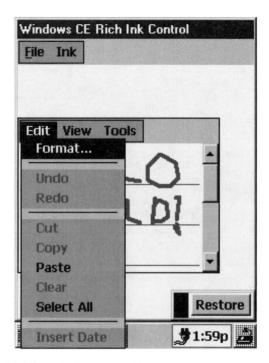

Figure 13.6 The rich ink control command bar.

```
InitInkX();
/* Code for registering the main window class
  and creating the main window omitted.
 */
hwndInk = CreateWindow(
 WC_INKX,
 NULL,
 WS_BORDER|WS_CHILD|WS_VISIBLE,
 0,75,200,150,
 hwndMain,
 (HMENU)IDC_INK,
 hInstance,
 NULL
 );
/* Hide the command bar on the control */
SendMessage(hwndInk, IM_SHOWCMDBAR,
  (WPARAM)FALSE, 0);
}
```

The application initializes the rich ink control class and then creates an instance of the rich ink control. It then sends the control an IM_SHOWCMDBAR message. This message programmatically hides or shows the command bar (Figure 13.6) associated with the specified

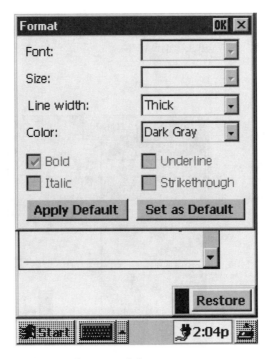

Figure 13.7 The rich ink control Format dialog.

rich ink control. The effect of the IM_SHOWCMDBAR message in this case is to make the command bar invisible when the rich ink control is created. The IM_SHOWCMDBAR message is described in Table 13.2.

Table 13.1 Rich Ink Control Messages

MESSAGE	MEANING
IM_SHOWCMDBAR	Hides or shows the rich ink control command bar.
IM_GETDATALEN	Returns the length of the ink data in bytes.
IM_SETDATA	Sets the contents of the specified rich ink control to the specified data.
IM_GETDATA	Retrieves the ink data currently displayed by the rich ink control.
IM_CLEARALL	Erases the rich ink control contents.

Table 13.2 The IM_SHOWCMDBAR Message

PARAMETER	MEANING
wParam	If TRUE, the command bar is made visible. If FALSE, the command bar is hidden.
lParam	Not used, should be 0.

Working with Inking Data

As users draw in a rich ink control, the control stores the ink data in an internal data structure. Users need to be able to store and retrieve what they input into the control as needed.

For example, one application of the rich ink control might be a simple notepad application. Users make handwritten notes on a "page" of the notepad and then save the note for later reference. The application obviously needs to be able to store and retrieve inking data in persistent storage.

To demonstrate how to save and restore inking data, let's look at how the INK.EXE application saves and reads ink data files. The application stores inking data in files with the extension .INK.

Saving and restoring inking data requires the two rich ink control messages IM_GETDATA and IM_SETDATA. The meanings of their parameters are shown in Tables 13.3 and 13.4.

To implement the inking data file save and retrieval functionality, INK.EXE defines the function *OnOpenSave*. This function is responsible for both opening and displaying existing .ink files and for saving .ink files to the object store.

The prototype of *OnOpenSave* is found in the application header file INK.H:

Table 13.3 The IM_GETDATA Message

PARAMETER	MEANING
wParam	Integer indicating the length of the inking data to be retrieved from the rich ink control.
lParam	Pointer to an array of bytes that receives the inking data from the control.

Table 13.4 The IM_SETDATA Message

PARAMETER	MEANING
wParam	Integer indicating the length of the data buffer that contains the rich ink control data.
lParam	Pointer to an array of bytes that contains the rich ink control inking data.

```
void OnOpenSave(HWND hwndApp, HWND hwndInk,
  BOOL bOpen);
```

The *hwndApp* and *hwndInk* parameters are the main application window and the rich ink control window, respectively. The *bOpen* parameter tells the function if it is being called to open a file or save a file.

We will break further discussion of this function into two sections. The first describes how ink files are saved. The second discusses how INK.EXE opens and reads ink data files.

Saving Inking Data

The portion of the *OnOpenSave* function that saves .ink files is shown below. All of the code that fills the OPENFILENAME structure has been left out for brevity.

```
DWORD dwLen, dwSize;
HANDLE hFile, hFind;
LPBYTE lpByte;
OPENFILENAME ofn;
if (GetSaveFileName(&ofn))
{
  dwLen = SendMessage(hwndInk, IM_GETDATALEN, 0, 0);
  /* Get the ink data if there is any
    (i.e., if dwLen != 0) */
  if (dwLen)
  {
   lpByte = (LPBYTE)LocalAlloc(LPTR, dwLen+1);
   SendMessage(hwndInk, IM_GETDATA,
     (WPARAM)dwLen, (LPARAM)lpByte);
  }
  /* Now we revisit all of the file system API stuff
    as we create a file and write the ink data to it.
    */
  hFile = CreateFile(
  ofn.lpstrFile,
  GENERIC_READ|GENERIC_WRITE,
  0,
```

```
            NULL,
            CREATE_ALWAYS,
            FILE_ATTRIBUTE_ARCHIVE,
            NULL
            );
            WriteFile(hFile, lpByte, dwLen, &dwSize, NULL);
            CloseHandle(hFile);
            LocalFree(lpByte);
    }   //End of if (GetSaveFileName(&ofn)) block
```

The first thing the function does when saving a file is to get the length in bytes of the inking data from the rich ink control. This is accomplished in a single line of code:

```
dwLen = SendMessage(hwndInk, IM_GETDATALEN, 0, 0);
```

The IM_GETDATALEN message returns the number of bytes of inking data contained by the specified rich ink control. If the control has inking data, the value returned by the IM_GETDATALEN message will be non-zero. The IM_GETDATALEN message is detailed in Table 13.5.

The function next allocates *dwLen* bytes to the array *lpByte* and retrieves the control's inking data by sending an IM_GETDATA message:

```
lpByte = (LPBYTE)LocalAlloc(LPTR, dwLen+1);
SendMessage(hwndInk, IM_GETDATA,
   (WPARAM)dwLen, (LPARAM)lpByte);
```

When the IM_GETDATA message returns, *lpByte* will be filled with the inking data currently stored in the rich ink control *hwndInk*. The IM_GETDATA message also returns the actual number of bytes written to *lpByte* as the return value of the *SendMessage* function call.

Once the inking data has been extracted from the rich ink control, *OnOpenSave* proceeds by storing the data in the file specified by *ofn.lpstrFile*. This file name is specified by the user in the File Save common dialog box that is invoked by the *GetSaveFileName* function call. Since we covered the file system API in detail in Chapter 6, the

Table 13.5   The IM_GETDATALEN Message

PARAMETER	MEANING
wParam	Not used, should be 0.
lParam	Not used, should be 0.

preceding code that saves the data to the data file should not be mysterious.

Reading Inking Data Files

Reading and displaying an existing .ink file is very similar to saving an .ink file. As mentioned above, *OnOpenSave* both saves and reads .ink files. The portion of the function that reads existing inking data files is given below. As was the case with the presentation of the file save code, all logic required to initialize the OPENFILENAME structure has been left out.

```
if (GetOpenFileName(&ofn))
{
  WIN32_FIND_DATA fd;
  hFind = FindFirstFile(ofn.lpstrFile, &fd);
  if (hFind)
  {
   CEOIDINFO oidInfo;
   CeOidGetInfo(fd.dwOID, &oidInfo);
   dwLen = oidInfo.infFile.dwLength;
   dwSize = 0;
   lpByte = (LPBYTE)LocalAlloc(LPTR, dwLen+1);
  }
  hFile = CreateFile(
   ofn.lpstrFile,
   GENERIC_READ|GENERIC_WRITE,
   0,
   NULL,
   OPEN_EXISTING,
   FILE_ATTRIBUTE_NORMAL,
   NULL
   );
  ReadFile(hFile, lpByte, dwLen, &dwSize, NULL);
  SendMessage(hwndInk, IM_SETDATA,
   (WPARAM)dwSize, (LPARAM)lpByte);
  CloseHandle(hFile);
  FindClose(hFind);
 }  //End of if (GetOpenFileName(&ofn) block
```

FindFirstFile is called with the file name selected by the user to get WIN32_FIND_DATA information about the file to be opened. In particular, the *dwOID* member of this structure is necessary for getting further information about the file, such as the file size.

Note that *CeOidGetInfo* is called to get the length of the file in bytes. Compare this with using the IM_GETDATALEN message when the .ink file was saved. In the case of saving files, the application can ask the rich ink control for the length of the inking data it contains. But when reading files, the file must be queried for this information. The rich ink control only knows the length of the data it contains.

After getting the length of the file, the array *lpByte* is allocated. The file is then opened and all of the inking data is read into *lpByte*.

Finally, *OnOpenSave* must display the data read from the .ink file in the rich ink control. It does this by sending the control an IM_SETDATA message:

```
SendMessage(hwndInk, IM_SETDATA,
   (WPARAM)dwSize, (LPARAM)lpByte);
```

dwSize tells the control how many bytes of data to expect. *lpByte* points to the array of inking data. The rich ink control responds to the IM_SETDATA message by displaying the new data.

The IM_CLEARALL Message

The last rich ink control message to discuss is IM_CLEARALL.

This message removes all inking data from a rich edit control. IM_CLEARALL is a very simple message. As Table 13.6 shows, both message parameters are zero.

As an example, the INK.EXE application sends this message in response to the Clear Page option of the Ink menu. This single line erases the contents of the rich ink control *hwndInk*:

```
SendMessage(hwndInk, IM_CLEARALL, 0, 0);
```

Programming the Palm-size PC Navigation Buttons

Given that the Palm-size PC does not include a hardware keyboard, many application developers and users alike might lament the absence of keyboard accelerators on these devices.

Table 13.6   The IM_CLEARALL Message

PARAMETER	MEANING
wParam	Not used, should be 0.
lParam	Not used, should be 0.

However, the Palm-size PC product platform specifies four different types of *navigation buttons*. These are hardware buttons that can be used as accelerator keys for performing application-specific actions.

The four types of navigation buttons are detailed in Table 13.7. The first column of this table specifies the navigation button. The second column indicates the key on a standard PC or Handheld PC keyboard to which the navigation button corresponds.

Program buttons launch predetermined applications. Every Palm-size PC must have at least one program button that activates the voice recorder application.

Navigation buttons tell the Palm-size PC shell that they have been pressed or released by sending WM_KEYDOWN and WM_KEYUP messages to the shell. The shell in turn forwards these messages to the application that is currently running. Each WM_KEYDOWN or WM_KEYUP message is sent with a virtual key code. This mechanism is similar to that used to send virtual key messages to applications running on a desktop PC or other Windows-based device with a keyboard.

The different virtual key codes sent with the WM_KEYDOWN and WM_KEYUP messages allow applications to distinguish which navigation button is being pressed or released.

Programmers can implement application-specific responses to navigation button actions. This is done by responding to the WM_KEYDOWN and WM_KEYUP messages in the main application window's window procedure.

Navigation buttons may actually send a series of messages depending on the particular action involved. We take a closer look at these messages in the sections that follow.

Table 13.7   The Palm-size PC Navigation Buttons

NAVIGATION BUTTON	KEYBOARD EQUIVALENT
Action button	Enter key
Exit button	Escape key
Arrow button	Up or down arrow key
Program button	None

NOTE
NAVIGATION BUTTON MESSAGES MAY DIFFER

It is up to the particular Original Equipment Manufacturer (OEM) to map each navigation button action to a virtual key message or series of messages. This mapping is implemented in the navigation button device driver supplied with a particular manufacturer's Palm-size PC. Therefore the messages described below are typical navigation key mappings. The actual mappings on your particular device may differ.

Action Button

The Palm-size PC action navigation button sends one message when pressed and three different messages when released. These messages are detailed in Table 13.8. When the action button is released, it sends the three messages in a series: a WM_KEYUP message with *wParam* VK_F23, a WM_KEYDOWN message with *wParam* VK_RETURN, and a WM_KEYUP message with *wParam* VK_RETURN.

Exit Button

The exit navigation button sends the messages shown in Table 13.9.

Arrow Button

Arrow buttons behave somewhat differently from the navigation buttons described previously. The navigation button device driver implements an auto repeat feature for arrow buttons. When an arrow button is pressed and held down, the driver sends a pair of messages for each auto repeat cycle. Arrow button messages are listed in Table 13.10.

Sometimes there is a single rocker button on a Palm-size PC to take the place of the arrow buttons. In these cases, the rocker button can be

Table 13.8   Action Button Messages

ACTION	MESSAGE	VIRTUAL KEY CODE (WPARAM)
Press button	WM_KEYDOWN	VK_F23
Release button	WM_KEYUP	VK_F23
	WM_KEYDOWN	VK_RETURN
	WM_KEYUP	VK_RETURN

Table 13.9 Exit Button Messages

ACTION	MESSAGE	VIRTUAL KEY CODE (WPARAM)
Press button	WM_KEYDOWN	VK_F24
Release button	WM_KEYUP	VK_F24
	WM_KEYDOWN	VK_ESCAPE
	WM_KEYUP	VK_ESCAPE

clicked either up or down. Each of these states replaces the corresponding up or down arrow navigation button.

Nonetheless, this discussion will continue to refer to Up and Down Arrow buttons. You should interpret this as meaning whatever mechanism a particular device provides for Up and Down Arrow button functionality.

Applications can program the arrow buttons to perform actions such as scrolling windows or list boxes. For example, when a user presses and holds the Down Arrow button, the main window procedure receives two messages in series. First it gets a WM_KEYDOWN message with a *wParam* equal to VK_NEXT. It then receives a WM_KEYUP message with *wParam* VK_NEXT.

Table 13.10 Arrow Button Messages

ACTION	MESSAGE	VIRTUAL KEY CODE (WPARAM)
Press button	WM_KEYDOWN	VK_UP
Release Up Arrow	WM_KEYUP	VK_UP
Press and hold Up Arrow	WM_KEYDOWN	VK_PRIOR
	WM_KEYUP	VK_PRIOR
Press Down Arrow	WM_KEYDOWN	VK_DOWN
Release Down Arrow	WM_KEYUP	VK_DOWN
Press and hold Down Arrow	WM_KEYDOWN	VK_NEXT
	WM_KEYUP	VK_NEXT

Program Buttons

The Palm-size PC program buttons (also called application buttons) are used to launch applications. They can also be used as hot keys for performing application-specific functions.

The message mechanism used by the program button is a little different from that used by the other navigation buttons. Whenever a program button is pressed or released, a series of WM_KEYDOWN or WM_KEYUP messages is sent to the Palm-size PC shell. The *wParam* of the first message is VK_LWIN. This tells the shell to wait for the next WM_KEYDOWN or WM_KEYUP message to determine which application to launch. The *wParam* of the second message contains information for the shell about where to look in the Windows CE registry to find the name of the application to launch.

Let's look at an example to make this more clear. Assume that a user presses program button number 1. The series of messages shown in Table 13.11 is generated. The first message alerts the shell that a program button has been pressed. It now knows to look for the next WM_KEYDOWN message. This second message's *wParam* value contains a virtual key code which the shell uses to look up application information in the registry.

Specifically, upon receiving the second WM_KEYDOWN message, the shell responds by looking for the registry subkey \HKEY_LOCAL_ MACHINE\Software\Microsoft\Shell\Keys\40C1. The default value of this subkey is the full path name of the application to be launched. The shell launches the referenced application. Notice that the last two characters of the subkey name correspond to the virtual key code.

When the shell receives another message containing VK_LWIN in the *wParam*, it begins sending the program button messages that it receives to the current application. VK_LWIN therefore acts as a switch, toggling the shell between handling program button messages itself and sending them to the currently running application.

Table 13.11 Program Button 1 Messages

ACTION	MESSAGE	VIRTUAL KEY CODE (WPARAM)
Press button	WM_KEYDOWN	VK_LWIN
	WM_KEYDOWN	0xC1

NOTE

PROGRAM BUTTON VIRTUAL KEY CODES MAY BE DIFFERENT

Like the sequence of messages sent in response to navigation button actions, the virtual key codes that are sent with program buttons may be different on your device. The device driver provided by the OEM is responsible for making the mapping between program button and virtual key code. Refer to the documentation for the device driver on your specific device for details.

Optional Subkeys

There are other subkeys that may be present under an application's registry subkey. These subkeys are detailed in Table 13.12.

For example, an application that resides in the file \Windows\ MyApp.exe may have a Name registry subkey with the value "MyApp".

Launching a Different Application with a Program Button

The registry values that tell the Palm-size PC shell which application to launch in response to a particular program button can be changed. This allows users to redefine which applications are launched by the various program buttons on their devices.

The Button Properties dialog box allows users to redirect program buttons. Changing the mapping between a program button and the application it launches forces the shell to send a WM_WININICHANGE message to all running applications.

Adding Hot Keys

Program buttons can be programmed as hot keys to perform application-specific actions. For example, pressing and holding the program button that launches an application might invoke a particular menu item.

Hot keys must be *registered* with the Palm-size PC shell. To register, your application must first call the Palm-size PC shell API *ShGetApp-KeyAssoc* to determine if a program button is already assigned to the application:

```
SHGetAppKeyAssoc(ptszApp);
```

Table 13.12 Other Registry Subkeys Related to Program Navigation Buttons

STYLE	MEANING
Name	Name of the application, not including the full directory path or .EXE extension.
Icon	Full path name of the application's Start menu icon.
Flags	Program control flags.
ResetCmd	Default application command line.

ptszApp is a string containing the name of the application of interest. The function returns the virtual key code of the Program control associated with the application. If no program button is assigned to the specified application, *SHGetAppKeyAssoc* returns zero.

If no virtual key is assigned to the application you wish to register a hot key for, you can map a program button to the application using the Button Properties dialog.

Next, you register the hot key by calling *RegisterHotKey:*

```
RegisterHotKey(hWnd, id, fsModifiers,     vk);
```

hWnd is the window that is to receive the WM_HOTKEY messages. *id* is a unique hot key identifier.

fsModifiers indicates other keys that must be pressed at the same time as the program button to invoke the hot key. This really only makes sense for non–Palm-size PC platforms. For the Palm-size PC platform, *fsModifiers* can be MOD_KEYUP. This means that the WM_HOTKEY message is sent both when the corresponding program button is pressed and when it is released.

Finally, *vk* indicates the virtual key code of the hot key.

For example, to register a hot key with MyApp.exe, I could write:

```
BYTE bVirtKey;
bVirtKey = SHGetAppKeyAssoc(TEXT("\\Windows\\MyApp.exe"));
RegisterHotKey(hwndMain, 0, 0, bVirtKey);
```

This example assumes that the window procedure of the window *hwndMain* handles the WM_HOTKEY messages. It also assumes that a program button has been mapped to the application MyApp.exe.

NOTE
■■■■■ USING AYGSHELL.DLL

The implementation of the *SHGetAppKeyAssoc* function is in the dynamic link library AYGSHELL.DLL. In order to use this function, your application must include the header file AYGSHELL.H. It must also either link dynamically with AYGSHELL.DLL or statically with AYGSHELL.LIB.

Once registered, the shell sends WM_HOTKEY messages to the application whenever the particular program button is pressed. Parameters of these messages are explained in Table 13.13.

Adding Voice Input to Palm-size PC Applications

The Palm-size PC SDK includes support for recording voice input. This allows application programmers to add voice recording features to their applications. Voice data recorded using a voice recorder control is stored in a .WAV file in the object store.

NOTE
■■■■■ VOICE ON OTHER PLATFORMS

Windows CE devices other than the Palm-size PC support voice input. Most notably, the Auto PC platform is largely voice driven. This chapter introduces the features of voice input in the context of the Palm-size PC.

These voice recording capabilities are provided by the Windows CE voice recorder control. The control contains a Play button, and optional Stop, Record, OK, and Close buttons. There is no voice recording API. Instead, the voice recorder control responds to a set of messages that control recording and playback.

Table 13.13   The WM_HOTKEY Message.

PARAMETER	MEANING
(int)wParam	Identifier of the hot key that generated the message. This is the value originally passed as the *id* parameter of the *RegisterHotKey* function.
(UINT)LOWORD(lParam)	Hot key modifier flags. This is the same as the *fsModifiers* parameter of the *RegisterHotKey* call that registered the hot key.
(UINT)HIWORD(lParam)	Hot key virtual key code.

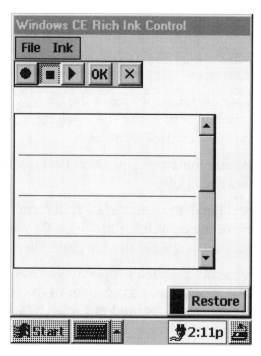

Figure 13.8 The voice recorder control.

Creating a Voice Recorder Control

An instance of the voice recorder control is created by calling the function *VoiceRecorder_Create*:

```
VoiceRecorder_Create(lpCMVR);
```

Like all other window creation functions, this function returns the HWND of the voice recorder control if control creation is successful. If *VoiceRecorder_Create* fails, it returns NULL.

lpCMVR is a pointer to a CM_VOICE_RECORDER structure that specifies styles and other attributes of the control (see Figure 13.8). This structure is defined as:

```
typedef struct tagCM_VOICE_RECORDER
{
  WORD cb;
  DWORD dwStyle;
  int xPos;
```

```
      int yPos;
      HWND hwndParent;
      int id;
      LPSTR lpszRecordFileName;
  } CM_VOICE_RECORDER, *LPCM_VOICE_RECORDER;
```

The *cb* member contains the size of the CM_VOICE_RECORDER structure. *hwndParent* specifies the voice recorder control's owner window. *id* is the voice control identifier.

xPos and *yPos* are the x and y position of the control with respect to the control's owner window.

The *lpszRecordFileName* member is a null-terminated string that specifies the name of the default file to which the control stores the recording. It is also used as the default playback file name.

The *dwStyle* member is used to specify various styles' bits for customizing the appearance and behavior of the voice recorder control. The available styles are detailed in Table 13.14.

NOTE

WHY DOES THE VOICE RECORDER CONTROL HAVE AN OWNER INSTEAD OF A PARENT?

Even though it's called a control, the voice recorder control is actually implemented as a WS_POPUP-style dialog box. Pop-up dialogs have owners, not parents. This is why the CM_VOICE_RECORDER structure specifies an owner.

Table 13.14 Voice Recorder Control Styles

STYLE	MEANING
VRS_NO_OKCANCEL	The OK and Close buttons are not displayed.
VRS_NO_NOTIFY	The control does not send notifications to the owner window.
VRS_MODAL	The control is implemented as a modal dialog instead of as a WS_POPUP-style dialog box. Thus, program control does not return to the calling application until the control is closed.
VRS_NO_OK	The Stop button is not displayed.
VRS_NO_RECORD	The Record button is not displayed.
VRS_PLAY_MODE	The control plays the file indicated by the *lpszRecordFileName* member immediately when the control is created.
VRS_NO_MOVE	The control's gripper handle is removed. The user therefore cannot move the control.

Voice Recorder Control Messages

Applications use the various voice recorder control features by sending messages to the control. The control supports messages for recording and playing back files, stopping recording, and dismissing the control. The messages are listed in Table 13.15.

The VRM_CANCEL, VRM_OK, and VRM_STOP messages take no parameters. The *wParam* and *lParam* parameters should be zero when sending or posting these messages with *SendMessage* or *PostMessage*.

Voice Recorder Control Notifications

The voice recorder control can also send notifications to its owner window at various times. If the control is created without the VRS_NO_NOTIFY style, the notifications described in Table 13.16 are sent to the owner window.

These notifications are sent via the WM_NOTIFY message just like any other common control notification. Notifications are sent using the NM_VOICE_RECORDER structure. This structure contains the usual NMHDR structure, as well as an error code. The error codes that can be sent are described in Table 13.17.

NOTE USING VOICECTL.DLL

The voice recorder control is implemented in the library VoiceCtl.DLL. To use the control, an application must include the file VoiceCtl.h and link (either statically or dynamically) with VoiceCtl.DLL.

Table 13.15 Voice Recorder Control Messages

MESSAGE	MEANING
VRM_CANCEL	Stops recording or playback. Also deletes any unsaved voice recorder files and closes the control.
VRM_OK	Same as VRM_CANCEL, except recorded data is saved to the current recording file.
VRM_PLAY	Plays the file specified by the string contained in the message *lParam*.
VRM_RECORD	Tells the control to begin recording. The message *lParam* contains the name of the file to which the recording is saved.
VRM_STOP	Stops recording or playback.

Table 13.16 Voice Recorder Control Notifications

NOTIFICATION	MEANING
VRN_ERROR	An error has occurred.
VRN_RECORD_START	The control has begun recording.
VRN_RECORD_STOP	The control has stopped recording.
VRN_PLAY_START	The control has begun playback.
VRN_PLAY_STOP	The control has stopped playback.
VRN_CANCEL	The Cancel button has been pressed.
VRN_OK	The OK button has been pressed.

A Real Example

Let's take a look at an example that uses some of the navigation button and voice recorder concepts. We will add some functionality to the INK.EXE application introduced earlier in this chapter.

Specifically, let's enhance the application to provide basic voice recording capability. The recording process is started by pressing and releasing the action button. The recording is stopped by pressing and releasing the action button again.

Table 13.17 Voice Recorder Control Error Codes

NOTIFICATION	MEANING
ER_SUCCESS	No error has occurred.
ER_FAIL	Unknown error.
ER_OUTOFMEMORY	Out of memory.
ER_INVALIDPARAM	An invalid parameter has been passed to a control function or message.
ER_WRITE_FILE_FAIL	Error occurred writing to file.
ER_OOM_STORAGE	Out of storage memory.
ER_MAX_FILE_SIZE	Maximum file size reached during record.
ER_BUSY	Control is busy recording or playing a file.
ER_UNUSED1	Reserved.
ER_UNUSED2	Reserved.
ER_UNUSED3	Reserved.

We must therefore make the application respond to the action button, and insert a voice recorder control.

To use the action button, INK.EXE registers the corresponding hot key and responds to subsequent WM_HOTKEY messages. It does so by calling *RegisterHotKey*:

```
RegisterHotKey(hwndMain, 0, 0, VK_RETURN);
```

The virtual key code associated with the action button is VK_RE-TURN. Hence, any time the action button is pressed, the main application window is sent a WM_HOTKEY message with the VK_RETURN virtual key code.

The main application window responds to the action button by turning voice recording on and off. This behavior is implemented by the WM_HOTKEY message handler of the window procedure (refer to Table 13.13 for details about the WM_HOTKEY message):

```
case WM_HOTKEY:
  UINT nKey;
  nKey = (UINT)HIWORD(lParam);
  switch(nKey)
  {
   case VK_RETURN:
   if (!bRecording)
   {
    bRecording = TRUE;
    SendMessage(hwndVoice,
     VRM_RECORD,
     0,
     (LPARAM)TEXT("\\My Documents\\Note.wav"));
   }
   else
   {
    bRecording = FALSE;
    SendMessage(hwndVoice, VRM_STOP, 0, 0);
   }
   break;
 /* Other message handlers */
```

bRecording is a global BOOL variable that indicates whether the voice recorder control *hwndVoice* is currently recording. If the action button has been pressed and the control is not recording, the application sends the control a VRM_RECORD message. This begins recording to a file called \\My Documents\Note.wav. If the voice recorder control is already recording, recording is stopped by sending a VRM_STOP message.

The code above of course implies that an instance of the voice recorder control has been created. The INK.EXE *WinMain* function creates the control, *hwndVoice*, as follows:

```
CM_VOICE_RECORDER cmvr;
memset(&cmvr, 0, sizeof(cmvr));
cmvr.cb = sizeof(CM_VOICE_RECORDER);
cmvr.dwStyle = VRS_NO_MOVE;
cmvr.xPos = 0;
cmvr.yPos = CommandBar_Height(hwndCB);
cmvr.hwndParent = hwndMain;
cmvr.lpszRecordFileName = TEXT("\\My Documents\\Note.wav");
hwndVoice = VoiceRecorder_Create(&cmvr);
```

The only style specified is VRS_NO_MOVE, meaning that the user cannot drag the voice recorder control to a new location. The y position is set to the height of the command bar that the INK.EXE application contains. This positions the recorder just below the command bar.

The action button now controls voice recording in the INK.EXE application. The voice recorder control buttons can of course be used as well.

The voice recording feature of this example is pretty limited. The application can only record and play back one sound file. You could enhance this program into a full-featured voice memo application that can record and play back a choice of files.

Concluding Remarks

We have reached the end of our discussion of Windows CE user interface programming. The most common techniques for implementing custom Windows CE user interfaces have been covered. At this point, you should be comfortable using owner draw controls and their close relative, the custom draw service. For cases where your applications require completely new controls, you can implement custom Windows CE controls as described in Chapter 11.

In addition, we have briefly described how to use the HTML viewer control, and how to program some of the unique input options provided by the Palm-size PC platform.

This user interface programming discussion has by no means been exhaustive. As you work with Windows CE and write applications, you will have plenty of opportunities to experiment with the techniques described in the previous five chapters. But these chapters provide what I hope is a good foundation in Windows CE user interface programming.

Desktop Connectivity and Memory Issues

One of the most useful features of Windows CE-based products is their ability to share data with a desktop computer. The success of many PC companion products on the market today owes much to this feature.

As the market for Windows CE-based devices continues to grow, the importance of desktop connectivity will grow as well. Doctors might collect patient data in hospital rooms with mobile diagnostic devices. Laboratory researchers will collect experimental data in electronic lab books. And all of this information will end up in large databases where powerful desktop computers perform complex analysis.

Part IV of this book introduces Windows CE desktop connectivity. We cover Microsoft's ActiveSync technology, and describe how to program the service providers necessary for synchronizing application data between Windows CE devices and desktop computers.

Next we discuss how to write file filters for transferring files and converting data between Windows CE and desktop computing platforms. We also discuss the Remote Application Programming Interface (RAPI), which allows desktop PC applications to access data or execute functions and applications on a Windows CE device.

Finally, we introduce Windows CE memory and power management in Chapter 16.

CHAPTER 14

Windows CE Data Synchronization

So far in this book, we have explored many of the features of Windows CE that allow you to create applications for a variety of uses. We have discussed how to design and implement user interfaces for such applications. We have also covered the various persistent storage options provided by Windows CE so that your applications can store information on the device for later use.

You could easily put this book down now and be well equipped to tackle many different Windows CE programming tasks. As long as your software users only needed to access their data on their Windows CE devices, everything would be fine. But this is not a realistic expectation.

The real power and advantage of Windows CE is that it provides ways for users to share data between a mobile device and a desktop computer. A user can enter data on the desktop and then transfer it to a Windows CE-based device. Likewise, data on a mobile device can be transferred to the desktop PC. This allows users to back up Windows CE application data to a PC.

The term *PC companion* came about because most users treat Windows CE-based devices such as Handheld PCs and Palm-size PCs as tools for carrying small subsets of the vast amounts of data on their desktop computers.

A typical user may maintain all of the contact information for friends and business associates in an application like Microsoft Outlook. The user may access contact information from his desktop computer while he's sitting right in front of it. But while away from the office, in meetings, or on the road, the user looks up information on the same business contacts on his Handheld PC using Pocket Outlook.

For this to be possible, the desktop computer must be able to transfer data from the contacts database on the desktop to the corresponding database on the Windows CE device. And once our user returns from an important business meeting, he must be able to transfer the contact information added on the Handheld PC to his desktop computer.

AFTER COMPLETING THIS CHAPTER YOU WILL KNOW HOW TO . . .

Write ActiveSync desktop service providers

Write ActiveSync device service providers

The Sample Code

For this chapter, probably more than any other chapter in this book, the complete programming example will help solidify the concepts discussed. To illustrate the nuances of ActiveSync programming, we revisit the phone list application introduced back in Chapter 7. This

Some Brief Caveats

Windows CE data synchronization is a large subject. An entire book could, and probably should, be dedicated to this subject. This chapter will cover the major aspects of writing Windows CE ActiveSync service providers. Covering every detail of data synchronization is impractical for a book of this size. It is expected that the accompanying sample application and service provider code, as well as the Microsoft on-line documentation, will be used to supplement your understanding of the subject.

application was first presented to demonstrate Windows CE database programming. It returns in this chapter along with a desktop PC version and complete desktop and device ActiveSync service providers. You can therefore enter, delete, and modify entries on either the PC or a Windows CE device and synchronize the data stores of the two applications.

The companion CD contains a directory called \Samples\datasync\ PhoneApp. This directory contains a Microsoft Developer Studio workspace called PHONEAPP.DSW. This workspace contains five projects:

DeskApp. Builds the desktop version of the phone list database application.

DeskSync. Builds the desktop ActiveSync service provider.

DevSetup. Builds a device application for registering the device service provider. Run this application to register the device service provider.

DevApp. Builds the device version of the phone list application.

DevSync. Builds the device ActiveSync service provider.

You will also find the registry file PHONEDESK.REG, which creates all of the registry subkeys and sets the necessary values to register the desktop service provider.

ActiveSync Technology Overview

The Windows CE solution to the data synchronization problem is a technology called *ActiveSync*. ActiveSync is based on a client/server architecture. The server is called the *ActiveSync service manager*. The client—or more accurately, clients, as we'll soon see—are called the *ActiveSync service providers*. For simplicity, we will refer to the former as the service manager, and the latter as the service providers.

The service manager is implemented by the Windows CE operating system. The service providers are programmed by the application programmer.

Synchronizing application data under Windows CE implies that there are two applications interested in the data being synchronized. One application resides on the Windows CE device, and the other resides on the user's desktop computer. Each of these applications implements some mechanism for storing a user's data. The particular data repository for each application is called a *data store*.

For example, the Windows CE version of a contacts database application might store its data in the Windows CE contacts database. The desktop version of the same application might store its data in a file in the Windows NT file system. In this case, the Windows CE contacts database acts as the data store for the device application. The file system data file is the data store for the Windows NT application.

Now that we have defined what a data store is, we can give a simple definition of data synchronization. Data synchronization is the process of keeping the desktop and device data stores of a given application up to date.

The ActiveSync Service Manager

The ActiveSync service manager is one of the components of the Windows CE Services package that a user installs on a desktop PC when configuring a device such as a Handheld PC. There is actually a service manager that resides on the desktop, and one that is part of the Windows CE operating system on the device. Both services are collectively called the service manager.

The service manager has several responsibilities. It detects changes to objects in the desktop or device data stores. It also detects when objects are added or deleted. The service manager also establishes the connection between the desktop and device and resolves data conflicts. It also facilitates the transfer of data between the desktop and device data stores.

To perform all of its tasks, the desktop service manager implements a COM interface called IReplNotify. The service manager interacts with the service providers on the desktop and Windows CE device to perform data synchronization tasks. Most of the data synchronization is performed by the desktop manager and service providers. As we will see later, the device service manager and provider roles are much simpler.

ActiveSync can be used to synchronize data from a wide variety of applications. Pocket Outlook and Pocket Word files, for example, can be synchronized with their desktop PC counterparts. More significantly, ActiveSync can be used to transfer data between your custom Windows CE applications and their desktop versions. All of these synchronization chores are performed by the same ActiveSync service manager. This is pretty amazing, considering that the service manager was written long before your applications that use it were designed.

This is possible because the service manager has no knowledge of the internal structure of the data objects used by the applications it is synchronizing. The service manager controls the flow of data between the desktop and device in the form of binary data *packets*. The service providers associated with a particular application are responsible for translating these packets into whatever form is used by the application. Similarly, the service providers convert internal application data into packets and hand them over to the service manager for transfer.

The role of the service manager can thus be described as orchestrating the synchronization process by requesting information or action from the service providers at the appropriate times.

The Service Manager Data Model

The ActiveSync service manager does not have information about the internal structure of data in the applications it synchronizes. It does not know, for example, that an entry in the phone list application contains strings for a first name, last name, and phone number, and an integer value representing an employee department number.

But the service manager does keep track of some information about each data object that it synchronizes. The service manager stores a handle identifying each synchronized object. Along with this handle, information uniquely identifying the object may be stored. This information might include a global unique identifier (GUID), a FILETIME stamp representing when the object was last modified, or an application-defined index. As we will see later, this additional information is instrumental in determining if a given object has changed since it was last synchronized.

Other information can be stored as well. It is common, for instance, to store information used by the service manager for resolving data conflicts, or to save a version number of the application data.

This information is stored in a file called REPL.DAT. You can think of this file as the service manager's synchronization log. It contains a handle and other related data for each object synchronized by ActiveSync.

The service manager models the objects contained in REPL.DAT as a collection of *folders*. Each folder contains all of the data objects synchronized for a particular application data type. Each of these objects is called an *item*. Windows CE defines handle types for each of these data types. HREPLFLD is the folder handle type, and HREPLITEM is the item handle type. Folders and handles are considered to be subtypes of the more generic *object* type, represented by the handle HREPLOBJ. As we will see, many of the methods implemented by ActiveSync service providers operate on data of these types.

To represent folders, objects, and items internally, the phone list application desktop service provider defines the following C++ classes in the file \samples\datasync\phoneapp\desktop\sync\store.h:

```
//Synchronization option flags
#define SO_ALL    0
#define SO_AM     1
#define SO_NZ     2
#define OT_ITEM   1
#define OT_FOLDER 2
class CReplObject
{
public:
  virtual ~CReplObject() {}
  UINT m_uType; //Object type (folder or item)
};
class CFolder: public CReplObject
{
public:
  CFolder()
  {
    m_uType = OT_FOLDER;
    m_uSyncOpt = SO_ALL;
    m_fChanged = FALSE;
  }
  virtual ~CFolder() {}
  UINT m_uSyncOpt; //Synchronization option
  BOOL m_fChanged; //Is the item changed?
};
class CItem: public CReplObject
{
public:
  CItem()
  {
    m_uType = OT_ITEM;
```

```
   memset(&m_ftModified, 0, sizeof(FILETIME));
   }
   virtual ~CItem() {}
   UINT m_uid; //Item / phone entry identifier
   FILETIME m_ftModified; //Time last modified
};
```

These classes model the information stored by the service manager in REPL.DAT for the various folders and items synchronized.

The ActiveSync Service Providers

Whereas the service manager is provided by the Windows CE Services, the service providers are implemented by the application programmer. The majority of the tasks required to carry out synchronization are implemented by the service providers.

For example, the service manager transfers data from the desktop to a connected Windows CE device and vice versa. But it is the service providers' responsibility to convert transferred data packets into a form useful to the application.

Application data can originate on either the desktop or the Windows CE device. Likewise, data can be changed or deleted either in the desktop or the device version of a particular application. There must therefore be a service provider on both the desktop computer and the Windows CE device corresponding to each type of data that can be synchronized.

ActiveSync service providers are implemented as in-process COM servers. Hence, service providers are implemented in dynamic link libraries. Each desktop service provider must implement two COM interfaces, IReplStore and IReplObjHandler. Device service providers must implement IReplObjHandler, as well as various exported functions.

IReplStore, simply called the store, is responsible for such tasks as enumerating objects in the application data store and converting these objects into HREPLITEM or HREPLFLD representations for the service manager. This interface takes care of any task related to the data store.

IReplObjHandler, or "the handler" for short, implements tasks such as converting object data into binary packets so that they can be transferred by the service manager.

Any application data type that can be synchronized between a Windows CE device and a desktop PC must implement both a device and a desktop service provider.

ActiveSync service providers generally implement the IReplStore and IReplObjHandler interfaces as C++ classes. In the phone list application, the desktop service providers implement these interfaces as the classes CStore and CDataHandler. On the device, the service provider also uses a class called CDataHandler to implement the IReplObjHandler interface.

ActiveSync service providers are registered in the registry. The desktop provider is registered in the desktop computer registry and the device service provider in the Windows CE registry of the device on which the service provider is installed.

The various methods defined by the service provider interfaces are listed in Tables 14.1 and 14.2. Since this chapter cannot possibly cover every ActiveSync detail, these tables will provide a useful reference for service provider capabilities.

NOTE
INTERFACE INSTANCES?

Throughout this chapter I refer to instances of COM interfaces. I am well aware that COM interfaces are not instantiated. Instead, clients create instances of components which implement COM interfaces. To prevent the discussion in this chapter from becoming more verbose than necessary, an instance of a particular COM component which implements interface IFoo is referred to as an instance of IFoo. I sometimes get even more succinct and call this component an IFoo instance.

The Synchronization Process from the 50,000-Foot Level

Writing ActiveSync service providers requires understanding a number of subtle programming steps. Understanding these steps will be much easier if we first examine the whole data synchronization process from a higher, more abstract level.

When a Windows CE device connects to a desktop PC, the following steps take place to synchronize a particular application data type:

Table 14.1   IReplStore Methods

METHOD	PURPOSE
Initialize	Called by the service manager to initialize the service provider.
GetStoreInfo	Retrieves information about an IReplStore instance.
ReportStatus	Called by the service manager to get synchronization status.
CompareStoreIDs	Compares data store identifiers.
CompareItem	Used to compare two data store objects.
IsItemChanged	Determines if a data store object has changed between synchronizations.
IsItemReplicated	Determines if an object is to be synchronized.
UpdateItem	Updates data stored in a data object handle.
GetFolderInfo	Creates a new folder for the given object type.
IsFolderChanged	Determines if any object in the specified folder has changed since the method was last called.
FindFirstItem	Called to recreate the first item in a folder during object enumeration.
FindNextItem	Called to recreate additional folder items during enumeration.
FindItemClose	Completes enumeration.
ObjectToBytes	Converts a data store object to bytes for storage in REPL.DAT.
BytesToObject	Converts an array of bytes from REPL.DAT into the corresponding data store object.
FreeObject	Frees the specified data store object.
CopyObject	Copies the specified data store object.
IsValidObject	Determines if the specified object handles are valid.
ActivateDialog	Invokes the synchronization options dialog box.
GetObjTypeUIData	Retrieves information to be used about a data type in the conflict resolution dialog box and the ActiveSync status window.
GetConflictInfo	Retrieves information to be displayed in the conflict resolution dialog box about two conflicting objects.
RemoveDuplicates	Removes duplicate objects from the data store.

1. The ActiveSync service manager determines what service providers are installed on the PC and the device by looking in the desktop and device registries.

2. With the help of the desktop service provider, the service manager reconstructs the data folder (HREPLFLD) and all of the items (HREPLITEM) it contained during the *previous* synchronization.

Table 14.2 IObjReplHandler Methods

METHOD	PURPOSE
Setup	Called by the service manager to prepare the service provider to receive a data packet.
Reset	Frees resources used during serialization or de-serialization.
GetPacket	Converts data store objects into data packets.
SetPacket	Converts data packets into data store objects.
DeleteObj	Deletes a data store object.

3. The desktop service provider enumerates all of the objects currently contained by the application data store, passing an HREPLITEM back to the manager for each enumerated data store object.

4. The service manager creates new entries in REPL.DAT for any new data objects returned by the service provider's object enumeration. For old objects, the service manager asks the service provider if the object has changed since the last synchronization. If an object has changed, the service manager gets the new object from the service provider.

5. New objects are transferred to the Windows CE device by the service manager. This is done with the help of the desktop service provider, which converts each object to be transferred into a binary data packet.

A similar set of operations take place over on the device side:

1. The device ActiveSync service manager enumerates all device data store objects.

2. For each enumerated object, the device service provider tells the service manager whether or not the object needs to be synchronized.

3. For each object requiring synchronization, the service provider converts the object data into a binary packet.

4. The packets are transferred by the service manager.

The steps above are executed by the service manager and service provider software to perform data synchronization. Data synchronization can also be looked at from the point of view of the data being synchronized:

1. The data that was synchronized during the last data synchronization operation is reconstructed. This is done to facilitate the comparison of current data store objects with those in REPL.DAT to decide what data needs to be synchronized.

2. Data store objects are converted into packets for transfer by the ActiveSync service manager.

3. Transferred data is converted from binary packets back into the data object format used internally by the application.

Registering ActiveSync Service Providers

In the previous section I said that service providers get registered in the desktop or device registry. This is required so that the ActiveSync service manager can determine what service providers to initialize in order to synchronize their corresponding application data. Let's look at how to register the service providers for the phone list application.

It might seem that this should be described after we have developed the service provider DLLs. However, understanding how service providers are registered will help you understand how the service manager initializes service providers. It will also make it easier to understand how the data synchronization process is started.

So, let's assume that we have implemented a device service provider in the dynamic link library PHDEVS.DLL. We also have the desktop provider, PHSYNC.DLL. These service providers are used by ActiveSync to synchronize phone database entries used by the phone list application.

Registering the Desktop Service Provider

Recall that the device service provider DLL is an in-process COM server implementing the COM interfaces IReplStore and IReplObjHandler. The service manager implements the IReplNotify COM interface. The service manager uses COM to create instances of the interfaces implemented by the service provider.

The service manager creates instances of the service providers it uses by finding the *class identifiers* for each of the service providers. This class identifier is a globally unique identifier value, or GUID. Using this identifier, the service manager can search the registry for the path of the DLL that implements the service provider interfaces.

To facilitate this process, a service provider must first be registered under the HKEY_CLASSES_ROOT registry key. The registry subkeys required are given in Figure 14.1.

<Class ID> represents the service provider's class identifier. This identifier is a globally unique identifier, or GUID. It can be generated by running the GUIDGEN.EXE program that ships with Microsoft Developer Studio. This program user interface is shown in Figure 14.2.

Selecting the registry format option as shown and pressing the New GUID button will create a new GUID in the format expected by the Windows registry. Next, press the Copy button. This copies the newly created GUID to the clipboard.

ProgID contains a *programmatic identifier* that uniquely identifies the service provider. This identifier typically consists of a company name followed by an application name. In our example, the service identifier is given the programmatic identifier **Wiley.PhoneApp**.

Finally, the InProcServer32 subkey contains the full path name of the DLL that implements the service provider.

Now create a file named PHONEDESK.REG and add the text shown in Figure 14.3. You should replace the GUID 025A8621-56FE-11d2-9BCC-000000000000 with the GUID you just created with GUIDGEN.EXE. If you copied your new GUID to the clipboard as described previously, you can simply paste your GUID over every occurrence of the GUID 025A8621-56FE-11d2-9BCC-000000000000.

What you now have is a registry file that will automatically create all of the registry subkeys shown in Figure 14.1. The path defined in the InProcServer32 subkey should be changed so that it contains the correct location of PHSYNC.DLL on your desktop computer.

```
HKEY_CLASSES_ROOT\CLSID\<Class ID>\InProcServer32
HKEY_CLASSES_ROOT\CLSID\<Class ID>\ProgID
HKEY_CLASSES_ROOT\<ProgID>\CLSID
```

Figure 14.1 Registry subkeys for registering a desktop ActiveSync service provider.

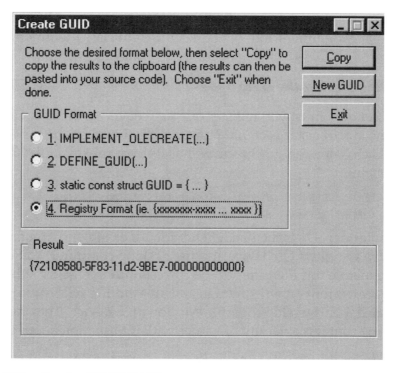

Figure 14.2 Running GUIDGEN.EXE.

```
REGEDIT4
; PhoneApp Active Sync Module Registration
[HKEY_CLASSES_ROOT\Wiley.PhoneApp]
@="Phone List Application Active Sync Module"
[HKEY_CLASSES_ROOT\Wiley.PhoneApp\CLSID]
@"{025A8621-56FE-11d2-9BCC-000000000000}"
[HKEY_CLASSES_ROOT\CLSID\{025A8621-56FE-11d2-9BCC-000000000000}]
@="Phone List Application Active Sync Module"
[HKEY_CLASSES_ROOT\CLSID\{025A8621-56FE-11d2-9BCC-000000000000}\ProgID]
@="Wiley.PhoneApp"
[HKEY_CLASSES_ROOT\CLSID\{025A8621-56FE-11d2-9BCC-000000000000}\Inproc-
Server32]
@="E:\\Samples\\datasync\\PhoneApp\\obj\\release\\phsync.dll"
```

Figure 14.3 The PHONEDESK.REG registry file.

Service providers for other applications will have different programmatic identifiers and, of course, different class identifiers.

Registering the Data Types

Not only must you register our ActiveSync service provider, but you need to register each data type synchronized by the service provider. Each data type synchronized has its own subkey in the following hierarchy:

```
HKEY_CURRENT_USER\Software\Microsoft\Windows CE Services\Partners\<Part-
nerID>\Services\Synchronization\Objects
```

<Partner ID> is the partnership identifier of the partnership between the Windows CE device and the desktop computer. You do not have to generate this identifier or the corresponding registry subkey. It was created for you when you installed Windows CE Services and first created a partnership for your Windows CE device. This Partner ID subkey contains a variety of values with information about the device.

Under the Objects subkey, you must create a new subkey for each data type synchronized by the ActiveSync service provider. Since the phone list application only uses one data type, you only need to create one data type subkey:

```
HKEY_CURRENT_USER\Software\Microsoft\Windows CE Services\Partners\<Part-
nerID>\Services\Synchronization\Objects\PhoneApp
```

Create three new string values in this subkey called Display Name, Plural Name, and Store. The first two values contain the singular and plural names of the data object represented by the PhoneApp subkey. These values will occasionally be used by the ActiveSync service manager in user interfaces it displays during synchronization.

The Store value is far more important. This contains the programmatic identifier of the service provider that implements the IReplStore and IReplObjHandler interfaces for this data type.

To complete the PHONEDESK.REG file, add the following:

```
[HKEY_CURRENT_USER\Software\Microsoft\Windows CE Services\Part-
ners\15616b0e\Services\Synchronization\Objects\PhoneApp]
@="PhoneApp"
"Display Name"="Phone Entry"
"Plural Name"="Phone Entries"
"Store"="Wiley.PhoneApp"
```

You now have a registry file that will create all the necessary registry subkeys and assign all of the right values to register the phone list application desktop service provider. This file will also properly register the data types to be synchronized.

To insert these values into the registry, run the following command from a DOS prompt:

```
REGEDIT PHONEDESK.REG
```

This command will import the subkeys and values defined in PHONEDESK.REG into the registry.

Registering the Device Service Provider

Registering the Windows CE device service provider is much simpler than registering the desktop service provider. You simply create a subkey for each synchronized data type under the following hierarchy:

```
HKEY_LOCAL_MACHINE\Windows CE Services\Synchronization\Objects
```

Each of these data type subkeys contains one required value called Store. This value contains the path name of the DLL that implements the desktop service provider.

The optional value Display Name can also be defined. This value is analogous to the Display Name values registered on the desktop PC.

In the case of the phone list application with a device service provider implemented in PHDEVS.DLL, the registry subkey and value you would add to the device registry are shown in Figure 14.4. Such a registration would require that the DLL PHDEVS.DLL be copied to the Windows directory of the device.

There is an alternative to registering the device service provider manually. The application DEVSETUP.EXE, created by the DevSetup project on the companion CD, is a Windows CE application that will register the device service provider for you. Simply build the application, download it to your device, and run it.

When the ActiveSync service starts, or when a user initiates a data synchronization, the ActiveSync service manager looks in the desktop and device registries to determine what data types to synchronize. On the desktop and device, the service manager gets the programmatic identifier for each registered synchronization data type. It then creates

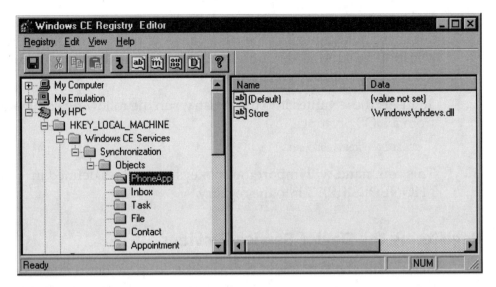

Figure 14.4 Registering a device service provider.

instances of the IReplStore and IReplObjHandler interfaces for each of the corresponding service providers.[1]

Desktop Service Provider Data Model

In the phone list application synchronization example presented in this chapter, the desktop service provider uses various application-defined data structures to represent the phone entry data. Individual phone entries are modeled as PHONEENTRY structures. The data store of all phone entries is modeled as a PHONEFILE structure.

The PHONEENTRY structure definition looks like this:

```
typedef struct tagPhoneObj
{
  UINT uidEntry; //Phone entry ID
  UINT uFlags;
  FILETIME ftLastModified; //Entry modification time
  char lpszLastName[MAX_STRING_LENGTH];
```

[1] In reality, this is done by COM. The service manager maps the programmatic identifier to the class identifier of the service provider. *CoCreateInstance* then gets called using this identifier to create the interface instances.

```
    char lpszFirstName[MAX_STRING_LENGTH];
    char lpszPhoneNumber[MAX_STRING_LENGTH];
    int nDept;
} PHONEENTRY, *PPHONEENTRY;
```

Notice that the last four members of this structure are the same members as in the PHONERECORD structure from the DBASE.EXE application of Chapter 7. This is because we are using the same database schema in this chapter as in the original phone list application.

uidEntry is used to assign a unique index to each database entry in the desktop data store. *ftLastModified* is a FILETIME value that contains the time that the entry was last modified. The *uFlags* member contains flags indicating the state of the entry, such as whether the entry has changed since the last synchronization.

The data store is modeled using the PHONEFILE structure:

```
#define MAX_ENTRIES 500 //Maximum number of entries
typedef struct tagPhoneFile
{
  UINT uidCurrEntry;
  UINT cChg, cDel;
  UINT rgidChg[MAX_ENTRIES], rgidDel[MAX_ENTRIES];
  UINT cEntries;
  PHONEENTRY rgEntries[MAX_ENTRIES];
} PHONEFILE, *PPHONEFILE;
```

uidCurrEntry contains the zero-based index of the phone entry currently being accessed. *cEntries* is the total number of phone entries in the data store. *rgEntries* is an array of all the data store phone entries.

One of the most important responsibilities of the desktop service provider is keeping track of what desktop data store entries have changed or been deleted between synchronizations. The service provider alerts the service manager when entries are changed or deleted so that the changes can be synchronized.

To make this easier, the PHONEFILE structure contains two additional arrays, *rgidChg* and *rgidDel*. These arrays contain the entry identifiers of the changed and deleted data store entries. The members *cChg* and *cDel* contain the number of entries in each of these arrays.

As phone entries are modified or deleted by the desktop application user, the identifiers are added to the appropriate array. We will see how the service manager is notified of these changes in the section "Notifying the Service Manager."

Initializing a Desktop Service Provider

The desktop service provider is initialized when the service manager calls the *IReplStore::Initialize* method:

```
HRESULT Initialize(pReplNotify, uFlags);
```

pReplNotify is a pointer to the IReplNotify instance created by the service manager. *uFlags* indicates why the store is initialized. This can be ISF_REMOTE_CONNECTED, indicating that the service provider is initialized while the device is connected. A *uFlags* value of ISF_SELECTED_DEVICE indicates that the provider is initialized for a particular selected device. This would occur when a PC with multiple partnerships is connected to a device, that is, if a particular PC has been set up to connect to more than one device. (Note that a given PC can connect with no more than two devices.)

Generally, a PC has a partnership with only one Windows CE device. Therefore *uFlags* will be zero, indicating that the PC is initializing a service provider for that one device.

Service providers use the *Initialize* method to open the data store for the particular application and read the data store objects into the IReplStore object's internal data structures.

In the case of the phone list application example in this chapter, the desktop service provider uses the *Initialize* method to read the phone entry data from the flat file in which the data is stored:

```
STDMETHODIMP CStore::Initialize(
  IReplNotify *pNotify,
  UINT uFlags)
{
  char pszFile[MAX_PATH];
  HRESULT hr = NOERROR;
  m_uFlags  = uFlags;
  m_pNotify = pNotify;
  hr = Open(TRUE);
  if (FAILED(hr))
  {
   /* Display a message box indicating the data store
      file could not be opened.
    */
  if (SUCCEEDED(hr))
  {
    m_uFlags |= ISF_INITIALIZED;
  }
```

```
    return (hr);
  }
```

This method stores the *pNotify* and *uFlags* parameters in two data members of the CStore class for later use.

The most important part of this function is the *Open* function call. *Open* is a method defined on CStore that opens the desktop file containing the phone entry data. The phone entry data is read into the *m_pEntries* data member of CStore. This member is an array of pointers to PHONEENTRY structures defined previously. Therefore, all access to store data is done through this *m_pEntries* member.

Reconstructing Folders and Items

After a connection between a Windows CE device and a desktop computer has been established and any ActiveSync service providers registered on the desktop computer have been initialized, the most recently synchronized data is reconstructed.

The service manager reconstructs this data snapshot by asking the desktop service provider to reassemble all data folders and their item contents from the data stored by the manager in REPL.DAT. The IReplStore method that the manager calls to accomplish this is called *BytesToObject*:

```
HREPLOBJ BytesToObject(lpb, cb);
```

lpb is a pointer to a BYTE array and *cb* is a UINT indicating the number of bytes in the *lpb* buffer. *lpb* contains data item information from REPL.DAT.

The service manager gets the bytes that it writes to REPL.DAT for a particular item by calling the IReplStore method *ObjectToBytes*.

```
UINT ObjectToBytes(hObject, lpb);
```

hObject is an HREPLITEM or HREPLFLD handle, and *lpb* is a pointer to the BYTE buffer in which the service provider should store the pertinent information. This method returns the number of bytes placed in the *lpb* byte array.

The phone list application desktop service provider implements *ObjectToBytes* as shown in the following code. From this code we can see that the service manager saves the object type (folder or item) and a synchronization option for folders. It saves the object type, object identifier, and last modified time in the case of an item, i.e., a phone entry.

```
STDMETHODIMP_(UINT) CStore::ObjectToBytes(
  HREPLOBJ hObject,
  LPBYTE    lpb)
{
  LPBYTE    lpbStart = lpb;
  CReplObject *pObject = (CReplObject *)hObject;
  CFolder   *pFolder = (CFolder *)pObject;
  CItem     *pItem = (CItem *)pObject;
  if (lpbStart)
  {
   *(PUINT)lpb = pObject->m_uType;
  }
  lpb += sizeof( pObject->m_uType );
  switch(pObject->m_uType)
  {
  case OT_FOLDER:
   if (lpbStart)
   {
    *(PUINT)lpb = pFolder->m_uSyncOpt;
   }
   lpb += sizeof(pFolder->m_uSyncOpt);
   break;
  case OT_ITEM:
   if (lpbStart)
   {
    *(PUINT)lpb = pItem->m_uid;
   }
   lpb += sizeof(pItem->m_uid);
   if (lpbStart)
   {
    *(FILETIME *)lpb = pItem->m_ftModified;
   }
   lpb += sizeof(pItem->m_ftModified);
   break;
  }
  return (lpb-lpbStart);
}
```

The service manager passes in the folder or item as an HREPLOBJ handle. *ObjectToBytes* first casts this handle to both a CItem pointer and a CFolder pointer. The function then writes the object type to the byte array pointed to by *lpb*, and then moves the pointer to the next free byte.

Next, depending on whether the object passed in is a folder or an item, the other pertinent object data is added to the byte array to be written out by the service manager.

It might seem strange that the service manager asks the service provider to fill the byte array that is written to REPL.DAT. After all, the service manager passed in a valid item or folder handle containing all of the item data. Why didn't the manager write the data itself?

The answer goes back to the original idea that the ActiveSync service manager only facilitates the entire synchronization process. The data stored in REPL.DAT is used to discover changes in the data store between synchronizations. But as we will see, the comparisons needed to detect data changes are done by the service provider at the request of the service manager.

Therefore, the service manager lets the service provider tell which specific pieces of information about a folder or item should be stored. Hence the calls to *ObjectToBytes*.

BytesToObject works in a similar way. Whenever synchronized data needs to be reconstructed, the service manager passes the entire set of data stored with a particular object to the service provider. The provider then extracts those pieces of information it will need for other synchronization tasks.

For example, the phone list application implements *BytesToObject* as follows:

```
STDMETHODIMP_(HREPLOBJ) CStore::BytesToObject(
  LPBYTE lpb,
  UINT cb)
{
  CReplObject *pObject = NULL;
  CFolder    *pFolder;
  CItem      *pItem;
  UINT  uType = *(PUINT)lpb;
  lpb += sizeof(uType);
  switch(uType)
  {
  case OT_FOLDER:
   pObject = pFolder = new CFolder;
   pFolder->m_uSyncOpt = *(PUINT)lpb;
   lpb += sizeof(pFolder->m_uSyncOpt);
   break;
  case OT_ITEM:
   pObject = pItem = new CItem;
```

```
   pItem->m_uid = *(PUINT)lpb;
   lpb += sizeof(pItem->m_uid);
   pItem->m_ftModified = *(FILETIME *)lpb;
   lpb += sizeof(pItem->m_ftModified);
   break;
   }
   return (HREPLOBJ)pObject;
}
```

The service manager passes a byte array of length *cb*. The service provider proceeds by extracting the parts of that array it is interested in as defined by the CItem and CFolder data members. Once it has finished, the provider returns a handle to the new object. As we will see in the next section, the service manager uses these handles during object enumeration.

Enumerating Objects

The ActiveSync service manager determines whether data objects have changed by the process of *enumeration*. As with all other synchronization steps, the manager controls the enumeration process. The desktop service provider is responsible for telling the manager if objects have changed since the last synchronization.

Before enumeration begins, the service manager sets a bit in each object handle stored in REPL.DAT. This bit will be used to indicate whether a particular object should be deleted from the device data store during synchronization.

During enumeration, the service manager asks the service provider for handles to each item in the desktop data store. The service manager compares each handle returned by the service provider to the handles stored in REPL.DAT. If a matching handle is found, the delete bit is turned off, and the service manager asks the service provider if the item has changed by calling the *IsItemChanged* method of the IReplStore interface.

If the service provider returns TRUE from *IsItemChanged*, the service manager obtains a copy of the new item handle by calling *CopyObject*. Finally, to determine if the new item should be transferred to the Windows CE device during synchronization, the service manager calls the IReplStore method *IsItemReplicated*.

The object enumeration itself is accomplished with the IReplStore methods *FindFirstItem*, *FindNextItem*, and *FindItemClose*.

FindFirstItem retrieves the first item from the specified folder:

```
HRESULT FindFirstItem(hFolder, phItem, pfExist);
```

hFolder is an HREPLFLD handle to the folder of interest. *phItem* is used by the method to return a pointer to the HREPLITEM handle of the first item in the folder. *pfExist* is also a return value. It is a pointer to a BOOL that the service provider returns indicating whether or not there are items in the folder.

The *FindNextItem* function has the same signature as *FindFirstItem*. This function is called by the service manager to obtain handles to subsequent data items. The service manager calls *FindNextItem* repeatedly until the service provider returns FALSE through the *pfExist* parameter after enumerating the last item in the folder.

Both *FindFirstItem* and *FindNextItem* return either E_FAIL or NOER-ROR. A service provider returns the E_FAIL error code to indicate that an error occurred during enumeration. In such a case, the contents of the folder in question are not synchronized. NOERROR indicates that no object enumeration problems occurred.

Once the last item has been enumerated, the service manager calls *FindItemClose* to give the service provider the opportunity to free any resources that were used during enumeration. The definition of *FindItemClose* is:

```
HRESULT FindItemClose(hFolder);
```

hFolder is the HREPLFLD handle of the folder whose items were previously enumerated.

Copying and Synchronizing Items

As mentioned previously, as items are enumerated, the service manager will copy changed data store items and ask the service provider if such items should be synchronized.

Items are copied with the IReplStore method *CopyObject*:

```
BOOL CopyObject(hObjSrc, hObjDst);
```

The method copies the item indicated by HREPLOBJ handle *hObjSrc* to the handle *hObjDst*. It returns TRUE if the copy is successful and FALSE if the operation fails.

During item enumeration, handles to new items are passed to the service manager. These item handles are copied to separate handles that are stored in REPL.DAT.

The service provider tells the service manager that a particular new item is to be synchronized by its response to the method *IsItemReplicated*:

```
BOOL IsItemReplicated(hFolder, hItem);
```

hItem is the HREPLITEM handle of the item in question, and *hFolder* is the folder that contains the item. Desktop service providers use this method to implement rules for determining which items to replicate. If this method returns TRUE, the item will be synchronized during the next data synchronization. Returning FALSE tells the service manager not to synchronize the item.

The phone list application implements a simple synchronization rule using the synchronization option value that it stores with the phone entry data folder. The relevant parts of this method implementation are shown here:

```
STDMETHODIMP_(BOOL) CStore::IsItemReplicated(
  HREPLFLD hFolder,
  HREPLITEM hItem)
{
  CFolder *pFolder = (CFolder *)hFolder;
  CItem   *pItem = (CItem *)hItem;
  PPHONEENTRY pEntry;
  char cLastName;
  pEntry = FindPhoneEntry(pItem->m_uid);
  if (pEntry)
  {
   cLastName = pEntry->lpszLastName[0];
  }
  switch (pFolder->m_uSyncOpt)
  {
  case SO_ALL:
   return (TRUE);
  case SO_AM:
   return (cLastName >= 'A' && cLastName <= 'M');
  case SO_NZ:
   return (cLastName >= 'N' && cLastName <= 'Z');
  }
```

```
      return (FALSE);
  }
```

The method *FindPhoneEntry* obtains the PHONEENTRY structure corresponding to the specified entry identifier from the data store contained in the *m_pEntries* data member of CStore:

```
PPHONEENTRY CStore::FindPhoneEntry(
  UINT uidEntry,
  PUINT pIndex)
{
  UINT i;
  PPHONEENTRY pEntry = NULL;
  for (i = 0; i < m_pEntries->cEntries; i++)
  {
   if (m_pEntries->rgEntries[i].uidEntry == uidEntry)
   {
    break;
   }
  }
  if (pIndex)
  {
   *pIndex = ((i < m_pEntries->cEntries) ? i : -1);
  }
  if (i < m_pEntries->cEntries)
  {
   pEntry = &m_pEntries->rgEntries[i];
  }
  return (pEntry);
}
```

The *FindPhoneEntry* method is used extensively to retrieve the phone
entry from the data store corresponding to the specified object identifier. *m_pEntries* contains all the data store entries in its *rgEntries* array.
The method also returns the array index of the retrieved entry if the
caller passes a non-NULL value in the *pIndex* parameter.

Depending on the synchronization option associated with the folder,
the *IsItemReplicated* method decides if the item should be
replicated. For example, the synchronization option SO_ALL means
that all items are synchronized. In this case *IsItemReplicated* always
returns TRUE.

The SO_AM option, however, means that only those items with a last
name value that begins with the letters A through M are replicated.
Likewise, SO_NZ means only last names beginning with N through Z
get synchronized.

Setting Synchronization Options

As we have seen, the *IsItemReplicated* method can be used to implement synchronization rules using service provider–specific synchronization options. This section describes how the service provider obtains such options from the user.

To specify synchronization options for a particular installed desktop service provider, the user must choose the ActiveSync Options menu item from the Mobile Devices window Tools menu. The dialog box shown in Figure 14.5 is displayed after this menu option is selected. This dialog lists all of the installed service providers. The check box next to each indicates if the provider is active, that is, if the data corresponding to that provider is synchronized.

Double-clicking on any of the service providers in the list will invoke another dialog box if the provider includes synchronization options that the user can specify. Double-clicking on PhoneApp will invoke

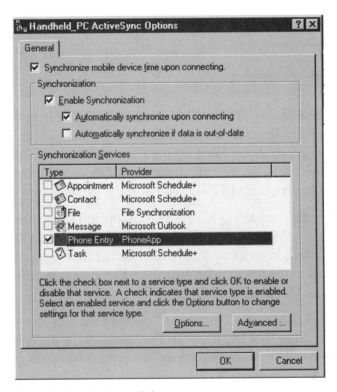

Figure 14.5 The ActiveSync Options dialog.

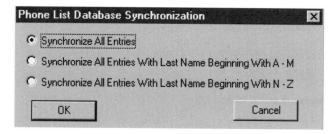

Figure 14.6 Phone list service provider Synchronization Options user interface.

the phone list application service provider synchronization options dialog, as shown in Figure 14.6.

The three radio buttons correspond to the three synchronization options defined by the service provider, SO_ALL, SO_AM, and SO_NZ.

A synchronization options dialog is implemented just like any other dialog box. The service provider includes the dialog template in its resource file, and implements the dialog procedure for the dialog box. The dialog box is invoked when the ActiveSync service manager calls the *ActivateDialog* method of the data store CStore interface:

```
HRESULT ActivateDialog(uDlg, hwndParent, hFolder, penum);
```

hFolder specifies the data folder whose options are to be specified by the service provider. *hwndParent* is the parent window that the service manager wants the provider to use as the parent of the dialog box. *penum* points to an enumerator for the items contained in *hFolder*.

uDlg is an input flag indicating which dialog to invoke. Currently the only value this parameter can take is OPTIONS_DIALOG. In future versions of ActiveSync, *ActivateDialog* may be used to invoke a variety of synchronization-related user interfaces.

The phone list service provider implements *ActivateDialog* as follows:

```
STDMETHODIMP CStore::ActivateDialog(
  UINT uDlg,
  HWND hwndParent,
  HREPLFLD hFolder,
  IEnumReplItem* penum)
{
  // Initialization code...
  if (DialogBox(v_hInst,
    MAKEINTRESOURCE(IDD_SYNCOPTIONS),
```

```
        hwndParent,
        (DLGPROC)dlgSyncOpt) == IDOK)
    {
      ((CFolder *)hFolder)->m_uSyncOpt = v_uSyncOpt;
      return NOERROR;
    }
    return RERR_CANCEL;
}
```

v_hInst contains the HINSTANCE of the service provider DLL. The dialog box procedure sets the global variable *v_uSyncOpt* to one of the synchronization options depending on which radio button is selected. If the user presses the OK button, that option is stored in the data folder.

ActiveSync places no restrictions on the number of synchronization options that can be defined for a particular data type. Further, your options dialog boxes may be as complicated as necessary for a user to specify the appropriate options.

Reporting Desktop Data Store Changes

The previous section described how the ActiveSync service manager and desktop service provider work together to enumerate objects in the desktop data store. We said that the primary purpose of this enumeration is to aid the service manager in detecting changes in data store objects.

The service manager compares the object handles returned by service provider *FindFirstItem* and *FindNextItem* calls to the handles stored in REPL.DAT. New objects are added by writing the handle and other item data to the file. But for each existing item, the service manager must determine if the item has been changed by the desktop application since the last data synchronization.

The service manager calls the *IsItemChanged* method on the IReplStore interface to make this determination:

```
    BOOL IsItemChanged(hFolder, hItem, hItemComp);
```

hFolder is the handle of the folder that holds the items to be compared. *hItem* and *hItemComp* are the two items to be compared.

When enumerating objects, *hItem* is the handle to the item returned by a *FindFirstItem* or *FindNextItem* call, and *hItemComp* is the handle to the corresponding item from REPL.DAT. In other words, *hItem* is the current item from the desktop data store; *hItemComp* contains the attributes of the same item, as of the last synchronization.

IsItemChanged can also be called by the service manager when actually transmitting data packets between the desktop and device. In such cases *hItemComp* will be NULL; the service provider compares the item in *hItem* to the corresponding item in the data store.

For example, the phone list service provider compares items as shown in the code below:

```
STDMETHODIMP_(BOOL) CStore::IsItemChanged(
  HREPLFLD hFolder,
  HREPLITEM hItem,
  HREPLITEM hItemComp)
{
  CFolder *pFolder = (CFolder *)hFolder;
  CItem  *pItem = (CItem *)hItem;
  CItem  *pItemComp = (CItem *)hItemComp;
  BOOL  bChanged = FALSE;
  if (pItemComp)
  {
   bChanged = CompareFileTime(&pItem->m_ftModified,
    &pItemComp->m_ftModified);
  }
  else
  {
   PPHONEENTRY pEntry;
   pEntry = FindPhoneEntry(pItem->m_uid);
   bChanged = pEntry &&
    CompareFileTime(&pItem->m_ftModified,
     &pEntry->ftLastModified);

  }
  return (bChanged);
}
```

To determine data store item equality, the phone list application service provider simply compares the modification times of the two items. For those cases when *hItemComp* is NULL, the service provider retrieves the data store item corresponding to *hItem*. This item modification time is compared to that of *hItem*.

The value returned by *IsItemChanged* indicates whether the item in *hItem* has changed. A TRUE return value means the item has changed, FALSE means it has not.

Transferring the Data

The ActiveSync service manager is responsible for transferring data store objects between Windows CE–based devices and desktop computers. For data to be transferred, it must first be converted into binary data *packets*. A packet in this context is simply an array of the bytes that make up the data store items.

The process of converting data store objects into packets is sometimes called *de-serialization*. Synchronized data packets are also converted back into data store objects once they reach their destination in a processes called *serialization*.

Data de-serialization involves three steps. These steps are performed by the service provider using three methods implemented by the IReplObjHandler interface. This is in contrast to all of the synchronization tasks seen so far, which are implemented by the IReplStore interface.

The three IReplObjHandler interface methods that perform de-serialization are:

Setup. Tells the service provider what object is to be de-serialized. This gives the provider an opportunity to allocate any resources required for de-serialization.

GetPacket. The service provider creates one or more packets.

Reset. Used by the service provider to free any resources used during de-serialization.

Similarly, serialization involves three steps:

Setup. Tells the service provider what object is to be serialized.

SetPacket. The service provider converts packets back into data store objects.

Reset. Used by the service provider to free any resources used during serialization.

Setup is called by the service manager for each and every object to be serialized or de-serialized by a service provider. Furthermore, it is important to note that a service manager request to serialize an object can occur before a previously de-serialized packet has been transferred. Likewise, a service provider can receive a request to de-serialize a transferred packet before a packet it has just serialized has been transferred by the service manager.

This means that the service provider programmer must make provisions to accommodate these possibilities. We will shortly see how this is typically done.

The *Setup* method takes a single parameter:

```
HRESULT Setup(pSetup);
```

pSetup is a pointer to a REPLSETUP structure that contains information about the item to be synchronized. This structure contains many members. Most relevant to synchronization are a BOOL member called *fRead* and *hItem*. *hItem* is the item handle of the data store object to be synchronized. *fRead* specifies whether the item is being serialized or de-serialized.

The *fRead* value is important in light of the fact that a service provider can be asked to serialize a packet before a previous packet is de-serialized and vice versa. A service provider should maintain separate storage for an item to be serialized and for an item to be de-serialized. If packets happen to be serialized and de-serialized at the same time, the service provider can then keep the two items straight.

For example, the phone list application service providers define two REPLSTORE pointer members on their IReplObjHandler interfaces, *m_pWriteSetup* and *m_pReadSetup*. The *Setup* method is then implemented like this:

```
STDMETHODIMP CDataHandler::Setup(PREPLSETUP pSetup)
{
  if (pSetup->fRead)
  {
   m_pReadSetup = pSetup;
  }
  else
  {
   m_pWriteSetup = pSetup;
  }
  return (NOERROR);
}
```

If the method is called by the service manager to prepare the service provider to serialize a packet, the REPLSETUP information is saved in *m_pReadSetup*. If called to prepare to de-serialize, the information is stored in *m_pWriteSetup*.

Then, when the service manager calls *SetPacket* or *GetPacket*, the service provider can be sure to serialize or de-serialize the right data store object.

The *GetPacket* IReplObjHandler method creates a packet from a data store item:

```
HRESULT GetPacket(lppbData, pcbData, cbRecommend);
```

lppdData is a pointer to a BYTE array. This is the data buffer where the service provider should put the packet data. *pcbData* points to a DWORD in which the service provider should return the packet size. *cbRecommend* is passed by the service manager to tell the service provider the maximum packet size.

A data store object may require more than one packet in order to be completely transferred by the service manager. The service manager will therefore call *GetPacket* repeatedly until the service provider returns RWRN_LAST_PACKET, indicating that the last packet for the object has been created.

The service provider's implementation can use the *cbRecommend* parameter to determine how many packets to create for a particular object. If the number of bytes to be transferred is greater than *cbRecommend*, the service provider should create packets and return NOERROR until the last packet has been created.

Notice that none of the parameters to *GetPacket* indicate which item is being packetized. This information is stored in the *hItem* member of the REPLSETUP structure that was saved in the *Setup* method.

In the case of the phone list application, the desktop service provider creates packets like this:

```
STDMETHODIMP CDataHandler::GetPacket(
  LPBYTE *lppbPacket,
  DWORD *pcbPacket,
  DWORD cbRecommend)
{
  PPHONEENTRY pEntry;
  if (m_pReadSetup->hItem == NULL)
  {
   return E_UNEXPECTED;
  }
```

```
memset(&m_packet, 0, sizeof(m_packet));
pEntry = m_pStore->FindPhoneEntry(
 ((PITEM)m_pReadSetup->hItem)->m_uid);
if (pEntry)
{
 MultiByteToWideChar(CP_ACP, 0, pEntry->lpszLastName,
  -1, m_packet.lpszLastName,
   sizeof(m_packet.lpszLastName) - 1);
 MultiByteToWideChar(CP_ACP, 0, pEntry->lpszFirstName,
  -1, m_packet.lpszFirstName,
   sizeof(m_packet.lpszFirstName) - 1);
 MultiByteToWideChar(CP_ACP, 0, pEntry->lpszPhoneNumber,
  -1, m_packet.lpszPhoneNumber,
  sizeof(m_packet.lpszPhoneNumber) - 1);
 m_packet.nDept = pEntry->nDept;
 m_packet.ftUpdated = pEntry->ftLastModified;
}
*pcbPacket = sizeof(m_packet);
*lppbPacket = (LPBYTE)&m_packet;
return (pEntry ? RWRN_LAST_PACKET : E_UNEXPECTED);
}
```

Since *GetPacket* is used to de-serialize an item, the implementation works with the item corresponding to the HREPLITEM handle from *m_pReadSetup*. The function retrieves the PHONEENTRY structure corresponding to the item, and then proceeds to copy the data from that structure into the CDataHandler member *m_packet*.

m_packet is of type PHONEOBJPACKET, a structure defined by the application to represent a phone entry data packet:

```
#define MAX_STRING_LENGTH 129
typedef struct tagPhoneObjPacket
{
  WCHAR lpszLastName[MAX_STRING_LENGTH];
  WCHAR lpszFirstName[MAX_STRING_LENGTH];
  WCHAR lpszPhoneNumber[MAX_STRING_LENGTH];
  int nDept;
  FILETIME  ftUpdated;
} PHONEOBJPACKET, *PPHONEOBJPACKET;
```

Notice that the members of this structure are very similar to those of the PHONEENTRY structure. The main difference is that the strings are all Unicode, as Windows CE only uses Unicode strings. This explains all of the *MultiByteToWideChar* calls that convert the ANSI string versions of the entry string data to Unicode.

After the packet has been filled with the phone entry data, the *Get-Packet* method executes these two lines of code:

```
*pcbPacket = sizeof(m_packet);
*lppbPacket = (LPBYTE)&m_packet;
```

This ensures that the packet data and packet data size can be referenced by the ActiveSync service provider, as *pcbPacket* and *lppbPacket* are *GetPacket* method return values.

Serializing packets is done similarly with *SetPacket*:

```
HRESULT SetPacket(lpbData, cbData);
```

In this case the service manager passes the data packet to the service provider to be converted back into a data store object. *lpdData* is a pointer to a BYTE array containing the packet data. *cbData* is the size of the array.

Serialization is almost the same as de-serialization. In the case of the phone list application, instead of filling a packet structure, the *SetPacket* method reconstructs a PHONEENTRY structure from the packet data.

Notifying the Service Manager

So far we have seen how the service manager and service provider work together to reconstruct synchronized data, enumerate items, and transfer data between desktop and Window CE device data stores.

Most of these operations were described in the context of synchronizing data when a device is initially connected to the desktop PC. However, a user can synchronize data at any time when a device is connected as well.

For example, a user may add, delete, or change phone list entries from the desktop phone list application while connected. The user can synchronize such changes with the Windows CE device by selecting the Synchronize Now option from the Mobile Devices folder Tools menu. Alternatively, the user can select the same option from the ActiveSync manager menu invoked by right-clicking the ActiveSync icon in the taskbar (Figure 14.7).

For this to be possible, ActiveSync service providers must have a way of telling the service manager when objects in their data stores have changed.

For desktop service providers, this notification is performed by calling the *OnItemNotify* on the service manager's IReplNotify interface. This

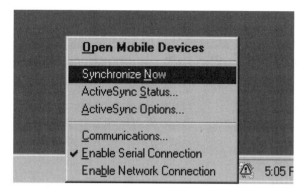

Figure 14.7   Invoking synchronization from the taskbar.

is the first time that we have seen a service provider call a method exposed by the service manager.

The *OnItemNotify* method looks like this:

```
HRESULT OnItemNotify(uCode, lpszProgId, lpszObjType, hItem,
   ulFlags);
```

uCode is a UINT containing a flag used to indicate why the notification is being made. This flag can be one of the four values shown in Table 14.3. *uFlags* is reserved. Service providers therefore typically pass zero in this parameter.

lpszProgID is a string containing the programmatic identifier of the data store. In the case of the phone list data store, this string would be "Wiley.PhoneApp". See the section "Registering ActiveSync Service Providers" for details.

lpszObjType is a string containing the name of the data store object type. You will recall that each data type synchronized by a service provider is registered. The subkey name used to register the data type is the data store object type. Thus, for the phone list application, *lpszObjType* would be "PhoneApp".

Finally, the *hItem* parameter is the HREPLITEM handle of the item in question.

We can now see why CStore, which implements the desktop service provider's IReplStore interface, has a data member of type PHONE-FILE. The PHONEFILE structure contains two arrays for storing the object identifiers of changed and deleted phone entries. Periodically the service provider can iterate through those arrays and send notifica-

Table 14.3 IReplNotify::OnItemNotify uCode Values

VALUE	MEANING
RNC_CREATED	Indicates that the object was created.
RNC_MODIFIED	Indicates that the object was changed (but not deleted).
RNC_DELETED	Indicates that the object was deleted.
RNC_SHUTDOWN	Indicates that the data store has been shut down. This tells the service manager to unload the service provider.

tions to the service manager, telling the service manager if data store items have been added or deleted.

For example, let's say a phone entry with identifier *nID* is deleted by the desktop application. The service provider could notify the service manager of this fact as follows:

```
CItem* pItem;
PPHONEENTRY pEntry;
pItem = new CItem;
pEntry = FindPhoneEntry(nID);
pItem->m_uid = nID;
pItem->m_ftModified = pEntry->ftLastModified;
m_pNotify->OnItemNotify(RNC_DELETED,
   "Wiley.PhoneApp", "PhoneApp", (HREPLITEM)pItem, 0);
```

Recall that a pointer to an instance of the service manager's IReplNotify interface was stored in the CStore member *m_pNotify* when CStore was initialized. The *FindPhoneEntry* call retrieves the phone entry with identifier *nID* from the data store. A CItem object is created with the relevant data and sent with the notification so that the service manager can mark it as deleted for the next synchronization.

Device service providers notify the service manager differently. We will look at device service manager notification in the next section.

Programming Device Service Providers

So far we have concentrated on programming desktop ActiveSync service providers. For synchronization to work for any given data type, there must also be a service provider installed on the Windows CE device capable of synchronizing the data type.

Device service providers are much easier to implement. The main reason is that the device service provider only implements one of the

COM interfaces implemented by its desktop counterpart. Device service providers must implement IReplObjHandler, but they do not implement IReplStore. The role of IReplStore is instead performed by four functions exported by the device service provider DLL. These functions are listed in Table 14.4. Of these four functions, *ObjectNotify* carries the majority of the device service provider responsibilities. We will therefore focus on this function first.

Synchronizing Device Data Store Changes

When data store objects on the Windows CE device change, or new objects are created, the service manager calls the device service manager *ObjectNotify* function. The service provider responds to this function call by telling the service manager if the corresponding object change should be synchronized during the next data synchronization.

The *ObjectNotify* function is defined as:

```
BOOL ObjectNotify(pNotify);
```

The *pNotify* parameter is a pointer to an OBJNOTIFY structure that contains information about the object that has changed. The service provider returns TRUE to indicate that the change should be synchronized. It returns FALSE if the change is not to be synchronized.

The OBJNOTIFY structure has the following definition:

```
typedef struct tagObjNotify
{
  UINT cbStruct;
  OBJTYPENAME szObjType[ MAX_OBJTYPE_NAME ];
  UINT uFlags;
```

Table 14.4 Device Service Provider Exported Functions.

FUNCTION	PURPOSE
InitObjType	Initializes the device provider IReplObjHandler interface instance.
GetObjTypeInfo	Called by the service manager to retrieve data type information from the device.
ObjectNotify	Called by the service manager when a device data store object changes.
ReportStatus	Called by the service manager to get status of device synchronization objects.

```
      UINT uPartnerBit;
      CEOID oidObject;
      CEOIDINFO oidInfo;
      UINT cOidChg;
      UINT cOidDel;
      UINT *poid
   } OBJNOTIFY, *POBJNOTIFY;
```

cbStruct contains the size of the structure in bytes. *szObjType* is the object type name (for example, "PhoneApp").

A desktop PC can connect to up to two Windows CE devices. Each connection is called a partnership. *uPartnerBit* indicates which partnership is connected.

oidObject and *oidInfo* contain the CEOID and CEOIDINFO data of the object in question.

The *cOidChg* and *cOidDel* members are returned by *ObjectNotify*. They tell the service manager the number of changed or deleted objects that should be synchronized.

poid is also returned by *ObjectNotify*. It points to an array of object identifiers corresponding to the objects to be synchronized.

The *uFlags* member contains flag bits that give the *ObjectNotify* function information about why the function is being called. *uFlags* can take on one or more of the values given in Table 14.5.

Table 14.5 ObjectNotify Function Flag Values

FLAG	MEANING
ONF_FILE	The object in question is a file.
ONF_DIRECTORY	The object in question is a directory.
ONF_RECORD	The object in question is a database record.
ONF_DATABASE	The object in question is a database.
ONF_CHANGED	Indicates that the object has changed.
ONF_DELETED	Indicates that the object was deleted.
ONF_CLEAR_CHANGE	Indicates that the service provider should mark the object as up to date.
ONF_CALL_BACK	If returned by the service provider, tells the service manager to call *ObjectNotify* again in two seconds.
ONF_CALLING_BACK	Indicates that the service manager is calling *ObjectNotify* in response to the ONF_CALL_BACK flag.

For example, a device service provider might tell the service manager to synchronize an object deletion as follows:

```
BOOL ObjectNotify(POBJNOTIFY pNotify)
{
  if (pNotify->uFlags & ONF_DELETED)
  {
   pNotify->cOidDel = 1;
   pNotify->poid = (UINT *)&pNotify->oidObject;
   return (TRUE);
  }
  /* Other ObjectNotify code ... */
}
```

A complete *ObjectNotify* example can be found in the phone list application device service provider. This is implemented in the companion CD file \samples\datasync\phoneapp\device\sync\phdevs.cpp.

Other Device Service Provider Functions

We will briefly describe the functions *InitObjType* and *GetObjTypeInfo*, which are exported by a device service provider. *ReportStatus* is an optional function and is not covered.

InitObjType

The function *InitObjType* is used to create the service provider's IReplObjHandler interface instance. It is also called when the service provider DLL is unloaded when ActiveSync terminates. This gives the service provider a chance to free any resources it may have allocated.

```
BOOL InitObjType(lpszObjType, ppObjHandler, uPartnerBit);
```

lpszObjType is the name of the object type being initialized. In the case of the phone list application, this is "PhoneApp." This string will be NULL if *InitObjType* is being called during termination.

ppObjHandler is used as an output parameter. It is used to return a pointer to the service provider's IReplObjHandler interface instance. *uPartnerBit* indicates which partner the desktop computer is connected as. A value of 1 indicates it is partner 1, while 2 indicates the desktop is connected as partner 2.

InitObjType returns TRUE if successful, and FALSE if unsuccessful.

The phone list device service provider uses *InitObjType* to store the partner bit in a global variable and to return the IReplObjHandler instance to the service manager:

```
BOOL InitObjType(LPWSTR lpszObjType,
  IReplObjHandler** ppObjHandler,
  UINT uPartnerBit)
{
  if (lpszObjType == NULL)
  {
   //Free resources if necessary
   return (TRUE);
  }
  *ppObjHandler = new CDataHandler;
  v_uPartnerBit = uPartnerBit;
  return (TRUE);
}
```

GetObjTypeInfo

This function is called by the service manager to get information about a particular type of data synchronized by the device service provider.

```
BOOL GetObjTypeInfo(pObjTypeInfo);
```

The parameter is a pointer to an OBJTYPEINFO structure. This structure is used to tell the service provider which data type the service manager wants information about. The service provider fills in various members of this structure to supply the requested information.

```
typedef struct tagObjTypeInfo {
  UINT cbStruct;
  OBJTYPENAMEW szObjType;
  UINT uFlags;
  WCHAR szName[ 80 ]
  UINT cObjects;
  UINT cbAllObj;
  FILETIME ftLastModified
} OBJTPYEINFO, *POBJTYPEINFO;
```

cbStruct contains the byte size of the structure. *uFlags* is reserved by Windows CE and is therefore not used.

szObjType is a string containing the name of the data type for which information is requested.

The service provider uses the other four members to report data type information to the service manager. *szName* is the name of the file or database containing the data store objects. *cObjects* is the number of objects of the requested type, and *cbAllObj* is the number of bytes used to store these objects. Finally, *ftLastModified* reports the last time any of the objects was modified.

For example, the phone list device service provider implements *GetObjTypeInfo* as follows:

```
BOOL GetObjTypeInfo(POBJTYPEINFO pInfo)
{
  CEOIDINFO oidInfo;
  //g_oidDB is the global handle to the phone list database
  CeOidGetInfo(g_oidDB, &oidInfo);
  lstrcpy(pInfo->szName, oidInfo.infDatabase.szDbaseName);
  pInfo->cObjects = oidInfo.infDatabase.wNumRecords;
  pInfo->cbAllObj = oidInfo.infDatabase.dwSize;
  pInfo->ftLastModified = oidInfo.infDatabase.ftLastModified;
  return (TRUE);
}
```

Conflict Resolution

Thus far in our discussion of data synchronization, we have talked about items that are changed either on the desktop computer or on the Windows CE device and then transferred to the other platform.

But what happens if the same data store object is modified on both the desktop and the device, and then the user attempts to synchronize? The ActiveSync service manager includes functionality for resolving such data conflicts. And as with all other synchronization operations, the service manager asks for help by calling various service provider methods.

Creating a Conflict

To demonstrate the ActiveSync conflict resolution scheme, I created the phone list entry shown in Figure 14.8 on my desktop PC.

I then synchronized with my Handheld PC to put this entry in the Handheld PC data store. Next, I changed the entry on both the desktop and the device. On the desktop, I changed the last name to "Users". On the device, I changed the first name to "Same". I then re-synchronized, and ActiveSync displayed the dialog box shown in Figure 14.9.

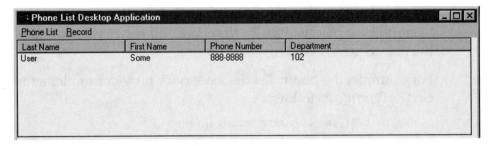

Figure 14.8   The original phone entry.

This conflict resolution dialog box is implemented by the ActiveSync service manager. It allows the user to decide which versions of conflicting data store objects should be saved.

The *GetConflictInfo* Method

The desktop service provider can first try and resolve conflicts programmatically. If it cannot, or otherwise chooses not to, the service provider supplies the service manager with the information to be displayed in the conflict resolution dialog box. It does this with its implementation of the IReplStore method *GetConflictInfo*:

```
HRESULT GetConflictInfo(pConfInfo);
```

The *pConfInfo* parameter points to a CONFINFO structure:

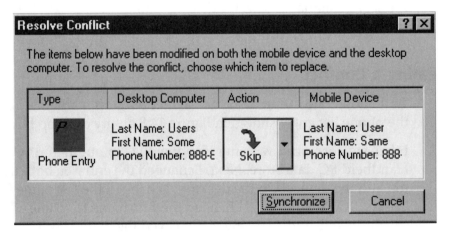

Figure 14.9   The conflict resolution dialog box.

```
typedef struct tagConfInfo{
  UINT cbStruct;
  HREPLFLD hFolder;
  HREPLITEM hLocalItem;
  HREPLITEM hRemoteItem;
  char szLocalName[ MAX_OBJTYPE_NAME ];
  char szLocalDesc[ 512 ];
  char szRemoteName[ MAX_OBJTYPE_NAME ];
  char szRemoteDesc[ 512 ];
} CONFINFO, *PCONFINFO;
```

cbStruct is the structure size, as usual. *hFolder* is the handle of the folder that contains the item for which there is a data conflict.

hLocalItem and *hRemoteItem* are the item handles of the conflicting desktop and device data store items.

When a data conflict is detected, the service manager transfers the conflicting device object to the desktop. This is done so that the desktop service provider has access to the conflicting device object data during conflict resolution.

szLocalName and *szLocalDesc* are string output values that the service provider fills with the name and description of the desktop object. These strings are displayed to the user in the conflict resolution dialog. *szLocalName* identifies the name of the data type and appears below the icon in the "Type" column.[1] *szLocalDesc* appears as the descriptive text in the "Desktop Computer" column.

szRemoteName and *szRemoteDesc* are supposed to play the same role for the device object. In reality, only the *szRemoteDesc* string is used in the conflict resolution dialog as the text in the Mobile Device column.

GetConflictInfo can return either NOERROR or RERR_IGNORE. NOERROR means that the service manager will display the conflict resolution dialog box with the text supplied by the service provider. RERR_IGNORE means that the *GetConflictInfo* implementation has determined that the items are in fact not conflicting. In such cases, the conflict resolution dialog box is not displayed, and the data items are assumed to be the same.

The phone list application desktop service provider implementation of *GetConflictInfo* is shown here:

---

[1] The icon used in the conflict resolution dialog and the ActiveSync Status windows are both specified by the *IReplStore::GetObjTypeUIData* method that gets called during data object enumeration.

```
STDMETHODIMP CStore::GetConflictInfo(PCONFINFO pConfInfo)
{
  lstrcpy( pConfInfo->szLocalName, "Phone Entry" );
  CItem* pLocalItem = (CItem*)pConfInfo->hLocalItem;
  CItem* pRemoteItem = (CItem*)pConfInfo->hRemoteItem;
  PPHONEENTRY pLocalEntry, pRemoteEntry;
  pLocalEntry = FindPhoneEntry(pLocalItem->m_uid);
  pRemoteEntry = FindPhoneEntry(pRemoteItem->m_uid);
  if (pLocalEntry)
  {
   wsprintf( pConfInfo->szLocalDesc,
   "Last Name: %s\r\nFirst Name: %s\r\nPhone Number:
   %s\r\nDept.: %d",
   pLocalEntry->lpszLastName, pLocalEntry->lpszFirstName,
   pLocalEntry->lpszPhoneNumber, pLocalEntry->nDept);
  }

  if (pRemoteEntry)
  {
   wsprintf( pConfInfo->szRemoteDesc, "Last Name:
   %s\r\nFirst Name: %s\r\nPhone Number: %s\r\nDept.: %d",
   pRemoteEntry->lpszLastName, pRemoteEntry->lpszFirstName,
   pRemoteEntry->lpszPhoneNumber, pRemoteEntry->nDept);
  }
  return (NOERROR);
}
```

The method retrieves the two conflicting items from the data store by calling *FindPhoneEntry*. The information to be displayed in the conflict resolution dialog box is then copied into the appropriate members of the CONFINFO structure.

If the user chooses to synchronize the desktop changes, the service manager deletes the conflicting device item, which it copied to the desktop when the conflict was originally detected.

Concluding Remarks

In this chapter we have covered the major aspects of data synchronization under Windows CE. A book of this scope cannot possibly cover every nuance and detail of a subject of this magnitude. In fact, an entire data synchronization book would not be unrealistic. However, with the overview provided by this chapter and the sample code on the companion CD, you will be well on your way to writing your own custom ActiveSync modules.

CHAPTER 15

Other Desktop Connectivity Topics

I n the previous chapter we tackled the rather enormous subject of Windows CE data synchronization using the ActiveSync technology. While ActiveSync is perhaps the most important desktop connectivity feature of Windows CE, it is by no means the only connectivity feature.

In this chapter we will briefly introduce two additional components of the Window CE desktop connectivity landscape. The first of these is the Remote Application Programming Interface, commonly known as the Remote API or RAPI. The second is file filters, also known as file converters.

The subjects covered in this chapter are considerably more straightforward than data synchronization. You may well ask why these subjects were not covered first. As you will soon see, writing file filters involves some of the same steps as writing ActiveSync modules. For example, file filters have various registry entries that must be set, and file filters are implemented as COM servers. It is my feeling that once you have read and absorbed the material on ActiveSync programming, the subject of file filters will require much less discussion.

As for the Remote API, almost all of the functions that make up the API are related to Windows CE functions we have already covered in detail. You therefore already understand almost everything there is to know about RAPI. One feature common to both the Remote API and file filters is that they are both desktop PC phenomena. You only make Remote API calls from a desktop application. File filter DLLs are implemented for and reside on the desktop. Therefore, all of the code samples in this chapter are Windows NT code.

AFTER COMPLETING THIS CHAPTER YOU WILL KNOW HOW TO . . .

Use the Remote API to access a Windows CE device from a desktop computer application

Implement filters for converting files transferred between a desktop PC and a Windows CE device

The Remote API

The Windows CE Remote API provides a way for desktop PC applications to access a connected Windows CE device. This includes the ability to access the object store on the device, as well as to invoke functions residing in modules on the device. Data synchronization allows the desktop PC to access device data as well. But synchronization requires that device data be transferred to the desktop. With RAPI, a desktop application simply reads data from the device.

The API includes functions for reading files or databases from the connected device. The API can also be used to read the registry of a Windows CE device. The desktop PC can also write to files, databases, or registry entries on the device.

Most of the Remote API functions are similar to Windows CE API functions we have already encountered. In many cases, the function names and arguments are exactly the same. For example, a Windows CE application opens a database in the object store by calling the Windows CE API *CeOpenDatabase*. A desktop application interested in accessing the same device database calls the RAPI function *CeOpenDatabase*.

Keep in mind that although the RAPI functions are similar or identical to their Windows CE counterparts, they are implemented in a library that resides on the desktop PC called RAPI.LIB. In short, the Remote API is a desktop PC feature for providing access to a remote device.

NOTE

━━━━ INCLUDE **RAPI.H** AND LINK WITH **RAPI.LIB**

To use any of the Remote API functions, your application must include the header file RAPI.H. It must also link with the library RAPI.LIB.

A RAPI Sample Application

As with all other subjects in this book, an example is worth a few thousand words. The project files in \Samples\rapisamp build an application called RAPISAMP.EXE that looks very similar to the FILES.EXE application of Chapter 6. Throughout this discussion, keep in mind that this application is a Windows NT desktop application. User actions cause RAPISAMP.EXE to call RAPI functions. These RAPI function calls allow RAPISAMP.EXE to communicate with a connected Windows CE device.

Figure 15.1 shows the RAPI sample application on the desktop PC. Expanding folders in the right-hand pane causes the application to read the contents of the corresponding directory on the connected Windows CE device. Tapping once on a folder forces the application to display the names of the files in the corresponding directory in the list view control pane on the right.

Don't be alarmed if you run this application and it does not display every file in a particular directory. Since RAPI calls are made across the serial connection to the device, they can be slow. The application therefore only displays 50 files or subdirectories for any one selected folder. This keeps the application from appearing to hang, which it might seem to do if it were to read every file from a large directory, such as the device Windows directory.

Using Remote API Functions

The complete set of RAPI functions can be found in the Microsoft Developer Studio on-line documentation. Since the majority of the functions are the same as the Windows CE API equivalents, listing them all here would be redundant.

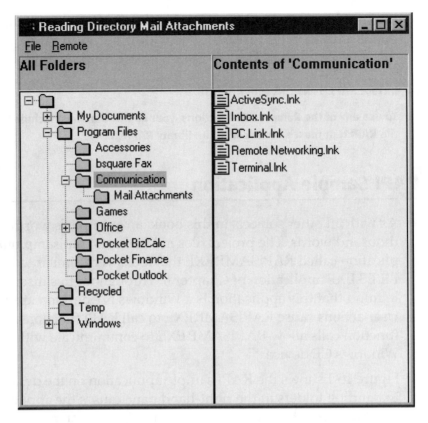

Figure 15.1 The RAPI sample application.

However, there are RAPI functions that correspond to Windows CE functions that we have not covered in this book. For example, RAPI includes a function called *CeCreateProcess* for creating processes on a connected Windows CE device. The Windows CE equivalent of this function, *CreateProcess*, has not been covered.

RAPI functions corresponding to Windows CE APIs that we have not discussed are shown in Table 15.1.

Initializing and Terminating a RAPI Session

To use any of the Remote API functions, an application must first initialize RAPI. There are two functions for doing this: *CeRapiInit* and *CeRapiIntiEx*. *CeRapiInit* looks like this:

```
HRESULT CeRapiInit();
```

This function simply initializes RAPI. For this function to succeed, a Windows CE device must be connected to the PC that is making the

Table 15.1   RAPI Functions with No Windows CE Equivalent

FUNCTION	PURPOSE
CeRapiFreeBuffer	Frees memory allocated by *CeFindAllDatabases*, *CeFindAllFiles*, or *CeReadRecordProps*.
CeRapiGetError	Reports RAPI errors.
CeRapiInit	Initializes RAPI synchronously.
CeRapiInitEx	Initializes RAPI asynchronously.
CeRapiInvoke	Calls functions in device DLLs.
CeRapiUninit	Terminates a RAPI session.
CeCheckPassword	Compares a string to the system password.
CeCreateProcess	Creates a new process on the connected device.
CeGetDesktopDeviceCaps	RAPI version of *GetDeviceCaps*.
CeGetLastError	RAPI version of *GetLastError*.
CeGetSpecialFolderPath	Gets the path to a shell folder.
CeGetSystemInfo	Gets information about the connected device.
CeGetSystemMetrics	Gets system metrics of connected device.
CeGetSystemPowerStatusEx	Gets connected device power status.
CeGetVersionEx	Gets information about the Window CE version running on the connected device.
CeGlobalMemoryStatus	Gets device memory information.
CeSHCreateShortcut	Creates a shortcut on the connected device.
CeSHGetShortcutTarget	Retrieves the path of a connected device shortcut.
CeGetClassName	Retrieves the registered class name of a window.
CeGetWindow	Retrieves a window handle.
CeGetWindowLong	RAPI version of *GetWindowLong*.
CeGetWindowText	RAPI version of *GetWindowText*.

CeRapiInit call. If the function is successful, it returns ERROR_SUCCESS. Otherwise it returns an error code.

CeRapiInit is a synchronous function call. That is, *CeRapiInit* does not return until RAPI is initialized or an error occurs. The asynchronous version of this function is *CeRapiIntiEx*.

To terminate a RAPI session, an application calls *CeRapiUninit*. This function takes no arguments and has no return value.

The sample application RAPISAMP.EXE calls *CeRapiInit* right before the message loop in *WinMain*. It terminates the RAPI session by calling *CeRapiUninit* in response to the Exit menu option.

Accessing a Remote File System

The sample application displays the directory structure of a connected Windows CE device. To do this, the application must be able to read the device file system.

Remote API file system functions are used just like the Windows CE versions. There is a *CeFindFirstFile* function, which plays the same role as *FindFirstFile*. *CeFindNextFile* is like *FindNextFile*.

These functions have arguments that are similar to the Windows CE versions as well. A major difference is that the RAPI versions use CE_FIND_DATA structures to report their results instead of WIN32_FIND_DATA structures. The only difference between these structures is that CE_FIND_DATA does not include an alternate file name member.

As an example, let's look at how the sample application reads the names of the files in a particular directory. The function *BuildFileList* takes a directory name argument, and iterates through the directory files by calling *CeFindNextFile*. The pertinent parts of this function are shown here:

```
void BuildFileList(WCHAR* pszPath)
{
  CE_FIND_DATA ced;
  HANDLE hFind;
  BOOL bContinue = TRUE;
  hFind = CeFindFirstFile(pszPath, &ced);
  if (hFind!=INVALID_HANDLE_VALUE)
  {
   while(bContinue)
    {
     //Add file name to list view control
     bContinue = CeFindNextFile(hFind, &ced);
    }
    CeFindClose(hFind);
   }
}
```

This example should illustrate how similar RAPI is to what you already know. Other than user interface code, there isn't a whole lot more than this to RAPISAMP.EXE.

Invoking Functions on a Windows CE Device

The Remote API allows desktop applications to call functions implemented by DLLs on a connected Windows CE device. This is done with the function *CeRapiInvoke*:

```
HRESULT CeRapiInvoke(pDLLPath, pFunctionName, cbInput, pInput,
    pcbOutput, ppOutput, ppIRAPIStream, dwReserved);
```

CeRapiInvoke is a remote *LoadLibrary, GetProcAddress,* and remote function call all in one. *pDLLPath* is the path to the DLL on the remote device that implements the function to be invoked. *pFunctionName* is the name of the function to invoke.

cbInput contains the number of bytes in the buffer *pInput. pInput* is a pointer to an array of bytes representing the arguments to the remote function.

Similarly, *pcbOutput* is a DWORD pointer through which RAPI returns the number of bytes in the return value array *ppOutput.*

ppIRAPIStream is a pointer to an IRAPIStream interface. This can be used to pass data to and from remote functions. Generally, this parameter will be NULL.

As an example, RAPISAMP.EXE includes the function *InvokeRemoteFunction*. This function simply calls the function *ShowDialogBox* in a DLL called DLLSAMP.DLL. This DLL function displays a message box on the remote device:

```
void InvokeRemoteFunction()
{
  DWORD dwOut;
  BYTE bOut[1];
  CeRapiInvoke(L"\\Windows\\dllsamp.dll", L"ShowDialogBox",
    0, NULL, &dwOut, (BYTE**)&bOut, NULL, 0);
}
```

DLLSAMP.DLL can be built from the project files included on the companion CD under \Samples\dllsamp. The Invoke Function option of the application's Remote menu invokes this feature.

Windows CE File Filters

With ActiveSync technology, programmers can transfer data between the Window CE device and desktop PC versions of their applications.

In the previous chapter, for example, we wrote ActiveSync service providers enabling the phone list database applications on the desktop and Windows CE device to share phone list entries.

There are often times when you want to transfer entire files between a PC and a Windows CE device. For instance, you will want to transfer applications or dynamic link libraries that you have built on the desktop to the devices on which they are meant to run. Or you may want to copy data files used by an application from one platform for use by the counterpart application on the other platform.

File filters, or *file converters*, are desktop COM components that convert files from one platform format to another. Whenever you drag a file from Windows NT Explorer to a Mobile Devices folder, Windows CE applies the filter registered for converting the file from the desktop to the device file format. Similarly, transferring files from a connected Windows CE device to a desktop computer invokes the appropriate filters for converting the device format files to the format used on the desktop PC. Figure 15.2 shows the file transfer dialog, invoked when files are copied between a desktop computer and a connected Windows CE device.

Programmers can implement two types of Windows CE file filters. An *import file filter* performs file conversion on a file copied from a desk-

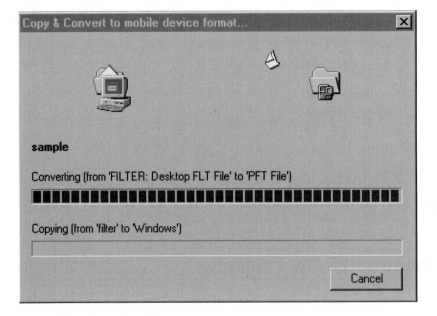

Figure 15.2 The file transfer dialog.

top computer to a Windows CE device. An *export file filter* converts a file copied from the device to the desktop computer.

One more definition is in order. A file being copied is sometimes called a *source file*. A filtered version of a source file that is created on the destination platform is called a *destination file*.

The Sample File Filters

The companion CD includes a project for building two sample Windows CE file filters. The files can be found in the directory \Samples\filter.

This project implements a COM in-process server DLL called FILTER.DLL. It implements two COM objects, CImportFilter and CExportFilter, both of which are derived from ICeFileFilter. CImportFilter transfers files with the .flt extension to an attached Windows CE device, where they are given the .pft extension. CExportFilter transfers .pft files from the device to the desktop, where they are given the .flt extension.

Although the import and export functionality could be implemented with one filter object, I chose to implement separate COM objects for each.

Both the .flt and .pft file types are simply text files. You can create any text file on the desktop, give it the .flt extension, and drag it to an attached Windows CE device to invoke CImportFilter. Similarly, you can create any text file on the device and give it the .pft extension. Copying it to the desktop by dragging it from the Mobile Device folder into Windows NT Explorer will invoke CExportFilter.

The file filters implemented by this sample are pretty boring. They simply copy a file from one platform to the other. But you can use the code as a starting point for any other file filter. All that needs to be changed is the file conversion method *NextConvertFile*.

The \Samples\filter directory also include two registry files, IMFILTER.REG, which will register the import file filter, and EXFILTER.REG, which registers the export filter.

NOTE

CHANGE THE PARTNER IDENTIFIER IN **FILTER.REG**

The FILTER.REG file registers the sample file filters quite well on my computer. You must change the partner ID in the registry keys to your own Windows CE device partnership ID.

The ICeFileFilter Interface

Just like ActiveSync service providers, Windows CE file filters are implemented as COM in-process server dynamic link libraries. Each file filter must implement the COM interface ICeFileFilter.

This interface only exposes three methods. These methods are listed in Table 15.2. Of these methods, *NextConvertFile* is by far the most important. This method is responsible for performing the actual file data conversion duties of the corresponding file filter.

The *NextConvertFile* method has this definition:

```
HRESULT NextConvertFile(nConversion, pci, psf,
    pdf,pbCancel,perr);
```

This cryptic set of parameters contains all the information a file filter needs to open the file being converted as well as to write the destination file.

NextConvertFile is called repeatedly by Windows CE Services until your filter code tells it to stop. *nConversion* is an integer that tells you how many times the method has been called. This parameter is used as a counter for converting a single file into multiple destination files.

Generally, you will write file filters that convert one source file to one destination file. Therefore, if *nConversion* is not zero, you need to tell Windows CE Services to stop calling *NextConvertFile*. You do this by returning HRESULT_FROM_WIN32(ERROR_NO_MORE_ITEMS).

pbCancel is a pointer to a BOOL indicating if the user has pressed the cancel button in the file transfer dialog. Implementations of *NextConvertFile* should periodically check this value to see if the user has aborted file conversion.

perr is a pointer to an error value that can be returned. This value is in turn passed to *FormatMessage*.

The remaining parameters contain all of the information about the source and destination file and file conversion information.

pci is a pointer to a CFF_CONVERTINFO structure. This structure supplies the filter with information about the file conversion. *psf* is a CFF_SOURCEFILE structure pointer. This structure defines the source file. Finally, the *pdf* parameter is a pointer to a CFF_

Table 15.2 ICeFileFilter Methods

METHOD	PURPOSE
NextConvertFile	Converts file data from one format to another.
FilterOptions	Displays a dialog box allowing the user to select supported file filter options.
FormatMessage	Formats a message string for user interface display. This method is analogous to the Win32 *FormatMessage* API.

DESTINATIONFILE structure, which contains information about the destination file.

These three new data types are described in the following sections.

NOTE
THE ICEFILEFILTEROPTIONS INTERFACE

For a Windows CE file filter to include user-selectable conversion options, it must implement the ICeFileFilterOptions interface as well as ICeFileFilter. We do not cover the ICeFileFilterOptions interface in this chapter.

NOTE
FILE FILTER TYPE NAMES

As you write file filters and browse through the Microsoft Developer Studio online documentation, you will see type names like PFF_CONVERTINFO and IPegasusFileFilter. These were the type names assigned back in the Windows CE 1.0 beta days, when the operating system was code-named Pegasus. As with the Windows CE database APIs, the new names like CFF_CONVERTINFO have been created as aliases for the old names with typedef statements throughout the header file CEFLTMAP.H.

The CFF_CONVERTINFO Structure

The definition of the CFF_CONVERTINFO structure is:

```
typedef struct tagCFF_CONVERTINFO
{
  BOOL bImport;
  HWND hwndParent;
  BOOL bYesToAll;
```

```
        ICeFileFilterSite *pffs;
    } CFF_CONVERTINFO;
```

The *bImport* member indicates whether the *NextConvertFile* function is being called to import or export a file. This allows a particular ICeFile-Filter implementation to act as both an import and an export file filter. By checking this member, *NextConvertFile* can decide which file conversion code to execute.

hwndParent can be used as the parent window for dialog boxes that might need to be displayed during conversion. *bYesToAll* is used by *NextConvertFile* to tell Windows CE Services whether to include a Yes To All button in the Confirm File Replace dialog. This would be done if a source file is to be converted into more than one destination file which must be overwritten. Figure 15.3 shows a Confirm File Replace dialog without this button.

Finally, the *pffs* member points to an ICeFileFilterSite interface instance. Among the methods exposed by this interface are methods for opening and closing source and destination files.

For example, the *OpenSourceFile* method opens the source file:

```
HRESULT OpenSourceFile(nHowToOpenFile, ppObj);
```

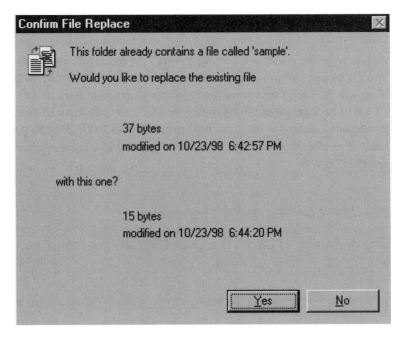

Figure 15.3 The Confirm File Replace dialog.

nHowToOpenFile is an integer describing how the file should be opened. Passing PF_OPENFLAT opens the file as a flat file and returns an IStream interface pointer to the file data through *ppObj*.

The *CloseSourceFile* method of ICeFileFilterSite closes a file opened by an *OpenSourceFile* call.

The CFF_SOURCEFILE and CFF_DESTINATIONFILE Structures

CFF_SOURCEFILE describes the source file being copied and filtered.

```
typedef struct tagCFF_SOURCEFILE
{
  TCHAR szFullpath[_MAX_PATH];
  TCHAR szPath[_MAX_PATH];
  TCHAR szFilename[_MAX_FNAME];
  TCHAR szExtension[_MAX_EXT];
  DWORD cbSize;
  FILETIME ftCreated;
  FILETIME ftModified;
} CFF_SOURCEFILE;
```

These members are all pretty self-explanatory. *szFullPath* is the fully qualified path name of the file, including the file name. *szPath* is the directory name part of *szFullPath*. *cbSize* is the size of the source file in bytes. *ftCreated* and *ftModified* are the creation and last-modified times of the file, respectively.

The CFF_DESTINATIONFILE structure is very similar. It contains the first four members of the CFF_SOURCEFILE structure.

```
typedef struct tagCFF_DESTINATIONFILE
{
  TCHAR szFullpath[_MAX_PATH];
  TCHAR szPath[_MAX_PATH];
  TCHAR szFilename[_MAX_FNAME];
  TCHAR szExtension[_MAX_EXT];
} CFF_DESTINATIONFILE
```

An Example

To make this all more clear, let's look at an example. The *NextConvertFile* implementation from the sample filter FILTER.DLL looks like this:

```
STDMETHODIMP CImportFilter::NextConvertFile(
  int nConversion,
  CFF_CONVERTINFO* pci,
  CFF_SOURCEFILE* psf,
  CFF_DESTINATIONFILE* pdf,
  volatile BOOL *pbCancel,
  CF_ERROR *perr)
{
  ICeFileFilterSite* pffs; //Pointer to input file filter
                //site interface
  IStream *pSrcFile, *pDstFile;
  PF_ERROR pfError;
  HRESULT hResult, hResClose;
  if (nConversion)
  {
   return (HRESULT_FROM_WIN32(ERROR_NO_MORE_ITEMS));
  }
  pffs = pci->pffs;
  //Open the source file for reading
  hResult = pffs->OpenSourceFile(PF_OPENFLAT,
   (LPVOID*)&pSrcFile);
  if (!SUCCEEDED(hResult))
  {
   pfError = HRESULT_TO_PFERROR(hResult,
     ERROR_ACCESS_DENIED);
  }
  else //Open the desination file for writing
  {
   hResult = pffs->OpenDestinationFile(
     PF_OPENFLAT,
     NULL,
     (LPVOID*)&pDstFile);
   if (!SUCCEEDED(hResult))
   {
    pfError = HRESULT_TO_PFERROR(hResult,
      ERROR_ACCESS_DENIED);
   }
   else
   {
    hResult = _NextConvertFile(pSrcFile, pDstFile, pffs,
      psf, pbCancel, perr);
    hResClose =
      pffs->CloseDestinationFile(SUCCEEDED(hResult),
       pDstFile);
    if (SUCCEEDED(hResult))
    {
     pfError = HRESULT_TO_PFERROR(hResult,
       ERROR_ACCESS_DENIED);
     hResult = hResClose;
    }
```

```
    }
    }    //End of else open destination file block
    pffs->CloseSourceFile(pSrcFile);
    *perr = pfError;
    return (hResult);
}
```

The first thing this function does is check the value of the *nConversion* parameter. If this value is not zero, it returns the HRESULT value, which tells Windows CE Services to stop calling the function.

Next, the source and destination files are opened. If either file open operation fails, an appropriate error code is returned. Otherwise the *_NextConvertFile* method is called. This method simply reads the source file data and writes it to the destination file. It is a pretty straightforward function that uses the Win32 file system API. Since we are mainly concentrating on the high-level design of Windows CE file filters, we do not discuss *_NextConvertFile* here.

Finally, files are closed with the *CloseDestinationFile* and *CloseSourceFile* calls.

Registering File Filters

Like ActiveSync service providers, Window CE file filters must be properly registered before they can be used. Since file filters are only implemented on the desktop, they require no device registry entries.

Like any COM object, file filters are registered under their class identifier. The following registry entries must be made under the filter's CLSID:

```
[HKEY_CLASSES_ROOT\CLSID\{11732CC1-65D8-11d2-9BF2-000000000000}]
@="Windows CE Import File Filter Sample"
[HKEY_CLASSES_ROOT\CLSID\{11732CC1-65D8-11d2-9BF2-000000000000}\InProc-
Server32]
@="e:\\Samples\\filter\\Release\\filter.dll"
"ThreadingModel"="Apartment"
[HKEY_CLASSES_ROOT\CLSID\{11732CC1-65D8-11d2-9BF2-000000000000}\Pegasus-
Filter]
"Import"=""
"Description"="FILTER File"
"NewExtension"="pft"
```

```
[HKEY_CLASSES_ROOT\CLSID\{11732CC1-65D8-11d2-9BF2-000000000000}\Default-
Icon]
@="e:\\Samples\\filter\\release\\filter.dll,-101"
```

These are the usual registry key settings for a COM object, except for the PegasusFilter and DefaultIcon keys.

PegasusFilter contains three named values. Import tells Windows CE Services that the filter is for importing files from a desktop computer to a Windows CE device. If instead the named value Export was used, the filter is an export file filter. Description contains a file type description string. NewExtension specifies the file extension to be assigned to a file after it is transferred with this filter.

The DefaultIcon subkey specifies the icon to use with the file filter. This icon appears, for example, in the File Conversion dialog box property sheets describing the filter.

A file filter must also be registered under the appropriate Windows CE Services subkeys. For example, the import filter for converting .flt files to .pft files includes these registry settings:

```
[HKEY_CURRENT_USER\SOFTWARE\Microsoft\Windows CE
Services\Partners\<Partner ID>\Filters\.flt\InstalledFilters]
"{11732CC1-65D8-11d2-9BF2-000000000000}"=""
[HKEY_CURRENT_USER\SOFTWARE\Microsoft\Windows CE
Services\Partners\<Partner ID>\Filters\.flt]
"DefaultImport"="{11732CC1-65D8-11d2-9BF2-000000000000}"
```

The InstalledFilters subkey lists the class identifiers of all filters that can convert the corresponding file type. The DefaultImport value under the .flt subkey identifies which filter is to be used by default.

Finally, to complete the registration of our .flt file filter, these registry entries are required:

```
[HKEY_CLASSES_ROOT\.flt]
@="fltfile"
[HKEY_CLASSES_ROOT\fltfile]
@="FILTER: Desktop FLT File"
[HKEY_CLASSES_ROOT\fltfile\DefaultIcon]
@="e:\\Samples\\filter\\release\\filter.dll,-101"
```

These values specify the file type description and the icon used in the Windows NT Explorer for files of type .flt. The HKEY_CLASSES_ ROOT\.flt key simply identifies which subkey the description and icon values are found under.

The files IMFILTER.REG and EXFILTER.REG on the companion CD can be used to make all of the registry entries necessary to use the file filters built by the sample project. Just be sure to replace the partnership identifier in those files with your own. You should also replace the CLSIDs in these files with your own unique identifiers generated with GUIDGEN.EXE.

Concluding Remarks

The previous two chapters have provided you with an overview of how to program some of the most important Windows CE desktop connectivity features. The ActiveSync technology can be used for synchronizing application-specific data between a desktop PC and a Windows CE device. The sample code provided in Chapter 14 should give you a good head start on implementing your own ActiveSync service providers.

We also covered the Remote API and Windows CE file filters. RAPI allows you to access data and functionality of your Windows CE devices from desktop applications. File filters can be used to convert files from one format to another when transferring them between Windows CE devices and a PC.

Of course the discussion of these subjects in this book is only an introduction. As you experiment with the sample code, you will gain more and more insight into the subtleties of these Windows CE connectivity technologies.

CHAPTER 16

Memory and Power Management

As we have seen throughout this book, Windows CE provides many powerful features that allow product designers and application developers to create highly complex devices based on this operating system. However, the Windows CE operating system was designed primarily for small platforms, to encourage its use in the mobile computing arena.

Windows CE is particularly suited to the needs of small desktop PC companion products such as the Handheld PC and the Palm-size PC. The design emphasis on most *successful* handheld computing products on the market today has been small and convenient size and low price. Also, even though many Windows CE devices can be powered with an AC adapter, a key feature of successful products is long battery life.

Maintaining low competitive prices for mobile computing devices means reducing the cost of the hardware used in a given product. This generally means that mobile devices have much less memory than a desktop computer. Smaller and cheaper batteries are also commonly used to reduce the overall bill of materials.

Reduced memory budgets translate into devices that are very often run in low memory conditions. Relying on battery power means that devices must be designed with power efficiency in mind. In this chapter we discuss the memory and power management features of Windows CE. The memory and power APIs are explored, as well as ways in which applications can be written to handle low memory states.

AFTER COMPLETING THIS CHAPTER YOU WILL KNOW HOW TO . . .

Use the Windows CE memory management APIs to use available memory efficiently

Use Windows CE memory mapped files

Programmatically get power status diagnostics about a Windows CE device

Write applications capable of handling low memory conditions

The Sample Application

A simple application demonstrating the concepts covered in this chapter is included on the companion CD. The directory \Samples\memory contains the project files necessary to build MEMORY.EXE. The screen shots in this chapter all show various features implemented by this application.

Windows CE Memory Basics

Memory on Windows CE devices is divided into read-only memory (ROM) and random access memory (RAM).

Windows CE device RAM is divided into two sections. The first is *program memory*. Applications that you write and download to a Windows CE device get stored in program memory. Program memory also provides the memory for application heaps and stacks. For example, whenever you allocate memory using the function *LocalAlloc*, the memory allocated comes from the device program memory.

The second section of RAM is devoted to the *object store*. This is the memory that is used for the Windows CE file system, the registry, and Windows CE databases. These subjects are covered in detail in Part II of this book, "Windows CE Persistent Storage." We therefore will not discuss the object store further in this chapter.

The amount of RAM devoted to each of these memory sections can be changed by the user. The Memory tab in the System Control Panel provides an interface for adjusting the memory boundary between program memory and object store memory.

ROM typically stores the entire operating system as well as any applications that are included with the device. For example, when you buy a Handheld PC, Microsoft Pocket Word is included as part of the software that comes pre-installed on the device. This application, and all other software that comes pre-installed on the product, is in ROM.

Applications stored in ROM are run in-place by Windows CE. This means that the application code is run directly from ROM and does not need to be paged into program memory. ROM-based applications therefore run much faster than applications in program memory.

The Windows CE Address Space

As a 32-bit operating system, Windows CE defines a 4 GB address space. Two gigabytes of this space are reserved by Windows CE for hardware access. The other 2 GB block is the virtual memory space shared by all applications.

Windows CE divides 1.056 GB of this virtual address space into 33 process slots. Each of these slots occupies 32 MB of the 2 GB application virtual address space. Except for a small amount reserved by Windows CE, the rest of the virtual address space is used for memory mapped files.

The Windows CE API provides a number of functions for determining the global state of a Windows CE device. These functions can be used to determine the current physical and virtual memory usage, as well as current object store memory status.

The GlobalMemoryStatus *Function*

The Windows CE API provides a number of functions for determining the global state of a Windows CE device. These functions can be used to determine the current physical and virtual memory usage, as well as current object store memory status.

The function *GlobalMemoryStatus* gives information about physical and virtual memory:

```
GlobalMemoryStatus(lpmst);
```

The parameter *lpmst* is a pointer to a MEMORYSTATUS structure. *GlobalMemoryStatus* fills this structure with information about the current device memory status. The structure is defined as:

```
typedef struct _MEMORYSTATUS {
    DWORD dwLength;
    DWORD dwMemoryLoad;
    DWORD dwTotalPhys;
    DWORD dwAvailPhys;
    DWORD dwTotalPageFile;
    DWORD dwAvailPageFile;
    DWORD dwTotalVirtual;
    DWORD dwAvailVirtual;
} MEMORYSTATUS, *LPMEMORYSTATUS;
```

The caller of *GlobalMemoryStatus* must set the *dwLength* member to the size, in bytes, of the structure.

When the function returns, *dwLoad* contains the percentage of total memory in use. *dwTotalPhys* and *dwAvailPhys* give the total amount of physical memory on the device and the amount of that memory not in use, respectively. *dwTotalVirtual* and *dwAvailVirtual* give similar diagnostics for the virtual memory status.

The *dwTotalPageFile* and *dwAvailPageFile* members will always be zero. This is because Windows CE does not use a page file.

NOTE

▬▬▬ No Page File Support under Windows CE

Unlike Windows NT, Windows CE does not use a page file to manage virtual memory.

The GetStoreInformation *Function*

The function *GetStoreInformation* returns the current state of object store memory:

```
GetStoreInformation(lpsi);
```

lpsi is a pointer to a STATUS_INFORMATION structure. This structure contains two DWORD members. The first is *dwStoreSize*, which *GetStoreInformation* uses to return the total size of the object store. The second, *dwFreeSize*, returns the amount of the total not currently in use.

The application MEMORY.EXE includes options under the Memory menu for displaying the memory status using *GlobalMemoryStatus* and *GetStoreInformation*. For example, the Physical Memory Status option displays the total and available physical device memory (Figure 16.1). Object Store Status displays the status of the object store memory (Figure 16.2).

The GetSystemInfo *Function*

A final system status function, *GetSystemInfo*, is useful for obtaining global memory information about a connected Windows CE device. Of particular interest to us here is that this function returns the virtual memory page size, as well as the highest and lowest memory addresses accessible to applications and dynamic link libraries.

The function syntax is:

```
GetSystemInfo(lpSystemInfo);
```

lpSystemInfo is a pointer to a SYSTEM_INFO structure. For example, an application might use this function as follows to display system diagnostics to the user:

```
SYSTEM_INFO si;
TCHAR pszText[257];
memset(&si, 0, sizeof(si));
GetSystemInfo(&si);
wsprintf(pszText, TEXT("Page Size: %d\nMax Address: %ld\nMin
  Address: %ld"), si.dwPageSize,
    si.lpMinimumApplicationAddress,
      si. lpMaximumApplicationAddress);
MessageBox(NULL, pszText, TEXT("System Info"), MB_OK);
```

Figure 16.1 Physical Memory Status display.

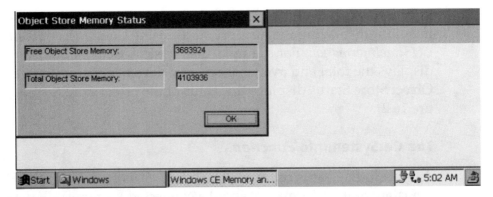

Figure 16.2   Object Store Memory Status display.

Windows CE Application Address Space

In the previous section we saw that the Windows CE address space breaks about half of shared virtual application address space into 33 process slots of 32 MB each. Each application running on a Windows CE device occupies one of these slots.

Slot 0 is reserved for the currently active process. As users switch between applications, the current application is swapped into slot 0. There can therefore be a maximum of 32 applications running at any one time.

The practical implication of this architectural detail is that each running Windows CE application can only access the virtual memory within its 32 MB slot. This limitation can be overcome through the use of memory mapped files, which are discussed later.

Allocating Memory

An application can allocate virtual memory (as long as there is virtual memory available within its 32 MB slot boundary). It can allocate memory from its default heap, or create new heaps. Finally, applications can use stack memory.

Each Windows CE thread has its own stack. Whenever a thread declares a variable, the memory to store the contents of that variable comes from the thread's stack. Parameters passed to a function call are also placed on the stack.

Can You Say "Code Bloat"?

Not too long ago, a total of 32 MB of RAM on a desktop PC was more than enough for even a serious Windows NT workstation. Software development tools, word processors, e-mail packages, and a Web browser could all run at the same time on such a machine with no serious limitations.

It is now common for even a low-priced PC to come equipped with 64 MB or more of RAM. One implication of this, other than greater application execution speed, is that applications can get larger, more complex, and handle ever larger amounts of data.

A similar trend is emerging in the world of Windows CE devices. Originally, Windows CE devices were designed as simple desktop companions for carrying phone numbers, addresses, and the like with you when away from your computer. Today, Windows CE devices are growing more complex and beginning to more closely resemble the desktop computers that Windows CE hoped to get away from.

The new Jupiter platform, for example, is used to produce Windows CE devices that are like pared-down laptop computers, with greater memory budgets and screen real estate than previous generation devices such as the handheld PC.

As this trend continues, I would expect the design of Windows CE to change such that the 32 MB application virtual memory limit is removed. As applications grow more complex, programmers will expect to have full access to the 2 GB virtual address space they are used to working with under Windows NT. And consumers will start asking themselves why they don't just buy that laptop instead.

The next sections cover Windows CE virtual memory and heaps in more detail.

Virtual Memory

Windows CE uses a paged virtual memory model. Page sizes vary depending on the processor used by the particular Windows CE device. The size of a page can be determined by calling the *GetSystemInfo* API discussed earlier.

As is the case under Windows NT, virtual memory pages under Windows CE can be committed, reserved, or free. *Committed* means that physical memory has been allocated for the memory in question.

Reserved means that the range of memory addresses corresponding to the virtual memory in question has been set aside for an application; however, no physical memory has yet been allocated. Finally, pages that are *free* are not committed or reserved, and therefore any application can allocate them.

A page of virtual memory can be allocated by an application by calling the *VirtualAlloc* function:

```
VirtualAlloc(lpAddress, dwSize, flAllocationType, flProtect);
```

If successful, *VirtualAlloc* returns the base address of the allocated region of virtual memory pages. Otherwise it returns NULL.

lpAddress specifies the starting address of the region of memory to allocate. This parameter can be NULL, in which case Windows CE determines where to start.

dwSize indicates the number of bytes of virtual memory to be allocated. Like Windows NT, Windows CE will round this value up to the nearest page boundary. Therefore, if the size you specify is even one byte over a page limit, the entire next virtual memory page will be allocated for your application.

flAllocationType specifies the memory allocation type. This can be any combination of the values shown in Table 16.1. Note that Windows CE includes a new allocation type, MEM_AUTO_COMMIT.

When a virtual memory page is allocated with the MEM_AUTO_COMMIT flag, the page is reserved as would be done by specifying MEM_RESERVE. However, the memory is automatically committed by Windows CE the first time the page is accessed.

Table 16.1 Virtual Memory Allocation Type Flags

FLAG	MEANING
MEM_COMMIT	Allocates physical memory for the region of pages being allocated.
MEM_RESERVE	Reserves virtual memory, but does not allocate physical memory.
MEM_TOP_DOWN	Allocates memory at the highest possible address.
MEM_AUTO_COMMIT	Reserves virtual memory, which is then automatically committed by Windows CE when accessed.

flProtect specifies the type of access protection to be granted to the allocated virtual memory. The values PAGE_READONLY, granting read-
only access, and PAGE_READWRITE, granting read-write access, are
most common.

Freeing virtual memory is done by calling the Windows CE API *VirtualFree*:

```
VirtualFree(lpAddress, dwSize, dwFreeType);
```

lpAddress specifies the base address of virtual memory space to be
freed. This value would be the return value of a previous *VirtualAlloc*
call. *dwSize* is the size of the region to be freed.

dwFreeType tells the function what to do. A value of MEM_
DECOMMIT decommits the committed virtual memory pages.
MEM_RELEASE tells *VirtualFree* to release previously reserved
memory.

If *VirtualFree* succeeds, it returns TRUE. Otherwise, it returns FALSE.

NOTE

INTER-PROCESS VIRTUAL MEMORY ACCESS

**Windows CE does not allow applications to access virtual memory in the address
space of other processes. Therefore, the virtual memory APIs *VirtualAllocEx*, *Virtual-
FreeEx*, *VirtualProtextEx*, and *VirtualQueryEx* are not supported under Windows CE.**

Using Heaps

In some sense, allocating virtual memory pages is the most basic form
of Windows CE memory allocation. As we have seen, *VirtualAlloc*
never allocates a block of virtual memory smaller than the page size
defined for the particular processor powering the device.

There are obviously times when an application needs to dynamically
allocate much less memory than this. For example, an application
might need to allocate memory to hold the contents of a file to be read
from the Windows CE file system. After determining the size of the
file, the application would allocate that number of bytes and read the
file. The memory would be freed when the application is done using
the file.

Applications typically use heaps for such dynamic memory allocation
needs. Every Windows CE application has a default heap, created by

the operating system when the application is launched. Applications can also create additional heaps that are separate from the default heap as needed.

An application's default heap contains 384 memory pages reserved by Windows CE. These memory pages are committed by Windows CE only as needed, that is, as memory is allocated on the default heap.

Allocating Memory on the Default Heap

An application allocates memory on its default heap by calling the function *LocalAlloc*. Memory is freed from the default heap with *Local-Free*.

LocalAlloc is defined as follows:

```
LocalAlloc(uFlags, uBytes);
```

uBytes indicates the number of bytes to be allocated on the default heap. *uFlags* contains one or more flags indicating how the memory is to be allocated. The allowable flag values are specified in Table 16.2.

LocalAlloc returns a handle to the allocated memory if the function is successful. Otherwise it returns NULL.

Applications typically specify the LPTR flag to allocate fixed heap memory, which is initialized to zero. The value returned by *LocalAlloc* in this case is a pointer to the allocated memory block. An application can therefore simply cast the return value to the proper pointer type and reference the allocated memory through that pointer.

For example, let's say that we want to allocate enough default heap space to hold a 256-character Unicode string, including NULL terminator. The string is then filled with the contents of an edit control specified by *hwndEdit*. Our application would include the following code:

Table 16.2 LocalAlloc Memory Allocation Flags

FLAG	MEANING
LMEM_FIXED	Allocates fixed memory.
LMEM_ZEROINIT	Initializes each byte of the allocated memory block to zero.
LPTR	Combines the LMEM_FIXED and LMEM_ZEROINIT flags, i.e., equals LMEM_FIXED | LMEM_ZEROINIT.

```
TCHAR* pszString; //Pointer to the string memory
int nCount = 257; //String length, plus NULL terminator
pszString = (TCHAR*)LocalAlloc(LPTR, nCount*sizeof(TCHAR));
if (pszString)
{
  GetWindowText(hwndEdit, pszString, nCount);
}
```

NOTE
WINDOWS CE ONLY SUPPORTS FIXED MEMORY HEAPS

Unlike Windows NT, Windows CE only allows fixed heap memory allocation. The LMEM_MOVEABLE flag is therefore not supported by the *LocalAlloc* function.

To prevent memory leaks from accumulating in your applications, dynamically allocated memory must be freed when it is no longer needed. Default heap memory is freed with the *LocalFree* API:

```
LocalFree(hMem);
```

hMem is the pointer to the block of heap memory to be freed. If successful, LocalFree returns NULL. Otherwise it returns back the *hMem* pointer.

Creating and Using Additional Application Heaps

Applications can create their own heaps in addition to the default heap created by Windows CE. Using such heaps may be advantageous in situations where an application needs to temporarily allocate lots of small pieces of memory.

The classic example is a word processing application. A heap can be created to store the contents of each open document. As the documents are closed, the corresponding heaps are freed.

Using such custom heaps is similar to working with the application's default heap. The primary difference is that the application must create and destroy such heaps.

An application creates a new heap by calling *HeapCreate*:

```
HeapCreate(flOptions, dwInitialSize, dwMaximumSize);
```

The only *flOptions* flag allowed is HEAP_NO_SERIALIZE. If specified, only the calling thread can allocate and free memory on the heap.

flOptions can also be zero, in which case multiple threads can access the heap.

dwInitialSize specifies the amount of memory initially allocated for the heap. *dwMaximumSize* specifies the maximum size of the heap.

If *dwMaximumSize* is zero, the heap can grow, and Windows CE grows the heap if more than *dwInitialSize* bytes are allocated. If *dwMaximumSize* is not zero, the heap cannot grow larger than this size.

If successful, *HeapCreate* returns a handle to the newly created heap. Otherwise it returns NULL.

NOTE
HEAPCREATE OPTIONS

The heap APIs under Windows CE do not support the HEAP_GENERATE_EXCEPTIONS flag.

A heap is destroyed by calling *HeapDestroy*. This is done when the heap is no longer needed. All heap memory is decommitted and released by this function.

```
HeapDestroy(hHeap);
```

The *hHeap* parameter is the handle to the heap to be destroyed.

Allocating and freeing memory on an application heap are done with the *HeapAlloc* and *HeapFree* functions, respectively.

HeapAlloc works very much like *LocalAlloc*:

```
HeapAlloc(hHeap, dwFlags, dwBytes);
```

Whereas *LocalAlloc* always operates on the application's default heap, *HeapAlloc* can be used to allocate memory on any heap an application creates with *HeapCreate*. You specify which heap to allocate memory in by passing the handle to the heap in the *hHeap* parameter. *dwFlags* specifies how the heap is created. *dwSize* is the number of bytes to allocate.

dwFlags can be any combination of the values HEAP_NO_SERIALIZE and HEAP_ZERO_MEMORY. HEAP_NO_SERIALIZE has the same meaning as it does when used with the *HeapCreate* function. HEAP_ZERO_MEMORY tells *HeapAlloc* to initialize all allocated memory to zero.

Freeing a heap is done with *HeapFree*:

```
HeapFree(hHeap, dwFlags, lpMem);
```

hHeap is the heap containing the memory to be freed. *lpMem* points to the block of memory to be freed. *dwFlags* can be 0, or HEAP_NO_SERIALIZE. Generally this parameter will be zero.

Windows CE Memory Mapped Files

Earlier in the chapter I said that only about half of the 2 GB virtual address space shared by applications is dedicated to the process slots in which running processes reside. What about the rest of this space?

The rest of the 2 GB application address space is used for *memory mapped files*. A memory mapped file is a block of physical memory that can be shared by different applications. This memory is called a *file* because memory mapped files are often used to access the contents of files in the Windows CE file system.

Memory mapped files do not have to correspond to a file system file. Memory mapped files can be created to hold data that is shared between processes. As we will see, this provides a powerful technique for inter-process communication in Windows CE.

Memory Mapped File Fundamentals

To use a memory mapped file, an application must create a *file mapping object*. A file mapping object associates, or maps, the contents of a file to a region of an application's virtual address space.

The file mapping object is a kernel object that Windows CE uses to maintain the file mapping. This object does not provide any access to the mapped file data. To access the physical memory containing the file contents, an application must create a *view* of the memory mapped file.

The file view is that portion of the application's virtual address space which the application references to get to the contents of the file. The actual file data is somewhere in physical memory.

The memory mapped file memory is accessed by referencing this file view object. Applications treat file views as they would data pointers.

Any change to the data pointed to by the file view is reflected in the memory mapped file. If the memory mapped file is backed by a real file, writing data to the view has the effect of writing to the actual file. Likewise, reading data from the address specified by the view reads data from the file system file.

If the memory mapped file is not backed by a file, reading or writing data through the view reads or writes data to the physical memory corresponding to the file mapping.

Memory mapped files are often used instead of the file system API for file access. This is much faster because, as the name suggests, the memory mapped file resides in memory. Windows CE takes care of writing the data to the actual file efficiently.

Memory mapped files can be *named* or *unnamed*. Since the Windows CE kernel maintains file mapping objects, naming a file mapping makes it unique throughout the system. In short, this means that different processes that create views into the same file mapping have access to the same physical memory. This is why memory mapped files can be used for communicating between Windows CE processes.

Finally, memory mapped files do not have to be backed up by a real file in the file system. Applications can create memory mapped files simply to access regions of physical memory.

Creating a File Mapping

A file mapping is created with the Windows CE API *CreateFileMapping*:

```
CreateFileMapping(hFile, lpFileMappingAttributes, flProtect,
    dwMaximumSizeHigh, dwMaximumSizeLow, lpName);
```

The *lpFileMappingAttributes* parameter is not used under Windows CE and must therefore be NULL.

hFile is a file handle. If the file mapping object is being created to access a physical file, this parameter will be the file handle returned by a *CreateFileForMapping* call. To create a file mapping not backed by a file, pass –1 to the *hFile* parameter.

CreateFileForMapping has exactly the same signature as the file system API *CreateFile*. It returns a handle to a file just as *CreateFile* does, except that this handle can be used to create a file mapping. See Chapter 6 for details on using the *CreateFile* function.

If the mapping is not backed by a file, you must specify the size of the memory mapped region via the *dwMaximumSizeLow* and *dwMaximumSizeHigh* parameters. The first specifies the low-order 32 bits of the region size, while the second specifies the upper 32 bits.

lpName can be used to pass a string used to name the file mapping. This is particularly important for inter-process communication. For two applications to gain access to the same physical memory using memory mapped files, they must both create views into the same file mapping. Naming a mapping provides a way to uniquely identify it throughout the Windows CE system.

Finally, *flProtect* is used to specify the type of access that is granted to the memory mapped by the file mapping object. PAGE_READONLY gives read-only access, PAGE_WRITECOPY gives write access, and PAGE_READWRITE grants read and write access.

If successful, *CreateFileMapping* returns a handle to the file mapping object. If the function fails, it will return NULL.

If *CreateFileMapping* is called and the mapping object already exists, it will return a handle to the existing object. Calling *GetLastError* in this case will return the error code:

```
ERROR_ALREADY_EXISTS
```

Creating a File View

Accessing the physical memory that corresponds to a file mapping object requires a view into the memory mapped file. The function *MapViewOfFile* is used for this purpose:

```
MapViewOfFile(hFileMappingObject, dwDesiredAccess,
    dwFileOffsetHigh, dwFileOfsetLow,
      dwNumberOfBytesToMap);
```

hFileMappingObject is the mapping object handle returned previously by *CreateFileMapping*. *dwDesiredAccess* specifies the access the view will have of the memory mapped by the file mapping. Allowed values are listed in Table 16.3.

dwFileOffsetLow and *dwFileOffsetHigh* are used to specify the file offset where the view starts. These parameters are useful when an applica-

Table 16.3 MapViewOfFile Access Flags

FLAG	MEANING
FILE_MAP_WRITE	The view has read-write access to the mapped file.
FILE_MAP_READ	The view has read-only access to the mapped file.
FILE_MAP_ALL_ACCESS	Same meaning as FILE_MAP_WRITE.

tion only needs to view a section of a memory mapped file. These parameters specify the low- and high-order 32 bits of the offset address, respectively.

dwNumberOfBytesToMap specifies the number of bytes of the file to map. This parameter can be zero, in which case the entire file is mapped.

MapViewOfFile returns a handle to the view of the memory mapped file. Physical memory corresponding to the file is accessed via this handle.

An Inter-process Communication Example

Let's put all of these concepts to work in an example. We will look at a simple example of using named memory mapped file for sharing data between two different applications.

The companion CD directory that contains the MEMORY.EXE project also contains a subdirectory called Helper. This directory contains the project files for building an application, called HELPER.EXE, with which MEMORY.EXE shares data.

HELPER.EXE is pretty boring. It consists of nothing but a main window with a title bar. Once the application is started, it cannot be closed except from MEMORY.EXE (or the task manager). HELPER.EXE's only role in life is helping MEMORY.EXE demonstrate memory mapped files.

MEMORY.EXE includes a feature for entering a simple text note. This note can be read by HELPER.EXE through the use of a named memory mapped file.

Launch MEMORY.EXE and select the Enter a Note option from the Notes menu. An edit box appears for entering note text (Figure 16.3).

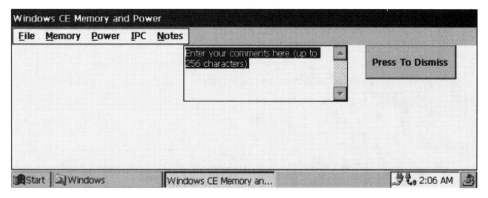

Figure 16.3 Entering a note in MEMORY.EXE.

The text you enter is limited to 256 characters. Once you have entered your note, press the Press To Dismiss button.

Next, choose the Create Helper Process option from the IPC menu (Figure 16.4). This automatically launches the HELPER.EXE application. Windows CE will switch the active process to HELPER.EXE. Go back to MEMORY.EXE by pressing its button on the taskbar.

Finally, to copy your note text to HELPER.EXE, select the Copy Note option from the Notes menu. If you then switch back to HELPER.EXE, you will see that the main window now contains your note text (Figure 16.5).

To terminate HELPER.EXE, choose the Terminate Helper Process option from the IPC menu.

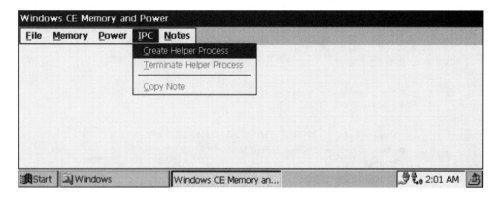

Figure 16.4 Launching the Helper Process.

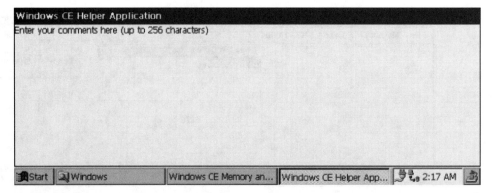

Figure 16.5 Note text successfully copied to the Helper Process.

How It Works

This simple example of Windows CE inter-process communication is accomplished using a named memory mapped file. Both applications include the following definition, which is used to name a file mapping:

```
#define MAPPED_NOTE_FILE_NAME TEXT("Note")
```

After launching MEMORY.EXE, note text is copied to the helper process by selecting the Copy Note menu option. This causes the application-specific function *OnCopyNote* to be called:

```
#define NOTE_LENGTH 257
TCHAR* pszNoteText;
HANDLE hNoteFile;
void OnCopyNote()
{
  int nSize = NOTE_LENGTH*sizeof(TCHAR);
  hNoteFile = CreateFileMapping(
   (HANDLE)-1,
   NULL,
   PAGE_READWRITE,
   0,
   nSize,
   MAPPED_NOTE_FILE_NAME);
  if (hNoteFile)
  {
   pszNoteText = (TCHAR*)LocalAlloc(LPTR, nSize);
   pszNoteText = (TCHAR*)MapViewOfFile(
    hNoteFile,
    FILE_MAP_WRITE,
    0, 0, 0);
   //Copy note text into the memory mapped file
```

```
    lstrcpy(pszNoteText, pszString);
    SendMessage(HWND_BROADCAST, nCopyMsgID, 0, 0);
  }
}
```

This looks like a lot of code, but it's actually pretty straightforward. *CreateFileMapping* creates a named file mapping object. The mapping has the name Note. Note that –1 is passed to the *hFile* parameter, indicating that the file mapping is not backed by a file system file. The mapping has read-write access, and its size is large enough to hold a 256-character note, including NULL terminator.

Next we allocate enough heap space for the string *pszNoteText* to hold 257 Unicode characters. The next step is the critical one. *MapViewOfFile* is called, and the return view handle is cast to a TCHAR pointer and assigned to *pszNoteText*. In other words, the TCHAR array defined by *pszNoteText* is the view into the file mapping created by the *CreateFileMapping* call.

Therefore, any string operation performed on *pszNoteText* is reflected in the memory owned by the file mapping *hNoteFile*. This is how the next line of code copies the text contained in *pszString* not just to *pszNoteText*, but to the named file mapping *hNoteFile,* which can be accessed by any other Windows CE process. (*pszString* contains the note text entered in the edit control shown in Figure 16.3.)

MEMORY.EXE notifies the helper process that the note has been copied by broadcasting the registered window message identified by *nCopyMsgID*.[1]

Over in HELPER.EXE, the main window procedure handles the message *nCopyMsgID* by calling *CopyNoteFromOtherProcess*:

```
void CopyNoteFromOtherProcess()
{
  int nSize = NOTE_LENGTH*sizeof(TCHAR);
  hNoteFile = CreateFileMapping(
   (HANDLE)-1,
   NULL,
   PAGE_READWRITE,
   0,
```

[1] The HWND_BROADCAST argument to *SendMessage* or *PostMessage* sends or posts the specified message to all top-level windows in the system. Notifying the helper process in this way is not ideal, as it assumes that HELPER.EXE is the only application that responds to the message being sent. But as our goal is to demonstrate the use of memory mapped files, HWND_BROADCAST is fine for our current purpose.

Registered Window Messages

The inter-process communication example in this chapter uses a special window message to notify the helper process that text has been copied into a named memory mapped file. The message used is called a *registered window message*.

Every window message is defined by a unique integer identifier. Browsing through the header file WINUSER.H, one finds definitions like this:

```
#define WM_PAINT          0x000F
```

Since every Windows CE application includes WINUSER.H (by including WIN-DOWS.H), WM_PAINT messages in any application are identified by the same unique integer.

But what if you want to define a custom window message without requiring every application that might use it to reserve the same integer identifier? The function *RegisterWindowMessage* provides a mechanism for defining messages with a unique string name:

```
RegisterWindowMessage(lpString);
```

Any time this function is called with the same string during the same Windows CE session, it returns the same unique integer identifier. *RegisterWindowMessage* returns an integer in the range 0xC000 and 0xFFFF. This range of message identifiers is reserved by Windows CE specifically for registered window messages.

Therefore, any application that calls *RegisterWindowMessage* with a specific string message name will get the exact same integer identifier as any other application calling the function with the same message name. Thus, applications can define custom messages by defining some descriptive string name. Other applications needing to respond to this message only need to know the string name. The unique integer identifier will be faithfully returned by *RegisterWindowMessage*.

Note that the value returned by *RegisterWindowMessage* cannot be used in the switch statement of a window procedure. Case values in switch statements must be compile-time constants. Your window procedures must test for registered window message identifiers with if statements, and let the switch statement handle only the standard Windows CE messages.

Message name strings can be stored in the Windows CE registry. This way applications needing to send or respond to such a message only need to know the name of the registry subkey and value under which the message name is stored. Requiring applications to know registry subkey and value names is much more standard than forcing them to reserve the same message identifiers.

```
    nSize,
    MAPPED_NOTE_FILE_NAME);
    if (hNoteFile)
    {
    pszNoteText = (TCHAR*)LocalAlloc(LPTR, nSize);
    pszNoteText = (TCHAR*)MapViewOfFile(
      hNoteFile,
      FILE_MAP_READ,
      0,0,0);
    }
  }
```

This function is almost exactly the same as *OnCopyNote* of MEMORY
.EXE. It creates a file mapping with the name Note, so that it can access the same memory as was written by MEMORY.EXE. A read-only access view of this file is created, and the contents of the named file mapping are assigned to the string *pszNoteText*.

When this function returns, the HELPER.EXE main window procedure invalidates the client area. The WM_PAINT handler draws the note text:

```
LRESULT CALLBACK WndProc(
  HWND hwnd,
  UINT message,
  WPARAM wParam,
  LPARAM lParam)
{
  RECT rc;
  HDC hdc;
  //Handle the nCopyMsgID message
  //...
  switch(message)
  {
  //Other window messages
  //...
  case WM_PAINT:
   HDC hdc;
   RECT rc;
   PAINTSTRUCT ps;
   hdc = BeginPaint(hwnd, &ps);
   GetClientRect(hwnd, &rc);
   rc.bottom = (rc.top+50);
   DrawText(hdc, pszNoteText, -1, &rc, DT_LEFT);
   EndPaint(hwnd, &ps);
   return (0);
  default:
   return (DefWindowProc(hwnd, message, wParam, lParam));
  }
}
```

Handling Low Memory Conditions

Our final subject in the area of Windows CE memory management is how to handle low memory conditions in your applications.

As was discussed at the beginning of this chapter, Windows CE devices are often designed with very low memory requirements. For example, the Handheld PC on which I tested all of the applications in this book has only 8 MB of RAM. With many applications running at the same time, it is possible for system RAM to be consumed very quickly. Writing Windows CE applications in a memory-efficient manner certainly helps. But with devices with as little memory as this, low memory conditions should always be expected.

Windows CE defines a special message for notifying applications that system memory resources are getting low. This message, WM_HIBERNATE, is sent to all active applications when a *hibernation threshold* is crossed. The hibernation threshold is defined as 128 KB of free memory on systems with 1 KB memory pages, and 160 KB for systems with 4 KB pages.

Applications that receive WM_HIBERNATE messages should respond to the message by closing applications that are no longer in use, freeing unused memory, or performing other operations that free memory resources. The parameters are explained in Table 16.4.

Windows CE also defines a low and critical memory state. These states are entered as available RAM drops below certain thresholds. For systems with 1 KB page sizes, the low memory state is triggered when available RAM drops below 64 KB. For 4 KB page systems, the threshold is 96 KB. The critical memory state is triggered if available RAM drops below 16 KB for 1 KB page systems, and if available RAM drops below 48 KB for 4 KB page systems.

Table 16.4 The WM_HIBERNATE Message

PARAMETER	MEANING
wParam	0, not used
lParam	0, not used

In these memory states, Windows CE limits the amount of memory that applications can allocate in an attempt to equally share remaining memory resources across all active applications.

In the low memory state, *VirtualAlloc* calls are limited to allocating 16 KB of memory. In the critical memory state, this limit drops to 8 KB.

The GetSystemPowerStatusEx Function

We close this chapter with a brief look at Windows CE power issues.

Windows CE supports the function *GetSystemPowerStatusEx*. This function provides information about such things as the main and backup battery levels of a Windows CE device. *GetSystemPowerStatusEx* also indicates whether the device is currently running on AC or battery power.

```
GetSystemPowerStatusEx(pSystemPowerStatusEx, fUpdate);
```

The first parameter is a pointer to a SYSTEM_POWER_STATUS_EX structure. This structure contains members that are filled by Windows CE to report remaining battery life, whether the device is running on AC power, and the like.

fUpdate is a BOOL specifying where the function gets the power information. If TRUE, the function gets the latest power information directly from the device driver. If *fUpdate* is FALSE, the information returned is cached information that may be a few seconds out of date.

One use of *GetSystemPowerStatusEx* is to drive user interfaces that report battery charge status. The sample application MEMORY.EXE includes a simple demonstration of this function's use. Selecting the Power Status option from the Power menu displays the dialog box shown in Figure 16.6.

The small icon in the lower left of the dialog indicates if the device is powered by battery or AC. (In Figure 16.6, the indicator shows that the device is running on battery power.) The two progress bars indicate the current power level of the main batteries and the backup battery. The code for displaying this information is straightforward. The pertinent parts of the power dialog's dialog procedure are shown as follows:

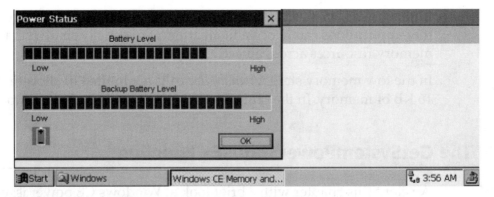

Figure 16.6 The MEMORY.EXE Power Status dialog box.

```
#define IDT_TIMER 128
BOOL CALLBACK PowerStatusDlgProc(
  HWND hwndDlg,
  UINT message,
  WPARAM wParam,
  LPARAM lParam)
{
  SYSTEM_POWER_STATUS_EX sps;
  HWND hwndBatteryLife; //Main battery power progress bar
  HWND hwndBackupLife; //Backup battery power progess bar
  HWND hwndStatic;   //Power source bitmap static control
  UINT nID;
  HBITMAP hBmp;
  switch(message)
  {
  //Other dialog messages
  //...
  case WM_INITDIALOG:
   GetSystemPowerStatusEx(&sps, TRUE);
   nID = (sps.ACLineStatus) ? IDB_ONLINE : IDB_OFFLINE;
   hBmp = LoadBitmap(ghInst, MAKEINTRESOURCE(nID));
   hwndStatic = GetDlgItem(hwndDlg, IDC_AC_POWER);
   SendMessage(hwndStatic, STM_SETIMAGE,
     IMAGE_BITMAP, (LPARAM)hBmp);
   SetTimer(hwndDlg, IDT_TIMER, 1000, NULL);
   return (TRUE);
  case WM_TIMER:
   GetSystemPowerStatusEx(&sps, TRUE);
   if (sps.ACLineStatus == 0)
   {
    hwndBatteryLife = GetDlgItem(hwndDlg,
      IDC_BATTERY_LIFE);
    SendMessage(hwndBatteryLife, PBM_SETPOS,
      (WPARAM)sps.BatteryLifePercent, 0);
    hwndBackupLife = GetDlgItem(hwndDlg,
```

```
      IDC_BACKUP_BATTERY_LIFE);
    SendMessage(hwndBackupLife, PBM_SETPOS,
      (WPARAM)sps.BackupBatteryLifePercent, 0);
  }
  return (0);
default:
  return (FALSE);
 }  //End of switch(message) statement
}
```

The WM_INITDIALOG message handler sets the bitmap in an SS_BITMAP-style static control. The handler calls *GetSystemPowerStatusEx*, and assigns the UINT *nID* to the identifier of a bitmap resource according to the AC power status of the Windows CE device. Next, it starts a timer identified by IDT_TIMER.

Every time the timer fires, the WM_TIMER message handler updates the progress bars, which report the device battery status. The *BatteryLifePercent* and *BackupBatteryLifePercent* member of the SYSTEM_POWER_STATUS_EX structure contain, respectively, the percentage of main and backup battery charge remaining.

Concluding Remarks

In this chapter, we have examined various Windows CE memory management techniques. We discussed basic features of Windows CE memory organization, such as the operating system and application address spaces. We looked at how to use application and custom heaps to allocate memory on an as-needed basis. We also looked at how to use memory mapped files for inter-process communication.

This chapter also introduced the WM_HIBERNATE message, which is used to report low memory conditions on Windows CE devices. The chapter concluded with a brief look at Windows CE power management issues.

What's on the CD-ROM?

The CD-ROM that accompanies this book contains a number of sample applications that illustrate the programming topics covered in the book. The table below lists the name of the directory in which the project and source files for each application are found. The table also lists the name of the executable application or DLL that is generated and gives a brief description of what it does.

Companion CD Contents

DIRECTORY	MODULE NAME	DESCRIPTION
\Samples\bands	BANDS.EXE	Demonstrates command band controls
\Samples\button	BUTTON.EXE	Owner draw button example
\Samples\cmdbar	CMDBAR.EXE	Demonstrates menus and command bands
\Samples\controls	CONTROLS.EXE	Demonstrates child control programming
\Samples\custdraw	CUSTDRAW.EXE	Custom draw service example
\Samples\custom	CUSTOM.EXE	Client application that uses CONTROL.DLL
\Samples\custom\ control	CONTROL.DLL	Custom control example
\Samples\datasync\ PhoneApp	various	ActiveSync module and client application samples

\Samples\datetime	DATETIME.EXE	Date time control example
\Samples\dbase	DBASE.EXE	Sample database application
\Samples\dialogs	DILAOGS.EXE	Dialog box programming examples
\Samples\files	FILES.EXE	File system programming example
\Samples\filter	FILTER.DLL	Sample file filters
\Samples\html	HTML.EXE	Demonstrates the HTML viewer control
\Samples\ink	INK.EXE	Rich ink control, voice recorder control, and Palm-size PC navigation button programming examples
\Samples\kiosk	KIOSK.EXE	Kiosk user interface example
\Samples\memory	MEMORY.EXE	Demonstrates memory, inter-process communication, and power techniques
\Samples\month	MONTH.EXE	Month calendar control example
\Samples\rapisamp	RAPISAMP.EXE	RAPI programming example
\Samples\rebar	REBAR.EXE	Demonstrates the rebar control
\Samples\registry	REGISTRY.EXE	Registry programming example
\Samples\tab	TAB.EXE	Tab control/common control example
\Samples\template	TEMPLATE.EXE	Template/boilerplate application

Hardware Requirements

To use this book, it is assumed that you have a desktop PC running Windows NT version 4.0 or later with Microsoft Developer Studio Visual C++ version 5.0 or later. It also assumes that you have installed the Windows CE Toolkit for Visual C++ version 2.0 or later.

The companion CD provides a number of sample applications illustrating the programming concepts discussed in this book. If you are interested in running any of these on a Windows CE device such as a Handheld PC or Palm-size PC, it is assumed that you have installed Windows CE Services on your desktop PC. This book also assumes that you are familiar with concepts such as connecting the device to the PC and copying files to the device.

Installing the Software

To install the software provided on the companion CD, simply follow these steps:

1. Insert the CD into your desktop PC CD-ROM drive.

2. Open Windows NT Explorer, and open the folder corresponding to your CD-ROM drive.

3. Copy the sample software by dragging the Samples folder from X: (use the proper designation for your CD-ROM drive) to the root directory on your hard drive.

Using the Software

The purpose and use of each of the applications on the companion CD are described in the chapter in which the application's concepts are introduced.

User Assistance and Information

The software accompanying this book is being provided as is without warranty or support of any kind. Should you require basic installation assistance, or if your CD is defective, please call our product support number at (212) 850-6194 weekdays between 9 AM and 4 PM Eastern Standard Time. Or, we can be reached via e-mail at: wprtusw@wiley.com.

To place additional orders or to request information about other Wiley products, please call (800) 879-4539.

To use this CD-ROM, your system must meet the following requirements:

Platform/Processor/Operating System. Desktop PC running Windows NT version 4.0 or later with Microsoft Developer Studio Visual C++ version 5.0 or later. It also assumes that you have installed the Windows CE Toolkit for Visual C++ version 2.0 or later.

RAM. 15 MB to copy sample programs to your hard drive.